METEOR OF WAR
THE JOHN BROWN STORY

"It is thought by the slaves . . . that the meteors from the heavens are sparks that . . . strike upon the craters of volcanoes, and that is the cause of their eruption. From the firmament of Providence today, a meteor has fallen . . . upon the volcano of American sympathies"

[Reverend J. S. Martin, 1859]

"If a fragment of an exploding aerolite had fallen down out of the air, while the meteor swept on, it would not have been more sudden, or less apparently connected with a cause or an effect."

[Henry Ward Beecher, 1859]

"John Brown's career for the last six weeks of his life was meteor-like, flashing through the darkness in which we live."

[Henry David Thoreau, 1860]

"But the streaming beard is shown
(Weird John Brown),
The meteor of the war."

[Herman Melville, 1866]

"Year of meteors! brooding year! . . .
I would sing how an old man, tall, with white hair, mounted the
scaffold in Virginia,
(I was at hand, silent I stood with teeth shut close, I watch'd,
I stood very near you old man when cool and indifferent, but trembling
with age and your unheal'd wounds you mounted the scaffold;) . . .
Nor forget I to sing of the wonder, the ship as she swam up my bay, . . .
Nor the comet that came unannounced out of the north flaring in heaven,
Nor the strange huge meteor-procession dazzling and clear shooting
over our heads,
(A moment, a moment long it sail'd its balls of unearthly light over
our heads,
Then departed, dropt in the night, and was gone;) . . .
Year of comets and meteors transient and strange—lo! even here one
equally transient and strange!
As I flit through you hastily, soon to fall and be gone, what is this chant,
What am I myself but one of your meteors?"

[Walt Whitman, 1881]

"Like the French country maiden who went to Paris to plunge her dagger
into a bloody ruler's heart, he meant to rescue good morals from the
usurpation of human laws. Corday fulfilled her solitary plan because it
was reasonable; John Brown failed in his plan because it was unreasonable; but as actors and martyrs, flashing upon the world's
attention like new meteors, they left examples of self-sacrifice"

[James Schouler, 1891]

"I soon found that he was a very thorough astronomer and he
enlightened me on a good many matters in the starry firmament
above us. He pointed out the different constellations and their
movements. "Now," he said, "it is midnight," and he pointed
to the finger marks of his great clock in the sky."

[William A. Phillips, 1879]

METEOR OF WAR
THE JOHN BROWN STORY

**EDITED AND WITH INTRODUCTION
AND COMMENTARY BY**

Zoe Trodd
and
John Stauffer

Brandywine Press • Maplecrest, NY

CONTENTS

PART TWO / 76

The Road to Kansas, and Harpers Ferry. 77

PART THREE / 108

The Harpers Ferry Raid and Aftermath 109

PART FOUR / 172

LIST OF ILLUSTRATIONS

ACKNOWLEDGMENTS

Zoe Trodd would like to thank David Burner, Susan Senter and Renzo Melaragno for superb work on this project; Charles Rosenberg for careful research into the identities of artists working for *Harper's Weekly* and *Leslie's Illustrated*; Victor Verney, Jean Libby and Phillip Beidler for much-appreciated efforts; Gabriel Trodd for excellent work as a research assistant; Tristan Jones, Rahul Sagar and Lawrence Groo for comments and suggestions; Bartosz Ostrowski and Richard Blow for thoughtful contributions; Benjamen Walker (yourlight.org) for ideas on John Brown as the first American terrorist; Emi Nakamura and Jon Steinsson for generous summer accommodation; Yael Schacher and Eduardo Canedo for hospitality; Jean Kelley and Christine McFadden for their care; Tom Rob Smith for writerly inspiration; Beatrice Trodd for sharing me with this book; Clare Pettitt, Ian Patterson, Stefan Collini, and Jean Gooder for their intellectual and pedagogic examples; Onora O'Neill for her continued interest and support; the Kennedy Memorial Trust for the scholarship of a lifetime; and Werner Sollors and Margot Gill for their gift of faith and opportunity in 2002–03. Most of all, thanks to John Stauffer, a meteor himself, brighter than all others; and to Lyn Jenkinson-Trodd and Geoff Trodd for an idyllic working and resting place, and a lifetime's education in idealism and empathy, the likes of which John Brown would have approved.

John Stauffer would like to thank Steve Mintz, whose own examples of anthologies served as a model for me; David Brion Davis, Michael Fellman, David Blight, Timothy Patrick McCarthy, Louis Menand, Jim Stewart, Robert Forbes, Larry Buell, and Werner Sollors, who helped clarify my understanding of John Brown; Joe Gerber, my research assistant; and especially Zoe Trodd, whose extraordinary efforts made the book possible. A number of people offered support and encouragement along the way, including Casey King; John Wood; Bill and Jean Stauffer; Rachel Stauffer and Jim Lawson; Mark, Rebecca, and Connor LeFavre; and Eliza Graham.

In October 1859 John Brown, an abolitionist, tanner, farmer and failed businessman, launched an attack against the institution of slavery. With a band of sixteen whites and five blacks he captured the town of Harpers Ferry and its federal arsenal, about 60 miles northwest of Washington, D.C., at the confluence of the Potomac and Shenandoah rivers, intending that blacks using arms from the arsenal rise up and claim their freedom. He was 59 years old. The poet Richard Realf later said of him: "His faith was very simple. He desired society to be pure, free, unselfish—full of liberty and love. He believed it capable of such realization."

Brown planned the raid while living in the black community at North Elba, New York. His training ground was the guerrilla warfare of Bleeding Kansas, where he fought with his sons against proslavery settlers. He murdered five men at Pottawatomie Creek in May 1856, inciting further retaliatory bloodshed, and in June of that year was victorious at the battle of Black Jack, Kansas, a clash regarded by many as the first of the Civil War.

Successful in Kansas, his mission at Harpers Ferry turned out differently. Federal forces led by Robert E. Lee overwhelmed Brown and his remaining men after thirty-six hours. Brown was tried and then executed in December 1859. His behavior in the face of death impressed even his captors and caught the imagination of the country as it hurtled toward a greater conflict. His raid foreshadowed the bloodshed of the coming war, and his life and death highlighted some of the central tensions and contradictions of the nineteenth century.

INTRODUCTION

I

". . . such a man as it takes ages to make, and ages to understand"
[Thoreau, 1860]

After all the noise and drama of his explosive life and death, John Brown's body finally hung, eerily silent and ominously swaying in the crisp Virginia air of December 1859. Jacob Lawrence's interpretation of this eternal moment, the cover illustration to our anthology, places Brown between two worlds, the heavens opening behind to let him in. Lawrence's Brown is a shape and emblem, a timeless and abstract figure more important for what he represents than for his individual humanity, transformed in death from man to myth. The white cloud behind the figure suggests a landmass and the blue sky the ocean around North America: Brown feels like a national symbol, lifted above and superimposed onto the United States.

It is as though Jacob Lawrence had Frederick Douglass's famous address at Storer College in mind when he painted the overpowering sky behind his hanging figure, for this speech of 1881 returns again and again to images of the sky: "Mighty with the sword of steel, he was mightier with the sword of the truth, and with this sword he literally swept the horizon . . . when John Brown stretched forth his arm the sky was cleared." And at another point in the speech: "Science now tells us when storms are in the sky, and when and where their violence will be most felt. Why may we not yet know with equal certainty when storms are in the moral sky, and how to avoid their desolating force?"[1] The abolitionist orator Wendell Phillips saw, like Douglass and Lawrence, an archetypal sign and a symbol in the image of sky and gallows. "As time passes, and these hours float back into history, men will see against the clear December sky that gallows. . . . Thank God for our emblem," said Phillips in his eulogy at Brown's funeral.[2]

Metaphors that draw on images of the sky are among John Brown's most consistent emblematic and symbolic forms. For Henry David Thoreau, Walt Whitman, Herman Melville, Henry Ward Beecher, James Schouler, and the Reverend J. S. Martin, Brown is a meteor, a bright and mysterious element in the wide canvas of the sky, described as such in this anthology's opening quotations. As meteor, portentous symbol and unearthly object, Brown exits in historical or real time, his actions "sudden . . . [un]connected with a cause or an

1

effect," himself sent "from the firmament of Providence," as Beecher and Martin put it.[3] "Meteor-like," Brown crosses the skies of human or national consciousness, a cosmic or universal force, a "flash of radiance," "transient and strange," "flashing upon the world's attention," or so Thoreau, Whitman, and Schouler perceive.[4]

This trail across the sky retraces periodically, for as a universal force outside of history Brown is an archetype or prototype, as Thoreau explained in his essay, "The Last Days of John Brown":

> I meet him at every turn. He is more alive than ever he was. He has earned immortality. He is not confined to North Elba nor to Kansas. He is no longer working in secret. He works in public, and in the clearest light that shines on this land.

Brown is "such a man as it takes ages to make, and ages to understand," who "died lately in the time of Cromwell [the seventeenth-century English Puritan and revolutionary], but . . . reappeared here," and it is "in vain to kill him," Thoreau continues. The meteor, as perceived by Brown's admirers, blazes through time, visible in the skies above Moses, Jesus, and Cromwell before him, and Brown's continual resurrection and reinterpretation since 1859 confirms that the meteor's trail blazes forward as well as back.

Noting this mythical trail, Brown's friend and biographer, Franklin Sanborn, described the process of myth-making to which he himself had contributed: "[Brown] was one of those rare types, easily passing into the mythical. Born of the people, . . . every blow struck at them only made them dearer to the hearts of the humble. . . . In heroes, faults are pardoned, crimes forgotten, exploits magnified—their life becomes a poem or a scripture—they enter on an enviable earthly immortality."[5] An *Atlantic Monthly* review of Sanborn's 1885 biography of John Brown recognized the power of the John Brown myth, observing: Brown's "apotheosis is due to the fact that his character and deeds have that quality which stirs the imagination, and moves the poetic feeling. He is seen walking far apart from the usual ways of men, in strange and solitary paths . . . seeking a peculiar goal by a forbidden route." Meteor-like, strange and solitary, Brown seemed elevated above the earthy plane: "like those whom the Greeks of old called heroes, human, yet in certain respects elevated above the customary and familiar plane of humanity."[6]

Brown belongs to "the imagination," as the review put it; to the realm of stories, national memory and myth-making; "to the ages," as did Lincoln after his own death, or so said his war secretary as he watched the President die. And Brown's mark on that realm, on American consciousness and imagination, is deep and wide. Hundreds of biographies, novels, poems, plays, speeches, sermons, literary essays, anthologies, and folk ballads have interpreted him. He is broad abstraction and metaphor, and a kaleidoscope of antonyms swirls around him: he is humanitarian, genius, saint, and patriot, but also murderer, egomaniac, fanatic, and extremist. For John Wilkes Booth, Lincoln's assassin, Brown was "a man inspired, the grandest character of the century," but also a despised traitor and murderer. Faced with the enigma that is the John Brown myth, we start to feel that he somehow embodies the German philosopher Friedrich Nietzsche's sense about humanity, that man is "material, fragment, excess, filth, nonsense, and chaos. But . . . also creator, image-maker, hammer-hardness, spectator-divinity, and day of rest."

It is probably due in part to Brown's unprecedented dependence on a sensational single act for his place in the pantheon of heroes that writers reach so readily for historical and mythic parallels. And these parallels come thick and fast. Through the rhetoric of nineteenth- and twentieth-century writers and speakers, of the United States, England, and Continental Europe, Brown morphs into Socrates, Ironsides, Spartacus, Martin Luther, John Milton, Charlotte Corded, Oliver Cromwell, William Tell, Sir Walter Raleigh, Washington, Garibaldi, Marquis de Lafayette, Longfellow, Jesus, Moses, David, Saint Paul, and numerous other Biblical figures. In an article for the *New York Tribune* on July 29, 1906, Sanborn put Brown alongside King Arthur and Joan of Arc; and the anonymous extended pamphlet of 1859, "The Life, Trial and Execution of Captain John Brown," ranks Brown with Don Quixote, who was persuaded "that he had a mission to rescue all the persecuted damsels in Spain." "The World's Homage," a poem of 1882 by Oliver Wendell Holmes, Sr., makes Brown as unreal, or real, as Harriet Beecher Stowe's fictional character Uncle Tom:

> . . . All through the conflict, up and down,
> Marched Uncle Tom and Old John Brown,
> One ghost, one form ideal;
> And which was false and which was true,
> And which was the mightier of the two,
> The wisest sibyl never knew,
> For both alike were real. . . .

Yet while myth endows Brown with timelessness, the metaphor of the meteor's trajectory across the skies recalls a figure whose legend *changes* as it flashes through history. Both Lawrence's painting and Herman Melville's poem, "The Portent," put their subject into movement: the coattails of Lawrence's Brown suggest motion, extended as they are on the right, and so does Melville's "slowly swaying" figure on the gallows.[7] Far from hanging passively, Brown continues to swing on the "scaffold [that] sways the future," the "Old Brown liberty-ball [kept] in motion"; the motion of his body on that December morning in 1859 pressing the ship of slavery, as Hermann von Holst phrased it, with "a mighty shove away from the shore" and over a "Niagara Falls."[8] Born of Bleeding Kansas, that complex struggle between supporters and opponents of slavery in a territory that seemed a mythical microcosm of the American experience, the John Brown legend was never taken off the scaffold of history to be lain in firm, still ground, so remaining a shape darkly swinging against the sky, as Edna Dean Proctor's poem, "The Virginia Scaffold," has it: "They may hang him on the gibbet; they may raise the victor's cry, / When they see him darkly swinging like a speck against the sky. . . ." A Puritan echo, an Old Testament Patriarch, a warrior-prophet transplanted into the nineteenth century, but also a man ahead of his time, anticipating the course of history and civil war, and reminiscent of late twentieth-century attitudes towards African Americans, Brown seems to belong anywhere but 1859. So he wanders through time, as homeless as a meteor.

* * * *

Examining the John Brown myth in all its fluctuations reinforces William James's assertion that "the world is full of partial stories that run parallel to one another, beginning and ending at odd times. They mutually interlace and interfere at points, but we cannot unify them completely in our minds."[9] John Brown's myth might also be a fit subject for Nietzsche, who, in *The Use and Abuse of History*, defines history's "real value" this way: to see "one thing with another, and weave the elements into a single whole," to find "ingenious variations on a probably commonplace theme." Brown, with his Janus-face, resembles the "great head" of Melville's whale that assumes "different aspects, according to your point of view," or Hawthorne's scarlet letter that comes to mean something different to everyone.[10]

Muriel Rukeyser's poem of 1940 offers "three images" of Brown, three versions of the myth.[11] But we can identify *four* particularly widespread and repeated phases in the "John Brown cycle," as the journalist William Allen White called it: the Force of Nature, the Christian Martyr, the Mad Villain, and the American Hero. Exploring these four myths, or phases, of John Brown might answer the question asked by Stephen Vincent Benét in his long poem of 1928, *John Brown's Body*: "You can weigh John Brown's body well enough / But how and in what balance weigh John Brown?"

II

"an elemental force"
[Lerone Bennett, Jr., 1964]

The first of these four phases is John Brown the Force of Nature, and it contains as one of its features the idea of Brown as meteor. In this legend, Nature, History, or Fate powered Brown in his meteoric flight across the skies, and he was "pure passion, pure transcendence . . . an elemental force like the wind, rain and fire . . . a man for all seasons, a pillar of fire by night and a cloud by day."[12] One of several Transcendentalists who helped construct this myth, Thoreau embraced Brown as a natural force, referring to him in "A Plea for Captain John Brown" as a "volcano," and "clear as lightning," an image employed also by one minister: "a volcanic blaze, that rises as if to 'lick the stars.'"[13] Another noted: "Where heroism comes, where self-devotion comes, where the sublime passion for the right comes, there God comes; there a will immeasurable by all prudential gauges is executed, and we may as well question the moral propriety of a streak of lightning or an earthquake as of that deed." And Wendell Phillips, in "The Lesson of the Hour," described Brown as a cosmic force and a "central sun."[14] And when not an "elemental force," Brown is the cycle of nature itself, also imagined by Thoreau in the "Plea": "when good seed is planted, good fruit is inevitable, and does not depend on our watering and cultivating it . . . when you plant or bury a hero in his field, a crop of heroes is sure to spring up. This is a seed of such force and vitality, that it does not ask our leave to germinate."[15]

Closely related to these images of the natural world is the theme of Brown as an episode in an inevitable historical process: Brown not as force of nature but as forced *by* nature. Wendell Phillips, in "The Puritan Principle," portrays Brown as a catalyst in history, with a predefined place in the evolution of the American mind. He is the "Puritan Principle" embodied, and Phillips imagines Brown proclaiming: "Posterity will summon the State to judgment and will admit my principle."[16] Frederick Douglass's "Address at Storer College" presents Brown as a vessel through whom "the judgment of God" can act. His meteoric flight historically determined, Brown's character is unimportant, the details of his biography, personality, and self-image as irrelevant as the myth-making tends to render them. He is beyond the historical course of the nation. Caught in an inexorable current, Brown is the agent of a larger elemental force.

For Transcendentalists like Thoreau and Emerson, who emphasized intuitive thought, inspiration, and experience, this larger force was history and nature but also the universal moral law. Brown seemed an agent of universal justice, his actions the embodiment of their political philosophy. These two figures were particularly active spokesmen on Brown's behalf, lecturing often throughout New York and Massachusetts between October 1859 and early 1860. Thoreau and Emerson recognized Brown's close relationship to nature, were impressed by his fire for abolitionism, and claimed him as a Transcendentalist. On his New England trips, Brown had fashioned a Transcendentalist persona, and this self-creation served him well from prison: his violent methods seemed relatively unimportant next to his romantic image as a self-educated, self-reliant New England common-man rebelling justly and patriotically against oppressive institutions. Brown made the Transcendentalists' abstractions concrete and in return they lent him their Transcendental imagery. He rises above the nation's law, again a force higher than ground level, a moral meteor in the national sky.

Brown becomes an allegorical and tragic figure in a large morality play in Robert Penn Warren's 1928 biography, *John Brown: The Making of a Martyr*. Brown's life and death, and the American Civil War, are tragedies, clashes of higher law with statutory law. Warren's Brown is ambitious and egocentric, his character tragically flawed, and so is toppled by his own *hubris:* "He was alone, and always acted alone, for his egotism would permit nothing else."[17] In Warren's representation, Brown has very little self-knowledge, and so, like many of the Greek tragic heroes, makes an arrogant attempt at godhead. His blindness, presumption, and self-worship leads, in Aristotelian terms, to his *hamartia*, his fatal, destructive error.

Other observers set the John Brown story in the mold of a drama by the Greek tragedian Sophocles, whose particular genius was to portray characters who seem to choose their path and yet be helplessly swept along by Fate. Reviewing Oswald Garrison Villard's compendious biography of Brown in 1910, the *Atlantic Monthly* noted: "the story has the movement of a Greek tragedy," and fifty years earlier the *Edinburgh Caledonian Mercury* had suggested a Shakespearean tragedy; Brown was an Othello "who loved his fellow man not wisely but too well."[18] The social drama of the nineteenth century had Brown's Harpers Ferry raid as the necessary dramatic link between the climax of war in the 1860s and earlier events like the Missouri Compromise and the passing of the Fugitive Slave Law, and the traditional mix of pity and terror that defined Greek tragedy was abundant in Brown's portion of this drama. The terror of Kansas lay wounded and pathetic in the courtroom, barely able to hear his trial's proceedings; the murderer penned sad and Biblically-infused missives to his cherished family during imprisonment; the monster stooped to kiss a slave child on the way to the gallows. Brown performed the over-reaching of Icarus, who flew too close to the sun; the flailing of Shakespeare's Lear alone on a heath; the calm fatalism of Sophocles' Oedipus, who inflicted damage upon himself in a passion and was serene in the sacrificial aftermath. It is not hard to understand how the *Atlantic Monthly* reviewer of 1910 saw "Greek tragedy" in the John Brown story. The strange spectacle of raid, trial, and execution was an almost choreographed process of violence, punishment, conversion, redemption, and catharsis. And through trial and execution by ritual Brown moved from degradation to sainthood.

In 1937 John Steuart Curry brought together these three elements of the first phase in the John Brown cycle. His Kansas mural, *The Tragic Prelude* (fig. 1), which he painted between 1937 and 1942, links Brown visually to the prairie fire and tornado that rage in the background, so making the ten-foot figure of Brown in the painting's foreground a powerful force of nature. Indeed, during his lifetime Brown was popularly known as the "Cyclone of Kansas." Curry's concept of Brown's actions in Kansas as a "Prelude" to the Civil War also sets down Brown's life as part of a historical process, like the movement westward enacted by the figures behind Brown as they move across the canvas from right to left. The "Prelude" is laid out like music, one section following inevitably another: once Brown had played his part in Kansas, the Civil War would surely follow. Curry's title ("Tragic") and the possible visual allusion to Shakespeare's Lear, "bound upon a wheel of fire," infuse the mural with tragedy.[19] Linking these three strands, of nature, history, and tragedy, Curry adds a religious element too: his Brown is reminiscent of Moses and Christ, so connecting him to the second major phase in the John Brown cycle, Brown as Christian Martyr.

III

"gallows glorious like the cross"
[Emerson, 1860]

Brown the Force of Nature resembles Brown the Christian Martyr: still an instrument, though of God now rather than Nature, History, or Fate. Here "the perfectness and glory of [Brown's] protest—its completeness, its sublimity, its solemnity and firmness, even to the end" come to "surpass all possibility of mere human contrivance, and are at once the work of a Divine Providence, and the impulse of Divine Truth," as the Unitarian minister George B. Cheever noted.[20] This religious persona is one that Brown himself repeatedly offered the world, and others reinterpreted as he awaited execution and in the weeks after his death. His last speech before the court, the prison letters, and the note that he wrote on the morning of his execution fashioned him as a prophet, and his execution made him a Christ figure. He quickly became a symbol of idealism and self-sacrifice, and his Biblical rhetoric resonated with the religiosity deeply embedded in American political culture. Americans immediately recognized a potential martyr in Brown, as they would in Lincoln and Martin Luther King, Jr.

Presumably relishing the opportunity to add this first American to the sacred list of historical martyrs, New England ministers of 1859 sermonized Brown into the tradition of Christ's disciple Paul, the martyr Saint Stephen, and Joan of Arc. Once Lincoln became Christ in the popular imagination, Brown was more easily portrayed as John the Baptist, "the one who came to tell about the light," [John 1:8], the light being Lincoln. But as early as 1859 the black minister J. S. Martin put Brown alongside John the Baptist:

> Men say that his life was "a failure." I remember the story of one of the world's moral heroes, whose life was just such a "failure." I remember one who, having retired to the deserts of Judea, to wring from the hard, stony life of those deserts the qualifications, and with all this purity, was brought into a corrupt and voluptuous court . . . John Brown, like John the Baptist, retired into the hard and stony desert of Kansas, and there, by the weapons of heroism, by the principles of freedom, and the undaunted courage of a man, wrung from the bloody soil the highest encomiums of Freedom and the most base acknowledgements of slavery, that the one was right and the other wrong. I know that John Brown, in thus rebuking our public, in thus facing the monarch, has had to bear just what John the Baptist bore.[21]

Two particularly popular Brown parallels were the figures of Samson and Moses. Franklin Sanborn saw that Brown's death "like Samson's, was to be his last and greatest victory," and Hermann von Holst's narrative, *John Brown* (1888), also paints Brown as Samson.[23] The black abolitionist Frederick Douglass noted, "Like Samson," Brown "has laid his hands upon the pillars of this great national temple of cruelty and blood, and when he falls, that temple will speedily crumble to its final doom, burying its denizens in its ruins."[22] Douglass saw an American Moses in Brown too, and commented in a later speech: "forty long years this man was struggling with this one idea; like Moses he was forty years in the wilderness . . . this one thought, like the angel in the burning bush, had confronted him with its blazing light. . . . Like Moses, he had made excuses, and as with Moses his excuses were overruled."[24] The parallel also struck several artists, and Charles Sumner observed of Edwin A. Brackett's marble bust of Brown (fig. 2), sculpted after a visit to Brown in prison: "This is like the Moses of Michelangelo." The same imagery is at work in de Blezar's bronze bust of 1870 (fig. 3).[25] Curry would even use Michelangelo's "Moses" rather than John Brown himself as a model for Brown in *The Tragic Prelude*, in which Brown's arms are stretched as wide as his myth, of course also evoking a figure on a cross. Curry's Brown wears a patriarchal Moses-like beard, which Brown did not in fact have until after the moment in

Figure 1: John Steuart Curry, *The Tragic Prelude,* 1937–42, detail of John Brown, north wall of the East Corridor, Kansas Statehouse murals. (*Courtesy, Kansas State Historical Society.*)

Figure 2: Edwin A. Brackett, John Brown bust, 1863 (*Courtesy, Boston Athenaeum.*)

Figure 3: Joseph-Charles de Blezar, *John Brown,* 1870. (*Courtesy, Library of Congress.*)

Kansas to which the mural refers. Curry extended the comparison in another work: his painting, *Moses and the Eleventh Commandment,* is alternatively titled *John Brown Depicted as a Saint.*

The most controversial and widespread parallel, however, was to Jesus himself, and commentators drew it repeatedly, forging from Brown's gallows the cross at Calvary, or what the novelist Louisa May Alcott called Brown's "stepping-stone to heaven." Victor Hugo's sketch of Brown on the gallows was inscribed "Pro Christo sicut Christus" ("For Christ just as Christ") and, after Lincoln's assassination, Hugo wrote: "Let not America weep for Lincoln. This martyr has his place between John Brown and Jesus Christ as the third redeemer of humanity." The Italian patriot Garibaldi also remarked on this triumvirate of saints after the Emancipation Proclamation in 1863, calling Lincoln the "heir of the aspirations of Christ and John Brown."

The New England intellectuals pushed the comparison between Brown and Christ. Thoreau observed, for example, that "some eighteen hundred years ago Christ was crucified. This morning perchance John Brown was hung. These are the two ends of a chain, not without links," and Emerson agreed: "that new saint, than whom none purer or more brave was ever led by love of men into conflict and death—the new saint awaiting his martyrdom, and who, if he shall suffer, will make the gallows glorious like the cross."[26] Several New England ministers saw nothing blasphemous about the comparison, and made it themselves: "The gallows from which he ascends into heaven will be in our politics what the cross is in our religion—the sign and symbol of supreme self-devotedness," noted one. "From his sacrificial blood the temporal salvation of four millions of our people shall yet spring."[27]

In 1861 Charles Robinson gave the link a new twist, commenting: "To the superficial observer John Brown was a failure. So was Jesus of Nazareth. Both suffered ignominious death as traitors to the government, yet one is now hailed as the Savior of the world from sin, and the other of a race from bondage."[28] During the twentieth century this link between Brown and Christ remained strong. In 1909 W. E. B. Du Bois reiterated the theme of Brown's divine sacrifice: "On the second of this month he was crucified, and on the 8th he was buried and on the 25th, fifty years later, let him rise from the dead in every Negro-American house. Jesus Christ gave his life as a sacrifice for the lowly. So did John Brown."[29] Brown was a holy hero in the African American tradition for the rest of the twentieth century: Langston Hughes insisted that "John Brown's name is one of the great martyr names of all history," and Countee Cullen, another great black writer of the 1920s Harlem Renaissance, made Brown an archangel in "A Negro Mother's Lullaby": "His sons are high fellows; / An Archangel is he; / They doff their bright halos / To none but the Three."[30]

Both supporters and opponents of slavery had predicted such longevity for the myth of Brown as martyr. Southern newspapers worried that "to hang a fanatic is to make a martyr of him and fledge another brood of the same sort."[31] Abolitionists gloried in the same logic of transformation: "To all outward appearances all is defeat and ruin. Yet in reality what a glorious success! What a splendid martyrdom," proclaimed Lydia Maria Child, writer and activist, a few weeks before Brown's death; "The scaffold will be as glorious as the Cross of Calvary."[32] And, more than anyone, John Brown himself understood the power of the martyr myth. As the journalist and politician William A. Phillips explains, "in his humble way [Brown] endeavored to pattern [himself] after the man of Galilee," and to make sure the world saw the pattern.[33] While in prison, Brown read a copy of Henry Ward Beecher's sermon at Plymouth Church, given on the Sunday before Brown's sentencing, and found the following section:

> Let no man pray that Brown be spared. Let Virginia make him a martyr. Now he had only blundered. His soul was noble; his work miserable. But a cord and a gibbet would redeem all that, and round up Brown's failure with a heroic success.[34]

In the margin, Brown marked, simply, "good."

Brown's prison letters are one of the best sources through which to see the mythologizing process at work. In the letter he wrote to the Reverend McFarland, on November 23, 1859, he compared himself to the apostle Paul while also slipping in a direct but unacknowledged quote from Jesus on the cross ("they know not what they do"): "I think I feel as happy as Paul did when he lay in prison. He knew if they killed him, it would greatly advance the cause of Christ; that was the reason he rejoiced so. On that same ground 'I do rejoice, yea, and will rejoice.' Let them hang me; I forgive them, and may God forgive them, for they know not what they do."[35]

For many years Brown had felt himself to be an instrument of God. For example, John Jr. recalled that his father once began to punish him with lashes for the moral debts accumulated in his "account book" of transgressions, but ended up taking two-thirds of the lashes on his own back, to pay his son's debt and enact the doctrine of Atonement before John Jr.'s eyes. But until October 1859 he had identified with several roles. Now, in prison, he was wholly focused on martyrdom. He exchanged his weapon for a pen and shifted from his most recent role of warrior-hero to that of martyr-hero. Brown's legendary martial prowess and his reputation for terror, when combined with his persistently dignified and calm bearing, lent his trial and execution a sense of exquisite farce—as though he could break free at any moment but simply chose to remain. He worked to give the impression that he chose death willingly: his execution could be a martyrdom only if he seemed to die voluntarily as punishment for his beliefs. The likeness is that of Buddha calmly eating his last meal while knowing it to be poisonous, or of Christ on the cross, taunted: "if you are the son of God, climb down and save yourself."

IV

"a criminal paranoiac"
[Thomas Dixon, 1921]

Brown's self-conscious martyrdom served the cause of abolitionism. Nowhere is there evidence that he sought a martyr's death for its own sake and for the sake of vanity. While Brown saw himself as an instrument of God, which indicates the opposite of egomania, his detractors denied his prophecy, and attributed his actions to a fiendish ego and destructive monomania. This third unsympathetic phase of the "John Brown cycle," Brown as the Mad Villain, prevailed mainly in the conservative years of post-Reconstruction and McCarthyism, and again when the terrorist Timothy McVeigh explicitly cast himself as a modern-day John Brown. Allan Nevins, in *The Emergence of Lincoln*, published in 1950, portrayed Brown as mentally disturbed, and in the same decade C. Vann Woodward looked at Brown's family history and continued this line of thought, concluding that Brown had inherited a genetic disorder. Later commentator Robert McGlone claimed in 1988 that Brown was bipolar, and recent criticism has dealt with whether Brown was a manic-depressive or an obsessive-compulsive, whether marked by the death of his mother or broken beyond repair by his business failures.[36]

Though this hostility towards Brown was particularly pronounced during the 1940s and 50s, he had been from the 1920s onwards a lens through which Americans reflected their fears about militant politics, and the Russian Revolution in particular. *The Torch*, Thomas Dixon's motion picture screenplay of 1927, subtitled *The Story of the Paranoiac Who Caused a Great War*, portrays Brown as a crazed demagogue, but, unlike his novel *The Clansman,* upon which D. W. Griffith based *Birth of a Nation* twelve years earlier, *The Torch* was never made into a film. Dixon's novel, *The Man in Gray*, was extremely popular, however, and made Brown into a manipulative and lunatic anti-American bent on corrupting the people—a "criminal paranoiac": "Within thirty days he could work with his pen the miracle that would transform a nation into the puppets of his will," Dixon writes. "His soul on fire with the fixed idea that he had been ordained by God to drench a nation in blood, he joyfully began the task of cementing the mob mind."[37]

Biographies by Hill Peebles Wilson in 1913, Robert Penn Warren in 1929, and James C. Malin in 1942, did not grant Brown such significant status. They dismiss everything from the sincerity of his religious beliefs to his motives for seeking freedom for blacks. Brown was for them a small-time con man and hypocrite, an unbalanced but irrelevant lone gunman. Malin in particular intended to show that the myth of Brown is far larger than the man, while Peebles Wilson reduced Brown to a "soldier of fortune" and a pirate. Brown was a relative nobody whose greatest insanity was that he thought he was a somebody: a Captain Kidd aspiring to be a Washington or a Jesus.[38]

All of this attention to Brown's state of mind came in spite of the observation by one of Brown's greatest political enemies, Governor Wise, after an encounter with him, that "they are mistaken who take him to be a madman. He a bundle of the best nerves I ever saw—cut and thrust and bleeding in bonds. He is a man of clear head, of courage, of simple ingenuousness. He is cool, collected, and indomitable."[39] Brown's sane and respected Northern backers admired him as a perfectly sound individual. The letters from his comrades to their families just before the Harpers Ferry raid are passionate but clearheaded, and certainly not hypnotized or willfully suicidal. Affadavits claiming insanity in Brown's family *were* presented in his defense by his counsel at the trial, but originated from Brown's well-meaning neighbors and Asahel H. Lewis, an abolitionist newspaper editor in Ohio, in an attempt to mitigate Brown's crimes. Brown rejected these claims vehemently.

Brown had an extremely active fantasy life and a rich imagination—a sense of alternate reality more common to writers and artists than to militant political leaders—and in part this generated the complex responses to his life. However, though attached to his Millennialist vision of the world, he did not lose sight of the political situation as it was. Alongside the claim that he was insane must be set the possibility that Brown's tactics were meant to sow the seeds of sectional discord. "As a war measure, John Brown's murders were beyond doubt successful," Villard writes of Brown's murders in Kansas. "If Brown intended to set men at each other's throats, to make every man take sides, to bring matters in Kansas to a head, he was wholly successful."[40] The very gruesomeness of the murders that Brown ordered was meant to prompt reprisal. Pottawatomie was direct action.

Then at Harpers Ferry, Brown virtually destroyed the possibility of sectional reconciliation. His raid was an acknowledgement that moral suasion was useless. "The people of the North have said John Brown was a madman—I suppose mostly because it is on the eve of an election," the Reverend J. S. Martin commented, "but if he was mad, his madness not only had a great deal of method in it, but a great deal of philosophy and religion."[41] The North needed Brown to be a saint or a madman, but not a radical abolitionist; God's instrument rather than a political force; a martyr from another more romantic era rather than a hardheaded tactician and catalyst. Recognizing that he was more valuable as a martyr than as a political leader, Brown refused after his capture to discuss politics and his place in the world of Northern abolitionism. The Republican Party used the myth, and the myth did its work.

Hamlet

V

"in accord with what is best in American character"
[Franklin Sanborn, 1885]

Brown believed that slavery was an "unjustifiable War of one portion of its citizens upon another," that America was a lawless state, and that the slaves had a natural right to rebel.[42] He therefore put into practice Thomas Jefferson's belief that "the tree of liberty must be refreshed from time to time with the blood of patriots and tyrants." He reminded many in the North of Jefferson's warnings about the inevitability of God's justice for a slaveholding nation. He was a representation of the power of the individual and so of the American creed, recognized as such by numerous contemporaneous observers and later commentators. "So much was he in accord with what is best in the American character, that he will stand in history as one type of our people, as Franklin and Lincoln do," his friend Sanborn claimed. "He embodied the distinctive qualities of the Puritan, but with a strong tincture of the humane sentiments of later times."[43] Sanborn's invocation of the Puritans is characteristic of the many responses to Brown that rendered him as a quintessentially American hero, and this fourth and final phase of the Brown cycle, The American Hero, casts him as Puritan, revolutionary, and frontiersman; and as a revolutionary he was embraced by labor leaders and African Americans.

An avid reader of Oliver Cromwell's biography, which, according to his daughter, he enjoyed second only to the Bible, Brown was often compared to this British anti-monarchist Puritan. Emerson was intrigued by Brown's direct descent from Peter Brown, a Plymouth colonist of the Mayflower, and Wendell Phillips called Brown "a real Puritan Presbyterian . . . a regular Cromwellian dug up for two centuries—in the midst of our New England civilization."[44] Sanborn compared him to both Cromwell and the poet John Milton, and declared that Brown had "entered upon his perilous undertaking with deliberate resolution . . . as did the Pilgrims before they set forth from Holland to colonize America."[45] In interpreting Brown as a Yankee Puritan pioneer, with a "homely, Franklin-like wisdom and Connecticut shrewdness," but also the "romantic spirit" and primitivism of a man on an errand into the wilderness, Sanborn associated him with several myths of American identity.[46] Dressing like a frontiersman, Brown seemed a real-life frontier hero to the Massachusetts intellectuals, who loved his true tales of violence and heroism. One of the original stock, bred of American soil and ideals, Brown was one of their own on the Kansas frontier: a Leatherstocking among blacks rather than Indians; a freedom fighter fresh from the front lines and straight out of a romantic novel; an American Robin Hood. New England abolitionists and ministers spoke of him with sectional pride.

Thus born of and into myth and history, Brown was part of America's revolutionary heritage, of "old Puritan stock," and so with a "soul . . . steeped in revolutionary memories."[47] Harpers Ferry was "the Bunker Hill of our second Revolution," and Brown, "true to the logic of Lexington and Concord . . . no American is so loyal to the meaning of the Fourth of July as he."[48] Identifying Brown as a patriot, Wendell Phillips reminded Americans that "now, it may be treason; but the fact is it runs in the blood. We were traitors in 1776."[49] Some went even further, claiming Brown as a greater American patriot than George Washington, "armed only with his faith," and marching on to certain death.[50]

This theme of Brown as a soldier and war hero, one part of this fourth phase of Brown, the American hero, became more common after his violent end, which was subsumed into the larger violence of the war. Abolitionists used Brown's name to prepare the North for a holy war that would visit on the South divine retribution for the crime of slavery, and many claimed that the shots fired at Harpers Ferry were the first of the Civil War. Wendell Phillips summed up Brown's role in abolition in his funeral oration for Brown: "[He] abolished slavery in Virginia . . . History will date Virginia Emancipation from Harpers Ferry . . . John Brown has loosened the roots of the slave system. It only breathes—it does not live hereafter."[51] And Frederick Douglass declared some years later that "not Carolina, but Virginia, not Fort Sumter, but Harpers Ferry and the arsenal, not Col. Anderson, but John Brown, began the war that ended American slavery and made this a free Republic . . . The time for compromises was gone, the armed hosts of freedom stood face to face over the chasm of a broken Union—and the clash of arms was at hand."[52]

Once the fighting began, it was, as Emerson wrote in his journal in 1865, "impossible to keep the name of John Brown out of the war."[53] War vindicated Brown and made him a prophet. Union soldiers replaced the unappealing war cry of "preservation of the Union" with the marching song, "John Brown's

Body," making Brown a symbol of abolition, progress, and sacrifice; and their war aims were more inspiring than simply the protection of the status quo. If Brown was a Christ-figure, then the death and destruction of war could be a holy crusade. And if his soul marched on, lifted out of the mouldering grave, then so too could the nation's soul march, out of the wasteland of war and into victory and reconstruction. "The apotheosis of old John Brown is fast taking place," noted a newspaper in 1862. "All over the country [the Old John Brown song] may be heard at all times of the night or day in the streets of Chicago and all other cities; it is the pet song among the soldiers in all our armies."[54] Men needed a hero in order to fight, and symbolism in order to stay emotionally committed, and so, as the image of the nation's soul and the first Unionist fatality of war, Brown became a quintessential Northern war hero. For anyone too exhausted by the storm and stress of war to consider the path of gradual abolitionism not taken, Brown was reason and root, and as abstractly symbolic as the American flag. From then on, as Theodore Roosevelt explained in 1910, "the name of John Brown" was forever "associated with . . . the nation's history." Roosevelt expanded on the theme of Brown the Civil War hero:

> John Brown stands to us now as representing the men and the generation who rendered the greatest service ever rendered this country. He stood for heroic valor, grim energy, fierce fidelity to high ideals. A great debt is owed to John Brown because he is one of the most striking figures in the mighty struggle which was to keep us forever a free and united nation, which was to secure the continuance of the most tremendous democratic experiment ever tried. He did much in his life and more in his death; he embodied the aspiration of the men of his generation; his fate furnished the theme of the song which most stirred the hearts of the soldiers. John Brown's work was brought to completion by the men who bore aloft the banner of the Union.[55]

The Brown symbol of American liberty and democracy also included a role as labor hero in the early part of the twentieth century. Seized upon as "the inspiration of the Union armies in the emancipation war," as Charles Robinson explained in 1861, Brown then easily translated into "the inspiration of all men in the present and distant future who may revolt against tyranny and oppression."[56] Between 1880 and 1940 the Northern worker was often cast as the equivalent of the antebellum Southern slave—enslaved by capitalism, though politically free, and by the capitalist bosses who were the slave-owners of the era. When labor reformers looked back to abolitionism for a model, Brown seemed the "spirit incarnate of the Revolution," as Eugene V. Debs explained in his piece, "December 2, 1859." Debs and others in the anarchist and socialist movements often referenced Brown, asking, as did Debs in the essay, "History's Greatest Hero," "Who shall be the John Brown of Wage-Slavery?"

On December 2, 1881, the Labor Standard American Auxiliary Association held a meeting in New York to commemorate Brown's execution and raised him up as a symbol of the aims and struggles of the Association, offering cards on which were written "Yesterday—the abolition of chattel slavery. Tomorrow—the abolition of wage slavery. His soul is marching on!" The president of the Association called upon the participants to "celebrate the memory of a man—not he of Nazareth, but one who will also live forever in the hearts of the working people; he of Ossawatomie, John Brown the labor martyr."[57] Brown's name was invoked in 1910 in Theodore Roosevelt's "Progressives, Past and Present" and in 1921 in John Dos Passos's *Three Soldiers*. The relevance of Brown for labor reformers was challenged somewhat in the late 1920s when the recently executed Sacco and Vanzetti seemed likely to replace Brown as leftist symbols and martyrs, but in 1935 Brown appeared in Sinclair Lewis's *It Can't Happen Here;* and five years later in Muriel Rukeyser's "The Soul and Body of John Brown," among numerous other works that sought a symbol for leftist politics. Kenneth Porter, in his poem, "To the Jayhawkers of the International Brigade," equated Brown's struggles to those of the Left in the Spanish Civil War, and wrote: "John Brown of Kansas . . . goes marching on / his tread is on the plains of Aragon."[58] Michael Blankford and Michael Gold wrote the 1936 play *Battle Hymn* that connected their present moment to 1856. Blankford explained: "The left creative movement had a great burden to bear and that is the Russian burden. Lenin was hero . . . or Trotsky was hero. . . . It seemed to us then that we had to find our own roots in our own revolutionary past . . . and Brown was such a perfect example of that because he wasn't an import. . . . He was a rock of American rock."[59] Many radicals in the 1930s viewed Brown as a proto-Marxist revolutionary, and articles in the *New Masses* and the *Daily Worker* frequently mentioned his name. In 1953 a huge crowd in Beijing greeted W. E. B. Du Bois with a rendition of "John Brown's Body."

Brown, the unknown farmer and the simple working man, was such a potent symbol of revolution and change and able to speak so effectively to other working men precisely because of his "natural" simplicity and "instincts" as one of the common men, as Clarence Darrow explained:

> His natural instincts were never warped or smoothed or numbed by learning . . . like all men who deeply impress the generation in which they live . . . He was of the type of Cromwell, of Calvin, of Mahomet; not a good type for the peace of the world, but a type that here and there, down through the ages has been needful to kindle a flame that should burn the decaying institutions and ancient wrongs in the crucible of the world's awakening wrath.[60]

Again a "type," belonging to the realm of myth and symbol, Brown was also, for Michael Gold, "the greatest man the common people of America have yet produced . . . a hard-working, honest Puritan farmer with a large family, a man worried with the details of poverty," and though "a legend," still visible in "the simple, obscure heroes who fight for freedom today in America." Gold continues, in this biography of Brown:

> That is why I am telling his story. It is the story of thousands of men living in America now, did we but know it. John Brown is still in prison in America; yes, and he has been hung and shot down a hundred times since his first death. For his soul is marching on; it is the soul of liberty and justice, which cannot die or be suppressed.[61]

Brown was especially present when black Americans were "hung or shot down." African Americans are the one group in American history who, from

Brown's death to the present day, have consistently praised him as a hero. More than any other white man in the historical record, Brown devoted his life to their cause and saw in their sufferings his own. He was, as African Americans have always recognized, the blackest white man ever lived: many Southern slaves who heard about the Harpers Ferry raid assumed that Brown was black. In 1882 one of the first black historians, George Washington Williams, recognized the movement of the John Brown cycle but thought that Brown, among the world's greatest heroes, was "rapidly settling down to his proper place in history . . . 'the madman' has been transformed into a 'saint'."[62] In this third subphase of Brown the American Hero, Brown became the hero of African Americans, and again the guardian of the American democratic experiment.

During the Niagara Movement, W. E. B. Du Bois, Reverdy Ransom, and Francis Grimké spoke of Brown's efforts on behalf of blacks. And at the second annual meeting of the Movement, held at Harpers Ferry in 1906, Ransom compared Brown to Moses, David, Joshua, Cromwell, and Toussaint L'Ouverture; the last a martyr to the successful black revolution in Haiti in 1791. "The Negroes who are aggressively fighting for their rights have the same spirit that animated the founders of this nation. In them the soul of John Brown goes marching on," Ransom declared. "Like the ghost of Hamlet's father, the spirit of John Brown beckons us to arise and seek the recovery of our rights, which our enemy . . . has sought forever to destroy."[63] Du Bois used Brown as a rallying call in his own time, asking in his biography of Brown: "Has John Brown no message—no legacy, then, to the twentieth century? He has and it is this great word: the cost of liberty is less than the price of repression." As an American hero, the symbol of liberty, Brown was still relevant, as Du Bois explained in the last chapter of *John Brown*:

> Not only is the cost of repression to-day large—it is a continually increasing cost: the procuring of coolie labor, the ruling of India, the exploitation of Africa, the problem of the unemployed. . . . The memory of John Brown stands to-day as a mighty warning to his country. He saw, he felt in his soul the wrong and danger of that most daring and insolent system of human repression known as American slavery.[64]

In the 1930s Muriel Rukeyser reappropriated Brown on behalf of African Americans. Her poem, "The Trial," about the Scottsboro case, and the article, "Trial of the 'Scottsboro Boys,'" have Brown present in the Alabama courtroom. "John Brown, Nat Turner, [and] Toussaint L'Ouverture . . . watch the trial from the corner."[65] Arthur Covey's New Deal mural, *John Brown* (fig. 4), depicts Brown as a pioneering leader of the black people. And in the 1960s, amid centennial commemorations of the Harpers Ferry raid, civil rights groups plucked Brown from the political wilderness of the 1950s and reclaimed him as a hero to blacks. As debates unfolded on the role of the white man in black America's struggle for equal rights, it seemed that another civil war loomed unless white America could finally follow in Brown's ever-marching footsteps. The activist Truman Nelson, in *The Right of Revolution*, examined the "John Brown principle," quoting Malcolm X: "If you are for me and my problem . . . then you have to be willing to do as old John Brown did." Robert Williams

Figure 4: Arthur Covey, *John Brown,* mural in the U.S. Post Office in Torrington, Conn. (*Courtesy, Library of Congress.*)

echoed this thought: "We do not need paternal white 'Big Daddies' for our friends now. What we need are some fighting John Browns." Nelson himself believed that there was a "John Brown in every man's conscience," ready to push America to another Harpers Ferry.[66] And Lerone Bennett, Jr.'s essay, "Tea and Sympathy: Liberals and Other White Hopes," points to the recognition by blacks that Brown identified completely with their people. The essay concludes:

> There was in John Brown a complete identification with the oppressed. It was his sister that a slave-owner was selling . . . his wife who was being raped in the gin house. It was not happening to Negroes, it was happening to him . . . John Brown *was* a Negro, and it was in this aspect that he suffered."[67]

Brown, in this "complete identification with the oppressed," was also a hero for black South Africans during the 1960s. In a speech to the UN, on October 9, 1963, R. H. Amonoo of Ghana referred to the "great American whose soul still goes marching on throughout the world . . . taken prisoner at Harpers Ferry over one hundred years ago." Amonoo quoted Brown's words to his captors: "'You may dispose of me very easily; I am nearly disposed of now; but the question—this negro question I mean—the end of that is not yet,'" and continued: "Mr. Chairman, John Brown's soul still goes marching on in South Africa today. It will find no rest until it has seen justice done."

So the fourth and final phase of the "John Brown cycle" encompasses Brown as Puritan and frontier hero of American liberty; Brown as military hero and symbol of America's greatest conflict; Brown as simple working-class hero of American labor and reform; and Brown as empathetic hero of oppressed races in America and abroad. He seemed, in Sanborn's words, "in accord with what is best in American character" and perhaps in all human character and conscience; an eternal principle.

VI

"the representative man"
[Stearns, 1860]

The persistence of the John Brown cycle as it shifted through four major phases indicates the enormous impact Brown has had on American national consciousness. Enacting what Ralph Ellison believed to be its search for identity—the theme of *Invisible Man* and "THE American theme," as he put it—America found itself in different ways through the John Brown story. In the creation of a national history, Brown became a cultural symbol and a representative mythical American. His career offered a usable past to historical nationalists. The fervent search for America's identity and national character conducted by historians, writers, and artists in the first third of the twentieth century in particular swept the Brown legend along in its wake. He symbolized the crisis of the 1850s and 1860s, connected pre– and post–Civil War America to its revolutionary and heroic Puritan past, and represented the shift from one age to another: as the sentimental age ended and the age of industrial capitalism began, John Brown was a harbinger and, in accordance with the psychologist Carl Jung's explanation, a "wise man . . . savior or redeemer . . . one who is awakened whenever the times are out of joint and a human society is committed to a serious error."[68]

The "error" of slavery, the crisis of secession and the "out of joint" times of civil war and reconstruction propelled the John Brown myths. In a moment of absolutes and ideals, and the clash of two "ways of life" and types (Southerner and Northerner), Brown expressed the situation of a society, and that society elaborated around its hero much symbolic imagery and plot. As Jung explains, "when people go astray they feel the need of a guide or a teacher," and in such moments the whole weight of myth and history comes to bear on an individual: "primordial images . . . come to light in . . . the visions of artists and seers, thus restoring the psychic equilibrium to the epoch."[69] The artists, speech-makers, and commentators who saw in Brown an archetypal tragic character, martyr-figure or hero, a nineteenth-century Samson, Jesus, or Cromwell, sought to give shape and meaning to the chaos of their "epoch," and restore through such familiar and "primordial" symbolic imagery a "psychic equilibrium." Brown then remained a barometer to political climates in America: "I believe John Brown to be the representative man of this century, as Washington was of the last," said the abolitionist George Stearns in 1860, and Brown continued as the "representative man" of twentieth century moments and movements.[70]

And yet the very persistence of Brown in American consciousness, the extreme responses to his myth, and the contradictions and antonyms of the dialogue that surrounds his story, also indicate that something in John Brown the "representative man" unsettles America. Some of the tensions in his mythology are also those in American history: between idealism and pragmatism; the moral and the legal; the individual and community; revolution and evolution; the Declaration of Independence and the Constitution. Part of the same Protestant heritage as Emerson and William James, Brown is the ultimate example of a rugged individualist who lived by higher law yet acted in order to reconnect with his fellow men and his country's statutes rather than to deny or escape from them. He is an embodiment of the tension continuously present in American society between patriotism and individual rights, the law and principles, and so he himself remains continuously present. "But was he not a rebel, guilty of sedition and treason?" asked the Reverend Newhall in December 1859. "Yes, all this. But we are to remember that the words 'rebel' and 'treason' have been made holy in the American language. Are not our children fed on revolutionary reminiscences which make 'rebel' and 'patriot' synonymous in their childish apprehension?"[71] The combination of treason and patriotism in the John Brown story are the threads from which the historical fabric of America is woven, and this makes Brown's story difficult to confront without recourse to myths and symbols. Writers and artists return to him with such intensity and controversy, using such mythology and symbolism, because he dramatized a set of conflicts in American history and culture.

He is part of America's self-image as a violent redeemer nation. The literary critic Harold Bloom writes that "salvation for the American cannot come through the community or the congregation, but is a one-on-one act of confrontation," and the historian David Brion Davis notes that, as far as Europeans are concerned, America has "glorified personal whim and has ranked hardened killers with the greatest of folk heroes," one of those murderous folk heroes being John Brown.[72] Personal freedom secured by righteous violence through a sense of Biblical mission is part of the national teleology and the narrative behind America's founding and growth. Brown's form of violent heroism may in fact make his story difficult for Americans to confront at all even through myths and archetypes—hence the sheer number of contradictory images and reinterpretations in his mythology. For, viewed as part of the American culture of righteous violence and frontier justice, Brown's terrorism might force an acknowledgment of the centrality of violence to American history: from Indian Removal and the brutality of the American West to slavery and the lynchings of Reconstruction; the oppression of radicals throughout the twentieth century; the assassinations of four presidents and several other leaders; and of course the Civil War. The novelist Toni Morrison pointed out in an interview that America is "the land where the past is always erased," a country with an "innocent future," a place where "the past is absent or it is romanticized," for the "culture doesn't encourage dwelling on, let alone coming to terms with, the truth about the past."[73] The pervasive extremes of the John Brown myth indicate such an erasure or romanticization of the past; a cultural rationalization and an attempt to cling to a more attractive self-image than that lit up by Brown's meteor. Distanced through myth, defensively simplified, Brown's life and legend are prevented from speaking dangerous truths. Symbolism allows an uncomfortable narrative to exist, cloaked but expressed, and so the John Brown cycle beats on, boats against the current. To recognize that he was more than the "weird John Brown" of Melville's poem, not hero or villain but both and much in between, would be to see in Brown not a meteor out of time but a man whose character and actions were made possible and necessary *by* his time and his country; his meteor's path that of the nation.

VII

"the theatrical manager"
[Thoreau, 1859]

So John Brown is a mass-invention. Thus invented, made a symbol and representation, is he then, to use his own phrase, "a mere blank" upon which faces can be sketched?[74] Far from it. Though his legacy took on a life of its own, and he came to represent more than he envisaged, in fact Brown was a self-made man in the more literal sense of the expression, for he made and remade himself during his lifetime, with a keen eye for his own mythology. His various self-representational strategies were models for the discourse that came after his death. Called an enigma by several who knew him personally, including William Phillips, and notoriously difficult for biographers and historians to get to know after the fact, Brown relied on his self-constructed public image because he had no identity in a career, little education, and an unimpressive history of bankruptcy. To be an insider he needed a public persona, and sure enough power and influence came with the construction of personas and a legend, during and after his death. He used the chronic social upheaval and instability of his life as an opportunity to constantly redefine himself, and his self-definition was complex, multivalent, and fluid.

The perfect subject for the philosophy of biography, Brown resisted the "myth of coherent personality" and played multiple roles consciously, purposefully, and with great skill.[75] He loved disguise and indulged his romantic streak, embracing such roles as the Job-like loser, the philosophical Mayflower descendent, the simple farmer, the brutal Kansas terrorist. He played in particular on the expectations and self-conceptions of the New England abolitionists, invoking their Puritan heritage in his self-presentation. After his capture at Harpers Ferry, the national press used various images that Brown projected of himself—prophet, patriot, messiah, terrorist—and abolitionists were able to feed the myths only because Brown had converted himself so thoroughly into a suitable martyr.

Brown's vocation was in one sense that of actor, his world a stage. He wrote his autobiography in the third person, read John Foxe's *Book of Martyrs* repeatedly, and used a variety of stage names, for logistical reasons but perhaps also to express his shifting selfhood: in April 1857 he was Nelson Hawkins; in May 1857, James Smith; in June 1858, Shubel Morgan (complete with long white beard); and in May 1859, Isaac Smith. He understood the media theater of his trial and execution, even though his trial was the first in American history covered widely and on a daily basis by the national media. And he used his earlier courtroom experience in bankruptcy to his advantage. By the time of his execution, Thoreau could say of Brown's expert stagecraft: "no theatrical manager could have arranged things so wisely to give effect to his behavior and words."[76] More than a hundred years later the popular rock band,

Kansas, used as the cover illustration to their 1984 album, *The Best of Kansas*, an adaptation of John Steuart Curry's mural (fig. 5), where Brown the stage manager, in charge of the stage set, curtains, and lighting, points at the stage. The back cover to the album shows an inkwell and quill, presumably used by Brown when he writes the script for the performance. Brown stands between drama and audience, the mediator of his own story.

Brown always knew how to perform and mediate. He was acutely aware of his double audience or readership: young Stearns (the recipient of his autobiographical letter) and the boy's father (Brown's sponsor); the courtroom and the slaveholding South; his family and the newspaper-reading public in the North. Brown also understood the importance of symbolism in performance and so, at Harpers Ferry, sent his men to capture Colonel Lewis W. Washington, the great-grandnephew of George Washington, telling the hostage: "I wanted you particularly for the moral effect it would give our cause having one of your name as a prisoner." To complete the symbolism Brown then sent more men to seize the Colonel's sword, which Frederick the Great had given to George Washington, and wore it until overpowered by Lee's marines. The sword took valuable time to seize but had great symbolic value, indicating that Brown was a patriot and a revolutionary hero and that the mission at Harpers Ferry was historically important. Undoubtedly aware of the powerful legend of the gallant and compassionate slaveholder, Brown challenged this legend with a performative one of his own, almost working as a nineteenth-century spin doctor for the image of the abolitionist. His receptive audience responded

Figure 5: Steve Carver, musical record cover illustration (c. 1984), *The Best of Kansas*. (*Courtesy, Sony.*)

to his rhetoric and understood the excessive theater of his eventual transformation into Christ.

Another part of Brown's public self-fashioning was to describe himself in terms of myth, as in "Brown's Parallels," his letter of 1857. He likened himself to Samson upon several occasions, writing for example to Sanborn in 1858: "God has honored but comparatively a very small part of mankind with any possible chance for such mighty and soul-satisfying rewards . . . I expect to effect a mighty conquest even though it be like the last victory of Samson." Attempting to topple the pillars of slavery upon which the South rested, Brown was crushed as they fell. William A. Phillips recalls an occasion on which Brown compared himself to the gladiator Spartacus:

> [Brown told] me of Spartacus and his servile war, and was evidently familiar with every step in the career of the great gladiator. I reminded him that Spartacus and Roman slaves were warlike people in the countries from which they were taken . . . [that] the negroes were a peaceful, domestic, inoffensive race. In all their sufferings they seemed to be incapable of resentment or reprisal. "You have not studied them right," he said, "and you have not studied them long enough. Human nature is the same everywhere." He then went on in a very elaborate way to explain the mistakes of Spartacus, and tried to show me how he could easily have overthrown the Roman empire.[77]

Brown, according to Villard, "pictured himself a modern crusader as much empowered to remove the unbeliever as any armored researcher after the Grail," and underwent a "metamorphosis" from "staid, somber merchant and patriarchal family-head" to "John Brown of Osawatomie," a warrior with an Indian name.[78] He fashioned himself as a western hero in the tradition of the novelist James Fennimore Cooper's Leatherstocking tales, in which a virtuous white man blurs the boundaries between savagery and civilization in his quest for justice, and after the warfare in Kansas, during which he relied on the fighting tactics of the Kansas Indians, with whom he associated, he began referring to himself as Osawatomie Brown. He fixed his background, upbringing, and self-conception to the symbol of the savage Indian, telling Gerrit Smith on April 8, 1848, "I am something of a pioneer. I grew up among the woods and wild Indians of Ohio," and noting in his autobiography: "After getting in Ohio to 1805 he was for some time rather afraid of the Indians, & of their Rifles ; but this soon wore off : & he used to hang about them quite as much as was consistent with good manners ; & learned a trifle of their talk."[79]

In fact, Brown's sense of theater, while making him politically very effective and historically very enigmatic, also had deep implications for his attitudes towards race. His most authentic role, the one he remained committed to in thought, word, and deed, was that of African American. His various self-conscious metamorphoses occurred at a moment in time when an understanding of character as fixed shifted towards a notion of the self in a state of continuous flux. Significantly, whiteness as a superior category was tied to the idea that "character" is determined by heredity and one's place in the social hierarchy, rather than chosen or self-fashioned, and Brown continually sought to become black. He identified so closely with blacks that he chose to live among them and was willing to sacrifice his life for their cause, and in 1849 moved to the black community in the wilderness of Timbucto, in the Adirondacks, on land given to blacks by Gerrit Smith in 1846. He considered it his permanent home and final resting place.

Brown was therefore able to stand apart from widespread racism and white supremacy in part because of his ability to re-create himself and his sense that identity was subjective and ever-changing. He broke down racial hierarchies and envisaged an egalitarian society in which everyone, men and women, black and white, was free, equal, and judged not on the basis of sex, skin color, wealth, or family and heredity, but rather on adherence to the Declaration of Independence and the Golden Rule as sacred texts. Douglass recognized this as a genuine process in Brown, and after their first meeting in late 1847 described him in the *North Star* as someone who, "though a white gentleman, is in sympathy a black man, and as deeply interested in our cause, as though his own soul had been pierced with the iron of slavery." The editor of the *Ram's Horn*, Willis Hodges, published Brown's essay, "Sambo's Mistakes," which affects the voice and tone of an urban Northern black, and preserved Brown's black identity by publishing anonymously, because, like Douglass, he knew Brown's black persona to be authentic rather than a parody or caricature in the style of blackface minstrelsy. Du Bois commented later that Brown "worked not simply for Black Men—he worked with them; and he was a companion of their daily life, knew their faults and virtues and felt, as few white Americans have felt, the bitter tragedy of their lot." Many blacks throughout the twentieth century have acknowledged Brown's sincere blurring of racial categories.

Brown's desire to blur racial categories and reshape the world was well answered by daguerreotypes. Pictures allowed him to remake himself, and remaking himself was of course one step closer to remaking the world. He crossed racial lines visually, and established a black performative self, proving correct Douglass's statement in his article, "Pictures": "Poets, prophets, and reformers are all picture-makers—and this ability is the secret of their power and of their achievements. They see what ought to be by the reflection of what is, and endeavor to remove the contradiction."[80] The 1856 daguerreotype by John Bowles (fig. 6), one of numerous portraits taken of Brown while he was in Kansas, is perhaps deliberately underexposed, rendering Brown's tanned skin even darker and so blurring the line between black and white.

Like other abolitionists, Brown had his picture taken often. Modern visual culture emerged at the same time as the crisis over slavery accelerated, and image-making enhanced the sense abolitionists had of the contrast between ideal and reality. It spoke to their desire to transform the world and themselves. Brown, always willing to exchange past identities for new ones, recognized that he could remake himself through pictures. The period's new emphasis on present and future, and the fragmentation of past identities that had been stable phenomena, felt strongly by Brown throughout his tumultuous career, both reflected and furthered a visual culture of the mid-nineteenth century that asked

Figure 6: John Bowles, *John Brown*, daguerreotype, 1856. (*Courtesy, Boston Atheneum.*)

Figure 7: John Adams Whipple and James Wallace Black, *John Brown*, daguerreotype, 1857. (*Courtesy, Boston Atheneum.*)

Figure 8: John Brown, daguerreotype, 1857. (*Courtesy, Boston Atheneum.*)

the question "Who am I?" Brown seemed able to answer this question in several different ways with daguerreotypes, and others also used these images to answer the same question of him. The so-called "mad" photograph of 1857 (fig. 8), where the right side of Brown's face is blurred, and Brown has asymmetrical features and a sagging right lip, was either distorted by the daguerreotypist or else the lens or plate were damaged. Repeatedly cited as evidence that Brown was mad, the grotesque image made its way into mainstream literature on Brown when engraved as the frontispiece to James Redpath's biography (fig. 12). The frontispiece rebalances his face somewhat, though the influence of the distortion is still evident in the curved lip and asymmetrical eyes, features absent from all other daguerreotypes of Brown.

When able to answer the question "Who am I?" for himself, however, Brown seemed to do so with gusto. Like Douglass, Brown not only wrote himself into public existence and redefined himself continuously through language, but also updated his persona through photography. An early image of 1847 (fig. 10) records Brown taking an oath, and connects him to the flag held by his side, just at his height, its triangle shape also that of his shirt-front. Brown is at one with his oath. The daguerreotypes of 1856–58 (fig. 7) are uncompromisingly that of a warrior. In all the images, Brown stares intensely into the lens, disregarding portrait conventions of the time, challenging and penetrating with his gaze. The over-riding impression is one of boldness, with an emphasis on physicality. His hands often grip his elbows, in a classic posture of defiance, and his arms are forcefully crossed whenever in shot. His brow is furrowed dramatically, his lips tight. He rarely smiles, and his occasional half-smile is more knowing than warm.

In 1859, however, he adopted a different visual persona. In J. W. Black's Boston photograph of May 1859 (fig. 9), a bearded Brown affects a different posture: less aggressive, more statesman-like, his body more open and relaxed, though his gaze remains direct and challenging. The warrior has become a prophet. Perhaps by now, in the last months before Harpers Ferry, he felt more comfortable in his authority, less driven to impose a visual authority through an impression of force and defiance. Painters of the nineteenth and twentieth centuries based their representations of Brown on this late metamorphosis rather than on any of the earlier daguerreotypes. Nahum B. Onthank's painting of 1860 (fig. 11), the frontispiece to Villard's biography, is one example.

Brown perhaps enjoyed the image-making process because he envisioned an alternate reality that was more compelling to him than his material world. A dreamer and a visionary, he was able to construct alternate versions of himself in photographs, through letters, essays, and his autobiography, and in person. In a reminiscence that resonates powerfully with all the meteor and sky imagery in the John Brown literature, William A. Phillips recounts the occasion on which he realized that Brown was, in addition to a visionary, also "a very thorough astronomer": "he enlightened me on a good many matters in the starry firmament above us. He pointed out the different constellations and their movements. 'Now,' he said, 'it is midnight,' and he pointed to the finger marks of his great clock in the sky."[81] As his own scriptwriter, director, mythographer, and interpreter, Brown knew the constellations and movements of that

Figure 9: J.W. Black, *John Brown*, May 1859. (*Courtesy, Library of Congress.*)

Figure 10: Augustus Washington, *John Brown*, daguerreo-type, 1847. (*Courtesy, National Portrait Gallery, Washington, D.C.*)

Figure 11: Nahum B. Onthank, *John Brown*
[painting from a photograph by J. W. Black.]
(*Courtesy, Boston Athenaeum*)

Figure 12: Frontispiece Engrav-
ing, in James Redpath, *The Public
Life of Capt. John Brown,* 1860.
(*Courtesy, Boston Athenaeum*)

metaphorical canvas for American history. A meteor himself, he was also an observer and philosopher of meteors. He planned and executed his entrance onto the stage that he managed, and with perfect timing, blazed his own trajectory across the "great clock in the sky."

VIII

"the exact face of every case"
[David Utter, 1883]

Before becoming a myth, John Brown was of course a man. Between 1859 and 1900 there was very little interest in the details of his life or personality, though this changed somewhat towards the end of the century when American historiographic style shifted from idealistic narrative to scientific realism. For example, in 1883 the historian David Utter urged new historians to examine the real career of Brown and construct a version of him that better suited the current age.[82] But Franklin Sanborn helped to hold the new historical realists at bay with his own idealistic writings on Brown, and Utter's plea was not really answered until the last third of the twentieth century, when the first balanced biographies came out.[83]

Utter distinguished between John Brown's body, the "man himself," and his "soul," the myth of Brown's name. Acknowledging that the latter had more popular appeal, he maintained nonetheless that the focus should now shift to Brown's "body," in all its human realities. The four sections of sources in this anthology do exactly that, albeit with an attention to how Brown fashioned and presented his "soul" to others. John Brown's "body," in the years before his "soul" marched on alone, now comes to center stage. As Benét would have it, we have weighed "John Brown" in the "balance" and now turn to "weigh John Brown's body."[84] This is Brown's life as he lived it and wrote about it, and with his mythology laid out by way of introduction, the details of his life and letters take on a new meaning. With the legend outlined, his life story can begin, and this order confirms his story as also that of an age and a country, of the human need for heroes and villains, and of Brown's own ability to create narratives and construct identities. The drive to make of himself a myth is apparent and painfully human when traced through his life and letters. The end comes before the beginning because this is how John Brown has always been received: his last act, at Harpers Ferry, the first ever seen by the nation; his life defined by his death; his legend better known than his biography; his afterlife more significant than his sixty years on earth.

An examination of these years allows students to see the complexities and ambiguities that are often lost among competing symbols. The abolitionist George Gill wrote that his "intimate acquaintance" with Brown had demonstrated that "he was very human," that the "angel wings were so dim and shadowy as to be almost unseen." [85] The intimate acquaintance with Brown that comes through a reading of his letters and writings will also strip angel wings away to reveal the human behind the representative human type: Brown the individual, albeit one who set out to make himself an icon and symbol. This symbol has become bigger than the man, and Brown is like Hawthorne's Hester

Prynne, who stands in front of the mirror at the Governor's Hall and sees the symbol that defines her "in exaggerated and gigantic proportions, so as to be greatly the most prominent feature of her appearance."[86] By reading his writings we see where private and public meet, and are able to assess how Brown's self-image squares with the posthumous construction of his character. In particular we might understand why blacks of the period would so easily accept Brown into their hearts at a time when, disillusioned by years of promises and unproductive tactics, most were no longer willing to embrace whites as their leaders and spokesmen in the antislavery cause. Working toward rather than from a picture of his life and actions, allowing him to evolve as we read his letters and piece together the world as he saw and experienced it, we unearth a complex and contradictory life.

The selections cover his early life, the build-up to Harpers Ferry, the raid, and his imprisonment and execution. They also include writings on him by his contemporaries, and so lay out the beginnings of the John Brown myth, his afterlife in the national imagination. According to Douglass, "Slavery had so benumbed the moral sense of the nation," that "it was difficult for Captain Brown to get himself taken for what he really was."[87] In these initial responses, bewildered and otherwise, we witness how and why the legend took on so many different meanings, and can better understand the momentum behind the John Brown cycle.

With close readings of sources as well as historical contextualization, this anthology approaches Brown from the borderland of literature and history. Brown was rhetoric becoming violence, a human literalization of politics. He turned words into actions: when Douglass proclaimed that liberty "must either cut the throat of slavery or slavery would cut the throat of liberty," unbeknownst to him and his audience, Brown and his men had cut the throats of five proslavery settlers four days earlier.[88] With his death he turned actions back to words: his actions became myth and symbol, message and document; "his forty days in prison . . . all in all made the mightiest Abolition document that America has known," as Du Bois noted.[89] Knowing this complex relationship between words and actions in his life and afterlife and between symbol and reality in his mythology, close attention to his words seems all the more crucial.

Equally imperative is an attention to the history of his time. Heroes and madmen are generally banished to pedestals and attics, away from the world's action, and the raid at Harpers Ferry is consequently too often treated as an historical anomaly. In addition, frequent attempts to separate the man and his actions, and to balance the means and ends of his violence in Kansas and at Harpers Ferry, have created a sense that Brown is somehow beyond the reach of the historian's analysis. But this anthology's sources and their introductions collapse the historical vacuum around Brown.

Thus armed with the tools of literature and history, we have access to what Utter called "the exact fact of every case," and so can disagree with Douglass who, in 1881, argued that Brown, "our noblest American hero," "like the great and good of all ages, . . . must wait the polishing wheels of after-coming centuries" before his worth can be truly assessed. "The brightest gems shine at first with subdued light, and the strongest characters are subject to the same limitations."[90] But the John Brown cycle, the "polishing wheels of after-coming centuries," as Douglass has it, makes Brown shine with *less* clarity with each passing generation: the clear bright light of his biography and writings are a stark contrast to the sheer volume of his myths and symbols, the indistinct layering of his meanings and reinterpretations. In fact, Brown's light *fractures* the further we come from his life and times. Wendell Phillips's sentiment was closer to the truth: "The deeper you probe his life the brighter it shines," he commented in 1859.[91] This anthology's sources and their introductions probe Brown's life, and reveal his light as it shone before the wheels took up their polishing. It is not the light of a gem, or even of a star, for starlight is remote and mediated, long since disconnected from its source and reaching us though the star itself is burnt out. Rather, Brown's light in the pages that follow is like that of a meteor, flashing at the exact moment of perception across the night sky.

NOTES

1 See in this anthology: Frederick Douglass, "John Brown: An Address at the Fourteenth Anniversary of Storer College," 1881.

2 See in this anthology: Wendell Phillips, Eulogy for John Brown, December 8, 1859.

3 Henry Ward Beecher, Sermon of October 30, 1859, at Brooklyn's Congregationalist Plymouth Church. Reverend J. S. Martin, see in this anthology: speech given on John Brown in Boston on December 2, 1859, Martyr Day, and printed in *The Liberator* on December 9.

4 Henry David Thoreau, see in this anthology: "The Last Days of John Brown," July 4, 1860. Walt Whitman, see in this anthology: "Year of Meteors," 1881; James Schouler, *History of the United States of America Under the Constitution* (New York, 1891), pp. 443–44.

5 Franklin Sanborn, *Recollections of Seventy Years*, (Boston, R.G. Badger, 1909), I, 149.

6 Review in *Atlantic Monthly,* 37, January–June 1886, 272.

7 See in this anthology: Herman Melville, "The Portent" (1859), 1866.

8 The "scaffold [that] sways the future," from Wendell Phillips, lecture entitled "The Lesson of the Hour," Brooklyn, New York, November 1, 1859, printed in James Redpath, *Echoes of Harper's Ferry* (New York: Arno Press, 1969, lecture first published in 1860), pp.43–66 (p. 66). "Old Brown liberty-ball [kept] in motion," Mr. George Hannibal Parker, President of the Old Capt. John Brown Liberty League, on Martyr Day, Meeting in Detroit, December 2nd, 1859, as reported in *The Weekly Anglo-African*. See also Hermann von Holst, *John Brown* (Boston: Cupples, 1888).

9 William James, *Pragmatism* (Cambridge, Mass: Harvard University Press, 1975, first published 1907), p. 71.

10 Herman Melville, *Moby-Dick* (New York: Norton Critical Edition, 2002, first published 1951), p. 265. See also Nathaniel Hawthorne, *The Scarlet Letter* (1850). Janus, Roman god of beginnings, has two opposite faces.

11 Muriel Rukeyser, "The Soul and Body of John Brown" (1940):

> There! tall in October's fruition-fire stand
> three images of himself; one as he stood on the ground,
> one as he stood on sudden air, the third
> receding to our fatal topmost hills

faded through dying altitudes, and low
through faces living under the dregs of the air,
deprived childhood and thwarted youth and change
fantastic sweetness gone to rags
and incorruptible anger blurred by age.

12 Lerone Bennett, Jr., "Tea and Sympathy: Liberals and Other White Hopes," in *The Negro Mood and Other Essays* (Chicago, Johnson, 1964), p. 100–101, 102.

13 See in this anthology, Henry David Thoreau, "A Plea for Captain John Brown," October 30, 1859. Sermon by Fales Henry Newhall, entitled "The Conflict in America," December 4, 1859, printed in Redpath, pp. 195–211 (p. 195).

14 Reverend Moncure D. Conway, sermon of December 10, 1859, printed in Redpath, pp. 349–57 (p. 355).

15 See in this anthology: Henry David Thoreau, "A Plea for Captain John Brown," October 30, 1859.

16 Wendell Phillips, "The Puritan Principle," December 18, 1859, printed in Redpath, pp. 105–18 (p. 112).

17 Robert Penn Warren, *John Brown: The Making of a Martyr* (New York: Payson & Clarke Ltd., 1929), p. 62.

18 John Morse, review of Villard's biography *John Brown* in the *Atlantic Monthly*, 1910, 668. Article in the *Edinburgh Caledonian Mercury* on December 20, 1859, cited by Seymour Drescher, "Servile Insurrection and John Brown's Body in Europe," in the *Journal of American History*, 80 (1993), pp. 499–534 (p. 507).

19 William Shakespeare, *King Lear*, IV, I, 46.

20 Reverend George B. Cheever, "The Martyr's Death and the Martyr's Triumph," December 4, 1859, printed in Redpath, pp. 213–35 (p. 233).

21 For Biblical allusion, see the Gospel of John 1:8. For Martin, see in this anthology: Reverend J. S. Martin, speech, December 2, 1859.

22 See in this anthology: Frederick Douglass, "Capt John Brown Not Insane," *Douglass' Monthly*, November 1859.

23 Franklin Sanborn, *The Life and Letters of John Brown, Liberator of Kansas, and Martyr of Virginia.* (Boston: Roberts Brothers), 1885, p. 623.

24 See in this anthology: Frederick Douglass, "John Brown: An Address at the Fourteenth Anniversary of Storer College" (1881).

25 See Lydia Maria Child's account of the creation and reception of Brackett's bust, reprinted in "Lydia Maria Child: Holographs of 'The Hero's Heart' and 'Brackett's Bust of John Brown', by Robert H. Swennes, in *American Literature*, Vol. 40, No. 4. (Jan., 1969), pp. 539-542.

26 See in this anthology: Henry David Thoreau, "A Plea for Captain John Brown," October 30, 1859. Ralph Waldo Emerson, "Courage," Boston, November 8, 1859.

27 Reverend Edwin M. Wheelock, sermon in Boston, November 27, 1859, printed in Redpath, pp. 177–94 (p. 191).

28 Charles Robinson, first governor of Kansas after admission to the Union in 1861, speech at Osawatomie, as reported by *New York Tribune*, Sept 1, 1877.

29 W. E. B. Du Bois, article in *Horizon*, December 1909.

30 Langston Hughes, in the *Chicago Defender,* October 17, 1959. Countee Cullen, poem in *Opportunity,* January 1942. Printed in Benjamin Quarles, *Allies for Freedom: Blacks and John Brown* (New York: Oxford University Press), 1974.

31 *New York Journal of Commerce*, proslavery newspaper in the North, quoted in Oswald Garrison Villard, *John Brown, 1800–1859; a biography fifty years after.* (Boston: Houghton Mifflin Company, 1910), p. 501.

32 Lydia Maria Child, *Lydia Maria Child, Selected Letters, 1817–1888,* ed. Milton Meltzer and Patricia Holland (Amherst, University of Massachusetts Press, 1982), p. 329.

33 William A. Phillips, lecture to the Kansas Historical Society, "Lights and Shadows of Kansas History," in *Magazine of Western History* 12 (1890), 6–12.

34 Henry Ward Beecher, sermon on October 30, 1859, printed in Redpath, pp. 257–79 (p. 262).

35 See in this anthology: John Brown's Prison Letters, October 21–December 2, 1859.

36 See Bertram Wyatt-Brown, "Volcano Beneath a Mountain of Snow," ed., Paul Finkleman, *His Soul Goes Marching On: Responses to John Brown and the Harper's Ferry Raid* (Charlottesville: University Press of Virginia, 1995), for a full discussion of all the different judgments on Brown's sanity.

37 Thomas Dixon, *The Man in Grey: A Romance of North and South,*(New York: D. Appleton, 1921) pp. 90, 94.

38 Hill Peebles Wilson, *John Brown, Soldier of Fortune: A Critique* (Lawrence, Kansas: Hill P. Wilson, 1913), p. 407.

39 See in this anthology: Governor Henry Wise, speech in Virginia, October 21, 1859.

40 Villard, pp. 181–82.

41 See in this anthology: Reverend J. S. Martin, speech on December 2, 1859.

42 For Brown's statement, see in this anthology: John Brown, Provisional Constitution and Ordinances for the People of the United States, May 8, 1858, and Journal of Provisional Convention, May 8–10, 1858.

43 Sanborn, *The Life and Letters of John Brown*, p. 185.

44 Phillips, "The Lesson of the Hour," in Redpath, p. 55

45 Sanborn, *The Life and Letters of John Brown*, p. 117.

46 Ibid, pp. 86, 98.

47 Newhall, in Redpath, p. 207.

48 Ibid, pp. 183, 189.

49 Wendell Phillips, speech on December 15, 1859, New York City.

50 Conway, in Redpath, p. 355.

51 See in this anthology: Wendell Phillips, Eulogy for John Brown, December 8, 1859.

52 See in this anthology: Frederick Douglass: "John Brown: An Address at the Fourteenth Anniversary of Storer College" (1881).

53 Ralph Waldo Emerson, *Works: Journals and Miscellaneous Notebooks*, ed. Ronald A. Bosco and Glen Jackson (Cambridge, 1982), 15:468.

54 Editorial in *Illinois Weekly Mirror*, August 6, 1862.

55 Theodore Roosevelt, "The Progressives, Past and Present," in *The Outlook,* 3 September 1910.

56 Charles Robinson, first governor of Kansas after admission to the Union in 1861, speech at Osawatomie, as reported by *New York Tribune*, Sept 1, 1877.

57 For more details of this meeting, see James C. Malin, *John Brown and the Legend of Fifty-Six*, (Philadelphia: Lancaster Press, 1942),p. 17.

58 Kenneth Porter, "To the Jayhawkers of the International Brigade," *Kansas Magazine,* 1939, 97.

59 Michael Blankford quoted in M. Sue Kendell, *Rethinking Regionalism: John Steuart Curry and the Kansas Mural Controversy* (Smithsonian Institute Press, Washington D.C., 1986), p. 82.

60 Clarence Darrow, speech in 1913 to the San Francisco Radical Club.

61 Michael Gold, *The Life of John Brown: Centennial of His Execution.* (1924, rept. New York: Roving Eye Press, 1960), pp. 3, 4.

62 George Washington Williams, *History of the Negro Race in America* (New York, Arno Press, 1968, first published 1882), 2: 214–22.

63 Reverdy Ransom, "The Spirit of John Brown," *Voice of the Negro,* 3, 1906, 416–17.

64 Du Bois, *John Brown* (Philadelphia: G. W. Jacobs & Company, 1909), pp. 366, 384–86.

65 Muriel Rukeyser, in *New Massses,* June 12, 1934.

66 Truman Nelson, *The Right of Revolution* (Boston: Beacon Press, 1968), pp. 3, 6.

67 Lerone Bennett, Jr., "Tea and Sympathy: Liberals and Other White Hopes," in *The Negro Mood and Other Essays* (Chicago, Johnson, 1964), pp. 100–101.

68 C. G. Jung, "Psychology and Literature," in *Modern Man in Search of a Soul,* (New York: Harcourt, 1933), p. 197.

69 Jung, "The Archetypes," in *Psychological Reflections* (Bollingen Series, XXXI. Princeton: PUP, 1970), p.39.

70 George Luther Stearns, see in this anthology: The Mason Report: Harpers Ferry Invasion, June 15, 1860, from the Report of the Select Committee of the Senate appointed to inquire into the late invasion and seizure of the public property at Harpers Ferry.

71 Newhall, in Redpath, p. 204.

72 Harold Bloom, *The American Religion: The Emergence of the Post-Christian Nation* (New York: Simon, 1992), 33. David Brion Davis, *Homicide in American Fiction, 1798–1860: A Study in Social Values* (Ithaca: Cornell, 1957), viii.

73 Toni Morrison, "Living Memory," *City Limits* (31 Mar.–7 Apr. 1988): 10–11 (11).

74 See in this anthology: John Brown, "Sambo's Mistakes," for *The Ram's Horn,* 1848.

75 See James Clifford, "'Hanging up Looking Glasses at Odd Corners': Ethnobiographical Prospects," in *Studies in Biography,* ed. Daniel Aaron (Cambridge: Harvard University Press, 1978), 44.

76 See in this anthology: Henry David Thoreau, "The Last Days of John Brown," July 4, 1860.

77 See in this anthology: William A. Phillips, "Three Interviews with Old John Brown," December 1879.

78 Villard, p. 77.

79 Brown, quoted in Sanborn, *Life and Letters of Brown,* p. 97; see in this anthology: Autobiographical Letter of John Brown (To Henry L. Stearns, July 15, 1857).

80 Frederick Douglass, "Pictures," holograph, n.d. [ca. late 1864], DP, unpaginated.

81 See in this anthology: William A. Phillips, "Three Interviews with Old John Brown," December 1879.

82 David Utter, *North American Review*: 137, July-December 1883, 437.

83 These were Stephen B. Oates, *To Purge This Land with Blood* (1970), Jules Abels, *Man on Fire* (1971), and Richard O. Boyer, *The Legend of John Brown* (1973).

84 For Benet quotation, see end of part I of this introduction.

85 See in this anthology: George B. Gill, letter to Richard Hinton, July 7, 1893.

86 Nathaniel Hawthorne, *The Scarlet Letter* (New York: Norton Critical Edition, 1961, first published 1850), p. 73.

87 See in this anthology: Frederick Douglass, "John Brown: An Address at the Fourteenth Anniversary of Storer College" (1881)

88 Douglass quoted in John Stauffer, *The Black Hearts of Men* (Cambridge: Harvard University Press, 2002), p. 21.

89 Du Bois, *John Brown,* p. 365.

90 See in this anthology: Frederick Douglass, "John Brown: An Address at the Fourteenth Anniversary of Storer College," (1881).

91 Wendell Phillips, speech on December 15, 1859, New York City.

Part One includes Brown's autobiography, letters from as early as 1834, the creative piece he wrote for an antislavery journal, and reminiscences from other activists. These years were full of pain, as he struggled in business, faced bankruptcy, lost a wife and several children, and failed to make any mark in the abolitionist arena. But the sources are lit up by his inimitable hope and enthusiasm for each new business or political venture, the pleasure he took in his family, and his Job-like faith and endurance. This is "the John Brown little known to history."[1]

Figure 13: Jacob Lawrence, *The Life of John Brown*, 1941, No. 2: For 40 years, John Brown reflected on the hopeless and miserable condition of the slaves. (*Courtesy, Jacob and Gwendolyn Lawrence Foundation.*)

---

1 See in this anthology: Salmon Brown (son), Reminiscences.

THE MAKING OF A MAN AND
A MILITANT

* * * *

Autobiographical Letter of John Brown
(To Henry L. Stearns, July 15, 1857)

In 1857, two and a half years before his execution, John Brown wrote a biographical sketch of his early life and sent it to Henry Stearns, the twelve-year-old son of George Luther Stearns, an abolitionist and benefactor who helped fund the raid at Harpers Ferry. In January of that year Brown had visited the Stearns' Boston home and, in response to a request from Henry, promised to write an account of his childhood, also accepting the boy's pocket money as a proffered "contribution in aid of the cause in which I serve," as phrased in the letter's postscript. In this third-person autobiographical essay he offers his early years as an alternative youthful existence upon which Henry Stearns might reflect.

The first paragraph sets up the account as a morality tale, of "follies and errors . . . which it is to be hoped you may avoid," and also a success story, "calculated to encourage any young person to persevering effort." Brown sees in Henry and the imaginary "young person" of the first paragraph parallel childhood realities to his own, and explores other alternate existences, where, for example "the want of [contact with women] might under some circumstances, have proved his ruin. He is again aware of the metaphysical fragility of "circumstances" when he encounters his black double, a slave "fully if not more than his equal," a boy his own age who shares the pain of being "Motherless" (the same word Brown uses to describe himself). He and this double live in entirely different worlds; for while "the Master made a great pet of John," the other boy "was badly clothed, poorly fed ; & lodged in cold weather." It is likely that this confrontation with racial difference and inequality helped form his sense of counterworlds and so fed his self-division.

Certainly it must have been difficult to represent his white past from the vantage point of his black present, for by 1857 he had integrated with African Americans and defined himself as a black man. The letter's third person voice, which was an unusual method of representation at the time, creates distance between the narrator and the subject, to the degree that the narrator does not always know what his subject felt and did, as when he can only guess that the child John cried about the loss of his marble: "I think he cried at times about it." The third person voice thus allows a separation of self and creates two different personalities. Brown's interest in multiple identities is apparent when he frequently uses nouns instead of verbs to describe new skills or habits: instead of 'he learned to ramble,' or 'he did the cooking,' he writes, "John began to be quite a rambler," "he did not become much of a schollar," "John was left a Motherless boy," "he officiated as Cook," or "he began to be a practical Shepherd," so allowing various distinct roles and identities to take shape.

His self-construction is deliberate and self-aware. He knows that he might be judged inconsistent, and in his description of his first wife there is perhaps a recognition that the most powerful difference between them was her consistency. He carefully reinvents himself to the degree that his business failings vanish behind a trajectory of determination and success. Pain and disappointment are rarely his own fault; he is instead "placed in the School of adversity," passive while "the Heavenly Father sees it best to take all the little things out of his hands which he has ever placed in them." He knows and accepts that he built himself through "reading the lives of great, wise & good men," from talking with the Indians, from observing the "boy Five years older (who had been adopted by his Father & Mother)."

Of course, the letter is, in one sense, a very practical self-construction, written to impress George Sterns, and so win his support. But it is also a playing out of Brown's imaginative fantasy life and lifelong ability to sense counterworlds, empathize with the otherness of a slave existence, and adjust and develop his various public personae as necessary. In the autobiography he calls this a "verry bad & foolish habbit to which John was somewhat addicted . . . telling lies" and adds, "I now think had he been oftener encouraged to be entirely frank . . . he would not have been so often guilty in after life of this fault." Alone throughout much of his childhood, for "to be sent off through the wilderness alone to very considerable distances was particularly his delight," and possessing a "taste for reading : which . . . diverted him in a great measure from bad company," John used books to help create himself, in the manner of many such lonely and artistic children and adults.

His "habit" of self-creation ("lies") and the relationship of this habit to books is nowhere more apparent than in the use he makes of Biblical symbolism throughout the letter. He is "very familiar" with the Bible, possessing "a most unusual memory of its entire contents," and uses various Biblical stories as parallels to the "story" of John. Brown's childhood is Genesis in miniature, when the temptation of "Three large Brass Pins" takes him from innocent pre-memory to the "wilderness" inhabited by snakes. The "Rattle Snakes" and the "Oxteam," "Cows," and "wild beasts" of Brown's narrative recalls this passage from Genesis 3:14–15: "God said to the serpent, 'Because you have done this, cursed *are you above all cattle, and above all wild animals." In a letter to his wife written around the same time as the autobiography, he more directly compares to the creatures of the Bible the snakes and beasts in the wilderness around him, this instance making it seem even more likely that his autobiography is also symbolic: "we have, like David of old, had our dwelling with the serpents of the rocks and wild beasts of the wilderness; being obliged to hide away from our enemies."*

Biblical imagery reappears in the death of the "little Ewe Lamb," a Christ symbol and gift from that other person of the Trinity, his Father, seemingly sacrificed so that John might "became to some extent a convert to Christianity," and later be a "Shepherd ; it being a calling for which in early life he had a kind of enthusiastic longing." Finally, as Frederick Douglass notes in his 1881 address at Storer College, the twelve-year-old John witnessing his host beat the slave boy repeats the experience of the child Moses, who reached an equivalent turning-point upon seeing an Egyptian beat a Hebrew slave.

RED ROCK, IOWA 15th July, 1857

MR. HENRY L. STEARNS,

MY DEAR YOUNG FRIEND I have not forgotten my promise to write you: but my constant care, & anxiety : have obliged me to put if off a long time. I do not flatter myself that I *can* write anything that will very much interest you : but have concluded to send you a short story of a certain boy of my acquaintance : & for convenience & shortness of name, I will call him John. This story will be mainly a naration of follies and errors ; which it is to be hoped *you may avoid ;* but there is one thing connected with it, which will be calculated to encourage any young person to persevering effort ; & that is the degree of success *in accomplishing his objects* which to a great extent marked the course of this boy throughout my entire acquaintance with him ; notwithstanding his moderate capacity ; & still more moderate acquirements.

John was born May 9th, 1800, at Torrington, Litchfield Co. Connecticut ; of poor but respectable parents : a decendant on the side of his Father of one of the company of the Mayflower who landed at Plymouth 1620. His mother was decended from a man who came at an early period to New England from Amsterdam, in Holland. Both his Fathers and his Mothers Fathers served in the war of the revolution : His Father's Father ; died in a barn at New York while in the service, in 1776.

I cannot tell you of anything in the first Four years of John's life worth mentioning save that at that *early age* he was tempted by Three large Brass Pins belonging to a girl who lived in the family & *stole them.* In this he was detected by his Mother ; & after having a full day to think of the wrong ; received from her a thorough whipping. When he was Five years old his Father moved to Ohio ; then a wilderness filled with wild beasts, & Indians. During the long journey which was performed in part or mostly with an *Oxteam ;* he was called on by turns to assist a boy Five years older (who had been adopted by his Father & Mother) & learned to think he could accomplish *smart things* in driving the Cows; & riding the horses. Sometimes he met with Rattle Snakes which were very large ; & which some of the company generally managed to kill. After getting in Ohio in 1805 he was for some time rather afraid of the Indians, & of their Rifles ; but this soon wore off : & he used to hang about them quite as much as was consistent with good manners ; & learned a trifle of their talk. His father learned to dress Deer Skins, & at 6 years old John was installed a young Buck Skin. He was perhaps rather observing as he ever after remembered the entire process of Deer Skin *dressing ;* so that he could at any times dress his own leather such as Squirel, Raccoon, Cat, Wolf or Dog Skins ; and also learned to make Whip Lashes : which brought him some change at times ; & was of considerable service in many ways. At Six years old John began to be quite a rambler in the wild new country finding birds and Squirrels and sometimes a wild Turkeys nest. But about this period he was placed in the School of *adversity ;* which my young friend was a most necessary part of his early training. You may *laugh* when you come to read about it ; but these were *sore trials* to John whose earthly treasures were very *few, & small.* These were the beginning of a severe but *much needed course* of dicipline which he afterwards was to pass through ; & which it is to be hoped has learned him before this time that the Heavenly Father sees it best to take all the little things out of his hands which he has ever placed in them. When John was in his Sixth year a poor *Indian boy* gave him a Yellow Marble the first he had ever seen. This he thought a great deal of ; & kept it a good while ; but at last *he lost it* beyond recovery. *It took years to heal the wound* & I *think* he cried at times about it. About Five months after this he caught a young Squirel tearing off his tail in doing it & getting severely bitten at the same time himself. He however held on *to the little bob tail Squirrel ;* & finally got him perfectly tamed, so that he almost idolized his pet. *This too he lost ;* by its wandering away ; or by getting killed ; & for year or two John was *in mourning ;* and looking at all the Squirrels he could see to try & discover Bobtail, *if possible.* I must not neglect to tell you of a verry *bad & foolish* habbit to which John was somewhat addicted. I mean *telling lies ;* generally to screen himself from blame ; or from punishment. He could not well endure to be reproached ; & I now think had he been oftener encouraged to be entirely frank ; *by making frankness a kind of atonement* for some of his faults ; he would not have been so often guilty in after life of this fault ; nor have been obliged to struggle *so long* with *so mean* a habit.

John was *never quarrelsome ;* but was *excessively* fond of the *hardest & roughest* kind of plays ; & could *never get enough* [of] them. Indeed when for a short time he was sometimes sent to School the opportunity it afforded to wrestle, & Snow ball & run & jump & knock off old seedy Wool hats ; offered to him almost the only compensation for the confinement, & restraints of school. I need not tell you that with such a feeling & but little chance of going to school *at all :* he did not become much of a schollar. He would always choose to stay at home & work hard rather than be sent to school ; & during the Warm season might generally be seen *barefooted & bareheaded :* with Buck skin Breeches suspended often with one leather strap over his shoulder but sometimes with Two. To be sent off through the wilderness alone to very considerable distances was particularly his delight ; & in this he was often indulged so that by the time he was Twelve years old he was sent off more than a Hundred Miles with companies of cattle ; & he would have thought his character much injured had he been obliged to be helped in any such job. This was a boyish kind of feeling but characteristic however. At Eight years old, John was left a Motherless boy which loss was complete & permanent for notwithstanding his Father again married to a sensible, inteligent, and on many accounts a very estimable woman ; yet he never *adopted her in feeling ;* but continued to pine after his own Mother for years. This opperated very unfavorably uppon him ; as he was both naturally fond of females ; &, withall, extremely diffident ; & deprived him of a suitable connecting link between the different sexes ; the want of which might under some circumstances, have proved his ruin. When the war broke out *with England :* his Father soon commenced furnishing the troops with beef cattle, the collecting & driving of which afforded him some opportunity for the chase (on foot) of wild steers & other cattle through the woods. During this war he had some chance to form his own boyish judgment of *men & measures :* & to become somewhat familiarly acquainted with some who have figured before the country since that time. The effect of what he saw during the war was to so far disgust him with Military affairs that he would neither train, *or drill ;* but paid fines; & got along like a Quaker untill his age finally has cleared him of Military duty. During the war with England a circumstance occurred that in the end made him a most *determined Abolitionist :* & led him to declare, *or Swear : Eternal war* with Slavery. He was staying for a short time with a very gentlemanly landlord since a United States Marshall who held a slave boy near his own age very active, inteligent, and good feeling ; & to whom John was under considerable obligation for numerous little acts of kindness. *The Master* made a great pet of John : brought him to table with his first company ; & friends ; called their attention to every little smart thing he *said or did :* & to the fact of his being more than a hundred miles from home with a company of cattle alone ; while the *negro boy* (who was fully if not more than his equal) was badly clothed, poorly fed ; & *lodged in cold weather ;* & beaten before his eyes with Iron Shovels or any other thing that came first to hand. This brought John to reflect on the wretched, hopeless condition, of *Fatherless & Motherless* slave *children :* for such children have neither Fathers or Mothers to protect & provide for them. He sometimes would raise the question *is God their Father?* At the age of Ten years, an old friend induced him to read a little history, & offered him the free use of a good library ; by ; which he acquired some taste for reading : which formed the principle part of his early education : & diverted him in a great measure from bad company. He by this means grew to be verry fond of the company & conversation of old & inteligent persons. He never attempted to dance in his life ; nor did he ever learn to know *one* of a pack of *Cards* from *another.* He learned nothing of Grammar ; nor did he get at school so much knowledge of comm[on] Arithmetic as the Four grand rules. This will give you some general idea of the first Fifteen years of his life ; during which time he became very strong & large of his age & ambitious to perform the full labour of a man ; at almost any kind of hard work. By reading the lives of great, wise & good men their sayings, and writings ; he grew to a dislike of vain & frivolous *conversation & persons ;* & was often greatly obliged by the kind manner in which older & more inteligent persons treated him at their houses : & in conversation ; which was a great relief on account of his extreme bashfulness. He very early in life became ambitious to excel in doing anything he undertook to perform. This kind of feeling I would recommend to all young persons both *Male & female :* as it will certainly tend to secure admission to the company of the more inteligent ; & better portion of every community. By all means endeavour to excel in some laudable pursuit. I had like to have forgotten to tell you of one of John's misfortunes which set rather hard on him while a young boy. He had by some means *perhaps* by gift of his Father become the owner of a little Ewe Lamb which did finely till it was about Two Thirds grown ; & then sickened and died. This brought another protracted *mourning season :* not that he felt the pecuniary loss so heavily : for that was never his disposition ; but so strong & earnest were his attachments. John had been taught from earliest childhood to "fear God & keep his commandments;" & though quite skeptical he had always by turns felt much serious doubt as to his future well being ; & about this time became to some extent a convert to Christianity & ever after a firm believer in the divine authenticity of the Bible. With this book he became very familiar, & possessed a most unusual memory of its entire contents.

Now some of the things I have been *telling of ;* were just such as I would recommend to you : & adopted them as part of your own plan of life ; & I wish you to have *some deffinite plan.* Many seem to have none ; & others never to stick to any that they do form. This was not the case with John. He followed up with *tenacity* whatever he set about so long as it answered his general purpose : & hence he rarely failed in some good degree to effect the things he undertook. This was so much the case that he *habitually expected to succeed* in his undertakings. With this feeling *should be coupled ;* the consciousness that our plans are right in themselves.

During the period I have named, John had acquired a kind of ownership to certain animals of some little value but as he had come to understand that the *title of minors* might be a little imperfect : he had recourse to various means in order to secure a more *independent ;* & perfect right of property. One of these means was to exchange with his Father for something of far less value. Another was by trading with other persons for something his Father had never owned. Older persons have sometimes found difficulty with *titles.*

From Fifteen to Twenty years old, he spent most of his time working at the Tanner & Currier's trade keeping Bachelors hall ; & he officiating as Cook ; & for most of the time as foreman of the establishment under his Father. During this period he found much trouble with some of the bad habits I have mentioned & with some that I have not told you of : his conscience urging him forward with great power in this matter : but his close attention to *business ;* & success in its management ; together with the way he got along with a company of men, & boys ; made him quite a favorite with the serious & more inteligent portion of older persons. This was so much the case ; & secured for him so many little notices from those he esteemed ; that his vanity was very much fed by it : & he came forward to manhood quite full of self-conceit ; & self-confidant ; notwithstanding his *extreme* bashfulness. A younger brother used sometimes to remind him of this : & to repeat to him *this expression* which you may somewhere find, "A King against whom there is no rising up."

The habit so early formed of being obeyed rendered him in after life too much disposed to speak in an imperious or dictating way. From Fifteen years & upward he felt a good deal of anxiety to learn ; but could only read & studdy a little; both for want of time ; & on account of inflammation of the eyes. He however managed by the help of books to make himself tolerably well acquainted with common Arithmetic ; & Surveying ; which he practiced more or less after he was Twenty years old. At a little past Twenty years led by his own inclination & *prompted also* by his Father, he married a *remarkably plain* ; but industrious & economical girl ; of excellent character ; earnest piety ; & good practical common sense ; about one year younger than himself. This woman by her mild, frank, & *more than all else ;* by her very consistent conduct ; acquired & ever while she lived maintained a most powerful ; & good influence over him. Her plain but kind admonitions generally had the right effect ; without arousing his haughty obstinate temper. John began early in life to discover a great liking to fine Cattle, Horses, Sheep, & Swine ; & as soon as circumstances would enable him he began to be a practical *Shepherd ; it being* a calling for which *in early life* he had a kind of *enthusiastic longing :* together with the idea that as a business it bid fair to afford him the means of carrying out his greatest or principal object. I have now given you a kind of general idea of the early life of this boy ; & if I believed it would be worth the trouble ; or afford much interest to any good feeling person ; I might be tempted to tell you something of his course in after life ; or manhood. I do not say that I *will do it.*

You will discover that in using up my *half sheets to save paper ;* I have written Two pages, so that one does not follow the other as it should. I have no time to write it over ; & but for unavoidable hindrances in traveling I can hardly say when I should have written what I have. With an honest desire for your best good, I subscribe myself ,

Your Friend, J. BROWN.

P.S. – I had like to have forgotten to acknowledge your contribution in aid of the cause in which I serve. God Allmighty *bless you ;* my son. J. B.

* * * *

John Brown to Brother Frederick, November 21, 1834

This letter of 1834 to his brother Frederick is John Brown's first written reference to any strategy for helping blacks, though he claims in the last paragraph that he has reflected upon the issue "for years." While this may be true, it is also likely that the intensification of the abolition movement prompted the ideas outlined; William Lloyd Garrison's recent editorials about manual labor schools for blacks, and the controversy over the establishment of a library and school for blacks in Cincinnati, may have contributed.

He wrote the letter soon after Frederick returned home to Hudson after visiting Randolph in October, and calls Frederick away from Hudson, a place of "conflicting interests and feelings" (Ohio denied black residents full rights as citizens). Nothing came of the ideas outlined in this letter: Brown took no blacks into his family and received no help from "first-rate abolitionist families." By the end of the year his busi-

ness was barely afloat and he was in no position to follow through on his offer to "make . . . any arrangement of our temporal concerns that shall be fair." The letter hints at Brown's sense that his abolitionist interests may not be compatible with his business and family life, for he emphasizes, a touch defensively, that he "fully consulted the feelings of [his] wife and three boys" and that his son Jason expressed interest in the subject of slavery. Brown would struggle for many years to balance with his commitment to his family his devotion to the abolitionist cause.

At this moment in 1834 he is also struggling with what it might mean to "effect" change, returning to this word repeatedly as he tries to balance human actions with divine will, always tempering any assertion of his own initiative with a reference to God's plan: "using means in order to effect, in the confident expectation that God is about to bring them all out of the house of bondage"; "our united exertions alone might soon, with the good hand of our God upon us, effect it all"; and "perhaps we might, under God, in that way do more towards breaking their yoke effectually than in any other."

Randolph, Nov. 21, 1834.

Dear Brother,—As I have had only one letter from Hudson since you left here, and that some weeks since, I begin to get uneasy and apprehensive that all is not well. I had satisfied my mind about it for some time, in expectation of seeing father here, but I begin to give that up for the present. Since you left me I have been trying to devise some means whereby I might do something in a practical way for my poor fellow-men who are in bondage, and having fully consulted the feelings of my wife and my three boys, we have agreed to get at least one negro boy or youth, and bring him up as we do our own,-viz., give him a good English education, learn him what we can about the history of the world, about business, about general subjects, and, above all, try to teach him the fear of God. We think of three ways to obtain one : First, to try to get some Christian slave-holder to release one to us. Second, to get a free one if no one will let us have one that is a slave. Third, if that does not succeed, we have all agreed to submit to considerable privation in order to buy one. This we are now using means in order to effect, in the confident expectation that God is about to bring them all out of the house of bondage.

I will just mention that when this subject was first introduced, Jason had gone to bed; but no sooner did he hear the thing hinted, than his warm heart kindled, and he turned out to have a part in the discussion of a subject of such exceeding interest. I have for years been trying to devise some way to get a school a-going here for blacks, and I think that on many accounts it would be a most favorable location. Children here would have no intercourse with vicious people of their own kind, nor with openly vicious persons of any kind. There would be no powerful opposition influence against such a thing; and should there be any, I believe the settlement might be so effected in future as to have almost the whole influence of the place in favor of such a school. Write me how you would like to join me, and try to get on from Hudson and thereabouts some first-rate abolitionist families with you. I do honestly believe that our united exertions alone might soon, with the good hand of our God upon us, effect it all.

This has been with me a favorite theme of reflection for years. I think that a place which might be in some measure settled with a view to such an object would be much more favorable to such an undertaking than would any such place as Hudson, with all its conflicting interests and feelings; and I do think such advantages ought to be afforded the young blacks, whether they are all to be immediately set free or not. Perhaps we might, under God, in that way do more towards breaking their yoke effectually than in any other. If the young blacks of our country could once become enlightened, it would most assuredly operate on slavery like firing powder confined in rock, and all slaveholders know it well. Witness their heaven-daring laws against teaching blacks. If once the Christians in the free States would set to work in earnest in teaching the blacks, the people of the slaveholding States would find themselves constitutionally driven to set about the work of emancipation immediately. The laws of this State are now such that the inhabitants of any township may raise by a tax in aid of the State school-fund any amount of money they may choose by a vote, for the purpose of common schools, which any child may have access to by application. If you will join me in this undertaking, I will make with you any arrangement of our temporal concerns that shall be fair. Our health is good, and our prospects about business rather brightening.

Affectionately yours, John Brown

* * * *

John Brown to George Kellogg, August 27, 1839

Two months before writing this letter to George Kellogg, Brown had received $2800 from the New England Woolen Company, for whom Kellogg worked as an agent. It was money intended for the purchase of wool. At the same time Brown was on tenterhooks, anticipating a loan from Boston that would pay off several other creditors. Letters to his family confirm that he did expect this loan to come, but by June 12 his hopes were fading a little: he wrote that "things have looked more unfavorable for a few days," asking though that his family not be "discouraged," for "tomorrow may be a much brighter day."

He had been farmer, tanner, land speculator, and now wool merchant, but never financially successful, and the financial crash of 1837 hit him hard. John Jr. would explain much later that with the panic "down came all of father's castles, and buried the reputation he had achieved of possessing at least good common-sense in respect to business matters." In 1839 Brown was still digging himself out from under the rubble, and when the loan didn't arrive from Boston he used the money from the New England Woolen Company to pay off a creditor, the cattle firm Wadsworth and Wells, and thus avoid a jail sentence. Now unable to repay the $2800 to Kellogg, and with no wool to show for it, he writes to excuse himself and promise settlement. The letter is dignified, humble, and sorrowful, and Kellogg was impressed by it. Respecting Brown's honesty and contrition, he concluded that the panic of 1837 had ruined many such men of integrity, and decided not to prosecute. In his reply on September 12, *however, he did advise Brown to remember that his business affairs might reflect badly on the abolitionist cause to which his name was increasingly attached.*

Franklin Mills, 27th Aug 1839

George Kellogg, Esqr
Dear Sir:
   Yours of the 2nd was received in season, & I have no excuse for not answering it promptly, except that I have found it hard to take up my pen to record, & to publish, my own shame, & abuse of the confidence of those whom I esteem, & who have treated me as a friend, & as a brother. I flattered myself till now, with the hope that I might be able to render a more favorable account of myself, but the truth, & the whole truth, shall be told. When I saw you at Vernon, I was in dayly expectation of receiving a number of thousands of dollars from Boston, something over five of which I owed for money I had used belonging to our cattle company, (viz Wadsworth, Wells & myself). On the day I was to set out for home, as I was disappointed of the money I expected, I found no alternative but to go to jail, or to pledge the money the money [sic] you had confided to my trust, & in my extremity I did so with the most of it, pledging it for thirty days, believing that in less than that time I could certainly redeem it, as I expected a large amount from a source I did believe I could depend uppon. Though I have been waiting in painful anxiety I have been disappointed still, & as the best course I could take, I have made an assignment of all my real & personal property for the benefit of my creditors generally, as our laws forbid any preference. I think my property much more than sufficient to satisfy all demands, & that I shall not have to subject you to anything worse in the end than disappointment & delay. I am determined that shall be all, if I & my family work out by the month, & by the day, to make up a full return. I have yet hopes of relief from Boston, & should that be, it will set matters in measure to right again. I have disposed of about 40 yards of your cloth, & find it would go well if my affairs had stood as I expected. Wool has sold at much higher prices here than was expected, & higher than I should have dared to pay had your money been in my possession when I got home.

Unworthily yours, JOHN BROWN

* * * *

John Brown, Declaration of Bankruptcy, October 17, 1842

Brown's business ventures did not recover from the crash of 1837. He was unable to repay loans and fulfill contracts. Hoping for a new start in the Ohio Valley of West Virginia surveying and settling on land owned by Oberlin College, an institution that admitted women and blacks, Brown was disappointed when the Oberlin officials didn't hire him. Creditors foreclosed and took him to court, and dark days followed. In 1841 he was arrested when he tried to prevent the eviction of his family from Westlands farm, where he raised cattle. After barricading himself in a cabin, with three of his sons, John Jr., Jason, and Owen, he was jailed briefly by the local sheriff. His farms were sold at public auction, and he lost almost everything he owned in various settlements.

Even after this he owed thousands of dollars, and in the fall of 1842 he applied for bankruptcy. There were lawsuits against him in several states, and, while he was always considered honest, most involved thought him shortsighted and sloppy in his business dealings. He was declared bankrupt on September 28, 1842, and things didn't improve until 1844, when he went into the wool business with Simon Perkins Jr. After the bankruptcy, presumably remembering the humanity of Kellogg towards him in 1839 (see previous source), he insisted on paying his debts to the New England Woolen Company, and signed the agreement here, of October 17, 1842, also attaching a letter to Kellogg. He wanted, as he wrote to Kellogg in 1841, to "make amends for all the wrong [he had] done." But he hadn't paid the debt by the time of his death in 1859, and left $50 towards it in his will.

The crash, bankruptcy, and eviction had transformed Brown's outlook and beliefs, and he moved closer to the spiritual realm, seeking an escape from the values of the material world around him. He became more and more of an outsider, and looked with an even greater fervor for a new age.

Richfield, Oct. 17, 1842

Whereas I, John Brown, on or about the 15th day of June, A.D. 1839, received of the New England Company (through their agent, George Kellogg, Esq.), the sum of twenty-eight hundred dollars for the purchase of wool for said company, and imprudently pledged the same for my own benefit, and could not redeem it; and whereas I have been legally discharged from my obligations by the laws of the United States,—I hereby agree (in consideration of the great kindness and tenderness of said Company toward me in my calamity, and more particularly of the moral obligation I am under to render to all their due), to pay the same and the interest thereon, from time to time, as Divine Providence shall enable me to do. Witness my hand and seal, John Brown

To the agreement was attached this letter:

* * * *

John Brown to George Kellogg, October 17, 1842
Richfield, Summit Country, Ohio, Oct. 17, 1842

George Kellogg, Esq.

Dear Sir,—I have just received information of my final discharge as a bankrupt in the District Court, and I ought to be grateful that no one of my creditors has made any opposition to such discharge being given. I shall now, if my life is continued, have an opportunity of proving the sincerity of my past professions, when legally free to act as I choose. I am sorry to say that in consequence of the unforseen expense of getting the discharge, the loss of an ox, and the destitute condition in which a new surrender of my effects has placed

me, with my numerous family, I fear this year must pass without my effecting in the way of payment what I have encouraged you to expect (notwithstanding I have been generally prosperous in my business for the season).
Respectfully your unworthy friend, John Brown

* * * *

John Brown to John Jr., September 25, 1843

In 1843 dysentery cut a swathe through the Brown household. Four children, aged one, three, six and nine years, died during September, three of them in as many days. Salmon Brown's reminiscences complete the picture of these children: he remembers that "Charles was very swift and strong, his legs and arms straight as broomsticks, of sandy complexion, quiet as a cat, but brave as a tiger. Peter was very stout, darker, the best-looking member of the family." (See in this anthology: Salmon Brown (son), Reminiscences.)

In his letter to John Jr., two days after the fourth death, Brown informs his eldest son of these latest heartbreaks. There is a powerful and understated pathos to some of his phrasing, in particular the following line: "They were all children towards whom perhaps we might have felt a little partial but they all now lie in a little row together." The hesitancy and use of "perhaps" and "might", and the repetition of "little", are part of a self-protective attempt to telescope the situation, though actually serve to emphasize its magnitude. The repetition of "little" draws attention to the word, and so to the attempt at stoicism, giving it pathos. We know from Salmon Brown's account of the event that it was "a calamity from which father never fully recovered."

When describing the behavior of Sarah Brown on her death-bed, Brown was likely also instructing himself in the correct way to behave. He admires and perhaps envies her "great composure of mind, and patience, together with strong assureance at times of meeting God in Paradise." It is noticeable that several accounts of Brown's conduct at Harpers Ferry, and his trial and execution, describe a "composure of mind" similar to that of his daughter. For example, Thoreau, in his "Plea for Captain John Brown," describes Brown's "utmost composure" at the moment of capture, and a correspondent for the Washington National Intelligencer *notes that "Brown received the sentence with composure" at the end of his trial on November 2. Mary Brown had apparently developed the skill of composure also, for John T. L. Preston represents her "absolute composure of manner" at Brown's execution in his letter of December 2, 1859.*

In recounting his daughter's deathbed attitude and reminding himself of the importance of such qualities as faith, composure and patience, Brown probably had Job in mind as a model. Bereft of home, business and children, this was certainly the moment in his life when he must have felt most like the long-suffering Biblical character. Job, losing everything, struggled to maintain composure of mind, and heard of various losses to his estate sedately, but cracked when tidings were brought of the death of his children, whereupon he "arose and rent his mantle, and shaved his head, and fell down upon the ground" (Job 1:20). But even then he kept faith with God, saying as he lay and mourned, "the LORD gave, and the LORD hath taken away; blessed be the name of the LORD" (Job 1:21). Brown's weary affirmation that "still the Lord reigneth and blessed be his great and holy name forever" is almost an exact echo.

Richfield 25th Sept 1843

Dear Son

God has seen fit to visit us with the pestilence since you left us, and Four of our number sleep in the dust, and Four of us that are still living have been more or less unwell but appear to be nearly recovered. On the 4th Sept Charles was taken with the Dysentery and died on the 11th, about the time that Charles died Sarah, Peter, & Austin were taken with the same complaint. Austin died on the 21st, Peter on the 22d & Sarah on the 23d and were all buried together in one grave. This has been to us all a bitter cup indeed, and we have drunk deeply, but still the Lord reigneth and blessed be his great and holy name forever. In our sore affliction there is still some comfort. Sarah (like your own Mother) during her sickness discovered great composure of mind, and patience, together with strong assureance at times of meeting God in Paradise. She seemed to have no idea of recovering from the first, nor did she ever express the least desire that she might, but rather the reverse. We fondly hope that she is not disappointed. They were all children towards whom perhaps we might have felt a little partial but they all now lie in a little row together. Jason wants to add a few lines & I shall be short. I am yet feeble from the same disorder which may account for some of my blunders. We hope to see you when your term is out, it perhaps will not be best before. May you be enabled to cleanse your way. [signature cut out]

* * * *

Business Agreement between John Brown and Simon Perkins, January 1844

As an outcome of his sheep farming, Brown began a business partnership with Simon Perkins, and on January 9, 1844, formed with him the company Perkins & Brown, wool merchants, the terms of which are given here. In April he moved with his family to Akron, Summit County, Ohio, into a cottage on Perkins' property, just across from his partner's house. The Perkins family mansion still stands across the street from Brown's home. Perkins was said to resemble Moses in his head and beard, and, though less religious than Brown, was widely considered honorable. Brown was grateful for the risk that Perkins took, writing to his son John on January 11, 1844, that "it is certainly endorsing the poor Bankrupt and his family three of whom were but recently in Akron jail in a manner quite unexpected; . . . our industrious and steady endeavours to maintain our integrity and our character have not been wholly overlooked."

It was Brown's most successful business venture and he was excited about it, writing in the same letter that "Divine Providence seems to smile on our works at this time." The firm had Merino sheep, the best of the finewools, and Brown was an expert grader of wool. Salmon Brown remembers that "while running sheep with Simon Perkins, he took first prize at the first world's Fair ever held. Frederick Douglass, who first met Brown in Springfield, noted in a speech of 1881 that Brown was "a good judge of wool, as a wool-dealer ought to be," and a story circulated that while Brown was in England on business in 1849, an Englishman tested his knowledge of wool by handing him the fleece of a shorn poodle. Brown rolled it between his fingers for a few seconds and said: "Gentlemen, if you have any machinery in England that will work up dog's hair, I advise you to put this into it."

Even so, the partnership was not particularly profitable and the company was soon in trouble. In 1846 Brown moved to Springfield, Massachusetts, where the firm had a warehouse to sell Western Reserve wool. He bought and sold wool on commission, but blundered when he tried to force the value of wool higher, for this attempt to dictate prices prompted the New England manufacturers to combine against him. He traveled to Europe in August 1849 with a large cargo, but eventually sold it for much less than it would have brought in Springfield and returned, bankrupt, several months later. Though encouraged by Perkins to remain in the wool trade, Brown dissolved his part of the partnership in 1854, and joined his family in Timbucto (now North Elba), a black community founded on land donated by the wealthy antislavery campaigner, Gerrit Smith.

AGREEMENT – JOHN BROWN & SIMON PERKINS

The undersigned, Simon Perkins, Jr. and John Brown have this day agreed as follows viz. They agree to place the flocks of sheep which they each now have in a joint concern at their value, and to share equally the gain or loss yearly, commencing on the 15th day of April of each year.

Said Perkins agrees to furnish all the food and shelter that shall be necessary for the good of the flock from the 1st of December of each year to the 15th of April of each year.

Said Brown agrees on his part to furnish throughout the year all the care and attention of every description which the good of the flock may require, wash the sheep, shear the wool, sack and ship the same for market in the neatest and best manner, an equal set-off against the food &c. necessary for the wintering of the flock.

The said parties agree to share equally the pasturing, and all other expenses of said flock yearly, and to improve and increase the same from time to time as the business will justify, and they may agree.

Said Perkins agrees to let said Brown the frame dwelling-house on his farm (south of the house in which he now lives) door-yards, garden grounds, and the privilege of getting wood for fuel, for the rent of thirty-dollars a year commencing on the First of April next.

Said Brown agrees to pay that amount yearly, so long as he may continue to occupy said house, from his share of the proceeds of said flock.

Said Brown agrees to harvest the turnips and potatoes which said Perkins may raise yearly for the use of said flock.

This agreement to remain in force for full years until the parties shall think proper to alter or dissolve it.

Witness our names this ninth day of January 1844, [Signed]

Simon Perkins, Junior

John Brown

* * * *

John Brown to Mary Brown (wife), March 7, 1844

Mary Brown carried the following letter with her for many years (dated wrongly as March 7, 1844, probably written during 1847). It is Brown's most tender love-letter to her, free of his usual practical instructions, and full of intriguing revelations about the Brown family dynamics: the different roles of John and Mary (he writes, "I want your face to shine, even if my own should be dark and cloudy"); the unexpected use of pet-names for his children ("Little Chick and that strange Anna"); and his absolute yearning for "the quiet of home"—a less well-known side to the legendary hero-warrior.

Often homesick, as his letters of 1846 and 1847 testify, Brown imagines an alternative reality in which he is at home, as on November 29, 1846, when he states: "In imagination I seem to be present with you." In the letter here he feels himself so present at home that he is able to converse with Mary: "It is once more Sabbath evening, and nothing so much accords with my feelings as to spend a portion of it in conversing with the partner of my choice." He explains that, like Jesus, though "absent in body, I am very much of the time present in spirit."

His love of the third person where first or second person would be usual, most notably expressed in his autobiography of 1857, prompts him to use it here, writing to Mary: "I do not forget the firm attachment of her who has remained my fast and faithful affectionate friend." The device is reminiscent of his letter to Ruth of 1847 that proceeds at length in the third person, though asking questions of Ruth herself: "What feelings and motives govern her? In what manner does she spend her time?"

A final interesting feature of this letter is the confluence of Brown's homesickness and his pain on behalf of slaves, expressed as well in another letter of around the same time (see John Brown to His Afflicted Wife and Children, November 8, 1846). Just as his awareness of the emotional poverty of others increases his gratitude for his family, so his love of his family drives his desire to help those "millions" with no home. By the end of the letter it is ambiguous whether "those about me" are his immediate family or the human race.

Springfield, Mass, March 7, 1844.

My dear Mary,

It is once more Sabbath evening, and nothing so much accords with my feelings as to spend a portion of it in conversing with the partner of my choice, and the sharer of my poverty, trials, discredit, and sore afflictions, as well as of what comfort and seeming prosperity has fallen to my lot for quite a number of years. I would you should realize that, notwithstanding I am absent in body, I am very much of the time present in spirit. I do not forget the firm attachment of her who has remained my fast and faithful affectionate friend, when others said of me, "Now that he lieth, he shall rise up no more." . . . I now feel encouraged to believe that my absence will not be very long. After being so much away, it seems as if I knew pretty well how to appreciate the quiet of home. There is a peculiar music in the word which a half-year's absence in a distant country would enable you to understand. Millions there are who have no such thing to lay claim to. I feel considerable regret by turns that I have lived so many years, and have in reality done so little to increase the amount of human happiness. I often regret that my manner is no more kind and affectionate to those I really love and esteem; but I trust my friends will overlook my harsh, rough ways, when I cease to be in their way as an occasion of pain and unhappiness. In imagination I often see you in your room with Little Chick and that strange Anna. You must say to her that father means to come before long and kiss somebody. I will close by saying that it is my growing resolution to endeavor to promote my own happiness by doing what I can to render those about me more so. If the large boys do wrong, call them alone into your room, and expostulate with them kindly, and see if you cannot reach them by a kind but powerful appeal to their honor. I do not claim that such a theory accords very well with my practice; I frankly confess it does not; but I want your face to shine, even if my own should be dark and cloudy. You can let the family read this letter, and perhaps you may not feel it a great burden to answer it, and let me hear all about how you get along.

Affectionately yours,

John Brown

* * * *

John Brown to His Afflicted Wife and Children, November 8, 1846

Living and working in Springfield from 1846 onwards, Brown often felt as though he had abandoned his family, feeling them to be far away "in a distant country," as he put it in a letter to his wife (see John Brown to Mary Brown (wife), March 7, 1844). He regularly worried that some mishap had befallen them, writing once to check that the house hadn't burned down, and on another occasion that snow hadn't been "left to pile on the roof of the shed till it breaks down, and kills the cattle or some person" (letter of January 22, 1850). His constant dread and sense of helplessness must have made all the more testing the news of another death in the family, this time of one-year old Amelia Brown through accidental scalding by her older sister Ruth. Franklin Sanborn, writing in the April 1872 edition of Atlantic Monthly, *insists that when away from home Brown "did not by any means forget or neglect his family," but biographers differ on the issue of how neglected they were. Salmon Brown's reminiscences of his own childhood suggest that, at least until Brown began work in Kansas in the 1850s, he was much involved with all aspects of family life (see Salmon Brown (son), Reminiscences).*

Certainly at this particular moment Brown found his work for Perkins & Brown incompatible with family life. But he discovered that at least

Figure 14: Mary Brown and two daughters, dauguerreotype, 1859. (*Courtesy, Library of Congress.*)

his calling to free slaves was in harmony with his feelings for his wife and children (see John Brown to Mary Brown (wife), March 7, 1844, for another example of this harmony). His frequent homesickness made him "feel the more for the vast numbers who are forced away from their dearest relatives," as he wrote on January 8, 1847. Perhaps sensing this harmony, he opens out the letter here to a more general philosophizing about the power of small actions and little words to effect great change, so that it becomes an eerie prophesy of his raid and martyrdom. Equally, his assertion that "everything worthy of being done at all; is worthy of being done in good earnest, & in the best possible manner," might easily be applied to the manner in which he embraced death, for his was a death done carefully and well, so as to force the issue of slavery.

The letter is also interesting because, though he uses the same phrase as on September 25, 1843 to encapsulate his grief for the loss of life ("a bitter cup indeed"), it is more fluently emotional than the earlier letter to his son John announcing the deaths of four of his children. He writes to his wife and younger children now: "I seem to be struck almost dumb. One more dear little feeble child I am to meet no more till the dead small & great shall stand before God." This difference in tone may be due to the shift in readership, from eldest son to wife, or it may be that, far

from home, more and more confident in his calling, and in a less des-
perate financial situation than three years previous, Brown no longer felt
like a modern day Job lying among the ruins of his life and home and,
accordingly, did not adopt a Job-like stoic attitude.

Springfield 8th Nov 1846

Sabbath evening

MY DEAR AFFLICTED WIFE & CHILDREN

I yesterday at night returned after an absence of several days from this place & am uterly unable to give any expression of my feelings on hearing of the dreadful news contained in Owens letter of the 30th & Mr. Perkins of the 31st Oct. I seem to be struck almost dumb.

One more dear little feeble child I am to meet no more till the dead small & great shall stand before God. This is a bitter cup indeed, but blessed be God a brighter day shall dawn; & let us not sorrow as those that have no hope. Oh that we that remain, had wisdom wisely to consider; & to keep in view our latter end. Divine Providence seems to lay a heavy burden; & responsibility on you *my dear Mary;* but I trust you will be enabled to bear it in some measure as you ought. I exceedingly regret that I am unable to return, & be *present* to share your trials with you : but anxious as I am to be once more at home I do not feel at liberty to return yet. I hope to be able to get away before verry long; but cannot say when. I trust that none of you will feel disposed to cast an unreasonable blame on my dear Ruth on account of the dreadful trial we are called [to] suffer; for if the want of proper care in each, & all of us has not been attended with fatal consequenses it is no thanks to us. If I had a right sence of my habitual neglect of my familys Eternal interests; I should probably go crazy. I humbly hope this dreadful afflictive Providence will lead us all more properly to appreciate the amazeing, unforseen, untold, consequences; that hang upon the right or wrong doing of things seemingly of trifling account. Who can tell or comprehend the vast results for good, or for evil; that are to follow the saying of one little word. Evrything worthy of being done *at all;* is worthy of being done in good *earnest,* & in the best possible manner. We are in midling health & expect to write some of you again soon. Our warmest thanks to our kind friends Mr. & Mrs. Perkins & family. From your affectionate husband, & father JOHN BROWN

* * * *

John Brown to Mary Brown, November 29, 1846

"When the day comes that will afford me an opportunity to return I
shall be awake to greet the earliest dawn; if not its midnight birth."
Brown's letter of November 29, 1846 contains some of his most beauti-
ful prose. It has much of the character of the letter of November 8. We
continue to see the man behind the myth, his concern with mundane de-
tails—"whether you have received the cloth, fish & Tea I had tried to
send you or not"—and the tension between his work and family. He ex-
presses once more his desire to "share" his family's trials, and makes
clear again that he misses them.

But the letter has, at points, an entirely different tone from the ear-

lier letter. Two weeks on, clearly still in mourning for his daughter, Brown is less accepting and patient in his attitude towards "the bitter cup" that God keeps offering. Only happy thoughts of his family keep him feeling that God has not "forsaken us utterly." He is cheered though by the news that his sons John and Jason have written to Mary: "Nothing is scarsely equ[a]l with me; to the satisfaction of seeing that one portion of my remaining family are not disposed to exclude from their sympathies, & their warm affections, another portion." This is a fascinating insight into the dynamics of Brown's family, the potentially fraught relations between Dianthe's children and Brown's second wife, which of course might also be applied to Brown's abolitionism: his desire that blacks, part of the human family, as he believed, not be excluded from it.

Springfield 29th Nov 1846

Dear Mary

It is once more Sabbath evening, & kneed I say that with its return my mind is more than ever filled with the thoughts of home, of my wife, & my children. In immagination I seem to be present with you; to share with you the sorrows, or joys you experience. Your letter dated the 20th was received last night, & afforded one *a real* though a mournful satisfaction. That you had received; or were to receive a letter from either John, or Jason, I was in perfect ignorance of; till you informed me; & I am glad to learn that wholly uninfluenced by me; they have shown a disposition to afford you all the comfort in your *deep affliction* which the nature of the case would admit of. Nothing is scarsely equ[a]l with *me;* to the satisfaction of seeing that one portion of my *remaining* family are not disposed to exclude from their sympathies, & their warm affections, another portion. I accept it as one of the most grateful returns that can be made to me; for any care or exertions on my part to promote either their present or their future well being; & while I am able to discover such a feeling I feel assured that notwithstanding God has chastised us *often, & sore;* yet he has not *himself* entirely withdrawn from us, nor forsaken us *utterly.* The sudden, & dreadful manner in which he has seen fit to call *our dear little Kitty* to take her leave of us, is I kneed not tell you how much on mind; but before *Him;* I will bow my head in submission, & hold my peace. I suppose Jason is with you before this can reach you, & I trust that nothing on his part, or on the part of *any one* of my older children will be wanting to render your situation as comfortable as may be. Of the motives that lead one into such business as will, or does deprive me of the society of my family I will say nothing, but any ideas that *to me* the separation is not a painful one are wholly mistaken ones. I have sailed over a somewhat stormy sea for nearly half a century, & have experienced enough to teach me thoroughly that I may most reasonabl[y] buckle up & be prepared for the tempest. Mary let us try to maintain a cheerful self command while we are tossing up & down, & let our motto still be Action, Action; as we have but one life to live. How long I shall yet feel constrained to stay *here,* I am not yet able to foresee, sometimes the prospect seems quite disheartening, & at other times it brightens. Since Jason left things look a little more encourageing than at that time. When the day *comes* that will afford me an opportunity to return I shall be awake to greet the earliest dawn; if not its *midnight birth*. I want to have you write me often; & as there is another man belonging in Springfield of the same name as myself, & son, who sometimes opens my letters; you might direct to care of Perkins & Brown. I want to hear how Jason got home, (as he appeared lately to be in rather a poor state of health) & whether you have received the cloth, fish & Tea I had tried to send you or not. Mr. Perkins has done us a great kindness in writing us so often; & has manifested the kindest feeling in all that he has written, & in being midling particular about things at home. I hope he will not get tired of it. I mean to write him again shortly. I neither forget him, nor Mrs. P, or any of their family.

Affectionately Yours
JOHN BROWN

I think Ruth promised to write me again

* * * *

John Brown to His Father, December 10, 1846

Brown and his father Owen wrote to each other often. Brown would outline the latest developments in his business and recount domestic incidents, large and small, and he and his father reassured one another in their journeys toward God, for they shared a deep religious sympathy. There is an honest vulnerability in Brown's confession that he hasn't attended to the spirituality of his friends as he should have done. This is one of the many times that he sought his father's reassurance and approval in matters spiritual and political.

Owen was an important political influence, and Brown claimed that his father's abolitionism made him a "dyed-in-the-wool Abolitionist." Owen had been affected by a sermon given by Jonathan Edwards, Jr., which discussed slavery as a sin against God, and identified himself as an abolitionist throughout his life. Like Brown, who was involved with Oberlin College, a coed interracial institution, Owen was interested in the education of blacks. He sat on the board of trustees at Western Reserve University because the first college president was an abolitionist and took several black students. Owen resigned from the board when a later president cut the number of blacks offered places by the college.

Between Brown and his father dependence and respectful vulnerability were mutual. Though here Brown seeks his father's wisdom, he refers to Owen earlier in the letter as his "kind . . . old father," and in other letters addresses him almost as though he were the father and Owen his son: his affectionate pride is apparent when he writes to the seventy-six-year-old Owen on April 2, 1847: "It affords me a great satisfaction to get a letter from you at this period of your life, so handsomely written, so well-worded, and so exactly in point." (As he notes in the letter of December 1846, he saved the entire thirty-year correspondence.) Eventually of course Owen would be entirely vulnerable and their roles absolutely reversed (See in this anthology: Salmon Brown (son), Reminiscences).

Springfield, Mass, Dec 10, 1846

Dear Father—Yours, dated 2d and 3d December, we received this evening. It is perhaps needles for me to say that I am always grateful for everything of that kind I receive from you, and that I think I have your whole correspondence for nearly thirty years laid up to remember you by—I mean of course, what you have directed to me. I would further say, that I feel grateful to you, and my brother, for calling to see my dear afflicted wife and children in their calamity. It is a great comfort that *I can* in my imagination *see* my always kind and affectionate old father with them, while at the same time the responsibilities I have assumed constrain me to be absent, very contrary to my feeling (and it may be contrary to my duty, too, but trust not). I meant to return some time in February, and should feel like one out of prison could I leave tomorrow. I hope you will visit my family as often as you *can* during my absence, and that you will write us often while here. We will endeavor, one of us, to reply promptly at least. We are getting along with our business slowly, but prudently, I trust, and as well as we could reasonably expect under the circumstances; and so far as we can discover, we are in favor with this people, and also with the many we have had to do business with. I sent home a good supply of excellent cloth of pantaloons, from which you can have some if it suits you, and should arrive safe. If it does not, please write me without delay. Jason took the cloth with him (cost eight-five cents per yard). I can bring more cloth of almost any kind when I return, should there be need.

When I think how very little influence I have even tried to use with my numerous acquaintances and friends, in turning their minds toward God and heaven, I feel justly condemned as a most wicked and slothful servant; and the more so, as I have very seldom had any one refuse to listen when I earnestly call him to hear. I sometimes have dreadful reflections about having fled to go down to Tarshish.

Affectionately yours, JOHN BROWN

* * * *

John Brown, "Sambo's Mistakes," for The Ram's Horn, 1848

In 1848, while still living in Springfield, Brown contributed this essay to The Ram's Horn, *a short-lived black abolitionist journal based in New York. The editor knew he was white but preserved his black identity and printed the essay anonymously. In it he poses as a black moralist offering constructive criticism by way of autobiographical example. The message is that blacks need to help themselves and not be dependent on whites, a conclusion similar to that of several self-critical black newspapers to which Brown had subscriptions. The narrator embodies the oft-repeated criticism that blacks were submissive and held back by sectionalism, and also conforms to the stereotype of the self-indulgent and imprudent black man.*

The piece has been called heavy-handed by biographers and critics, but in fact has much humor and artistic merit. Brown alludes throughout to Exodus 32, Moses calling to the Israelites to rid themselves of idols and overthrow their masters. He also engages in a relentless parody, affecting an apologetic, garrulous style, and so a self-effacing and nervous narrator. The essay differs in cadence from his letters, which are never breathless and tend to have short sentences or longer sentences built with neat, short clauses. We soon ascertain that there is little use in the narrator's "seeing where he missed it," for the repetition of this phrase nine times undermines the narrator's claim to "quickness of perception," and the refrain, which begins as a believable if vague statement of self-knowledge and self-criticism, is, by the third or fourth repetition, a joke. After all nine repetitions it is almost musical.

The narrator's reiteration that he can see "where he missed it" distinguishes him from the real Brown, who rarely paused on his errors, instead reinventing himself and moving on as a different character: from business man to shepherd to Indian warrior to black man to martyr. The narrator of "Sambo's Mistakes" chooses repetition over reinvention. Of course Brown's exploration of this type of behavior is another example of his interest in different characters, the "variety" and "experience of millions of others of all ages" that he mentions in this essay. As an exercise in creative autobiography it predates his autographical letter to Stearns by nine years and is perhaps a playing out of the kind of man the young John Brown could have become: the narrator, unable to shake his childish love of "Canes, Watches, Safety Chains, Finger rings, Breast Pins," is like the five year-old John who covets Three large Brass Pins and a Yellow Marble.

Chapter 1st.

For the *Ram's Horn*

Sambo's Mistakes

Mess Editors   Notwithstanding I may have committed a few mistakes in the course of a long life like others of my colored brethren yet you will perceive at a glance that I have always been remarkable for a seasonable discovery of my errors & quick perception of the true course. I propose to give you a few illustrations in this & the following chapters. For instance when I was a boy I learned to read but instead of giving my attention to sacred & profane history by which I might have become acquainted with the true character of God & of man learned the true course for individuals, societies, & nations to pursue, stored my mind with an endless variety of rational and practical ideas, profited by the experience of millions of others of all ages, fitted myself for the most important stations in life & fortified my mind with the best & wisest resolutions, & noblest sentiments, & motives, I have spent my whole life devouring silly novels & other miserable trash such as most newspapers of the day & other popular writings are filled with, thereby unfitting myself for the realities of life & acquiring a taste for nonsense & low wit, so that I have no rellish for sober truth, useful knowledge or practical wisdom. By this means I have passed through life without proffit to myself or others a mere blank on which nothing worth peruseing is written But I can see in a twink where I missed it. Another error into [which] I fell in early life was the notion that chewing & smoking tobacco would make a man of me but little inferior to some of the whites. The money I spent in this way would with the interest of it have enabled me to have relieved a great many sufferers supplyed me with a well selected interesting library, & pa[i]d for a good farm for the support & comfort of my old age; whereas I have now neith[er] books, clothing, the satisfaction of having benefited others, nor where to lay my hoary head. But I can see in a moment where I missed it. Another of the few errors of my life is that I have joined the Free Masons Odd Fellows Sons of Temperance, & a score of other secret societies instead of seeking the company of inteligent wise & good men from whom I might have learned much that would be interesting, instructive, & useful & have in that way squandered a great amount of most precious time; & money enough sometime in [a] single year which if I had then put the same out on interest & kept it so would have kept me always above board given me character, & influence amongst men or have enabled me to pursue some respectable calling so that I might employ others to their benefit & improvement, but as it is I have always been poor, in debt, & now obliged to travel about in search of employment as a hostler shoe black & fidler. But I retain all my quickness of perception I can see readily where I missed it.

Chapter 2d

Sambo's Mistakes

Another error of my riper years has been that when any meeting of colored people has been called in order to consider of any important matter of general interest I have been so eager to display my spouting talents & so tenacious of some trifling theory or other that I have adopted that I have generally lost all sight of the business in hand consumed the time disputing about things of no moment & thereby defeated entirely many important measures calculated to promote the general welfare; but I am happy to say I can see in a minute where I missed it. Another small error of my life (for I never committed great blunders) has been that I never would (for the sake of union in the furtherance of the most vital interests of our race) yield any minor point of difference. In this way I have always had to act with but a few, or more frequently alone & could accomplish nothing worth living for, but I have one comfort, I can see in a minute where I missed it. Another little fault which I have committed is that if in anything another man has failed of coming up to my standard that notwithstanding he might possess many of the most valuable traits & be most admirably adapted to fill some one important post, I would reject him entirely, injure his influence, oppose his measures, & even glory in his defeats while his intentions were good, & his plans well laid. But I have the great satisfaction of being able to say without fear of contradiction that I can see *verry quick* where I missed it.

Chapter 3d

Sambo's Mistakes

Another small mistake which I have made is that I could never bring myself to practice any present self denial although my theories have been excellent. For instance I have bought expensive gay clothing nice Canes, Watches, Safety Chains, Finger rings, Breast Pins, & many other things of a like nature, thinking I might by that means distinguish myself from the vulgar as some of the better class of whites do. I have always been of the foremost in getting up expensive parties, & running after fashionable amusements, have indulged my appetite freely whenever I had the means (& even with borro[w]ed means) have patronized the dealers in Nuts, Candy, &c freely & have sometimes bought good suppers & was always a regular customer at Livery stables. By these & many other means I have been unable to benefit my suffering Brethren, & am now but poorly able to keep my own Soul & boddy together; but do not think me thoughtless or dull of appre[he]ntion for I can see at once where I missed it.

Another trifling error of my life has been that I have always expected to secure the favour of the whites by tamely submitting to every species of indignity contempt & wrong insted of nobly resisting their brutal aggressions from principle & taking my place as a man & assuming the responsibilities of a man a citizen, a husband, a father, a brother, a neighbour, a friend as God requires of every one (if his neighbour will allow him to do it) but I find that I get for all my submission about the same reward that the Southern Slaveocrats render to the Dough faced Statesmen of the North for being bribed & browbeat, & fooled & cheated, as the Whigs & Democrats love to be. & think themselves highly honored if they may be allowed to lick up the spittle of a Southerner. I say I get the same reward. But I am uncomm[only] quick sighted I can see in a minute where I missed it. Another little blunder which I made *is*, that while I have always been a most zealous Abolitionist I have been constantly at war with my friends about certain religious tenets. I was first a Presbyterian but I could never think of acting with my Quuaker friends for thay were the rankest heretiks & the Baptists would be in the water, & the Methodists denied the doctrine of Election, & of later years since becoming englightened by Garrison Abby Kelly & other really benevolent persons I have been spending all my force on my friends who love the Sabbath & have felt that all was at stake on that point just as it has proved to be of late in France in the abolition of Slavery in their colonies. Now I cannot doubt Mess Editors notwithstanding I have been unsuccessful that you will allow me full credit for my *peculiar* quick sightedness. I can see in one second where I missed it.

* * * *

John Brown to John Jr., December 6, 1850

Brown's letter to John Jr. on December 6, 1850 marks the beginning of the long process of winding up the firm's affairs, a process slowed by litigation such as the lawsuit for which Brown needs his son's testimony. Mr. Perkins, his business partner, and his eldest son, have both recently scolded him, and the letter has a conciliatory tone. He humorously tempers his skepticism towards the popular spiritualism of the day, most famously practiced by the Fox family of Rochester, New York, who held séances complete with "knocking spirits" in which John Jr. believed. And he admits that he has "often made mistakes by being too hasty." In fact, he seems to have given up on himself as a businessman, writing, "I most earnestly hope that should I lose caste, my family will at least prove themselves worthy of respect and confidence."

He is withdrawing psychologically from the business world and the company, Perkins & Brown, about which he had previously cared a great deal. The passing of the Fugitive Slave Act on September 18 of that year had shaken him deeply, and a month after writing this letter he would organize the United States League of Gileadites, aimed at reversing some of the tendencies of Sambo (see John Brown, Words of Advice, United States League of Gileadites, January 15, 1851 and John Brown, "Sambo's

Mistakes," for The Ram's Horn, *1848). Four years on, Perkins & Brown was finally dissolved, and by 1856 Brown the businessman had become Osawatomie Brown, warrior and legend. The "path of [his] feet" had led away from business for the final time.*

One of the most interesting features of the letter is this quotation from Proverbs 4:26, "ponder well the path of my feet." The Proverbs chapter to which Brown alludes is one of Solomon's more famous and powerful addresses to a "son." It opens, "Hear, ye children, the instruction of a father," and continues, "Hear, O my son, and receive my sayings; and the years of thy life shall be many. I have taught thee in the way of wisdom; I have led thee in right paths. . . My son, attend to my words; incline thine ear unto my sayings." Brown's otherwise conciliatory tone is diluted by this subtle reminder to his son about who captains the Brown family ship. He is gently pulling rank.

Springfield, Mass, Dec. 6, 1850.

Dear son John,— Your kind letter is received. By same mail I also have one from Mr. Perkins in answer to one of mine, in which I did in no very indistinct way introduce some queries, not altogether unlike those your letter contained. Indeed, your letter throughout is so much like what has often passed through my own mind, that were I not a little sceptical yet, I should conclude you had access to some of the knocking spirits. I shall not write you very long, as I mean to write again before many days. Mr. Perkins's letter, to which I just alluded, appears to be written in a very kind spirit; and so long as he is right-side up, I shall by no means despond; indeed, I think the fog clearing away from our matters a little. I certainly wish to understand, and I mean to understand, "how the land lies" before taking any important steps. You can assist me very much about being posted up; but you will be able to get hold of the right end exactly by having everything done up first-rate, and by becoming very familiar, and not by keeping distant. I most earnestly hope that should I lose caste, my family will at least prove themselves worthy of respect and confidence; and I am sure that my three sons in Akron can do a great job for themselves and for the family if they behave themselves wisely. Your letter so well expresses my own feelings, that were it not for one expression I would mail it with one I have just finished, to Mr. Perkins. Can you not all three effectually secure the name of good business men this winter? That you are considered honest and rather intelligent I have no doubt.

I do not believe the losses of our firm will in the end prove so very severe, if Mr. Perkins can only be kept resolute and patient in regard to matters. I have often made mistakes by being too hasty, and mean hereafter to "ponder well the path of my feet." I mean to pursue in all things such a course as is in reality wise, and as will in the end give to myself and family the least possible cause for regret. I believe Mr. Newton is properly authorized to take testimony. If so, I wish you to ascertain the fact and write me; if not, I want you to learn through Mr. Perkins who would be a suitable person for that business, a[n]d I expect before many weeks to want your testimony, and I want you to give me the name. I forgot to write to Mr. Perkins about it, and have sealed up my letter to him. I mentioned about your testimony, but forgot what I should have written.

Your affectionate father, John Brown

* * * *

John Brown to His Children, January 23, 1852

Brown's letter of January 23, 1852 is for Ruth and Henry Thompson, though addressed only to "Children." He wrote it while at Troy, New York, in the midst of the worst law suits of this career. Henry Warren, a New York wool farmer, claimed that Brown owed him several thousand dollars, and the Burlington Mills Company of Vermont claimed a $60,000 loss incurred when Brown delivered a lower grade of wool than promised. Seeking to escape these worldly dramas into the realm of religion, and to regain control in at least one area of his life, Brown began to express concern for his children's spiritual backsliding.

The letter is the first of a series in which he seems depressed about the spiritual state of his family, often blaming himself for their failings. One phrase in the letter echoes the refrain of his essay, "Sambo's Mistakes," of four years earlier, though meant here in earnest and so probably not a deliberate allusion: "I think I can clearly discover where I wandered from the Road," recalling the line of 1848: "I can see readily where I missed it." From feeling his family to be the source of his continued faith, in 1846, Brown has now lost faith in his family to the degree that even God cannot restore: "How to now get on it with my family is beyond my ability to see; or my courage to hope." The balance between his family and his calling has shifted again: he writes, "My attachments to this world have been very strong, & Divine Providence has been cutting me loose one Cord after another." Though affectionate, Brown is deadly serious in his reproaches.

Troy N Y 23 Jan, 1852

Dear Children

I returned here on the evening of the 19th inst & left Akron on the 14th the date of your letters to John. I was very glad to hear from you again in that way, not having received any thing from you while at home. I left all in usual health & as comfortable as could be expected; but am afflicted with you on account of your little Boy. Hope to hear by return mail that you are all well. As in this trouble you are only tasteing of a Cup I have had to drink of deeply, & very often; I need not tell how fully I can sympathize with you in your anxiety. My atachments to this world have been very strong, & Divine Providence has been cutting me loose one Cord after another, up to the present time, but notwithstanding I have so much to remind me that all ties must soon be severed; I am still clinging like those who have hardly taken a single lesson. I really hope some of my family may understand that this world is not the Home of man; & act in accordance. Why may I not hope this of you ? When I look forward as regards the religious prospects of my numerous family (the most of them) I am forced to say, & to feel too; that I have little, very little to cheer. That this should be so, is I perfectly well understand the legitimate fruit of my own planting; and that only increases my punishment. Some Ten or Twelve years ago, I was cheered with the belief that my elder children had chosen the Lord, to be their God; & I valued much on their influence & example in attoning for my deficiency, & bad example with the younger children. But; where are we now? Several have gone to where neither a good or bad example from me will better their condition or prospects or make them the worse. The younger part of my children seem to be far less thoughtful, & disposed to reflection than were my older children at their age. I will not dwell longer on this distressing subject but only say that so far as I have gone; it is from no disposition to reflect on anyone but myself. I think I can clearly discover where I wandered from the Road. How to now get on it with my family is beyond my ability to see; or my courage to hope. God grant you thorough conversion from sin, & full purpose of heart to continue steadfast in his ways through the very short season of trial you will have to pass.

How long we shall continue here is beyond our ability to foresee, but think it very probable that if you write us by return mail we shall get your letter. Something may possibly happen that may enable us, (or one of us) to go & see you but do not look for us. I should feel it a great privilege if I could. We seem to be getting along well with our business so far; but progress miserably slow. My journeys back & forth this Winter have been very tedious. If you find it difficult for you to pay for Douglas paper, I wish you would let me know as I know I took some liberty in ordering it continued. You have been very Kind in helping me, & I do not mean to make myself a burden   Your Affectionate Father, John Brown

* * * *

John Brown to His Son John, August 26, 1853

According to Salmon Brown, "The burden of [John Brown's soul] was the souls of his children, and he strove with them without ceasing." Brown's concern for his children's spirituality, expressed particularly strongly in 1852 and 1853, develops at length in a letter to John Jr., where he expresses his "pain and sorrow" at the attitudes of his sons. An attempt to convince his eldest son of Calvinist theology, it continues for several pages beyond the extract given, stringing together Biblical quotations and commenting on their language, ending with the call: "I beseech you to suffer the word of exhortation."

Salmon Brown acknowledged later that Brown "was greatly concerned over the spiritual welfare of us boys, whose beliefs were more or less reactionary. He constantly expostulated when with us, and in letters when away." John Jr.'s objection to Calvinism was far from reactionary, however. He felt there to be, as he put it in an account given to Franklin Sanborn, a "proslavery diabolism that had entrenched itself in the Church." He explains in the account that his "theological shackles were a good deal broken" in witnessing the segregationist treatment of blacks at a church. His sister, Ruth, also in an account given to Sanborn, remembers that her father saw blacks seated at the back of the church and settled them in his pew, to the anger of the congregation. She explains: "My brothers were so disgusted to see such a mockery of religion that they left the church, and have never belonged to another." Nonetheless Brown saw in his children's rejection of the church a more dangerous denial of God Himself. His verdict was that "their 'Eyes are blinded' to the real Truth, & that they have no right appreciation of his true character, nor of their own." Such pronouncements apparently did no damage to Brown's relationship with his skeptical children.

Akron, Ohio, Aug. 26, 1853.

Dear Son John,—Your letter of the 21st instant was received yesterday, and as I may be somewhat more lengthy than usual I begin my answer at once. The family have enjoyed as good health as usual since I wrote before, but my own health has been poor since in May. Father has had a short turn of fever and ague; Jason and Ellen have had a good deal of it, and were not very stout on Sunday last. The wheat crop has been rather light in this quarter; first crop of grass light; oats very poor; corn and potatoes promise well, and frequent rains have given the late grass a fine start. There has been some very fatal sickness about, but the season so far has been middling healthy. Our sheep and cattle have done well; have raised five hundred and fifty lambs, and expect about eighty cents per pound for our wool. We shall be glad to have a visit from you about the time of our county fair, but I do not yet know at what time it comes. Got a letter from Henry dated the 16th of August; all there well. Grain crops there very good. We are preparing (in our minds, at least) to go back next spring. Mrs. Perkins was confined yesterday with another boy, it being her eleventh child. The understanding between the two families continues much as formerly, so far as I know.

In Talmadge there has been for some time an unusual seriousness and attention to future interests. In your letter you appear rather disposed to sermonize; and how will it operate on you and Wealthy if I should pattern after you a little, and also quote some from the Bible? In choosing my texts, and in quoting from the Bible, I perhaps select the very portions which "another portion" of my family hold are not to be wholly received as true. I forgot to say that my younger sons (as is common in this "progressive age") appear to be a little in advance of my older, and have thrown off the old shackles entirely; after THOROUGH AND CANDID investigation they have discovered the Bible to be ALL a fiction! Shall I add, that a letter received from you some time since gave me little else than pain and sorrow? "The righteous shall hold on his way;" "By and by he is offended."

My object at this time is to recall your particular attention to the fact that the earliest, as well as all other, writers of the Bible seem to have been impressed with such ideas of the character of the religion they taught, as led them to apprehend a want of steadfast-ness among those who might profess to adhere to it (no matter what may have been the motives of the different writers). Accordingly we find the writer of the first five books putting into the mouth of his Moses expressions like the following,—and they all appear to dwell much on the idea of two distinct classes among their reputed disciples; namely, a genuine and a spurious class :—

"Lest there should be among you man, or woman, or family, or tribe, whose heart turneth away this day from the Lord our God to serve the gods of these nations; lest there should be among you a root that beareth gall and worm-wood." "Then men shall say, be-cause they have forsaken the covenant of the Lord God of their fathers." "But if thine heart turn away so that thou wilt not hear, but shalt be drawn away, and worship other gods, and serve them." [. . .]

The writer here makes his Moses to dwell on this point with a most re-markable solicitude, a most heart-moving earnestness. The writer of the next book makes his Joshua to plead with Israel with the same earnestness. "Choose you this day whom you will serve." "Ye are witnesses against yourselves that ye have chosen you the Lord, to serve him." The writer of the book called Judges uses strong language in regard to the same disposition in Israel to back-slide: "And it came to pass when the judge was dead, that they returned and corrupted themselves more than their fathers; they ceased not from their own doings, nor from their stubborn way." The writer of the book Ruth makes Naomi say to Orpah, "Thy sister-in-law is gone back unto her people and unto her gods." The writer of the books called Samuel represents Saul as one of the same spurious class. Samuel is made to say to him, "Behold, to obey is better than sacrifice; and to hearken, than the fat of rams"—clearly intimating that all service that did not flow from an obedient spirit and an honest heart would be of no avail. He makes his Saul turn out faithless and treacherous in the end, and finally consult a woman, "having a familiar spirit," near the close of his sad career. The same writer introduces Ahitophel as one whose counsel "was as if a man had inquired at the oracle of God;" a writer of the Psalms makes David say of him, "We took sweet counsel together, and walked to the house of God in company;" but he is left advising the son of David to incest publicly, and soon after hangs himself. The spot of those men seems not to be genuine. . . .

* * * *

John Brown, Jr. (son), Reminiscences

John Brown's first child, John Brown, Jr., less accomplished than his brother Salmon but his father's favorite nonetheless, provided historians with some of the most telling details we have about Brown as a parent and a man. He reminisced once, for example, about the time that his father began to punish him with lashes for the moral debts accumulated in his "account book" of transgressions: " I paid about one third of the debt. . . . Then, to my utter astonishment, father stripped off his shirt, and, seating himself on a block, gave me the whip and bade me 'lay it on' to on his bare back . . . until he received the balance of the account." It was the Doctrine of Atonement before his eyes.

Another famous story about John Brown, originating from an inter-view with his eldest son, concerns an incident of 1825 in Ohio. Though he was then only five years old, John Jr. would remember that Brown sheltered a fugitive slave and his wife, and when, during supper, "father heard the trampling of horses crossing a bridge on one of the main roads, half a mile off . . . he took his guests out the back door and down into the swamp near the brook to hide, giving them arms to defend them-selves."

John Jr. fought alongside his father in Kansas, though not at Pot-

Figure 15: John Brown Jr.,
daguerreotype, 1859. (*Courtesy,*
Library of Congress.)

tawatomie, staying behind with Jason while Owen, Frederick, and Salmon
accompanied Brown. He was also absent from the roll-call at Harpers
Ferry, dying on May 2, 1895 in Put-in-Bay, Ottawa County, Ohio. Yet
he was one of his father's most trusted allies, even bound by a formal
family oath to the struggle against slavery. He was devoted to Brown,
though very much his own person, as letters between the two reveal. A rad-
ical free-state man, he was elected to the free-state legislature at Topeka
and was responsible for bringing his father out to Kansas.

He witnessed and understood most of his father's troubles. The source
here is an interview covering the time before their antislavery alliance.
It deals with Brown's business years and his bankruptcy, and confirms
that Brown was crippled by the "pestilence" of borrowing. He is right
in his faith that Perkins has never disparaged his father, for the corre-
spondence between Perkins and Brown, if strained at times, was always
genuinely respectful, and Perkins tried to persuade Brown to remain in
the business.

1885

The bankruptcy of 1842 had little to do with any speculation in wool, for
at that time my father was not a wool-dealer on a large scale, but sold his own
"clip" as other farmers did. His failure, as I now remember, was wholly owing
to his purchase of *land* on credit,—including the Haymaker farm at Franklin,

which he bought in connection with Seth Thompson of Hartford, Trubull County, Ohio, and his individual purchase of three rather large adjoining farms in Hudson. When he bought those farms, the rise in value of his place in Franklin was such that good judges estimated his property worth fully twenty thousand dollars. He was then thought to be a man of excellent business judgment, and was chosen one of the directors of a Bank at Cuyahoga Falls. The financial crash came in 1837, and down came all of father's castles, and buried the reputation he had achieved of possessing at least good commonsense in respect to business matters. In his conversations with me in later years respecting the mistakes he had made, I have heard him say that "these grew out of one root—doing business on credit." "Where loans are amply secured," he would say, "the borrower, not the lender, takes the risks, and all the contingencies incident to business; while the accumulations of interest and the coming of pay-day are sure as death. Instead of being thoroughly imbued with the doctrine of *pay as you go*," he said, "I started out in life with the idea that nothing could be done without capital, and that a poor man *must* use his credit and borrow; and this pernicious notion has been the rock on which I, as well as so many others, have split. The practical effect of this false doctrine has been to keep me like a toad under a harrow most of my business life. Running into debt includes so much of evil that I hope all my children will shun it as they would a pestilence."

His imprisonment in the county jail had nothing to do with any of his wool matters, but related entirely to the affair of "the old log fort." The purchaser of the Hudson farm got out a warrant against father, Jason, Owen, and me for breach of the peace, alleging that he feared personal harm in his attempts at taking possession; and, alleging further that he could not obtain justice in Hudson, he swore out his warrant before a Justice in an adjoining township. We made no resistance whatever to the service of the writ, and appeared for examination before the Justice in that town, who was plainly in full sympathy with the complainant; and after a brief hearing he required us to enter into bonds for our appearance at the county court in Akron. These we would not give; and next day we went to jail. The sheriff, a friend of father, and who understood the merits of the case, went through the form of turning the jail-key on us, then opened the door and gave us the liberty of the town, putting us upon our honor not to leave it. We were then taken to board at a nice private residence, at county expense, for three or four days only, as it was just before the sitting of the Court. On calling the case it was "*nolled*," and we returned home. This scheme of the purchaser resulted in his getting possession of one of the fine farms which father then owned in Hudson, and that too within half an hour after our arrest. This is all there was in the matter of our having once been in Akron Jail.

In correction of what you told me Colonel Perkins said to disparage my father's skill as a shepherd, his success in business, etc., let me remark that the correspondence of Perkins & Brown, if exhibited, would not confirm these statements. Since father had become well known as a grower of the finest Saxony wool by the fine wool-growers of Pennsylvania and Ohio, and somewhat of Western Virginia, when these men all thought they were victimized by the manufacturers of fine wool, father was urged by these growers to undertake the work of grading their wool and selling it on commission, in hopes to obtain in this way fairer prices. Mr. Perkins not only "allowed" father to undertake this, but entered heartily into the plan, which for a year or two was successful, until the manufacturers discovered that Perkins & Brown were receiving a large share of the really fine wool grown in this country, and that if they bought it they must pay a fairer price for it. This would greatly diminish the profits heretofore made by the manufacturers of these very fine wools; and so this high-handed attempt, not to "control," as stated by Mr. Musgrave, but to *influence* the price somewhat "in the interest of the farmers" must be squelched. The manufacturers combined, and "boycotted" these upstart dealers. From the quoted prices in the London market of grades of wool not equal, as father well knew, to the wool he had, he became satisfied that rather than take the prices which the combination would pay it would be better to send the wool abroad. The clique had long arms, and finally bought at low rates and brought back the wool he shipped to London; and the farmers, most of whom had consented to the undertaking of sending it abroad, suffered great loss. Thus ended the wool business of Perkins & Brown.

* * * *

Salmon Brown (son), Reminiscences

Salmon Brown, John's eighth child, and third with his second wife Mary, was, in the judgment of his sister Sarah, "the sanest minded, level headedest one of the family." He helped persuade his father to join the Brown boys in Kansas, and then fought alongside his father in Kansas, taking a central role in the planning and execution of their campaigns there. He was opposed to the plans for the Harpers Ferry raid, however, and did not participate in the raid at all. Thomas Higginson believed that Salmon's non-participation was due to pressure from his wife, but Salmon himself claims that he knew his father would falter and trap himself and his men through delay, asserting in 1908, "I said to the buys before they left, 'you know father. You know he will dally till he is trapped.'" In the following account he explains that he "felt that the trip was a mistake."

Salmon's account touches on Brown's successes in business, and his concern for his children's spiritual welfare, prominent themes of earlier sources. John Brown the gentle and dedicated father is a figure almost lost to history, though apparent throughout his correspondence with his family and clearly emphasized by Salmon who calls him: "watchful, tireless, tender." His account emphasizes the multi-faceted nature of Brown, concluding that he was a "reckless adventurer" in the eyes of many but a "just and generous man" to his family.

1913

Perhaps the most striking characteristic of my father, as his children knew him, was his faith in God, his faith in his family, and his sense of equity. For whatever else may be said of John Brown, he was true to his God as he knew his duty, he was strongly devoted to the interests of his family, and he never wronged a man where the interests of justice—as he saw the situation—did not demand it of him. He was stern when need be, but sympathetic and just always.

Figure 16: Salmon Brown, daguerreotype. (*Courtesy, Library of Congress.*)

My memory goes back to the days long before the war, when slavery was not considered such a National sin as it was about the time Lincoln came on the scene. My early recollections of my father have to do with his hatred of slavery, his hatred for everything that would take from one man a single right and give to his fellow even a petty advantage. He was just in his conception of the rights of men, and could never understand why others were determined to reap where they had not sown, to profit unjustly by the efforts of others. My early recollections go back clearly to the old home at Hudson, Ohio, where I was born, October 2, 1836. Our home was an old-fashioned house, with a great rock nearly covering half an acre of land and nearly as high as the house. A spring bubbled out of the side of the rock, forming a basin and then running off in a "creek," as we called it. I have clear recollections of being chased by Aunt Martha and my sister Ruth all over the big rock in an effort to make me eat butter on my bread. Like my father, I have always disliked butter; why, I do not know.

In a large living-room was a fireplace ten feet long, with huge andirons and a crane and hooks to hang kettles upon. We boys would cut logs two and three feet through for the fireplace, and at night, in winter, two great back-logs were covered with ashes to hold fire. Father would sit in front of a lively fire and take up us children one, two, or three at a time, and sing until bedtime. We all loved to hear him sing as well as to talk of the conditions in the country, over which he seemed worried. A favorite song with father and us children was "Blow Ye the Trumpet, Blow."

We lived in an old whitewashed log house at Richfield, Ohio, with a mill-pond and creek dam, with mud-turtles, which we boys would fatten and eat. The turtles would jerk for twenty-four hours after being cooked, it seemed to us. At Richfield three children died—three in less than three weeks—a calamity from which father never fully recovered. Two years later, a year old, was burned to death. Of the three that died at Richfield, Charles was very swift and strong, his legs and arms straight as broomsticks, of sandy complexion, quiet as a cat, but brave as a tiger. Peter was very stout, darker, the best-looking member of the family.

Father had fine Saxony sheep at Richfield. Later in his career, at Akron, while running sheep with Simon Perkins, he took first prize at the first world's Fair ever held (at London, England) in competition with all countries, exhibiting one hundred fleeces of Saxony lambs.

Father was a strict observer of the Sabbath. Sunday evenings he would gather the family and hired help together, and have the Ten Commandments and the Catechism repeated. Sometimes he would preach a regular sermon to us. Besides we had prayers morning and night of every day, with Bible reading, all standing during prayer, father himself leaning on a chair upreared on the forward legs, the old-fashioned Presbyterian way. He was greatly concerned over the spiritual welfare of us boys, whose beliefs were more or less reactionary. He constantly expostulated when with us, and in letters when away. His expressed hope was "that ye sin not, that you form no foolish attachments, that you be not a "companion of fools."

Father had great confidence in us children. He never said "Don't tell," but simply trusted to our not telling. Before a child of seven or eight he would calmly discuss plans he would not have breathed before older persons.

Father was five feet ten inches in height, slightly stoop-shouldered after middle life, with eyes sky blue, hair dark brown till tinged with gray, nose-hawked and thin, skin florid, spare but muscular in build. His form and features attracted the attention of strangers quickly. He always dressed in snuff-colored broadcloth for good clothes, and was always neat. He wore boots, as was the custom of those days, and wore white shirts with a plait on each side of the bosom. Usually we walked with his hands clasped behind him, often with his eyes on the ground as if in deep thought. So far as I know he was never sick a day, and never missed a meal on account of his own illness. This was also true of his father.

Blood has always been thick in the Brown family. Family ties were firm, and the tendency has been strong to "stick together." I first noticed this family trait in my father's case when he would go to grandfather's bed—after he became old—and tuck the covers about him as a mother would do with her children.

Our old home was a model of orderliness, and quiet always prevailed when father was about. The meals were served leisurely, but with due order and silence. The long table where twelve children, the largest number ever living at any time (1843), sat down with keen appetites was a model of the time.

A favorite dish with us children was corn-meal mush cooked the whole afternoon long in a huge iron caldron, and served with rich milk or cream. It left a crust a half-inch thick in the caldron, and tasted, so I affirm to this day, like no other mush ever made. The table was always neatly set, never without a white tablecloth; the food was coarse, hearty farmers' food, always in abundance, and always well served. Frugality was observed from a moral standpoint; but, one and all, we were a well-fed, well-clad lot. Considerable hardship was entailed when father left to engage in the Kansas warfare; but real poverty never obtruded itself till his death.

There were no drones in the Brown hive. Little toddlers unable to help were at least not allowed to hinder; as soon as they had achieved a show of stable control of their uncertain little legs the world of work opened to them. There was no pampering, little petting. The boys could turn a steak or brown a loaf as well as their mother.

Despite his relentless sternness, and underlying it, cropping through in his later years, when paternalism of necessity gave way to comradeship, there ran in John Brown's nature a strain of intense tenderness. Suffering in himself he bore without a murmur; but every fiber of his being was wrung by the suffering of others. It brought out the woman in him, the John Brown little known to history, who sat around the great open fireplace at night with his children in his arms and sang them to sleep; who rose on the coldest night and paced the floor with a collicky child, while his wife, worn by childbearing and childrearing, lay in bed asleep; and who was ever the nurse in sickness, watchful, tireless, tender, allowing no one to lift the burden of the night watch from him. During a protracted illness of my mother he hovered over her night and day, sleeping for a fortnight only at intervals in his chair, unrelieved of his clothes, afraid to go to bed lest he oversleep.

His kindness toward dumb animals was proverbial. He was like the Israelite of old, sheltering the ninety-and-nine, but refusing shelter for himself till the straying hundredth was safely folded. A chilled and dying lamb was a spectacle upon which he would spend his energies till it either died or stood solidly upon its crooked legs. Even the Monday's wash, soaking in the tubs, was once put aside in order to thaw in the warm, soapy water the numbing death chill from a little straggler's bones.

Family worship was as inexorably a matter of habit as eating or sleeping. The burden of father's soul was the souls of his children, and he strove with them without ceasing. The day's work was ushered in and out with Scripture and prayer. Provided each with a Bible, we read in rotation, father leading with several verses from the large family Bible; mother following with several more from an old Bible bound in sheepskin which father himself had tanned; then on through the long line of children. During prayers all stood, father leaning against the back of a chair upreared on its forward legs, dead to the world and to the pranks of his unregenerate boys, who slyly prodded each other with pins and trampled upon each other's toes to relieve the tension. The week was opened by a Sunday service.

Our long trip from New York to Kansas brought many unusual experiences to the large family. Father outfitted well for the trip, which was beset with unforeseen hardships. But no one questioned the wisdom of the undertaking or feared the result.

At Brunswick, Missouri, we crossed the Missouri River. Near Independence was a slave pen, built like a chicken coop, only stronger and higher. Inside the pen was the auction block. This slave-selling stirred father to the depths of his soul. As he waited for the ferry he saw slaves handcuffed for the journey down the river to New Orleans. Cholera at that time was fearfully epidemic, people dying by hundreds on the boats. Jason's boy, four years old, contracted the disease and died there. The following spring father had the child's body removed to Kansas, thinking Jason would feel better to have the boy's body off Missouri soil.

On the first trip to Kansas father traded dogs with an old Quaker. The Quaker's dog was a ratter, which father wanted as a watch-dog. The trade was made on Sunday, but father would not exchange dogs till Monday. One day an old Missourian came up to our wagon. "Whar you going? " he asked.

"To Osawatomie."

"Whar you from?"

"New York."

"You'll never live to get thar," informed the Missourian.

"We are prepared not to die alone," answered father quietly, and the man slouched off.

Father was a man of intense earnestness in all things that interested him. Events which changed the course of his life occurred unexpectedly and even strangely. While he was living in Pennsylvania it was the custom for every farmer to have a barrel of whisky in the house. It was also the custom to have "bees" and barn-raisings. A tavern-keeper was to have a barn-raising, and father was to be there. The tavern-keeper needed more liquor and sent to Meadville father, then scarcely in middle life, for a three-gallon jug. The liquor cost twenty-five cents a gallon. On the road from Meadville father became thirsty and began taking "nips" from the jug. He was accustomed to drinking from his own barrel, and did not think the practice wrong. On the way to the barn-raising father realized that liquor was getting hold of him, and he became alarmed. He afterward spoke of the occurrence frequently. He reasoned that if liquor would lead him to drink from another man's jug it was surely gaining control over him—a thing he could not allow. Coming to a large rock by the roadway, he smashed the jug upon it, vowing that he would not be responsible for his neighbor's drinking at the barn-raising, where accidents might happen. He paid for the liquor, and when he reached home rolled his whisky barrel into the back yard and smashed it to pieces with an ax. No liquor was allowed about the house afterwards.

Father was strongly fixed in most of his habits. He worked with the same earnestness year after year; he ate regularly, and went to bed and arose at the same hours, whenever it was possible. It was always difficult for him to fit himself to circumstances; he wanted conditions to change for him—and he usually brought about the things he most desired. His persistence was as strongly developed as was his firmness. With it all the large family of boys usually held firmly to the idea that father was right; that his foresight was unusual.

Until the Harper's Ferry "trip" was planned father had never found reaction in the spirits of his boys. Where he had led we were glad to follow—and everyone of us had the courage of his convictions. Whatever else may be said of the Brown family, I feel that no one will charge us with lacking in bravery at the time when the shadows lowered and there was that dreadful feeling that a great mistake had been made. When death—and the gallows—enters a family it is a time that tries men's souls.

It may have been fear that led me to revolt against the proposed trip to Virginia, which father urged us boys to join him in. I thought the matter over and concluded that I would not go, that for the first time I could not go side by side with father. He urged and reasoned, and regretted my determination to stay at home, perhaps as he had never regretted the act of any of his children. But I felt that the trip was a mistake, that it was not the wise thing to do, and stayed at home. The slaughter at Harper's Ferry showed me clearly that father had miscalculated somewhere; I had no fears of death as the result of the effort against slavery. We never learned just how father accounted for his being trapped as he was.

Father never did anything that he thought was not worth doing well. As a boy he learned the lessons of thoroughness from his father, a tanner who lived in Ohio. Before father was fifteen years of age he learned something of tanning skins and determined to learn the trade of a tanner. He had not told his father of his intentions, but one day a currying-knife would not take an edge until father put it on the stone. In trying the knife father began graining a skin, and it was discovered that he had mastered much of the detail of the trade. Soon afterwards he was charged with a large part of the management of the tannery.

At eighteen the religious nature of father had developed until he determined to go to a New England college and study for the ministry. After a period of hard study he gave up the effort on account of inflammation of the eyes which had fastened itself upon him. At twenty he married and removed to Pennsylvania, where he took up wild land and built a tannery near Meadville. The land was covered with a heavy growth of hemlock, maple, and beech, and the task of clearing it was heartbreaking. The tannery was built of stone, and remains to this day. A great tan-bark yard—several acres of refuse—was soon developed, and here the first children had their playground. Every influence of the surroundings was rugged. While father operated the tannery successfully and engaged in the sheep business with profit, his spirit was constantly struggling with the problems of the National Life. He established at Springfield, Massachusetts, the first wool commission house in the United States, and operated it at a profit to himself and to wool-growers. When the Fugitive Slave Law was passed, he quickly made his warehouse a "station" on the "underground railway," sacrificing business and profit to principle. His blooded sheep industry was also sacrificed on the altar of freedom for the black man. Father may have been a fanatic, but he had some intensely practical and homely ideas which were lost sight of when his acts tended to throw the Nation into sectional strife and warfare. The country saw him as a reckless adventurer; his family knew him as a just and generous man.

Following the dark days at Harper's Ferry, the suffering of mother and the family was intense. Despised bitterly by all who sympathized with slavery and considered as the victims of a righteous wrath by many of the North, our family was long buffeted from pillar to post. Efforts to forget were fruitless. The passing years did not heal the horrible wounds made by the country father had tried so hard to help to a plane of higher living.

With nearly all my brothers and sisters gone to their reward, many of them before the Nation realized the importance of father's work, with more than half a century intervening since the tragedy at Harper's Ferry, during which time public judgment has calmed and changed materially. I feel that no apology is needed on behalf of John Brown, husband and father, kind and true, however much some may still doubt the saneness of his work for the abolition of that horrible National curse, slavery.

* * * *

Milton Lusk (brother-in-law), Reminiscence of Brown, 1882

Milton Lusk, brother of John Brown's first wife Dianthe, was not Brown's greatest admirer. He didn't approve of John as husband for his sister and in the account here, given to Franklin Sanborn in 1882, he paints a picture of an inflexible and austere man who chose to reach out to others only when it suited him, in Lusk's case when the two men finally saw eye-to-eye politically. Lusk may also have resented Brown because his sister was, by all accounts, not Brown's first choice of a wife. He settled for Dianthe only when rejected by another and "prompted . . . by his Father," as Brown confirmed in his autobiography.

However skewed by old tensions, Lusk's recollection does match descriptions given by Brown of himself. Lusk recalls "a commanding disposition" with "such force and mastery in what he did, that everything gave way before him," and Brown writes of himself in 1857: "The habit so early formed of being obeyed rendered him in after life too much disposed to speak in an imperious or dictating way." In a letter to Mary of 1844 he sighs: "I often regret that my manner is no more kind and affectionate to those I really love and esteem; but I trust my friends will overlook my harsh, rough ways, when I cease to be in their way as an occasion of pain and unhappiness." In a prison letter on November 24, 1859 he acknowledges that his son Jason "always has underrated himself; is bashful and retiring in his habits; is not (like his father) too much inclined to assume and dictate." Numerous testimonies, of family, friends and observers, confirm that Brown felt himself a man destined to lead others, like Napoleon or Cromwell. He gathered a group of unquestioningly loyal men around him at Harpers Ferry, and was able to do so because, according to Frederick Douglass, "no matter how inconsistent, impossible, and desperate a thing might appear to others, if John Brown said he would do it, he was sure to be believed."

Similarly, Lusk's description of his sister matches Brown's memory of her: Milton writes that "she was plain, but attracted John Brown by her quiet, amiable disposition," and Brown describes his wife as a "remarkably plain ; but industrious & economical girl . . . mild, frank," able to offer "plain but kind admonitions." Yet Lusk goes further in his praise for Dianthe than Brown ever went for either of his wives, perhaps reaching a level of romantic expression not accessible to Brown, saying of her: "She was my guiding star, my guardian angel."

1882

I am now seventy-nine years old, for I was born in 1803, my sister Dianthe in 1801, and Brown in 1800. I knew him from a boy, went to school with him, and remember well what a commanding disposition he always had. There was once a Democratic school and a Federal school in Hudson village, and the boys used to snow-ball each other. Brown and I were federalists, as our fathers, Squire Brown and Captain Lusk, were. One day the Democratic boys found a wet hollow in the battlefield of snow-balls, and began to throw wet balls, which were hard and hurt "masterly." John stood this for a while,—then he rushed alone upon the little Democrats, and drove them all before him into their schoolhouse. He did not seem to be angry, but there was such force and mastery in what he did, that everything gave way before him. He doted on his ability to hit the mark. Dianthe, my sister, was not tall like my father (who fought at the siege of Sandusky and died in the spring of 1813), but about her mother's height; she was plain, but attracted John Brown by her quiet, amiable disposition. She was my guiding star, my guardian angel; she sung beautifully, most always sacred hymns and tunes; and she had a place in the woods, not far from the house, where she used to go alone to pray. She took me there sometimes to pray with me. She was a pleasant, cheerful person, but not funny; she never said anything but what she meant. When mother and Dianthe were keeping house for John Brown at the old log-cabin where he had his tannery, I was working as a boy at Squire Hudson's in the village, and had no time to go up and see my mother and sister except Sundays. Brown was an austere feller, and he didn't like that; one day he said to me, "Milton, I wish you would not make your visits here on the Sabbath." I said, "John, I won't come Sunday, nor any other day," and I stayed away a long time. When Dianthe was married, I would not go to the wedding. I did not get along very well with him for some years; but when he was living in Pennsylvania and I had my controversy with the church in Hudson, he came and prayed with me, and shed tears, and said perhaps I was nearer right than he had thought. After my sister's death he said to John, his son, "I feel sure that your mother is now with me and influencing me." He was tasty in his dress,—about washing, bathing, brushing, etc.; when he washed him, he pushed his hair back from his forehead.

* * * *

Ruth Brown (daughter), Reminiscence of Brown

John Brown was particularly close to his eldest daughter Ruth, the unfortunate girl who, at the age of seventeen, had killed her one year old sister Amelia through accidental scalding, a surprisingly common cause of death at the time. She gave these recollections of his favorite books, Bible passages, and hymns, to Franklin Sanborn in 1882. To Ruth's list we can add that Brown also enjoyed writings by Jonathan Edwards, Benjamin Franklin, and Aesop.

Brown liked Rollins because the historian substantiated Old Testament history, and Josephus because he did the same for the New Testament. He was probably drawn to the account in Plutarch's Lives *of the slave revolt led by Spartacus. It seems likely that his interest in Napoleon was fed by his sense of being a man similarly destined to command great armies, but also by his more practical interest in the Spanish guerrillas who defeated Napoleon's veterans by using the mountains of the Iberian peninsula. Several associates and historians of Brown equate him with Napoleon, and there are countless direct comparisons between Brown and Cromwell, even before his death. Ruth's inclusion of* The Life of Oliver Cromwell *indicates that Brown may have modeled himself on the Englishman, a Puritan who saw himself as an instrument of God. Certainly his reading of another inspirational book,* Pilgrim's Progress, *spilled over into real life—in a prison letter just before his execution he imagined himself as "Bunyan's Pilgrim," on the "brink of Jordan."*

Ruth lists some of Brown's favorite Bible passages, and reconfirms the "perfect knowledge" of the Bible that Brown claimed in his autobiography. She mentions two other chapters not quoted in her account. The first verse of the Isaiah chapter functions as a concise summary of how Brown saw his role in American history: 58:1 "Cry aloud, spare not, lift up thy voice like trumpet, and shew my people their transgression, and the house of Jacob their sins." The first four verses of the passage from Ecclesiastes are eerily prophetic of the Civil War, for example, 12:3: "In the day when the keepers of the house shall tremble, and the strong men shall bow themselves, and the grinders cease because they are few, and those that look out of the windows be darkened. . . ."

My dear father's favorite books, of a historical character, were "Rollin's Ancient History," Josephus, Plutarch, "Napoleon and his Marshals," and the Life of Oliver Cromwell. Of religious books, Baxter's "Saints' Rest" (in speaking of which at one time he said he could not see how any person could read it through carefully without becoming a Christian), the "Pilgrim's Progress," and Henry "On Meekness." But above all others, the Bible was his favorite volume; and he had such a perfect knowledge of it, that when any person was reading it, he would correct the least mistake. His favorite passages were these, as near as I can remember:— "Remember them that are in bonds as bound with them."

"Whoso stoppeth his ear at the cry of the poor, he also shall cry himself, but shall not be heard." "He that hath a bountiful eye shall be blessed; for he giveth his bread to the poor." "A good name is rather to be chosen than great riches, and loving favor rather than silver or gold." "Whoso mocketh the poor, reproacheth his Maker; and he that is glad at calamities, shall not be unpunished." He that hath pity upon the poor lendeth to the Lord, and that which he hath given will He pay to him again." "Give to him that asketh of thee, and from him that would borrow of thee turn not thou away." "A righteous man regardeth the life of his beast; but the tender mercies of the wicked are cruel." "Withhold not good from them to whom it is due, when it is in the power of thine hand to do it." "Except the Lord build the house, they labor in vain that build it; except the Lord keepeth the city, the watchman walketh in vain." "I hate vain thoughts, but thy law I do love." The last chapter of Ecclesiastes was a favorite one, and on Fast-days and Thanksgivings he used very often to read the fifty-eighth chapters of Isaiah.

When he would come home at night, tired out with labor, he would, before going to bed, ask some of the family to read chapters (as was his usual course night and morning); and would almost always say "Read one of David's

Psalms." His favorite hymns (Watts's) were these: "Blow ye the trumpet, blow!" "Sweet Is Thy word, my God, my King!" "I'll praise my Maker with my breath;" "Oh, happy is the man who hears!" "Why should we start, and fear to die!" "With songs and honors sounding loud;" "Ah, lovely appearance of death!"

PART TWO

Fragile and indecisive in 1854, John Brown was born again as a fighter and leader by 1856. Part Two spans the years from 1854 to 1859, with a glance back to his League of Gileadites project in 1851. The section therefore covers his final months in business, the Kansas guerrilla warfare, the Pottawatomie murders, and the time spent gathering funds and support for the Harpers Ferry raid. It offers a selection of the important primary documents upon which the assorted and contradictory historical assessments about his campaigns in Kansas and the plans for Harpers Ferry are based. These documents include letters, eyewitness testimonies, and reminiscences, and reveal the development of his plans for the raid and the attitudes of some of the men who followed or funded him. At a crossroads, John Brown became the man he had always intended to be, and took the road to Kansas, and Harpers Ferry.

Figure 17: Jacob Lawrence, *The Life of John Brown*, 1941, No. 9: Kansas was now the skirmish ground of the Civil War. (*Courtesy, Jacob and Gwendolyn Lawrence Foundation.*)

THE ROAD TO KANSAS, AND HARPERS FERRY

* * * *

John Brown, Words of Advice, United States League of Gileadites, January 15, 1851

One of Brown's later identities was the fearsome Indian warrior Osawatomie Brown of Kansas. The phase of his life occupied with guerrilla warfare didn't begin in earnest until 1854, but we can see it on the horizon in January 1851, when he founded the League of Gileadites and launched the first (and only) branch in Springfield, Massachusetts. The passage on September 18, 1850 of the Fugitive Slave Law galvanized Brown and prompted the formation of the League. Brown does not condemn the Act in his "Words of Advice," or draw up a petition and discuss its relationship to the Constitution. His response is instead logical and practical. Years later his son Salmon commented: "he had some intensely practical and homely ideas which were lost sight of when his acts tended to throw the Nation into sectional strife and warfare" (see Salmon Brown (son), Reminiscences).

The League was named after the Biblical army whose numbers fell from thirty-two thousand to three hundred when tested by God before battle in order that Gideon would have no cowards fighting with him. The document comprises his "Words of Advice" to the new black self-defense unit, and the "Agreement" that was signed by forty-four black residents of Springfield, men and women. It should be compared to his Provisional Constitution of 1858 and to his essay, "Sambo's Mistakes." It is the more practical counterpart of this essay, aimed at reversing some of the tendencies of Sambo and blacks like him who, as he puts it in his "Words of Advice," "ape the follies and extravagances of their white neighbors" and "indulge in idle show, in ease, and in luxury". It is significant that the Springfield blacks accepted a white leader: another of Brown's identities was the white man with a black heart, and blacks accepted this identity as genuine.

WORDS OF ADVICE
Branch of the United States League of Gileadites.
Adopted January 15, 1851, as written and recommended by John Brown.
"Union is Strength"
Nothing so charms the American people as personal bravery. Witness the case of Cinques, of everlasting memory, on board the "Amistad." The trial for

life of one bold and to some extent successful man, for defending his rights in good earnest, would arouse more sympathy throughout the nation than the accumulated wrongs and sufferings of more than three millions of our submissive colored population. We need not mention the Greeks struggling against the oppressive Turks, the Poles against Russia, nor the Hungarians against Austria and Russia combined, to prove this. *No jury can be found in the Northern States that would convict a man for defending his rights to the last extremity. This is well understood by Southern Congressmen, who insisted that the right of trial by jury should not be granted to the fugitive.* Colored people have more fast friends amongst the whites than they suppose, and would have ten times the number they now have were they but half as much in earnest to secure their dearest rights as they are to ape the follies and extravagances of their white neighbors, and to indulge in idle show, in ease, and in luxury. Just think of the money expended by individuals in your behalf in the past twenty years. Think of the number who have been mobbed and imprisoned on your account. Have any of you seen the Branded Hand? Do you remember the names of Lovejoy and Torrey?

Should one of your number be arrested, you must collect together as quickly as possible, so as to outnumber your adversaries who are taking an active part against you. Let no able-bodied man appear on the ground unequipped, or with his weapons exposed to view; let that be understood beforehand. Your plans must be known only to yourself, and with the understanding that all traitors must die, wherever caught and proven to be guilty. 'Whosoever is fearful or afraid, let him return and depart early from Mount Gilead.' (Judges, vii. chap., 3 verse; Deut., xx chap., 8 verse.) Give all cowards an opportunity to show it on condition of holding their peace. *Do not delay one moment after you are ready you will lose all your resolution if you do. Let the first blow be the signal for all to engage, and when engaged do not do your work by halves ; but make clean work with your enemies, and be sure you meddle not with any others.* By going about your business quietly, you will get the job disposed of before the number that an uproar would bring together can collect; and you will have the advantage of those who come out against you, for they will be wholly unprepared with either equipments or matured plans; all with them will be confusion and terror. Your enemies will be slow to attack you after you have once done up the work nicely; and if they should, they will have to encounter your white friends as well as you, for you may safely calculate on a division of the whites, and may by that means get to an honorable parley.

Be firm, determined, and cool; but let it be understood that you are not to be driven to desperation without making it an awful job to others as well as to you. Give them to know distinctly that those who live in wooden houses should not throw fire, and that you are just as able to suffer as your white neighbors. *After effecting a rescue, if your are assailed, go into the houses of your most prominent and influential white friends with your wives, and that will effectually fasten upon them the suspicion of being connected with you, and will compel them to make a common cause with you, whether they would otherwise live up to their profession or not. This would leave them no choice in the matter.* Some would, doubtless, prove themselves true of their own choice; others would flinch. That would be taking them at their own words. You may make a tumult in the court-room where a trial is going on by burning gunpowder freely in paper packages, if you cannot think of any better way to create a momentary alarm, and might possibly give one or more of your enemies a hoist. But in such case the prisoner will need to take the hint at once and bestir himself and so should his friends improve the opportunity for a general rush.

A lasso might possibly be applied to a slave-catcher for once with good effect. Hold on to your weapons, and never be persuaded to leave them, part with them, or have them far away from you. *Stand by one another, and by your friends, while a drop of blood remains ; and be hanged, if you must, but tell no tales out of school. Make no confession.*

Union is strength. Without some well-digested arrangements nothing to any good purpose is likely to be done, let the demand be never so great. Witness the case of Hamlet and Long in New York, when there was no well-defined plan of operations or suitable preparation beforehand.

The desired end may be effectually secured by the means proposed; namely, the enjoyment of our inalienable rights.

AGREEMENT

As citizens of the United States of America, trusting in a just and merciful God, whose spirit and all-powerful aid we humbly implore, *we will ever be true to the flag of our beloved country, always acting under it.* We, whose names are hereunto affixed, do constitute ourselves a branch of the United States League of Gileadites. We will provide ourselves at once with suitable implements, and will aid those who do not possess the means, if any such are disposed to join us. We invite every colored person whose heart is engaged for the performance of our business, whether male or female, old or young. The duty of the aged, infirm, and young members of the League shall be to give instant notice to all members in case of an attack upon any of our people. We agree to have no officers except a Treasurer and Secretary, *pro tem.,* until after some trial of courage and talent of able-bodied members shall enable us to elect officers from those who shall have rendered the most important services. Nothing but wisdom and undaunted courage, efficiency, and general good conduct shall in any way influence us in electing our officers.

* * * *

John Brown to John Brown, Jr., August 21, 1854

In August of 1854 John Brown first heard about John Jr.'s plans to move to Kansas, and considered his son's invitation to join him. In the letter here he refuses, though reluctantly, writing that he feels "committed to operate in another part of the field." Some historians have assumed that this part of the field is Virginia, and Harpers Ferry, but he simply means his commitment to the settlers at North Elba: to the sermons he gave at the church there, the black farmers he taught about husbandry, his intimate friends and neighbors and the mountainous terrain and clean air that he loved so much. The writer and antislavery activist

Richard Henry Dana, Jr., visited Brown and his family in their North Elba home in 1849, and described the natural beauty of the region and the simplicity of Brown's life there in his journal (vol. 1): "Brown is a thin, sinewy, hard flavored, clear headed, honest minded man, who had spent all his days as a pioneer farmer." He is "well informed on most subjects, especially in the natural sciences, [with] an unlimited family of children. . . ."

Knowing he would thrive in North Elba, Brown had told Gerrit Smith in 1848: "I am something of a pioneer. I grew up among the woods and wild Indians of Ohio, and am used to the climate and the way of life that your colony find so trying." He had promised to live with the blacks on the land given by Smith and to encourage them, and had spent much of the period from 1851 onwards away on business or fighting lawsuits elsewhere. He was desperate to return. So he implies, with a tired dignity, that he has an important battle-front to defend, and hopes instead that others of his sons will go; in particular that Jason will leave "The Rock," his farm in Akron that had little fertile soil, hence its nickname. Exhausted after numerous lawsuits and feeling old, he talked and wrote more frequently about death, and the peace he believed he would find in retirement to North Elba, his refuge and retreat. He advised Henry Thompson about how to construct a log-house for himself on the farm, and added in the same letter that he might not "live to occupy it."

But John, Jason, Owen, Frederick, and Salmon, the youngest eighteen and the eldest thirty-three, were committed to the move. Kansas was the hub of the fight against slavery, and the Brown boys, very much their father's sons, wanted to join other settlers keen to keep the state free and farm the new territory. The Kansas-Nebraska Bill, passed on May 25 of 1854, placed the issue of slavery into the hands of those settling the new territories. The people would decide in 1855, by popular vote, whether to be "free" or "slave," and proslavery "Border Ruffians" and antislavery Free-Staters were pouring into Kansas. Brown's sons wanted to be part of this decisive moment.

For nearly a year Brown wavered, not sure what his part in the struggle against slavery would be. Though often imagined as a consistently unfaltering machine, he was, after all, a man—and an old one. He would be born again, but not yet. Far from coercing them into joining the campaign in Kansas, as is sometimes claimed, Brown's sons had to drag him there.

Akron, August 21, 1854

If you or any of my family are disposed to go to Kansas or Nebraska, with a view to help defeat *Satan* and his legions in that direction, I have not a word to say; *but I feel committed to operate in another part of the field.* If I were not so committed, I would be on my way this fall. Mr. Adair [married to Brown's half sister] is fixing to go, and wants to find "good men and true" to go along. I would be glad If Jason would give away his Rock and go. Owen is fixing for some move; I can hardly say what.

* * * *

John Brown to Children, September 30, November 2, 1854

From September 1854 to May 1855 Brown was unable to let go of the idea that he might join his sons in their move to Kansas. The letters here, both sent to Ruth and Henry Thompson, his daughter and son-in-law, show him vacillating but clearly more keen to go than in August. In a gesture that contradicts the general assumption that he was consistently autocratic by nature, he suggests that a democratic "vote" should decide the next step in his life, asking Ruth and Henry to seek the opinions and votes of "Mr. Epps & all the colored people." He also mentions that he has asked "Gerrit Smith, Fredk Douglas, & Dr McCune Smith for their advice."[1] Genuinely torn, he hopes others will make the final decision for him.

The letter of September 30 confirms that the commitment to "operate in another part of the field," mentioned in his initial reply to John Jr.'s invitation (see John Brown to John Brown, Jr., August 21, 1854) was a commitment to North Elba. Brown loved life, and knew that death could inevitably follow any militant engagement in the antislavery struggle. He had a new daughter, Ellen, his twentieth and last child and it was tempting to embrace family life and the farmland of his sanctuary in the Adirondacks. But leaving for Kansas would be the right decision. He wrote to Franklin Sanborn several years later: "I felt for a number of years, in earlier life, a steady, strong desire to die; but since I saw any prospect of becoming a 'reaper' in the great harvest, I have not only felt quite willing to live, but have enjoyed life much; and am now rather anxious to live for a few years more." His love of life was renewed, not dampened, by his decision to choose the blood of Kansas over the peace of North Elba.

Akron, Ohio, 30th Sept 1854
Dear Children
After being hard pressed to go with my family to Kansas as more likely to benefit the colored people *on the whole* than to return with them to North Elba; I have consented to ask for your *advice & feeling* in the matter; & also to ask you to learn from Mr. Epps & all the colored people (so far as you can) how they would wish, & advise me to act in the case, all things considered. As I volunteered in their service; (or the service of the colored people); they have a right to vote, as to the course I take. I have just written Gerrit Smith, Fredk Douglas, & Dr McCune Smith, for their advice. We have a new daughter now Five days old. Mother & child are both doing well to appearance. Other friends well so far as I know. John & Wealthy are still with us. Will you write as soon as you can? Have not received your reply to my other questions.

Your Affectionate Father   John Brown

* * * *

---

1 See John Stauffer, *The Black Hearts of Men: Radical Abolitionists and the Transformation of Race* (Harvard University Press, 2002), for a full discussion of the interracial alliance between Gerrit Smith, Frederick Douglass, James McCune Smith, and John Brown.

Akron, Nov 2, 1854

Dear Children,—I feel still pretty much determined to go back to North Elba; but expect Owen and Frederick will set out for Kansas on Monday next, with cattle belonging to John, Jason, and them-selves, intending to winter some-where in Illinois. . . . Gerrit Smith wishes me to go back to North Elba; from Douglass and Dr. McCune Smith I have not yet heard. . . .Your affectionate father, John Brown

* * * *

John Brown, Jr., to John Brown, May 20, 24, 1855

On February 13, 1855 Brown wrote to John W. Cook, of Connecticut, with the news that he was moving to Kansas, but evidently changed his mind, for nothing came of the scheme that he mentions as "the opperations of a Surveying, & exploring party." But in May of that year came the call that ended Brown's period of indecision. Writing from Kansas, as the period of civil war known as "Bleeding Kansas" began, John Jr. describes the conditions in a long and detailed letter, begun on May 20 and finished on May 24. It is clear that the brothers' motives are not purely political: the "present prospect for health, wealth, and usefulness" exceeds his expectations, and the "start" has been "easy."

Of course it was his description of the political conditions that galvanized Brown. His son asks for help in procuring weapons for the fight against slavery. After a confrontation with a squad of Missourians, and as hundreds of proslavery and antislavery advocates moved into the area, he had recognized the current limitations of their operation. Though no longer expecting his father to come in person, wondering instead if Gerrit Smith could provide some weapons, John Jr. had nevertheless touched the right nerve. Renewed by his decision to go, Brown gave an impassioned address at the Syracuse Convention of Radical Political Abolitionists, and secured funds for weapons.

Upon leaving for Kansas, Brown turned at the door and said to his weeping family: "If it is so painful for us to part with hope of meeting again, how of poor slaves." He was to return to North Elba in 1857, with the tombstone of his grandfather and namesake, also recently inscribed with an epitaph for his son Frederick who had died in Kansas, and lay it in the place where he wanted his own grave to be. Executed in December 1859, he would finally retire there forever. But in May 1855, after a year of painful indecision, he read John Jr.'s letter and knew that he would sleep only when dead. From the vantage point of 1881 Frederick Douglass looked back on Brown's life and saw a parallel with the life of Moses. Douglass remembered: "forty years passed between [Brown's] thought and his act . . . this man was struggling with this one idea; like Moses he was forty years in the wilderness . . . Like Moses he had made excuses, and as with Moses his excuses were overruled." Brown was on his way to Kansas.

May 20

Salmon, Fredk and Owen say that they never was in a country that begun to please them as well. And I will say, that the present prospect for health, wealth, and usefulness much exceeds even my most sanguine anticipations. I know of no country where a poor man endowed with a share of common sense & with health, can get a start so easy. If we can succeed in making this a free State, a great work will be accomplished for mankind.

May 24

And now I come to the matter, that more than all else I intended should be the principal subject of this letter. I tell you the truth, when I say that while the interest of despotism has secured to its cause hundreds and thousands of the meanest and most desperate of men, armed to the teeth with Revolvers, Bowie Knives, Rifles and Cannon,—while they are not only thoroughly organized, but under pay from Slave-holders—the friends of freedom are *not one fourth* of them *half armed,* and as to *Military Organization* among them it *no where exists in this territory* unless they have recently done something in Lawrence. The result of this is that the people here exhibit the most abject and cowardly spirit, whenever their dearest rights are invaded and trampled down by the lawless bands of Miscreants which Missouri has already at a moment's call to pour in upon them. This is the *general* effect upon the people here so far as I have noticed, there are a few, and but a few exceptions. Of course these foreign Scoundrels know what kind of '*Allies*' they have to meet. They boast that they can obtain possession of the polls in any of our election precincts without having to fire a gun. I enclose a piece which I cut from a St. Louis paper named the St. Louis '*Republican;*' it shows the spirit which moves them. Now Missouri is not alone in the undertaking to make this a Slave State. Every Slaveholding State from Virginia to Texas is furnishing men and money to fasten Slavery upon this glorious land, by means no matter how foul. . . .

Now the remedy we propose is, that the Anti slavery portion of the inhabitants should *immediately, thoroughly arm* and *organize themselves* in *military companies.* In order to effect this, some persons must begin and lead in the matter. Here are 5 men of us who are not only anxious to fully prepare, but are thoroughly determined to fight. We can see no other way to meet the case. As in the language of the memorial lately signed by the people here and sent to Congress petitioning help, 'it is no longer a question of negro slavery, but it is the enslavement of ourselves.'

The General Government may be petitioned until the people here are grey, and no redress will be had so long as it makes slavery its paramount interest.—We have among us 5, 1 Revolver, 1 Bowie Knife, 1 middling good Rifle 1 poor Rifle, 1 small pocket pistol and 2 slung shot. What we need in order to be thoroughly armed for each man, is 1 Colts large sized Revolver manufactured at Worcester, Mass, 1 *Minnie Rifle*—they are manufactured somewhere in Mass or The real Minnie Rifle has a killing range almost equal to Cannon and of course is more easily handled, perhaps enough so to make up the difference. Now we want you to get for us these arms. We need them more than we do bread. Would not Gerrit Smith or someone, furnish the money and loan it to us for one, two or three years, for the purpose, until we can raise enough to refund it from the *Free* soil of Kansas? . . .

* * * *

John Brown to Wife and Family, June 28, 1855

On June 26, 1855, by now committed to joining his sons in Kansas, John Brown arrived in Syracuse at the first day of the inaugural convention of the Radical Political Abolitionists, a group that existed for five years. He wanted to raise money for arms and seek encouragement from such sympathizers as Frederick Douglass, Gerrit Smith, and James McCune Smith: in fact the three-day antislavery convention is the only recorded moment at which all four men, a uniquely interracial quartet of friends and allies, were in the same place.

Gerrit Smith read John Jr.'s letters of May and then Brown spoke. He quoted Hebrews 9:22, insisting that "without the shedding of blood there is no remission of sin," asked for money and arms for his sons, and recommended to the other delegates that they help arm all the free-state settlers in Kansas. There was some argument over whether the convention wanted to encourage violence, but eventually only one delegate—Lewis Tappan—dissented. Douglass remembers that "the collection was taken up with much spirit . . . for Capt. Brown was present and spoke for himself; and when he spoke men believed in the man." The delegates agreed that the only way forward was Brown's way: the combination of moral suasion with bloodshed. By the end of the convention they had defined themselves as God's disciples and declared slavery a state of war. They passed a resolution to resist any attempted return of fugitive slaves.

With money and arms from the convention, John Brown headed to Kansas in mid-August with his son-in-law Henry Thompson and his son Oliver Brown. They arrived on October 6. There was, as he wrote to his wife on September 4, no "other way to answer the end of [his] being," or else he would be "quite content to be at North Elba." He was more at peace than even a retirement to North Elba could have enabled him to be.

Syracuse, June 28, 1855

Dear Wife and Children,—I reached here on the first day of the convention, and I have reason to bless God that I came; for I have met with a most warm reception from all, so far as I know, and—except by a few sincere, honest peace friends—a most hearty approval of my intention of arming my sons and other friends in Kansas. I received today donations amounting to a little over sixty dollars,— twenty from Gerrit Smith, five from an old British officer; others giving similar sums with such earnest and affectionate expressions of their good wishes as did me more good than money even. John's two letters were introduced and read with such effect by Gerrit Smith as to draw tears from numerous eyes in the great collection of people present. The convention has been one of the most interesting meetings I ever [at]tended in my life; and I made a great addition to the number of warm-hearted and honest friends.

* * * *

John Brown to Wife and Children, Everyone, June 1856

Throughout the period known as "Bleeding Kansas," Brown fought proslavery Missourians and their border ruffian allies, and in this was flanked by his sons. As Salmon later explained, "until the Harper's Ferry 'trip' was planned father had never found reaction in the spirits of his boys. Where he had led we were glad to follow." Salmon remembers that is was a hard time for the rest of the Brown clan: "Considerable hardship was entailed when father left to engage in the Kansas warfare."

In the letter Brown touches on his complicated relationship with the Free Slave men and offers details of his interactions with the Government and Army. But the letter's real importance is that it deals with the famous Pottawatomie murders. Brown neither denies nor confirms his role in the recent massacres at Pottawatomie Creek. He had apparently led a party of eight in the killing of five proslavery men, but here writes ambiguously: "We feel assured that He who sees not as men see, does not lay the guilt of innocent blood to our charge." The verb "see" here means both "to view," so suggesting that God, as an accurate eyewitness, present at the murders, knows that Brown wasn't present. "To understand" implies that God, with access to the bigger picture, recognizes the necessity of Brown's involvement in the murders and so excuses him. Once arrested, in October 1859, he said that he did not kill anyone at Pottawatomie, and that he killed men only in self-defense or a "fair fight." This letter is meant as a defensive and public account, aimed at his supporters in the North.

Near Brown's Station, K. T., June 1856

DEAR WIFE AND CHILDREN, EVERYONE—It is now about five weeks since I have seen a line from North Elba, or had any chance of writing you. During that period we here have passed through an almost constant series of very trying events. We were called to the relief of Lawrence, May 22, and every man (eight in all), except Orson turned out; he staying with the women and children, and to take care of the cattle. John was captain of a company over night. Next day our little company left, and during the day we stopped and searched three men.

Lawrence was destroyed in this way: Their leading men had (as I think) decided, in a very *cowardly* manner, not to resist any process having any Government official to serve it, notwithstanding the process might be wholly a bogus affair. The consequence was that a man called a United States marshal came on with a horde of ruffians which he called his posse, and after arresting a few persons turned the ruffians loose on the defenceless people. They robbed the inhabitants of their money and other property, and even women of their ornaments, and burned considerable of the town.

On the second day and evening after we left John's men we encountered quite a number of proslavery men, and took quite a number prisoners. Our prisoners we let go; but we kept some four or five horses. We were immediately after this accused of murdering five men at Pottawatomie, and great efforts have since been made by the Missourians and their ruffian allies to capture us. John's company soon afterwards disbanded, and also the Osawatomie men.

Jason started to go and place himself under the protection of the Government troops; but on his way he was taken prisoner by the Bogus men, and is yet a prisoner, I suppose. John tried to hide for several days; but from feelings of the ungrateful conduct of those who ought to have stood by him, excessive fatigue, anxiety, and constant loss of sleep, he became quite insane, and in that situation gave up, or as we are told, was betrayed at Osawatomie into the hands of the Bogus men. We do not know all the truth about this affair. He has since, we are told, been kept in irons, and brought to a trial before a bogus court, the result of which we have not yet learned. We have great anxiety both for him and Jason, and numerous other prisoners with the enemy (who have all the while had the Government troops to sustain them). We can only commend them to God.

The cowardly mean conduct of Osawatomie and vicinity did not save them; for the ruffians came on them, made numerous prisoners, fired their buildings, and robbed them. After this a picked party of the Bogus men went to Brown's station, burned John's and Jason's houses, and their contents to ashes; in which burning we have all suffered more or less. Orson and the boy have been prisoners, but were soon set at liberty. They are well, and have not been seriously injured. Owen and I have just come here for the first time to look at the ruins. All looks desolate and forsaken,—the grass and weeds fast covering up the signs that these places were lately the abodes of quiet families. After burning the houses, this self-same party of picked men, some forty in number, set out as they supposed, and as was the fact, on the track of my little company, boasting, with awful profanity, that they would have our scalps. They however passed the place where we were hid, and robbed a little town some four or five miles beyond our camp in the timber. I had omitted to say that some murders had been committed at the time Lawrence was sacked.

On learning that this party were in pursuit of us, my little company, now increased to ten in all, started after them in company of a Captain Shore, with eighteen men, he included (June 1). We were all mounted as we travelled. We did not meet them on that day, but took five prisoners, four of whom were of their scouts, and well armed. We were out all night, but could find nothing of them until about six o'clock next morning, when we prepared to attack them at once, on foot, leaving Frederick and one of Captain Shore's men to guard the horses. As I was much older than Captain Shore, the principal direction of the fight devolved on me. We got to within about a mile of their camp before being discovered by their scouts, and then moved at a brisk pace, Captain Shore and men forming our left, and my company the right. When within about sixty rods of the enemy, Captain Shore's men halted by mistake in a very exposed situation, and continued the fire, both his men and the enemy being armed with Sharpe's rifles. My company had no long-shooters. We (my company) did not fire a gun until we gained the rear of a bank, about fifteen or twenty rods to the right of the enemy, where we commenced, and soon compelled them to hide in a ravine. Captain Shore, after getting one man wounded and exhausting his ammunition, came with part of his men to the right of my position, much discouraged. The balance of his men, including the one wounded, had left the ground. Five of Captain Shore's men came boldly down and joined my company, and all but one man, wounded, helped to maintain the fight until it was over. I was obliged to give my consent that he should go after more help, when all his men left but eight, four of whom I persuaded to remain in a secure position, and there busied one of them in shooting the horses and mules of the enemy, which served for a show of fight. After the firing had continued for some two to three hours, Captain Pate with twenty-three men, two badly wounded, laid down their arms to nine men, myself included—four of Captain Shore's men and four of my own. One of my men (Henry Thompson) was badly wounded, and after continuing his fire for an hour longer was obliged to quit the ground. Three others of my company (but not of my family) had gone off. Salmon was dreadfully wounded by accident, soon after the fight; but both he and Henry are fast recovering.

A day or two after the fight, Colonel Sumner of the United States army came suddenly upon us, while fortifying our camp and guarding our prisoners (which, by the way, it had been agreed mutually should be exchanged for as many Free States men, John and Jason included), and compelled us to let go our prisoners without being exchanged, and to give up their horses and arms. They did not go more than two or three miles before they began to rob and injure Free-State people. We consider this as in good keeping with the cruel and unjust course of the Administration and its tools throughout this whole Kansas difficulty. Colonel Sumner also compelled us to disband; and we, being only a handful, were obliged to submit.

Since then we have, like David of old, had our dwelling with the serpents of the rocks and wild beasts of the wilderness; being obliged to hide away from our enemies. We are not disheartened, though nearly destitute of food, clothing, and money. God, who has not given us over to the will of our enemies, but has moreover delivered them into our hand, will, we humbly trust, still keep and deliver us. We feel assured that He who sees not as men see, does not lay the guilt of innocent blood to our charge.

I ought to have said that Captain Shore and his men stood their ground nobly in their unfortunate but mistaken position during the early part of the fight. I ought to say further that a Captain Abbott, being some miles distant with a company, came onward promptly to sustain us, but could not reach us till the fight was over. After the fight, numerous Free-State men who could not be got out before were on hand; and some of them, I am ashamed to add, were very busy not only with the plunder of our enemies, but with our private effects, leaving us, while guarding our prisoners and providing in regard to them, much poorer than before the battle.

If, under God, this letter reaches you so that it can be read, I wish it at once carefully copied, and a copy of it sent to Gerrit Smith. I know of no other way to get these facts and our situation before the world, nor when I can write again.

Owen has the ague to-day. Our camp is some miles off. Have heard that letters are in for some of us, but have not seen them. Do continue writing. We heard last mail brought only three letters, and all these for proslavery men. It is said that both the Lawrence and Osawatomie men, when the ruffians came on them, either hid or gave up their arms, and that their leading men counselled them to take such a course.

May God bless and keep you all!

Your affectionate husband and father, John Brown
PS. Ellen and Wealthy are staying at Osawatomie.

The above is a true account of the first regular battle fought between Free-

State and proslavery men in Kansas. May God still gird loins and hold our right hands, and to him may we give the glory! I ought in justice to say, that, after the sacking and burning of several towns, the Government troops appeared for their protection and drove off some of the enemy.   J.B.

* * * *

Testimonies of Mrs. Doyle, Mrs. Wilkinson, and James Harris on the Pottawatomie Murders, May 24–25, 1856

The last week of May 1856 must have seemed like a bloody week to Americans. Pro-slavery settlers burned and pillaged the Kansas town of Lawrence on May 21, and Preston Brooks bludgeoned Charles Sumner in Washington as retribution for Sumner's speech, "Crimes Against Kansas," on May 22. Then, late at night on May 24, John Brown, and seven others, including four of his sons and his son-in-law Henry Thompson, entered the proslavery settlement at Pottawatomie Creek and hacked to death five unarmed settlers. Three of the men killed were father and sons, the Doyles, poor white folks, proslavery but never slave-owning. The eyewitness testimony of Mrs. Doyle from 1860 is printed in full here. The same Mrs. Doyle would later write to Brown whilst he was in prison, on November 20, 1859, by way of the New York Express, *to confess that "I do feel grateful to hear that you were stopped in your fiendish career at Harpers Ferry." She adds: "With the loss of your two sons you can now appreciate my distress in Kansas when you, then and there, entered my house at midnight and arrested my husband and two boys, and took them out of the yard and in cold blood shot them dead in my hearing. You can't say you did it to free our slaves. We had none and never expected to own one. It had only made me a poor disconsolate widow, with helpless children. While I feel for your folly, I do hope and trust that you will meet your just reward. Oh! How it pained my heart to hear the dying groans of my husband and children."*

Another man killed at Pottawatomie was named Wilkinson, a member of the proslavery legislature, with some education, and by all accounts an unpopular neighbor and a bully to his wife, the eyewitness testimony of whom follows that of Mrs. Doyle. The fifth man killed was William Sherman, a border ruffian and horse-thief. He was taken from the house of one James Harris, whose testimony is also here. All three accounts were given to Congressman Oliver for the Howard Committee Report. There is still some mystery surrounding the murders, caused in part by Brown's failure to confess formally. But testimonies from Henry Thompson and Salmon Brown, as well as from the wives of Doyle and Wilkinson, leave little room for the possibility that Brown was not involved. It seems Brown may not have slain anyone himself: most accounts concur that the younger Brown boys and Henry Thompson killed the five men, and Brown fired a shot only after the killing was done, possibly as a signal to those of his band waiting at a distance. Even so, the incident is the major sticking point for would-be admirers of Brown: the men Brown slaughtered had neither owned slaves nor participated in the sacking of Lawrence.

The bodies were apparently mutilated, and this also garnered much attention, in 1856 and after. But James Townsley, one of the men who took part in the Pottawatomie murders, wrote in an article for the Lawrence Daily Journal, *on December 10, 1879: "it is not true that there was any intentional mutilation of the bodies after they were killed. They were slain as quickly as possible and left, and whatever gashes they received were inflicted in the process of cutting them down with swords. I understand that the killing was done with these swords, so as to avoid alarming the neighborhood by the discharge of firearms." The killings were meant as a warning. They were designed to terrify the proslavery forces and build a wall of protection around the free-state settlers. And, perhaps their most important intention was to grab the attention of the rest of the country—and push America closer to the final conflict, and so to the end of slavery.*

Testimony of Mrs Doyle:

I am the widow of the late James P. Doyle. We moved into the Territory—that is, my husband, myself, and children—moved into the Territory of Kansas some time in November, A. D. 1855, and settled upon Musketo creek, about one mile from its mouth, and where it empties into Pottawatomie creek, in Franklin county. On Saturday, the 24th of May, A. D. 1855, about eleven o'clock at night, after we had all retired, my husband, James P. Doyle, myself, and six children, five boys and one girl—the eldest is about twenty-two years of age; his name is William. The next is about twenty years of age; his name is Drury. The next is about seventeen years of age; his name is John. The next is about thirteen years of age; her name is Polly Ann. The next is about eight years of age; his name is James. The next is about five years of age; his name is Henry. We were all in bed, when we heard some persons come into the yard, and rap at the door, and call for Mr. Doyle, my husband. This was about eleven o'clock on Saturday night, of the 24th of May last. My husband got up and went to the door. Those outside inquired for Mr. Wilkinson, and where he lived. My husband said he would tell them. Mr. Doyle, my husband, and several came into the house, and said they were from the army. My husband was a pro-slavery man. They told my husband that he and the boys must surrender; they were then prisoners. The men were armed with pistols and large knives. They first took my husband out of the house; then took two of my sons—William and Drury—out, and then took my husband and these two boys (William and Drury) away. My son John was spared, because I asked them, in tears, to spare him.

In a short time afterwards I heard the report of pistols; I heard two reports. After which I heard moaning as if a person was dying. Then I heard a wild whoop. They had asked before they went away for our horses. We told them that our horses were out on the prairie. My husband and two boys, my sons, did not come back any more. I went out next morning in search of them, and found my husband and William, my son, lying dead in the road, near together, about two hundred yards from the house. They were buried the next day. On the day of the burying, I saw the dead body of Drury. Fear of myself and the remaining children induced me to leave the home where we had been living. We had improved our claim a little. I left and went to the State of Missouri.

Testimony of Mrs. Wilkinson:

I was sick with measles, and woke up Mr. Wilkinson, and asked if he heard the noise and what it meant? He said it was only someone passed about, and soon after was again asleep. It was not long before the dog raged and barked furiously, awakening me once more; pretty soon I heard footsteps as of men approaching; saw one pass by the window, and some one knocked at the door. I asked, who is that? No one answered. I awoke my husband who asked, who is that? Someone replied, "I want you to tell me the way to Dutch Henry's." He commenced to tell them, and they said to him, "Come out and show us." He wanted to go, but I would not let him; he then told them it was difficult to find his clothes, and could tell them as well without going out of doors. The men out of doors, after that, stepped back, and I thought I could hear them whispering; but they immediately returned, and, as they approached, one of them asked my husband, "Are you a northern armist?" He said "I am!" I understood the answer to mean that my husband was opposed to the northern or freesoil party. I cannot say that I understood the question. My husband was a pro-slavery man, and was a member of the territorial legislature held at Shawnee Mission. When my husband said "I am," one of them said "you are a prisoner. Do you surrender?" He said, "Gentlemen, I do." They said, "open the door." Mr. Wilkinson told them to wait till he made a light; and they replied, "if you don't open it, we will open it for you." He opened the door against my wishes, and four men came in, and my husband was told to put on his clothes, and they asked him if there were not more men about; they searched for arms, and took a gun and powder flask, all the weapon that was about the house. I begged them to let Mr. Wilkinson stay with me, saying that I was sick and helpless, and could not stay by myself. My husband also asked them to let him stay with me, until he could get some one to wait on me; told them that he would not run off, but he would be there the next day, or whenever called for; the old man who seemed to be in command looked at me, and then around at the children, and replied, "you have neighbors." I said, "so I have, but they are not here, and I cannot go for them." The old man replied, "it matters not," and told him to get ready. My husband wanted to put on his boots, and get ready, so as to be protected from the damp and night air, but they would not let him. They then took my husband away. After they were gone I thought I heard my husband's voice in complaint, but do not know; went to the door and all was still. Next morning Mr. Wilkinson's body was found about one hundred and fifty yards from the house, in some dead brush. A lady who saw my husband's body said that there was a gash in his head and side. Others said he was cut in the throat twice.

Testimony of James Harris:

On Sunday morning, May 25, 1856, about two A.M., while my wife and child and myself were in bed in the house where we lived, near Henry Sherman's, we were aroused by a company of men who said they belonged to the Northern army, and who were each armed with a sabre and two revolvers, two of whom I recognized; namely, a Mr. Brown, whose given name I do not remember (commonly known by the appellation of "old man Brown"), and his son Owen Brown. They came into the house and approached the bedside where we were lying and ordered us, together with three other men who were in the same house with me, to surrender; that the Northern army was upon us, and it would be no use for us to resist. The names of these other men who were in the house with me were William Sherman and John S. Whiteman; the other man I did not know. They were stopping with me that night. They had bought a cow from Henry Sherman, and intended to go home the next morning. When they came up to the bed, some had drawn sabers in their hands, and some re-volvers. They then took into their possession two rifles and a bowie-knife, which I had there in the room (there was but one room in my house), and af-terwards ransacked the whole establishment in search of ammunition. They then took one of these three men, who were staying in my house, out. (This was the man whose name I did not know.) He came back. They then took me out, and asked me if there were any more men about the place. I told them there were not. They searched the place, but found no others but us four. They asked me where Henry Sherman was. (Henry was a brother to William Sher-man.) I told them he was out on the plains in search of some cattle which he had lost. They asked me if I had ever taken any hand in aiding proslavery men in coming to the Territory of Kansas, or had ever taken any hand in the last troubles at Lawrence; they asked me whether I had ever done the Free-State party any harm, or ever intended to do that party any harm; they asked me what made me live at such a place. I then answered that I could get higher wages there than anywhere else. They asked me if there were any bridles or saddles about the premises. I told them there was one saddle, which they took: and they also took possession of Henry Sherman's horse, which I had at my place, and made me saddle him. They then said if I would answer no to all the questions which they had asked me, they would let me loose. Old Mr. Brown and his son then went into the house with me. The other three men— Mr. William Sherman, Mr. Whiteman, and the stranger—were in the house all this time. After old man Brown and his son went into the house with me, old man Brown asked Mr. Sherman to go out with him; and Mr. Sherman then went out with old Mr. Brown, and another man came into the house in Brown's place. I heard nothing more for about fifteen minutes. Two of the Northern army, as they styled themselves, stayed in with us until we heard a cap burst, and then these two men left. That morning, about ten o'clock, I found William Sherman dead in the creek near my house. I was looking for him; as he had not come back, I thought he had been murdered. I took Mr. William Sherman out of the creek and examined him. Mr. Whiteman was with me. Sherman's skull was split open in two places, and some of his brains was washed out by the water. A large hole was cut in his breast, and his left hand was cut off ex-cept a little piece of skin on one side. We buried him.

* * * *

New-York Herald *Report of the Pottawatomie Murders, June 10, 1856*

The proslavery press response to the Pottawatomie murders was ex-treme. On June 8 the New York Herald *described the five bodies "cold and dead upon the ground, gashed, torn, hacked and disfigured to a de-gree at which even Indian barbarity would shudder." The article con-*

tinues: "*The windpipe of the old man, for instance, was entirely cut out, his throat cut from ear to ear. The body of one young man has the face and head sacrificed, and the hands are cut and chopped up with a bowie knife.*" *Brown and his men seemed "devils in human form" who ignored the "groans" and "cries" of women and children, "brutes [who] would disgrace the brutal Indian." This comparison to Indian "barbarity" is noteworthy because it reveals that Brown's self-fashioning, as the Indian warrior Osawatomie Brown, had gone too far, at least in the eyes of some. He fashioned himself in the tradition of James Fenimore Cooper's Leatherstocking, a white man able to blur racial boundaries and cross fluidly from savagery to civilization and back. Now apparently more savage than the Indians, one of Brown's identities besmirched all his others.*

While Brown's supporters professed to see the political value of the murders, most were shocked by the details. They concluded that his savagery had to be viewed within the context of war. Gerrit Smith, who read the Herald *regularly, and had also read of the midnight executions in a government circulation, probably experienced an intensification of doubts about Brown's course. Brown was consistently evasive about the night of May 26, and so his friends in the North had to trust that the reports were lying, or at least exaggerating. In fact, it is because of Brown's evasiveness that we know an article in the* Herald *on June 10 is misleading. It states: "the leader of this party showed the bloody dagger, and boasted that it did the bloody deed; his name is Brown." The elusive Brown is unrecognizable here.*

The Herald's *issue of June 10 included a collection of articles on the subject of the Pottawatomie murders, and these two are printed here. They are worth laying alongside the testimonies given by Brown, his son Salmon, and August Bondi. An article of May 30 mentions that one of Brown's sons "who feigns to be crazy, has just left in charge of the dragoons." Brown's very different account of this is in his letter to his family of June (see John Brown to Wife and Children, Everyone, June 1856).*

New York Herald June 10, 1856

The Free State Massacre
May 30, 1856.
Your correspondent is in the neighbourhood of the massacre. There are over one hundred Kansas militia here and fifteen United States dragoons. They are assembled for the purposes of catching the murderers, who are an organized band of abolitionists, armed and equipped to . . . murder. . . . Such is the free State party here. The free soilers, who are ashamed of their comrades, have slipped them and joined the pro-slavery party in ferreting out the criminals. The facts as related in my last letter, regarding the slaughter, are correct; the circumstances are more aggravated than was thought. No grudge existed between the parties . . . in fact, no cause whatever can be, or is attempted to be assigned for the savage barbarity, but that the deceased were pro slavery in their sentiments.
Thirteen prisoners supposed to be connected with the affair are here under

arrest. What will be done with them is not known. The witnesses are scattered about, and Judge Cato's Court, now in session at this place, will perhaps adjourn before they can be brought in. If ever Lynch law was, or could be justifiable, it is in these cases.

It is said that the murderers are fortified on the Marais des Cygnes in a cave, about twenty-five miles from here, and are receiving reinforcements from Lawrence and elsewhere. The leader of this party showed the bloody dagger, and boasted that it did the bloody deed; his name is Brown, two of whose sons are arrested. One of them, who feigns to be crazy, has just left in charge of the dragoons.

He is made to accompany them on foot, at a pretty rapid gait of course, as the troops are mounted. His day's march will help the craziness, and perhaps cool down the fanaticism which has laid five innocent men in their graves, and brought mourning on several families—on a sick wife and a widowed mother. The blood of Allen Wilkinson cries out for justice—all humanity demands it; and let it be visited on the offenders as soon as possible. The destroyed hotel and presses at Lawrence were nuisances, because a means of resisting law . . . this the fanatics claim as an excuse for cold blooded slaughter and theft.

How long will the honest people of the North be deceived?

FROM THE BORDER–RUFFIANS PREPARING TO ARM THEMSELVES
May 29, 1856

Information of a reliable character, in which the utmost confidence may be placed, has reached us that . . . the abolitionists have been committing the grossest outrages upon the pro-slavery settlers . . . houses have been burned, and the Southern settlers ordered out of the Territory. At Pottawatomie Creek, some eight murders have been committed on defenceless pro-slavery settlers and not satisfied with killing, their bodies have been brutally mutilated. In view of these facts it is but right, and justice and humanity demand that we should arm ourselves, and proceed at once to the help and protection of our fellow countryman. Many of the settlers of Kansas are our neighbors and friends, from our own State. It is apparent that this state of things cannot and must not be suffered longer to exist, unless we intend to fold our arms and silently and patiently see our people brutally assassinated and murdered, and eventually our own lives endangered, and our property sacrificed. Efforts are now making to organize a party for the help of the pro-slavery settlers of the Territory. What is done, must be done at once and without delay, and it is therefore suggested that all who desire to aid in this matter should at once make steps to have here, just as early as possible, such provisions as will be necessary for the subsistence of the persons going. We say to you, that eight murders have been committed. What ought to be done under such circumstances will suggest itself without any intimation from us. Neither should it be expected that Jackson county, alone and single-handed, can meet this affair as it deserves. Missouri and the whole South have an interest at stake. These murders are but the natural result of the substitution of rifles for Bibles, and it remains to be seen whether the South will tamely permit them to proceed.

* * * *

August Bondi, report on events of May 26, 1856

There were three immigrant Jews among Brown's Kansas men: Theodore Wiener from Poland, Jacob Benjamin from Bohemia, and August Bondi from Vienna. Bondi's family had settled in St. Louis in 1848 after the failure of a democratic revolution in Austria, and in 1855 Bondi moved to Kansas to help work as a free-state settler, quickly joining Brown's small band. He always identified strongly and publicly with his Judaism, and perhaps admired the Old Testament qualities in Brown.

In the account here, Bondi describes the journey to Prairie City two days after the massacres at Pottawatomie. Brown and his group of nine men had accepted the request of the free-state settlers there, to protect them against the proslavery Missourians. Thick with tension and drama, the source gives us a flavor of Brown's Kansas experience. The months were exhausting but full of adventure and, as Bondi later wrote, "unity as a band of brothers." A week after making the journey of May 26, the band fought and won the Battle of Black Jack, capturing forty-eight proslavery fighters. This clash was said to be the first of the Civil War, pitched as it was North against South. In a different testimony, Bondi remembers that during the battle he and Brown fought next to each other, and "walked with bent backs, nearly crawled, that the tall dead grass of the year before might somewhat hide us from the Border Ruffian marksmen, yet the bullets kept whistling. . . ."

There were ten of us,—Captain Brown, Owen, Frederick, Salmon, and Oliver Brown; Henry Thompson, Theodore Wiener, James Townsley, Carpenter, and myself. Our armament was this: Captain Brown carried a sabre and a heavy seven-shooting revolver; all his sons and his son-in-law were armed with revolvers, long knives, and the common "squirrel rifle;" Townsley with an old musket, Wiener with a double-barrelled gun, I with an old-fashioned flint-lock musket, and Carpenter with a revolver. The three youngest men—Salmon Brown, Oliver, and I—rode without saddles. By order of Captain Brown, Fred Brown rode first, Owen and Carpenter next; ten paces behind them, old Brown; and the rest of us behind him, two and two. Our way from Middle Creek to Ottawa Creek was along the old military road between Fort Scott and Fort Leavenworth. When we had nearly reached the crossing of the old California road we saw by the fading watch-fires of a camp, hardly a hundred and fifty steps before us, an armed sentinel pacing. While Fred Brown rode slowly forward, Carpenter turned back and told Captain Brown that here was probably a division of United States dragoons who were acting as a *posse* for the marshal. Brown thereupon gave Carpenter his instructions in a few words. We were to ride forward slowly with no indication of the least anxiety, and otherwise to imitate his example. The sentry let Fred Brown and Carpenter approach within twenty five paces, and then cried, "Who goes there?" Fred answered just as loud, "Free-State." The sentry called the officer of the guard, and while he was coming the rest of us rode, by Brown's order, within five paces of where Fred and Carpenter were halted, forming ourselves in an irregular group. When the officer appeared, Carpenter spoke up and said we were farmers, living not far from Prairie City, who had gone to Osawatomie upon invitation of the settlers to protect them against an expected invasion from Missouri; had been there two days, seen and heard nothing of the Missourians, and so had resolved to return home. Upon this Lieutenant McIntosh, the commanding officer, appeared, and Carpenter repeated what he had said. None of the rest of us said a word; but the deputy marshal came forward and requested the lieutenant to detain us till daylight, so that he might make further inquiries. McIntosh replied sternly: "I have no orders to stop peaceable travellers, such as these people are; they are going home to their farms;" adding to Carpenter and the rest of us: "Pass on! Pass on!" We defiled slowly through the camp, forded the stream, and when the soldiers were a mile behind us pushed on rapidly. About four o'clock in the morning of May 27 we reached the secluded spot on Ottawa Creek which Carpenter had indicated to us as a safe place for camping. In the midst of a primeval wood, perhaps half a mile deep before you come to the creek, we pitched our camp beside a huge fallen oak, and tethered our horses in the underwood. Old Brown inspected the region, and set guards; Carpenter brought corn for the horses and coarse flour for ourselves, and then Brown began to get breakfast.

* * * *

John Brown to Wife and Children, Everyone, September 7, 1856

Brown was deeply immersed in the Kansas civil war throughout 1856, fighting, organizing, and making headlines nationwide. In June he defeated a proslavery party led by Henry Clay Pate at the Battle of Black Jack. Brown's leadership was unquestioned: on September 13, for example, anticipating the attack of 2800 Missourians on the town of Lawrence, he gave a speech there that ended, in typically charismatic Brown-style: "you had better aim at their legs than at their heads. In either case, be sure of the hind sights of your guns. It is from the neglect of this that I myself have been so many times escaped; for if all the bullets that have ever been aimed at me had hit, I should have been as full of holes as a riddle."

While Brown's letter of June 1856 was aimed at an interested public (see John Brown to Wife and Children, Everyone, June 1856), his shorter letter of September 7, here, is likely meant just for his family: it is less fluent and careful, has spelling errors and oddities of presentation, and is much less detailed in its account of his actions and whereabouts. He had narrated the capture of sons Jason and John in the June letter, and we can see from the note here that Jason was now free (he was freed on June 26), while John awaited trial (he was freed in late September). Brown also describes the battle at Osawatomie, where he acquired his Indian name after defending his band of forty-strong against four hundred better-equipped men.

The trying times were testing Brown's relationships, and his sons were discovering that, as Watson Brown said to his father at Harper's Ferry, he wanted them to "be brave as tigers" but "still afraid of [him]," and obedient in their fear. While they were still somewhat tolerant of this in September 1856, the death of their brother Frederick, related in the let-

ter here, combined with their guilt over the Pottawatomie Massacre, began to take a toll. By March 1857 the Brown boys, suffering—as Brown was himself—from physical and psychological battle-wounds, as well as dysentery, had apparently had enough. Brown's wife wrote to him with news that their sons had resolved to "learn, and practice war no more," to which Brown responded defensively, in a letter on March 31, that it was not at his request that his sons had engaged in the initial Kansas campaigns. He added, presumably referring to a wider war: "I think there may be possibly in their day that which is more to be dreaded." Though some of his sons remained to follow their father and "practice war," several, most painfully the dependable Salmon, withdrew from Kansas shortly after Brown wrote the letter below, and did not return in the spring, also refusing to assist in the Harpers Ferry raid.

Lawrence K T 7th Sept. 1856

Dear Wife & Children every one

I have one moment to write you to say that I am yet alive that Jason & family were well yesterday, John & family I hear are well; (he being yet a prisoner. On the morning of the 30th Aug an attack was made by the ruffians on Osawatomie numbering some 400 by whose scouts our dear Fredk was shot dead without warning he supposing them to be Free State men as near as we can learn. One other man a Cousin of Mr Adair was murdered by them about the same time that Fredk was killed & one badly wounded at the same time. At this time I was about 3 miles off where I had some 14 or 15 men over night that I had just enlisted to serve under me as regulars. There I collected as well as I could with some 12 or 15 more & in about ¾ of an Hour attacked them from a wood with thick undergroth, with this force we threw them into confusion for about 15 or 20 Minuets during which time we killed & wounded from 70 to 80 of the enemy *as they say* & then we escaped as well as we could with one killed while escaping; Two or Three wounded; & as many more missing. Four or Five Free State men were butchered during the day in all. Jason fought bravely by my side during the fight & escaped with me being unhurt. I was struck by a partly spent Grape, Canister, or Rifle shot which bruised me some but did not injure me seriously. "Hitherto the Lord hath helped me" notwithstanding my afflictions. Things now seem rather quiet just now; but what another Hour will bring I cannot say—I have seen Three or four letters from Ruth & One from Watson of July or Aug which are all I have seen since in June. I was very glad to hear once more from you & hope you will continue to write to some of the friends so that I may hear from you. I am utterly unable to write you for most of the time. May the God of of [sic] our Fathers bless & save you all

Your Affectionate Husband & Father, John Brown

Monday Morning 8th Sept/56

Jason has just come in Left all well as usual Johns trial is to come off or commence today Yours ever John Brown

* * * *

Gerrit Smith to John Brown, December 30, 1856

Gerrit Smith, land baron and abolitionist politician, was one of John Brown's best allies, and in 1856 and 1857 Brown leaned on him particularly hard for financial and emotional support. Brown left Kansas in October 1856, and the next year was mainly given to fund-raising and speech-giving throughout the North. He returned to Kansas briefly in November 1857, but the area was peaceful and there was nothing for him to do there. His fund-raising had mixed results and by early 1857 he was already disillusioned. In April he penned the following bitter critique of his supposed supporters, entitled "Old Browns Farewell To The Plymouth Rocks, Bunker Hill Monuments, Charter Oaks, and Uncle Thomas Cabbins":

> *He has left for Kansas. Has been trying since he came out of the territory to secure an outfit or in other words; the means of arming and thoroughly equipping his regular Minuet men, who are mixed up with the people of Kansas, and he leaves the States, with a feeling of deepest sadness; that having exhausted his own small means and with his family and brave men; suffered hunger, cold, nakedness, and some of them sickness, wounds, imprisonment in irons; with extreme cruel treatment, and others death: that after lying on the ground for months in the most sickly, unwholesome, and uncomfortable places; some of the time with sick and wounded destitute of any shelter, and hunted like wolves; sustained in part by Indians; that after all this; in order to sustain a cause which every citizen of this "glorious Republic," is under equal moral obligation to do: and for the neglect of which, he will be held accountable by God: a cause in which every man, woman and child; of the entire human family has a deep and awful interest; that when no wages are asked; or expected; he cannot secure, amidst all the wealth, luxury, and extravagance of this "Heaven exalted," people; even the necessary supplied of the common soldier. "How are the mighty fallen?"*   *Boston, April, A.D. 1857.*

guilt trip.

In the same month, on April 15, he wrote to John Jr.: "I have had a good deal of discouragement, & have often felt quite depressed; but 'hither to God hath helped me.'" So had Gerrit Smith. In a letter to Franklin Sanborn on August 13, 1857, Brown detailed just one of Smith's numerous gifts: "At most places I raised a little; but it consumed my time, and my unavoidable expenses so nearly kept pace with my incomes that I found it exceedingly discouraging." Only "the help of Gerrit Smith" kept him afloat. Smith's wealth made Brown's campaigns possible. His belief in Brown's nobility buoyed up the guerrilla warrior in another way, too. His letter here, for example, in which he articulates his respect and admiration for his friend, was intended to reassure Brown that the rumors about brutality in Kansas had not shaken his faith in Brown's cause. Frederick Douglass, another of Brown's friends and supporters, also turned a faithfully blind eye to the blood-letting at Pot-

*tawatomie, explaining in a speech of 1860 that slaveowners had "com-
pelled [Brown] to adopt a desperate measure"; and in his autobiography
of 1892 that it was "a terrible remedy for a terrible malady." Douglass
continued to defend Brown beyond 1859, but Smith, when implicated in
the raid at Harpers Ferry, was not so stalwart. Now, though, at the end
of a turbulent year in Brown's life, and throughout the months to come
as he presented himself to the world and begged its dollars and approval,
Smith's encouraging words were gratefully received.*

Peterboro, Dec. 30, 1856

Captain John Brown—You did not need to show me letters from Governor
Chase and Governor Robinson to let me know who and what you are. I have
known you for many years, and have highly esteemed you as long as I have
known you. I know your unshrinking bravery, your self-sacrificing benevolence, your devotion to the cause of freedom, and have long known them. May
heaven preserve your life and health, and prosper your noble purposes!
GERRIT SMITH

* * * *

John Brown to Wife and Family, March 12, 1857

*By March 1857 Brown was deeply immersed in his effort at fund-rais-
ing. He had made speeches in Hartford, Boston, and Concord, and ended
several speeches in Connecticut with a bargain: "I was told that the
newspapers dressed in mourning on hearing that I was killed and scalped
in Kansas," he would say, then continue: "Much good it did me. . . .
If my friends will hold up my hands while I live, I will freely absolve
them from any expense over me when I am dead." In his attempt to win
the hearts of the North, and also because he enjoyed the role-playing,
he played the Cromwellian hero, and thrilled the ladies in their parlors.
Earnest, chivalrous, often in military dress, full of stories, he seemed at
the very center of things, hardly a solitary madman.*

Of course the canvassing took its toll. In a letter to the New York
Tribune, *on March 4, he described the "sacrifice of personal feeling"
that such begging entailed. Such letters did raise funds, however, and
friends like Gerrit Smith filled the remaining gaps in Brown's coffers.
This letter of March 12, 1857 to his family shows him thinking forward
to the inevitable result of his fundraising: death, and a headstone.*

Springfield, Mass., March 12, 1857

Dear Wife and Children all—I have just got a letter from John. All middling
well, March 2, but Johnny, who has the ague by turns. I now enclose another
from Owen. I sent you some papers last week. Have just been speaking for
three nights at Canton, Conn., and at Collinsville, a village of that town. At
the two places they gave me eighty dollars. Canton is where both father and
mother were raised. They have agreed to send to my family at North Elba
grandfather John Brown's old granite monument, about eighty years old, to be
faced and inscribed in memory of our poor Frederick, who sleeps in Kansas.

I prize it very highly and the family all will, I think. I want to see you all very much, but cannot tell when I can go back yet. Hope to get something from you here soon. Direct as before. May God bless you all!

Your affectionate husband and father, JOHN BROWN

* * * *

Gerrit Smith to Franklin Sanborn, July 26, 1858

Gerrit Smith always had qualms about his support of John Brown. He was keen that Brown live at North Elba, on land given by Smith to poor black New Yorkers, and funded him faithfully for years. But he didn't want culpability for any deaths. The letter here was written two months after Brown's Constitutional Convention at Chatham, Canada, which he declined to attend. He is writing to Franklin Sanborn, a young Harvard graduate, one of Brown's greatest admirers, his future biographer, and by 1859 a co-conspirator in the Harpers Ferry raid. To Sanborn, Smith indicates an apparently unconditional trust in Brown, but may actually be expressing a nagging feeling that the Chatham Convention of that May, and Brown's planned invasion of the South, originally scheduled for July 4, 1858, were measures too extreme: "I do not wish to know . . .," he writes.

Smith generally preferred not to know about the precise details of Brown's campaigns, only discussing the grand design and results. Earlier that year a man who had worked with Brown in Kansas had threatened to expose the plans for the Harpers Ferry raid, and Smith's role therein, and by July Smith was almost tempted to cut all connections with Brown. He and Brown's other Northern backers quickly formulated a new "blind" arrangement, in which Brown would keep details of his plans hidden from them, so that they might protect themselves with denial if necessary.

Smith was always much more ambivalent about the use of violence than Brown, and throughout the 1850s he experienced guilt about his sanction of it. Anxieties and doubts over the possibility of racial equality surfaced repeatedly, though he kept them relatively well-hidden until the attack on Harpers Ferry. After the raid he was driven mad by the idea that he might be responsible for the loss of life there. During October 1859, he destroyed all evidence connecting him to Brown's venture, fearing that Brown had not kept the plans—and most importantly Smith's part in the plans—well enough to himself. He was committed to a state lunatic asylum by his family in November and after his release drew back from radical abolitionism.

Peterboro, July 26, 1858

Mr. F.B. Sanborn.

My Dear Sir

I have your letter of the 23d instant. I have great faith in the wisdom, integrity, and bravery of Captain Brown. For several years I have frequently given him money toward sustaining him in his contests with the slave-power. Whenever he shall embark in another of these contests I shall again stand ready

to help him; and I will begin with giving him a hundred dollars. I do not wish
to know Captain Brown's plans; I hope he will keep them to himself. Can you
not visit us this summer? We shall be very glad to see you.
With best regards, your friend,

Gerrit Smith

* * * *

John Henri Kagi to his father and sister, September 23, 1858

*The men who followed Brown down the road to Harpers Ferry were
young, idealistic, and passionate about their leader. They knew of the
risks and were prepared to suffer the consequences. All but two were
under thirty and three were less than twenty-one years old at the time
of the raid. Three of Brown's sons fought beside him at the Ferry. Eventually numbering twenty-two including Brown himself, the raiders were
an interracial group, sixteen white and five black. There was no racial
conflict within the group, and Osborne Anderson, in his account of the
Harpers Ferry operation, A* Voice From Harpers Ferry *(1861), charac-
terized the band as "one company, wherein no hateful prejudice dared
intrude its ugly self". The black men were Lewis Sheridan Leary, John
A. Copeland, Jr., Osborne Perry Anderson, Dangerfield Newby, and
Shields Green, the last introduced to Brown by Frederick Douglass on
the occasion that Brown tried—unsuccessfully—to persuade Douglass
himself to join the group. Of the five black raiders only Osborne Anderson, who escaped into the mountains, survived both the raid itself and
the executions in its wake.*

*John Henry Kagi was the ablest and best educated of all the raiders.
He was Brown's lieutenant, for "no one was greater in the essentials of
true nobility of character and executive skill than John H. Kagi, the con-
fidential friend and adviser of the old man," explained Osborne Anderson in* A Voice From Harpers Ferry. *He added: "had the old gentleman
been slain at the Ferry, and Kagi been spared, the command would have
devolved upon the latter." Kagi was a lawyer, teacher, businessman, and
stenographer, and during the Kansas warfare a correspondent for the*
New York Tribune, *the newspaper of largest circulation in the country,
publishing his articles under the name "Mohawk." Like Brown, who had
the nickname Osawatomie Brown, Kagi explicitly linked with the Indians
the crusade for freedom in Kansas. He was twenty-four years old when
he died on October 17, 1859. His body is still unaccounted for.*

*The raiders are confident and excited in their last letters to their fam-
ilies. Jeremiah Anderson wrote on July 5, 1859: "Millions of fellow-be-
ings require it of us; their cries for help go out to the universe daily and
hourly . . . there are a few who dare to answer this call and dare to answer it in a manner that will make this land of liberty and equality shake
to the centre." Kagi himself was capable of quite beautiful prose. He
wrote to his sister on June 8, 1859 of the importance of "not thinking
that you were singled out by Fate from living chessmen in his game of*

horror and of death," adding: "follow this and you will never regret being alive." Also moving is the letter here, written to his father and sister on September 23, 1858. He was an agnostic, so explains his actions and idealism as a labor for "mankind" rather than God. It is not a holy cause, but a right one, and Harpers Ferry was his secular Armageddon. Less than thirteen months before the future trod on to meet him with strides so rapid that they overtook his own, Kagi looks ahead and sees it coming, "bright and good."

I believe there are better times dawning, to my sight at least. I am not now laboring and waiting without present reward for myself alone; it is for a future reward for mankind and for you all. There can be no doubt of the reward in the end, or of the drawing very near of the success of a great cause which is to earn it. Few of my age have toiled harder or suffered more in the cause than I, yet I regret nothing that I have done, nor am I in any discouragement at the future. It is bright and good, and treads on to meet the hopeful with rapid strides. Things are now quiet. I am collecting arms, etc., belonging to J.B., so that he may command them at any time.

* * * *

Edwin Morton to Franklin Sanborn,
April 13, 18, June 1, 30, 1859

The last year of Brown's life was one of intense fund-raising and planning for the raid in Virginia. He used the full effect of his mesmeric personality to fill the expedition coffers. Often dressed in an old corduroy suit, his hair in disarray, he was, as Edwin Morton relates to Franklin Sanborn in the letter here, "most impressively tremendous".

As usual, Gerrit Smith was at the center of it all, financing and politicizing the campaign through donations and speeches. Since March 1858 he had been one of the Secret Six, a committee formed with five other white abolitionists to advise Brown and raise money for his Harpers Ferry expedition. The other five were the minister and abolitionist Thomas Wentworth Higginson; the philanthropist and educational reformer Samuel Howe, who also worked to provide for Brown's defense and fled to Canada after the raid to escape arrest; the controversial Unitarian minister and abolitionist Theodore Parker; the schoolteacher and friend of Emerson and Thoreau, Franklin Sanborn; and the abolitionist George Luther Stearns, who funded the antislavery homesteaders in Kansas and defended Brown's actions before the Senate committee investigating the raid. He also unveiled a bust of John Brown at a party celebrating the signing of President Lincoln's Emancipation Proclamation of January 1, 1863.

The existence of this secret committee of men of the highest rank in American society proved Morton's point (in French) here, that "it is society that stages the crime; the guilty person is only the instrument that executes it." The full citation, from Quetelet, continues, prophetically: "The victim on the scaffold is in a certain way the expiatory victim of society. His crime is the fruit of the circumstance in which he finds himself." Brown's "crime," the fruit of the circumstance in which all of America found itself as it careened towards civil war, took him to the scaffold.

Though not one of the Secret Six, Morton was a prominent abolitionist and a close friend of Thoreau, also of Franklin Sanborn, to whom he sent all of the letters here. He spent a lot of time with Brown during 1859 and likely knew many of the details for the planned invasion of the South. He fled to Europe after Brown's raid in October 1859 in part to protect Gerrit Smith, and returned in the summer of 1860 to study law at Plymouth. In his 1881 address at Storer College, Frederick Douglass lists Morton as one of significant antislavery men who surrounded Brown, along with Gerrit Smith, Joshua R. Giddings, S. G. Howe, G. L. Stearns, and Franklin Sanborn.

Wednesday Evening, April 13, 1859

You must hear of Brown's meeting this afternoon—few in numbers, but the most interesting people I ever saw. Mr. Smith spoke well; G.W. Putnam read a spirited poem; and Brown was exceedingly interesting and once or twice so eloquent that Mr. Smith and some others wept. Some one asked him if he had not better apply himself in another direction, and reminded him of his imminent peril, and that his life could not be spared. His replies were swift and most impressively tremendous. A paper was handed about, with the name of Mr. Smith for four hundred dollars, to which others added. Mr. Smith, in the most eloquent speech I ever heard from him, said: "If I were asked to point out—I will say it in his presence—to point out the man in all this world I think most truly a Christian, I would point to John Brown." I was once doubtful in my own mind as to Captain Brown's course. I now approve it heartily, having given my mind to it more of late.

April 18

Brown left on Thursday the 14th and was to be at North Elba tomorrow the 19th. Thence he goes "in a few days" to you. He says he must not be trifled with, and shall hold Boston and New Haven to their word. New Haven advises him to forfeit five hundred dollars he has paid on a certain contract and drop it. He will not. From here he went in good spirits, and appeared better than ever to us, barring an affection of the right side of his head. I hope he will meet hearty encouragement elsewhere. Mr. Smith gave him four hundred dollars, I twenty-five, and we took some ten dollars at the little meeting. . . .

"L'expérience démontre, avec toute l'évidence possible, que c'est la société que prepare le crime, et que coupable n'est que l'instrument que l'exécute" Do you believe Quetelet?

June 1

Mr. Smith has lately written to John Brown at New York to find what he needed, meaning to supply it. He now sends to him according to your enclosed address; I suppose to know the place where this matter is to be adjusted. Harriet Tubman suggested the 4th of July as a good time to "raise the mill."

June 30

News from Andover, Ohio, a week or more since, from our friend. He had received two hundred dollars more from here, was full of cheer, and arranging his wool business; but I do not look for a result so soon as many do.

* * * *

Annie Brown Adams to Garibaldi Ross, December 15, 1887

From November 1857 onwards Brown focused on his plans for Virginia, and bringing about "the great work of his life," as he put in a letter to his family on January 30, 1858. He freed eleven slaves in Missouri in December 1858, and led them eleven hundred miles to Canada, reaching there in March 1859 after eighty-two days of traveling. He continued to fund-raise until October 1859, supported all the way by Gerrit Smith. On July 3 he arrived in Virginia with his two sons Owen and Oliver, and rented a farm five miles from Harpers Ferry belonging to Dr. Booth Kennedy. Harpers Ferry seemed the perfect location for Brown's plans. Liberated slaves could be outfitted from the armory, and it was close to the mountains in which he planned to hide after the raid. Also, it was only fifty miles from the free state of Pennsylvania, where abolitionists lived.

Preparations for the raid began. To his neighbors Brown was "Isaac Smith," a New York cattle buyer. Men gathered, and rifles, revolvers, and pikes arrived. Some men waited for several months, devoted to the endeavor but missing their families. Brown's son Watson wrote to his wife: "I think of you all day, and dream of you at night. I would gladly come home and stay with you always but for the cause," and she replied: "Now Watson, keep up good courage and do not worry about me and come back as soon as possible I think of you all night in my dreams." In August Brown summoned his daughter Anne and his daughter-in-law Martha Brown, Oliver's sixteen-year-old wife, to the farm, to keep house and make the scene seem less suspicious to prying eyes.

Anne, later Annie Brown Adams, was one of Brown's youngest children. Only Amelia, Sarah, Ellen, and an unnamed son were born after her, and of the youngest born, only Anne, Sarah, and Ellen survived into adulthood. Here, in the account Anne gave to Garibaldi Ross in 1887, she describes the period just before the raid. It is the most detailed picture painted of the months at the Kennedy Farm that preceded the raid, of the camaraderie and dynamics among the men (Annie's "invisibles," as she called them), and the boredom and frustrations of being "invisible." Though only fifteen in 1859, Annie had a part in Brown's great work—for, as Salmon explained in his reminiscence of 1913, "Father had great confidence in us children." She took care of the house and the men, and worked as a lookout for inquisitive neighboring townsfolk.

Such prying neighbors were responsible for the suddenness of the raid. Though Annie remembers that the Kennedy Farm was "far enough from neighbors to seclude" them, in fact the raid went ahead earlier than intended, on October 16 instead of the 24th, because a woman had seen one of the black men of the group moving in and out of the farm, and Brown thought suspicions might have been raised. On September 30 Brown sent Annie and Martha back home to North Elba. "The men then sobered down and acted like earnest men working hard preparing for the coming raid," remembered Osborne Anderson, one of the raiders, in his book A Voice From Harpers Ferry *(1861). In sixteen days Brown and his band of twenty-one men would step out from the Kennedy Farm into a damp night and walk five moonlit miles to the Ferry. Frederick Douglass called the venture "a perfect steel trap" from which Brown "would never get out alive," and had refused to participate. Franklin Sanborn, one of Brown's Northern backers, would later reflect: "[It was] an amazing proposition—desperate in its character, seemingly inadequate in its provision of means, and of very uncertain results . . . But no argument could prevail against his settled purpose . . . and he left us only the alternatives of betrayal, desertion, or support. We chose the last."*

1887

My father and two brothers, Owen and Oliver, John Henry Kagi and Jerry G. Anderson went down to Harper's Ferry some time in June [1859] to prepare for and get a place that would be quiet and secluded where they could receive their freight and men. They rented the Kennedy Farm situated about five miles north of Harper's Ferry as that seemed in all respects perfectly adapted to their purpose. . . . It was far enough from neighbors to seclude us, in a quiet woodsy place, less than a half mile from the foot of the Blue Ridge Mountains in Maryland, about two miles from Antietam and six miles from Sharpsburg—afterwards noted battlegrounds during the War . . .

After my father had selected his place, he found out . . . that he would be obliged to have some woman to help him, to stand between him and the curiosity of outsiders. . . . So he sent Oliver back to North Elba after Mother and I, never dreaming that Mother would not go. Oliver's girl wife, Martha, and I went back with him. Martha was sixteen and I was fifteen years old then . . .

I will first describe John Brown, not the one the world knew, but my father as I knew him. He was very strict in his ideas of discipline. We all knew from our earliest infancy that we *must* obey him . . .

We commenced housekeeping at Kennedy Farm sometime in July. . . . Our family at that time consisted of six persons. . . . Then followed the rest—one, two three and four at a time. These last arrivals all came secretly by way of Chambersburg, Father and some of the rest going there with a light covered wagon, in which they rode or else walked a part of the way. They would hide in the woods and come in to the house before daylight in the morning or else after dark at night. They all lived upstairs over the dining room, coming down at their meals, and at any time that there was no strangers or visitors about . . .

My father encouraged debating and discussions on all subjects among the men, often taking a lively part in the debate himself. Sometimes it would commence between two in the dining room, then others would join, those who were upstairs coming down into the room to listen or take a part, some sitting on the stairs ready to jump and run back out of sight, if the danger signal was given that someone was approaching. Although he did not always agree with them, he encouraged them to discuss religious questions with him, and to express themselves freely on the subject. It is claimed by many that they were a wild, ignorant, fanatical or adventurous lot of rough men. *This is not so*, they were sons from good families well trained by orthodox religious parents, too young to have settled views on many subjects, impulsive, generous, too good themselves to believe that God could possibly be the harsh unforgiving being HE was at that day usually represented to be. Judging them by the rules laid down by Christ, I think they were uncommonly good and sincere Christians if the terms Christian means follower of Christ's example, and too great lovers of freedom to endure to be trammeled by church or creed. Self interest or self aggrandizement was the farthest thing from their thoughts or intentions. It was a clear case of an effort to help those who were oppressed and [they] could not help [to] ask father one day if the money to pay the expenses was furnished by orthodox church members or liberal Christians. He said he must confess that it came from the liberal ones. Tidd spoke up and said "I thought so, the orthodox ones do not often do such things."

After breakfast Father usually read a chapter in the Bible and made a plain, short, sensible prayer, standing while praying. (I have seen him kneel, but not often.) This was his custom both at home and at Kennedy Farm. Evenings he usually sat on a stool in the kitchen because it was warm there, and he once told me he did not wish to disturb the "boys," or spoil their enjoyment and fun by his presence in the living room. He thought they did not feel quite so free when he was there.

As the table was not large enough for all to sit down at one time and the supply of dishes quite limited, Martha and I usually ate alone after all the rest were done. She "dished up" the victuals and washed dishes while I carried things into the room and waited on the table. There was no door between and . . . both rooms opened on to the porch, making a great deal of walking back and forth. After the meals I cleared off the table and washed the dishes and swept the floors of the room and porch, constantly on the look out for Mrs. Huffmaster, our nearest neighbour. She was a worse plague than the fleas. Of our supplies of food a few things were occasionally bought at Harper's Ferry when the men went to the post office after *The Baltimore Sun,* which father subscribed for. Most of the mail was sent to Kagi at Chambersburg— merely for appearance sake. The rest of our food supplies was purchased at the towns and all along the road from Chambersburg down, a few things at a time or place as not to arouse suspicion. Owen brought a barrel of eggs at one time because they were cheaper than meat. We had potatoes, onions and bacon. Then Martha was an extra good "light bread" maker. . . . We had a cookstove in the small kitchen off the porch upstairs, where we did our cooking. We used the basement kitchen and other cemented room on the ground floor only for storing purposes.

The middle room in the second story was used for dining and general living room as the stairway from above came down into that room. The men came down and took their meals at the table, except on special occasions when some stranger or neighbour was calling there. If he or she stayed too long something was carried up the ladder at the back end of the house and passed into the window to the men. Sometimes Mrs. Huffmaster with her brood of little ones would be seen coming while the men were at the table eating. They would gather up all the things, table-cloth and all, and go so quietly upstairs that no one would believe they existed, finish their meal up there and come back down bringing the things, when the visitor had gone. We did not have any stove or way of warming any of the rooms except the kitchen. The white men most of them, would watch their chance, when no one was in sight and skulk into the kitchen and stay and visit Martha awhile to relieve the monotony. If any one came they would climb the ladder into the loft over the kitchen and stay there until Mrs. Huffmaster (usually) was gone. The coloured men were never allowed to be seen in daylight outside of the dining room. After Mrs. Huffmaster saw Shields Green in that room, they stayed upstairs closely.

I was there to keep the outside world from discovering that John Brown and his men were in their neighbourhood. I used to help Martha with the cooking all she would let me. Father would often tell me that I *must* not let any work interfere with my *constant watchfulness*. That others could help do the housework, but he *depended* on me to watch. When I sat on the porch or just inside the door, in the day . . . , I either read or sewed, to appear occupied if any one came near the table, where I could see out of the window and open [the] door if anyone was approaching the house. I was constantly on the lookout while carrying the victuals across the porch, from the kitchen, and while I was sweeping and tidying the rooms, and always at my post on the porch while the men ate their meals, when not passing in and out from the kitchen with food, or waiting on them in other ways at the table. My evenings were spent on the porch or sitting on the stairs, watching, and listening.

The men did nearly all the washing; we spread the clothes on the fence and on the ground to dry. Martha and I would bring them in as fast as they dried, but Mrs. Huffmaster would have some excuse to come to the garden, which she had rented before we went there, and then she would notice the clothes and tell us, "Your men folks has a right smart lot of shirts." No one can ever imagine the pestering torment that little barefooted woman and her four little children were to us. Martha called them the little hen and chickens. We were in constant fear that people would become suspicious enough to attempt an investigation and try to arrest the men. The rifles were in boxes called "furniture" and were used to sit on and kept standing against the walls in the dining room, one box of pistols being in one bedroom near Martha's bed. She used it for a stand, table or dressing case, whatever name you wish to call it by. I had to tell people who called that: "My mother was coming soon and that she was very particular and had requested us to not unpack her furniture until she arrived," to account for the boxes in the room.

At the Kennedy Farm, my father wore a short beard, an inch or an inch and a half long. He had made this change a disguise, on his return from Kansas, thinking it more likely to disguise him than a clean face or than the long beard.

Hazlett and Leeman were the hardest ones to keep caged of all of "my invisibles," as I called them. They would get out and wander off in the woods and even go down to Harper's Ferry, going to Cook's home and back in daylight. We were so self-conscious that we feared danger when no man pursued or even thought of it. Watson, Oliver, Leeman and Kagi were all a little more than six feet in height, J.G. Anderson and Dauphin Thompson were next them in height but a little less than six feet; William Thompson and Stewart Taylor were above or about medium height but not quite as tall as the two last. Dangerfield Newby was I think above medium size, spare and showed a Scotch blood plainly in his looks and ways. His father was a Scotchman, who took his family of mulatto children into Ohio and gave them their freedom. Newby was quiet, sensible and very unobtrusive. Stevens and Stewart Taylor were the only ones who believed in "spiritualism" and their belief was more theoretical than otherwise. The latter was nearer to a "born crank" than any other man in the company. He believed in dreams and all sorts of "isms," and predicted his own death, which really came true. He talked as coolly about it as if he were going into another room. He considered it his duty to go to Harper's Ferry and go he did, although he knew he was going to his end. He was all the time studying and "improving his mind" as he called it. He had learned to write shorthand. O.P. Anderson was accustomed to being confined in the house, being a printer by trade, so that he was not so restive as some of the others.

William Thompson was an easy-going, good-natured person who enjoyed telling funny stories, mimicking old people for the amusement of any company he was in. But for all his nonsense he possessed an abundance of good common sense. When the occasion seemed to demand it, he knew how to use it to advantage. He was kind hearted and generous to a fault. Dauphin Thompson was the youngest one of a family of eighteen children. He was a quiet person, read a good deal, said little. He was perfectly blond, with yellow, curly hair and blue eyes, innocent as a baby, nearly six feet high, good size, well proportioned—a handsome young man. I heard Hazlett and Leeman, one day saying that "Barclay Coppoc and Dauphin Thompson were too nearly like good girls to make soldiers;" that they ought to have gone to Kansas and roughed it awhile to toughen them, before coming down there. To while away the time the men read magazines, sang, told stories, argued questions, played cards and checkers, studied military tactics, and drilled under Stevens. When there was a thunderstorm they would jump about and play, making all kinds of noise to rest themselves, as they thought no one could hear them then.

PART THREE

Late in the evening on Sunday, October 16, 1859, John Brown and twenty-one men, five black, the rest white, seized the federal arsenal at Harpers Ferry, Virginia. They held out against Virginia and Maryland militia for two nights but United States marines took it back on Tuesday morning. Brown was indicted on counts of assault, murder, conspiracy, and treason; tried, convicted, and, on November 2, sentenced to hang. He was executed in Charlestown a month later, on December 2, 1859. Part Three includes Brown's Provisional Constitution of 1858, his virtuoso prison letters, and excerpts from his trial and execution. This selection of sources reveals Brown's judgment of how successful the raid had been, and his hopes for the future of the abolitionist movement. Laid bare is his self-image, and his sense of where he belonged in the larger canvas of God's universe and American history.

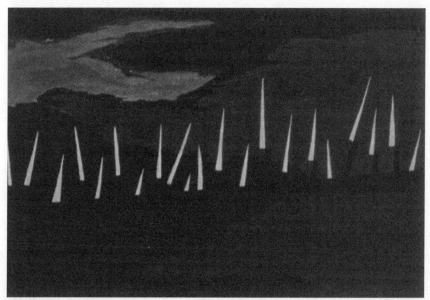

Figure 18: Jacob Lawrence, *The Life of John Brown*, 1941, No. 19: Sunday, October 16, 1859, John Brown with a company of men, white and black, marched on Harpers Ferry. (*Courtesy, Jacob and Gwendolyn Lawrence Foundation.*)

THE HARPERS FERRY RAID
AND AFTERMATH

* * * *

John Brown, Provisional Constitution and Ordinances for the People of the United States, May 8, 1858.

In April 1858 Brown went to Chatham in Ontario. There, a project he had contemplated for years would take definite form. He had drafted a "constitution" for a provisional government during a recent two-week stay at Frederick Douglass's home in Rochester, and now completed it, also organizing a convention for the following month.

The area had a large free black community, a number of whom attended the convention. The remainder of the forty-six black and white delegates were Brown's men, among them John H. Kagi, Aaron Stevens, Owen Brown, Richard Realf, George B. Gill, John E. Cook, Stewart Taylor, Richard Richardson, Charles P. Tidd, and J. S. Parsons. Frederick Douglass did not attend, though he kept a copy of the Constitution until the end of his life.

The "provisional constitutional convention" convened on May 8 and ran for two days. To the delegates, Brown outlined his plans to attack western Virginia, arm his men, and march south. He described the stronghold for escaping slaves that he intended to establish. After arming liberated slaves with stolen weapons, he would establish a free state under the constitution adopted at the convention. Freed blacks would be organized, and a new state would be founded in the southern Appalachian Mountains.

Brown then extemporized a government. Initially he presented a constitution for a separate state government within the Union, but the majority of members present objected that blacks were not equal under American law, approving instead a proposal for a new sovereign nation, an independent society, comparable to those of Native American tribes. By the end of the first day the convention had ratified a "provisional constitution and ordinances," elected Brown as commander-in-chief of the provisional forces, and other officers. On the 10th Brown appointed a committee with full power to fill all the executive, legislative, judicial, and military offices named in the constitution. John Kagi, the secretary, kept a journal of the proceedings.

Though efficient and formal, as the journal indicates, the convention was also an emotional affair, and Brown spoke passionately. The Chatham Convention became notorious in Brown's lifetime and beyond. Many who charge Brown with fanaticism return to the Provisional Constitution as their prime example. Those who interviewed Brown immediately after the Harpers Ferry raid were keen to question him about the document. The Constitution expresses a complicated attitude towards the United States government and there has been much debate around this issue. Though article XLVI states: "The foregoing Articles shall not be construed so as in any way to encourage the overthrow of any State Government of the United States," the preamble declares the current government to be "in utter disregard and violation of those eternal and self-evident truths set forth in our Declaration of Independence."

Most of Brown's biographers are, at best, embarrassed by the Constitution. A cursory examination of the period, however, reveals that revolutionary constitutions were drawn up all over the United States and Europe at this time, making embarrassed or hostile responses seem rather unfair. And many admired the principles behind the plans: the preamble casts the delegates in the mold of the patriots of 1776, and some may have enjoyed Brown's parody of the United States Constitution, complete with a three-branch government.

In organizing a Constitutional Convention, Brown proved his seriousness to the world and won the support of free blacks in America and Canada. The convention was a fundamental part of the Harpers Ferry raid, and Brown continued to plan the raid during the convention. When the meetings were all over, he printed and copied the document below. It was ready for distribution when he attacked on October 16, 1859.

Preamble:

Whereas slavery, throughout its entire existence in the United States, is none other than a most barbarous, unprovoked, and unjustifiable war of one portion of its citizens upon another portion—the only conditions of which are perpetual imprisonment and hopeless servitude or absolute extermination—in utter disregard and violation of those eternal and self-evident truths set forth in our Declaration of Independence:

Therefore we, citizens of the United States, and the oppressed people who, by a recent decision of the Supreme Court, are declared to have no rights which the white man is bound to respect, together with all other people degraded by the laws thereof, do, for the time being, ordain and establish for ourselves the following Provisional Constitution and Ordinances, the better to protect our persons, property, lives, and liberties, and to govern our actions:

ARTICLE I

Qualifications for membership

All persons of mature age, whether proscribed, oppressed, and enslaved citizens, or of the proscribed and oppressed races of the United States, who shall agree to sustain and enforce the Provisional Constitution and Ordinances of this organization, together with all minor children of such persons, shall be held to be fully entitled to protection under the same.

ARTICLE II
Branches of Government

The provisional government of this organization shall consist of three branches, viz. : legislative, executive, and judicial.

ARTICLE III
Legislative

The legislative branch shall be a Congress or House of Representatives, composed of not less than five nor more than ten members, who shall be elected by all citizens of mature age and of sound mind connected with this organization, and who shall remain in office for three years, unless sooner removed for misconduct, inability, or by death. A majority of such members shall constitute a quorum.

ARTICLE IV
Executive

The executive branch of this organization shall consist of a President and Vice-President, who shall be chosen by the citizens or members of this organization, and each of whom shall hold his office for three years, unless sooner removed by death or for inability or misconduct.

ARTICLE V
Judicial

The judicial branch of this organization shall consist of one Chief Justice of the Supreme Court and of four associate judges of said court, each constituting a circuit court. They shall each be chosen in the same manner as the President, and shall continue in office until their places have been filled in the same manner by election of the citizens. Said court shall have jurisdiction in all civil or criminal causes arising under this constitution, except breaches of the rules of war.

ARTICLE VI
Validity of Enactments

All enactments of the legislative branch shall, to become valid during the first three years, have the approbation of the President and the Commander-in-chief of the army.

ARTICLE VII
Commander-in-chief

A Commander-in-chief of the army shall be chosen by the President, Vice-President, a majority of the Provisional Congress, and of the Supreme Court, and he shall receive his commission from the President, signed by the Vice-President, the Chief Justice of the Supreme Court, and the Secretary of War, and he shall hold his office for three years, unless removed by death or on proof of incapacity or misbehavior. He shall, unless under arrest, (and until his place is actually filled as provided for by this constitution,) direct all movements of the army and advise with any allies. He shall, however, be tried, removed, or punished, on complaint of the President, by at least three general officers, or a majority of the House of Representatives, or of the Supreme Court; which House of Representatives, (the President presiding,) the Vice-President, and the members of the Supreme Court, shall constitute a court-martial for this trial; with power to remove or punish, as the case may require, and to fill his place, as above provided.

ARTICLE VIII
Officers

A Treasurer, Secretary of State, Secretary of War, and Secretary of the Treasury, shall each be chosen for the first three years, in the same way and manner as the Commander-in-Chief; subject to trial or removal on complaint of the President, Vice-President, or Commander-in-Chief, to the Chief Justice of the Supreme Court; or on complaint of the majority of the members of said court, or the Provisional Congress. The Supreme Court shall have power to try or punish either of those officers; and their places shall be filled as before.

ARTICLE IX
Secretary of War

The Secretary of War shall be under the immediate direction of the Commander-in-Chief; who may temporarily fill his place, in case of arrest, or of any inability to serve.

ARTICLE X
Congress or House of Representatives

The House of Representatives shall make ordinances for the appointment (by the President or otherwise) of all civil officers excepting those already named; and shall have power to make all laws and ordinances for the general good, not inconsistent with this Constitution and these ordinances.

ARTICLE XI
Appropriation of Money, etc

The Provisional Congress shall have power to appropriate money or other property actually in the hands of the Treasurer, to any object calculated to promote the general good, so far as may be consistent with the provisions of this Constitution; and may in certain cases, appropriate, for a moderate compensation of agents, or persons not members of this organization, for important service they are known to have rendered.

ARTICLE XII
Special Duties

It shall be the duty of Congress to provide for the instant removal of any civil officer or policeman, who becomes habitually intoxicated, or who is addicted to other immoral conduct, or to any neglect or unfaithfulness in the discharge of his official duties. Congress shall also be a standing committee of safety, for the purpose of obtaining important information; and shall be in constant communication with the Commander-in-Chief; the members of which shall each, as also the President, Vice-President, members of the Supreme Court, and Secretary of State, have full power to issue warrants returnable as Congress shall ordain (naming witnesses, etc.) upon their own information, without the formality of a complaint. Complaint shall be made immediately after arrest, and before trial; the party arrested to be served with a copy at once.

ARTICLE XIII
Trial of President and Other Officers
The President and Vice-President may either of them be tried, removed, or punished, on complaint made to the Chief-Justice of the Supreme Court, by a majority of the House of Representatives, which House, together with the Associate Judges of the Supreme Court, the whole to be presided over by the Chief-Justice in cases of the trial of the Vice-President, shall have full power to try such officers, to remove, or punish as the case may require, and to fill any vacancy so occurring, the same as in the case of the Commander-in-Chief.

ARTICLE XIV
Trial of Members of Congress
The members of the House of Representatives may any and all of them be tried, and on conviction, removed or punished on complaint before the Chief-Justice of the Supreme Court, made by any number of members of said House, exceeding one-third, which House, with the Vice-President and Associate Judges of the Supreme Court, shall constitute the proper tribunal, with power to fill such vacancies.

ARTICLE XV
Impeachment of Judges
Any member of the Supreme Court, tried, convicted, or punished by removal or otherwise, on complaint to the President, who shall, in such case, preside; the Vice-President, House of Representatives, and other members of the Supreme Court, constituting the proper tribunal (with power to fill vacancies); on complaint of a majority of said House of Representatives, or of the Supreme Court; a majority of the whole having power to decide.

ARTICLE XVI
Duties of President and Secretary of State
The President, with the Secretary of State, shall immediately upon entering on the duties of their office, give special attention to secure, from amongst their own people, men of integrity, intelligence, and good business habits and capacity; and above all, of first-rate moral and religious character and influence, to act as civil officers of every description and grade, as well as teachers, chaplains, physicians, surgeons, mechanics, agents of every description, clerks, and messengers. They shall make special efforts to induce at the earliest possible period, persons and families of that description, to locate themselves within the limits secured by this organization; and shall, moreover, from

time to time, supply the names and residence of such persons to the Congress, for their special notice and information, as among the most important of their duties, and the President is hereby authorized and empowered to afford special aid to such individuals, from such moderate appropriations as the Congress shall be able and may deem it advisable to make for that object. The President and Secretary of State, and in cases of disagreement, the Vice-President shall appoint all civil officers, but shall not have power to remove any officer. All removals shall be the result of a fair trial, whether civil or military.

ARTICLE XVII
Further Duties
It shall be the duty of the President and Secretary of State, to find out (as soon as possible) the real friends, as well as the enemies of this organization in every part of the country; to secure among them, innkeepers, private postmasters, private mail-contractors, messengers, and agents: through whom may be obtained correct and regular information, constantly; recruits for the service, places of deposit and sale; together with all needed supplies: and it shall be matter of special regard to secure such facilities through the Northern States.

ARTICLE XVIII
Duties of the President
It shall be the duty of the President, as well as the House of Representatives, at all times, to inform the Commander-in-Chief of any matter that may require his attention, or that may affect the public safety.

ARTICLE XIX
Duty of President—Continued
It shall be the duty of the President to see the provisional ordinances of this organization, and those made by Congress, are promptly and faithfully executed; and he may in cases of great urgency call on the Commander-in-Chief of the army, or other officers for aid; it being, however, intended that a sufficient civil police shall always be in readiness to secure implicit obedience to law.

ARTICLE XX
The Vice President
The Vice-President shall be the presiding officer of the Provisional Congress; and in cases of tie shall give the casting vote.

ARTICLE XXI
Vacancies
In case of death, removal, or inability of the President, the Vice-President, and next to him the Chief-Justice of the Supreme Court, shall be the President during the remainder of the term: and the place of Chief-Justice thus made vacant shall be filled by Congress from some of the members of said court; and places of the Vice-President and Associate Justice thus made vacant, filled by

an election by the united action of the Provisional Congress and members of the Supreme Court. All other vacancies, not heretofore specially provided for, shall, during the first three years, be filled by the united action of the President, Vice-President, Supreme Court, and Commander-in-Chief of the Army.

ARTICLE XXII
Punishments of Crimes
The punishment of crimes not capital, except in case of insubordinate convicts or other prisoners, shall be (so far as may be) by hard labor on the public works, roads, etc.

ARTICLE XXIII
Army Appointments
It shall be the duty of all commissioned officers of the army to name candidates of merit for office or elevation to the Commander-in-Chief, who, with the Secretary of War, and, in cases of disagreement, the President, shall be the appointing power of the army : and all commissions of military officers shall bear the signatures of the Commander-in-Chief and the Secretary of War. And it shall be the special duty of the Secretary of War to keep for constant reference of the Commander-in-Chief a full list of names of persons nominated for office, or elevation, by the officers of the army, with the name and rank of the officer nominating, stating distinctly but briefly the grounds for such notice or nomination. The Commander-in-Chief shall not have power to remove or punish any officer or soldier; but he may order their arrest and trial at any time, by court-martial.

ARTICLE XXIV
Courts-Martial
Courts-martial for Companies, Regiments, Brigades, etc., shall be called by the chief officer of each command, on complaint to him by any officer, or any five privates, in such command, and shall consist of not less than five nor more than nine officers, non-commissioned officers, and privates, one-half of whom shall not be lower in rank than the person on trial, to be chosen by the three highest officers in the command, which officers shall not be a part of such court. The chief officer of any command shall, of course, be tried by a court-martial of the command above his own. All decisions affecting the lives of persons, or office of persons holding commission, must, before taking full effect, have the signature of the Commander-in-Chief, who may also, on the recommendation of, at least, one-third of the members of the court-martial finding any sentence, grant a reprieve or communication of the same.

ARTICLE XXV
Salaries
No person connected with this organization shall be entitled to any salary, pay, or emolument, other than a competent support of himself and family, unless it be from an equal dividend, made of public property, on the establishment of peace, or of special provisions by treaty; which provision shall be

made for all persons who may have been in any active civil or military service at any time previous to any hostile action for Liberty and Equality.

ARTICLE XXVI
Treaties of Peace

Before any treaty of peace shall take full effect, it shall be signed by the President and Vice-President, the Commander-in-Chief, a majority of the House of Representatives, a majority of the Supreme Court, and a majority of all general officers of the army.

ARTICLE XXVII
Duty of the Military

It shall be the duty of the Commander-in-Chief, and all officers and soldiers of the army, to afford special protection when needed, to Congress, or any member thereof; to the Supreme Court, or any member thereof; to the President, Vice-President, Treasurer, Secretary of State, Secretary of Treasury, and Secretary of War; and to afford general protection to all civil officers, other persons having right to the same.

ARTICLE XXVIII
Property

All captured or confiscated property, and all property the product of the labor of those belonging to this organization and of their families, shall be held as the property of the whole, equally, without distinction; and may be used for the common benefit, or disposed of for the same object; and any person, officer or otherwise, who shall improperly retain, secret, use or needlessly destroy such property, or property found, captured, or confiscated, belonging to the enemy, or shall willfully neglect to render a full and fair statement of such property by him so taken or held, shall be deemed guilty of a misdemeanor and, on conviction, shall be punished accordingly.

ARTICLE XXIX
Safety or Intelligence Fund

All money, plate, watches, or jewelry, captured by honorable warfare, found, taken, or confiscated, belonging to the enemy, shall be held sacred, to constitute a liberal safety or intelligence fund; and any person who shall improperly retain, dispose of, hide, use, or destroy such money or other article above named, contrary to the provisions and spirit of this article, shall be deemed guilty of theft, and, on conviction, thereof, shall be punished accordingly. The Treasurer shall furnish the Commander-in-Chief at all times with a full statement of the condition of such fund and its nature.

ARTICLE XXX
The Commander-in-Chief and the Treasury

The Commander-in-Chief shall share power to draw from the Treasury the money and other property of the fund provided for in ARTICLE twenty-ninth, but his orders shall be signed also by the Secretary of War, who shall keep strict account of the same; subject to examination by any member of Congress, or general officer.

ARTICLE XXXI
Surplus of the Safety or Intelligence Fund

It shall be the duty of the Commander-in-Chief to advise the President of any surplus of the Safety or Intelligence Fund; who shall have power to draw such surplus (his order being also signed by the Secretary of State) to enable him to carry out the provisions of Article Seventeenth.

ARTICLE XXXII
Prisoners

No person, having surrendered himself or herself a prisoner, and who shall properly demean himself or herself as such, to any officer or private connected with this organization, shall afterward be put to death, or be subject to any corporal punishment, without first having had the benefit of a fair and impartial trial: nor shall any prisoner be treated with any kind of cruelty, disrespect, insult, or needless severity: but it shall be the duty of all persons, male and female, connected herewith, at all times and under all circumstances, to treat all such prisoners with every degree of respect and kindness the nature of the circumstances will admit of; and to insist on a like course of conduct from all others, as in the fear of Almighty God, to whose care and keeping we commit our cause.

ARTICLE XXXIII
Voluntaries

All persons who may come forward and shall voluntarily deliver up their slaves, and have their names registered on the Books of the organization, shall, so long as they continue at peace, be entitled to the fullest protection of person and property, though not connected with this organization, and shall be treated as friends, and not merely as persons neutral.

ARTICLE XXXIV
Neutrals

The persons and property of all non-slaveholders who shall remain absolute neutral, shall be respected so far as the circumstances can allow it; but they shall not be entitled to any active protection.

ARTICLE XXXV
No Needless Waste

The needless waste or destruction of any useful property or article, by fire, throwing open of fences, fields, buildings, or needless killing of animals, or injury of either, shall not be tolerated at any time or place, but shall be promptly and properly finished.

ARTICLE XXXVI
Property Confiscated

The entire and real property of all persons known to be acting either directly or indirectly with or for the enemy, or found in arms with them, or found willfully holding slaves, shall be confiscated and taken, whenever and wherever it may be found, in either free or slave States.

ARTICLE XXXVII
Desertion
Persons convicted, in impartial trial, of desertion to the enemy after becoming members, acting as spies, or of treacherous surrender of property, arms, ammunition, provisions, or supplies of any kind, roads, bridges, persons, or fortifications, shall be put to death and their entire property confiscated.

ARTICLE XXXVIII
Violation of Parole of Honor
Persons proven to be guilty of taking up arms after having been set at liberty on parole of honor, or, after the same, to have taken any active part with or for the enemy, direct or indirect, shall be put to death and their entire property confiscated.

ARTICLE XXXIX
All Must Labor
All persons connected in any way with this organization, and who may be entitled to full protection under it: shall be held as under obligation to labor in some way for the general good; and persons refusing, or neglecting so to do, shall on conviction receive a suitable and appropriate punishment.

ARTICLE XL
⚹ Irregularities
Profane swearing, filthy conversation, indecent behavior, or indecent exposure of the person, or intoxication, or quarrelling, shall not be allowed or tolerated; neither unlawful intercourse of the sexes.

ARTICLE XLI
Crimes
Persons convicted of the forcible violation of any female prisoner shall be put to death.

ARTICLE XLII
The Marriage Relation—Schools—the Sabbath
The marriage relation shall be at all times respected; and families kept together as far as possible; and broken families encouraged to re-unite, and intelligence offices established for that purpose, schools and churches established, as soon as may be, for the purpose of religious and other instructions and the first day of the week regarded as a day of rest and appropriated to moral and religious instruction and improvement; relief to the suffering, instruction of the young and ignorant, and the encouragement of personal cleanliness nor shall any persons [be] required on that day to perform ordinary manual labor, unless in extremely urgent cases.

ARTICLE XLIII
Carry Arms Openly
All persons known to be of good character, and of sound mind and suitable age, who are connected with this organization, whether male or female, shall be encouraged to carry arms openly.

ARTICLE XLIV
No Person to Carry Concealed Weapons
No person within the limits of the conquered territory, except regularly appointed policemen, express officers of the army, mail carriers, or other fully accredited messengers of the Congress, President, Vice-President, members of the Supreme Court, or commissioned officer of the army—and those only under peculiar circumstances—shall be allowed, at any time, to carry concealed weapons and any person not specifically authorized so to do, who shall be found so doing, shall be deemed a suspicious person, and may at once be arrested by any officer, soldier, or citizen, without the formality of a complaint or warrant, and may at once be subjected to thorough search, and shall have his or her case thoroughly investigated; and be dealt with as circumstances, on proof, shall require.

ARTICLE XLV
Persons to be Seized
Persons within the limits of the territory holden by this organization, not connected with this organization, having arms at all, concealed or otherwise, shall be seized at once; or be taken in charge of some vigilant officer; and their case thoroughly investigated : and it shall be the duty of all citizens and soldiers, as well as officers, to arrest such parties as are named in this and the preceding Section or Article, without the formality of complaint or warrant: and they shall be placed in charge of some proper officer for examination, or for safe keeping.

ARTICLE XLVI
These Articles Not for the Overthrow of Gov'm't
The foregoing Articles shall not be construed so as in any way to encourage the overthrow of any State Government of the United States: and look to no dissolution of the Union, but simply to Amendment and Repeal. And our flag shall be the same that our Fathers fought under in the Revolution.

ARTICLE XLVII
No Plurality of Offices
No two of the offices specially provided for, by this Instrument, shall be filled by the same person, at the same time.

ARTICLE XLVIII
Oath
Every officer, civil or military, connected with this organization, shall, before entering upon the duties of his office, make solemn oath or affirmation,

to abide by and support this Provisional Constitution and these Ordinances. Also, every Citizen and Soldier, before being fully recognized as such, shall do the same.

* * * *

John Brown's Interview with Senator Mason, Congressman Vallandigham and others, October 18, 1859

At midnight on the 16th Brown gave the order: "Men, get on your arms; we will proceed to the Ferry." He and his men took the armory and the arsenal, capturing the night watchmen and local militia leaders, including Colonel Lewis W. Washington, from whom they took a sword given to his grand uncle, George Washington, by Frederick the Great. The sword was first passed to Osborne Anderson, one of the black raiders, and then brandished by Brown until the moment that he fell. Throughout the attack, Brown and his men apparently tried hard not to kill anyone. Osborne Anderson recounts in A Voice From Harpers Ferry *that as the men prepared to attack Brown reiterated that they were not to shed blood unless their own lives were threatened.*

Brown's troops, barricaded in the engine-room, were overpowered early in the morning on the 18th by marines, led by Lieutenant Colonel Robert E. Lee and Lieutenant J. E. B. Stuart. Lee and Stuart had met with President Buchanan and Secretary of War John Floyd about the situation the day before. Beaten unconscious after he surrendered, the fifty-nine-year-old Brown was carried from the engine-house and taken to the armory. Soaked in blood and suddenly looking his age, he was laid out on the bare floor of the paymaster's office.

Figure 19: David Strother (a.k.a. Porte Crayon), "Militiamen rally to the defense of Harpers Ferry," *Harper's Weekly*, November 26, 1859. (*Courtesy, Library of Congress.*)

Now, less than a day later, Robert E. Lee, Governor Wise, Andrew Hunter, Senator Mason, Representatives Faulkner and Clement L. Vallandigham, and others clustered around their vanquished antagonist. Governor Wise later recalled that Brown looked like a "broken-wingd hawk lying upon his back, with fearless eye, and talons set for further fight if need be." They questioned him where he lay, "upon a miserable shake-down, covered with course old bedding," as a reporter for the New York Herald *wrote on October 21. The article, which also contained extracts of the interview, continues:*

> *Brown is fifty-five years of age, rather small-sized, with keen and restless gray eyes, and a grizzly beard and hair. He is a wiry, active man, and should the slightest chance for an escape be afforded, there is no doubt that he will yet give his captors much trouble. His hair is matted and tangled, and his face, hands, and clothes are smutched and smeared with blood. Colonel Lee stated that he would exclude all visitors from the room if the wounded men were annoyed or pained by them, but Brown said he was by no means annoyed; on the contrary, he was glad to be able to make himself and his motives clearly understood. He converses freely, fluently, and cheerfully, without the slightest manifestation of fear or uneasiness, evidently weighing well his words, and possessing a good command of language. His manner is courteous and affable, while he appears to be making a favorable impression upon his auditory, which, during most of the day yesterday averaged about ten or a dozen men.*

The Baltimore American *noted in an article excerpted by the* New York Tribune *on October 22 that "no sign [of] weakness was exhibited by John Brown," and continued:*

> *In the midst of enemies, whose home he had invaded; wounded and a prisoner, surrounded by a small army of officials, and a more desperate army of angry men; with the gallows staring him full in the face, he lay on the floor, and in reply to every question, gave answers that betokened the spirit that animated him. The language of Gov. Wise well expresses his boldness when he said "He is the gamest man I ever saw."*

Brown was, as Vallandigham told the Cincinnati Enquirer *on October 22, "anxious to talk and ready to answer anyone who chose to ask a question." The one question he wouldn't answer was that concerning the identities of his allies and co-conspirators. The Secret Six weren't so secret anymore: documents and letters of correspondence that exposed others had been found in Brown's hideout at the Kennedy Farm. But Brown repeatedly refused to confirm the names of anyone else involved in the raid, which must have greatly relieved his Northern backers.*

In spite of the dangers involved in talking too much, and though

*wounded and in a great deal of pain, Brown was eloquent and self-pos-
sessed from start to finish, remarking poignantly toward the end of the
three-hour interview: "You may dispose of me very easily,—I am nearly
disposed of now; but this question is still [to] be settled,—this negro
question I mean; the end of that is not yet." The interview over, Brown
traveled eight miles down the road to the prison at Charlestown. Of the
twenty-one men who fought beside him at the Ferry, ten died in the battle, six escaped, and five were later hanged. On October 25, a week after
his capture, he went on trial.*

*One character from this episode in the paymaster's episode made a
later appearance in the John Brown story. Eight months after the raid
James Mason and the United States Senate published a version of the
event. John Brown was arguably the first political subversive in American history, and this investigation was certainly the first Congressional
conspiracy investigation. A Select Committee of five, with Mason as the
chair, began its sessions on December 16, 1859, and ended them on June
14 the following year. In the intervening six months the members put together a report, and the majority of the committee—Mason, Jefferson
Davis of Mississippi, and Graham Fitch of Indiana—put their names to
what is commonly known as The Mason Report. Factual, concise, and,
in its own words, "not disposed to draw harsh, or perhaps uncharitable
conclusions," the Report went after relatively small quarries, attacking
the Massachusetts Committee and Congressman Giddings, and recom-
mending that military guards be kept at arsenals and armories. It attracted little attention: the Liberator commented only that the Mason
Committee "mountain" had produced a "mouse," and no other newspaper even mentioned it.*

*Franklin Sanborn commented later that Mason and the others asked
questions "unskilfully," and it seems that, as during Brown's interview
at Harpers Ferry, Mason and the others were verbally trumped. For example, George Stearns, one of the Secret Six (see p. 185), composed and
confident throughout his interview, commented to the Committee: "I believe John Brown to be the representative man of this century, as Washington was of the last—the Harper's Ferry affair, and the capacity shown
by the Italians for self-government, the great events of this age. One will
free Europe and the other America." At one point Mason asked, "Doesn't
your conscience trouble you for sending those rifles to Kansas to shoot
our innocent people?" to which Stearns replied: "Self-defence. You began
the game. You sent Buford and his company with arms before we sent
any from Massachusetts."*

*Later, with similar poise, feathers unruffled by the ineffectual dance
taking place around him, Stearns listened as Mason told him: "I think
when you go to that lower place, the Old Fellow will question you rather
hard about this matter and you will have to take it." "Before that time
comes," rejoined Stearns, "I think he will have about two hundred years
of Slavery to investigate, and before he gets through that, will say, we
have had enough of this business—better let the rest go." Bested by
Stearns as he was at the Ferry by Brown, Mason could only laugh.*

Senator Mason. Can you tell us who furnished money for your expedition?

John Brown. I furnished most of it myself: I cannot implicate others. It is by my own folly that I have been taken. I could easily have saved mysef from it, had I exercised my own better judgment rather than yielded to my feelings.

Mason. You mean if you had escaped immediately?

Brown. No. I had the means to make myself secure without any escape; but I allowed myself to be surrounded by a force by being too tardy. I should have gone away; but I had thirty odd prisoners, whose wives and daughters were in tears for their safety, and I felt for them. Besides, I wanted to allay the fears of those who believed we came here to burn and kill. For this reason I allowed the train to cross the bridge, and gave them full liberty to pass on. I did it only to spare the feelings of those passengers and their families, and to allay the apprehensions that you had got here in your vicinity a band of men who had no regard for life and property, nor any feelings of humanity.

Mason. But you killed some people passing along the streets quietly.

Brown. Well, sir, if there was anything of that kind done, it was without my knowledge. Your own citizens who where my prisoners will tell you that every possible means was taken to prevent it. I did not allow my men to fire when there was danger of killing those we regarded as innocent persons, if I could help it. They will tell you that we allowed ourselves to be fired at repeatedly, and did not return it.

A Bystander. That is not so. You killed an unarmed man at the corner of the house over there at the water-tank, and another besides.

Brown. See here, my friend; it is useless to dispute or contradict the report of your own neighbors who were my prisoners.

Mason. If you would tell us who sent you here,—who provided the means,—that would be information of some value.

Brown. I will answer freely and faithfully about what concerns myself,—I will answer anything I can with honor,—but not about others.

Mr. Vallandigham (who had just entered). Mr. Brown, who sent you here?

Brown. No man sent me here; it was my own prompting and that of my Maker, or that of the Devil,—whichever you please to ascribe it to. I acknowledge no master in human form.

Vallandigham. Did you get up the expedition yourself?

Brown. I did.

Vallandigham. Did you get up this document that is called a Constitution?

Brown. I did. They are a constitution and ordinances of my own contriving and getting up.

Vallandigham. How long have you been engaged in this business?

Brown. From the breaking out of the difficulties in Kansas. Four of my sons had gone there to settle, but because of the difficulties.

Mason. How many are there engaged with you in this movement?

Brown. Any questions that I can honorably answer I will,—not otherwise. So far as I am myself concerned, I have told everything truthfully. I value my word, sir.

Mason. What was your object in coming?

Brown. We came to free the slaves, and only that.

A Volunteer. How many men, in all, had you?

Brown. I came to Virginia with eighteen men only, besides myself.

Volunteer. What in the world did you suppose you could do here in Virginia with that amount of men?

Brown. Young man, I do not wish to discuss that question here.

Volunteer. You could not do anything.

Brown. Well, perhaps your ideas and mine on military subjects would differ materially.

Mason. How do you justify your acts?

Brown. I think, my friend, you are guilty of a great wrong against God and humanity,—I say it without wishing to be offensive,—and it would be perfectly right for any one to interfere with you so far as to free those you wilfully and wickedly hold in bondage. I do not say this insultingly.

Mason. I understand that.

Brown. I think I did right, and that others will do right who interfere with you at any time and at all times. I hold that the Golden Rule, "Do unto others as ye would that others should do unto you," applies to all who would help others to gain their liberty.

Lieutenant Stuart. But don't you believe in the Bible?

Brown. Certainly I do.

[. . .]

Mason. Did you consider this a military organization in this Constitution? I have not yet read it.

Brown. I did, in some sense. I wish you would give that paper close attention.

Mason. You consider yourself the commander-in-chief of these "provisional" military forces?

Brown. I was chosen, agreeably to the ordinance of a certain document, commander-in-chief of that force.

Mason. What wages did you offer?

Brown. None.

Stuart. "The wages of sin is death."

Brown. I would not have made such a remark to you if you had been a prisoner, and wounded, in my hands.

A Bystander. Did you not promise a Negro in Gettysburg twenty dollars a month?

Brown. I did not.

Mason. Does this talking annoy you?

Brown. Not in the least.

Vallandigham. Have you lived long in Ohio?

Brown. I went there in 1805. I lived in Summit County, which was then Portage County. My native place is Connecticut; my father lived there till 1805.

Vallandigham. Have you been in Portage County lately?

Brown. I was there in June last.

Vallandingham. When in Cleveland, did you attend the Fugitive Slave Law Convention there?

Brown. No. I was there about the time of the sitting of the court to try the Oberlin rescuers. I spoke there publicly on that subject; on the Fugitive Slave Law and my own rescue. Of course, so far as I had any influence at all, I was supposed to justify the Oberlin people for rescuing a slave, because I have my-self forcibly taken slaves from bondage. I was concerned in taking eleven slaves from Missouri to Canada last winter. I think I spoke in Cleveland before the Convention. I do not know that I had conversation with any of the Oberlin rescuers. I was sick part of the time I was in Ohio with the ague, in Ashtuba County.

Vallandigham. Did you see anything of Joshua R. Giddings there?

Brown. I did meet him.

Vallandigham. Did you converse with him?

Brown. I did. I would not tell you, of course, anything that would impli-cate Mr. Giddings; but I certainly met with him and had conversations with him.

Vallandigham. About that rescue case?

Brown. Yes; I heard him express his opinions upon it very freely and frankly.

Vallandigham. Justifying it?

Brown. Yes, sir; I do not compromise him, certainly, in saying that.

Vallandigham. Will you answer this; Did you talk with Giddings about your expedition here?

Brown. No, I won't answer that; because a denial of it I would not make, and to make any affirmation of it I should be a great dunce.

Vallandigham. Have you had correspondence with parties at the North on the subject of this movement?

Brown. I have had correspondence.

A Bystander. Do you consider this a religious movement?

Brown. It is, in my opinion, the greatest service man can render to God.

Bystander. Do you consider yourself an instrument in the hands of Provi-dence?

Brown. I do.

Bystander. Upon what principle do you justify your acts?

Brown. Upon the Golden Rule. I pity the poor in bondage that have none to help them: that is why I am here; not to gratify any personal animosity, re-venge, or vindictive spirit. It is my sympathy with the oppressed and the wronged, that are as good as you and as precious in the sight of God.

Bystander. Certainly. But why take the slaves against their will?

Brown. I never did.

Bystander. You did in one instance, at least.

[Stephens, the other wounded prisoner, here said, "You are right. In one case I know the negro wanted to go back."]

Bystander: Where did you come from?

Stephens. I lived in Ashtabula County, Ohio.

Vallandigham. How recently did you leave Ashtabula County?

Stephens. Some months ago. I never resided there any length of time; have been through there.

Vallandigham. How far did you live from Jefferson?

Brown. Be cautious, Stephens, about any answers that would commit any friend. I would not answer that.

[Stephens turned partially over with a groan of pain, and was silent.]

Vallandigham. Who are your advisors in this movement?

Brown. I cannot answer that. I have numerous sympathizers throughout the entire North.

Vallandigham. In northern Ohio?

Brown. No more than anywhere else; in all the free states.

Vallandigham. But you are not personally acquainted in southern Ohio?

Brown. Not very much.

A Bystander. Did you ever live in Washington City?

Brown. I did not. I want you to understand, gentlemen, and [to the reporter of the *"Herald"*] you may report that,—I want you to understand that I respect the rights of the poorest and weakest of colored people, oppressed by the slave system, just as much as I do those of the most wealthy and powerful. This is the idea that has moved me, and that alone. We expected no reward except the satisfaction of endeavoring to do for those in distress and greatly oppressed as we would be done by. The cry of distress of the oppressed is my reason, and the only thing that prompted me to come here.

Bystander. Why did you do it secretly?

Brown. Because I thought that necessary to success; no other reason.

Bystander. Have you read Gerrit Smith's last letter?

Brown. What letter do you mean?

Bystander. The "New York Herald" of yesterday, in speaking of this affair, mentions a letter in this way:—

"Apropos of this exciting news, we recollect a very significant passage in one of Gerrit Smith's letters, published a month or two ago, in which he speaks of the folly of attempting to strike the shackles off the slaves by the force of moral suasion or legal agitation, and predicts that the next movement made in the direction of negro emancipation would be an insurrection in the South."

Brown. I have not seen the "New York Herald" for some days past; but I presume, from your remark about the gist of the letter, that I should concur with it. I agree with Mr. Smith that moral suasion is hopeless. I don't think the people of the slave States will ever consider the subject of slavery in its true light till some other argument is resorted to than moral suasion.

Vallandigham. Did you expect a general rising of the slaves in case of your success?

Brown. No, sir; nor did I wish it. I expected to gather them up from time to time, and set them free.

Vallandigham. Did you expect to hold possession here till then?

Brown. Well, probably I had quite a different idea. I do not know that I ought to reveal my plans. I am here a prisoner and wounded, because I foolishly allowed myself to be so. You overrate your strength in supposing I could have been taken if I had not allowed it. I was too tardy after commencing the open attack—in delaying my movements through Monday night, and up to the time I was attacked by the government troops. It was all occasioned by my desire to spare the feelings of my prisoners and their families and the community at large. I had no knowledge of the shooting of the negro Heywood.

Vallandigham. What time did you commence your organization in Canada?

Brown. That occurred about two years ago; in 1858.

Vallandigham. Who was the secretary?

Brown. That I would not tell if I recollected; but I do not recollect. I think the officers were elected in May, 1858. I may answer incorrectly, but not intentionally. My head is a little confused by wounds, and my memory obscure on dates, etc.

Dr. Biggs. Were you in the party at Dr. Kennedy's house?

Brown. I was the head of that party. I occupied the house to mature my plan. I have not been in Baltimore to purchase caps.

Dr. Biggs. What was the number of men at Kennedy's?

Brown. I decline to answer that.

Dr. Biggs. Who lanced that woman's neck on the hill?

Brown. I did. I have sometimes practiced in surgery when I thought it a matter of humanity and necessity, and there was no one else to do it; but I have not studied surgery.

Dr. Biggs. It was done very well and scientifically. They have been very clever to the neighbors, I have been told, and we had not reason to suspect them, except that we could not understand their movements. They were represented as eight or nine persons; on Friday there were thirteen.

Brown. There were more than that.

Q. Where did you get arms?

A. I bought them.

Q. In what State?

A. That I will not state.

Q. How many guns?

A. Two hundred Sharpe's rifles and two hundred revolvers, a little under navy size.

Q. Why did you not take that swivel you left in the house?

A. I had no occasion for it. It was given to me a year or two ago.

Q. In Kansas?

A. No, I had nothing given to me in Kansas.

Q. By whom, and in what State?

A. I decline to answer. It is not properly a swivel; it is a very large rifle with a pivot. The ball is larger than a musket ball; it is intended for a slug.

Reporter. I do not wish to annoy you; but if you have anything further you would like to say, I will report it.

Brown. I have nothing to say, only that I claim to be here in carrying out a measure I believe perfectly justifiable, and not to act the part of an incendiary or ruffian, but to aid those suffering great wrong. I wish to say, furthermore, that you had better—all you people at the South—prepare yourselves for a settlement of this question, that must come up for settlement sooner than you are prepared for it. The sooner you are prepared the better. You may dispose of me very easily,—I am nearly disposed of now; but this question is still [to] be settled,—this negro question I mean; the end of that is not yet. These wounds were inflicted upon me—both sabre cuts on my head and bayonet stabs in different parts of my body—some minutes after I had ceased fighting and had consented to surrender, for the benefit of others, not for my own. I believe the Major would not have been alive; I could have killed him just as easy as a mosquito when he came in, but I supposed he only came in to receive our surrender. There had been loud and long calls of "surrender" from us,—as loud as men could yell: but in the confusion and excitement I suppose we were not heard. I do not think the Major, or any one, meant to butcher us after we had surrendered.

An Officer. Why did you not surrender before the attack?

Brown. I did not think it was my duty or my interest to do so. We assured the prisoners that we did not wish to harm them, and they should be set at liberty. I exercised my best judgment, not believing the people would wantonly sacrifice their own fellow-citizens, when we offered to let them go on condition of being allowed to change our position about a quarter of a mile. The prisoners agreed by a vote among themselves to pass across the bridge with us. We wanted them only as a sort of guarantee of our safety,—that we should not be fired into. We took them, in the first place, as hostages and to keep them from doing any harm. We did kill some men in defending ourselves, but I saw no one fire except directly in self-defence. Our orders were strict not to harm any one not in arms against us.

Q. Brown, suppose you had every nigger in the United States, what would you do with them?

A. Set them free.

Q. Your intention was to carry them off and free them?

A. Not at all.

A Bystander. To set them free would sacrifice the life of every man in this community.

Brown. I do not think so.

Bystander. I know it. I think you are fanatical.

Brown. And I think you are fanatical. "Whom the gods would destroy they first make mad," and you are mad.

Q. Was it your only object to free the negroes?

A. Absolutely our only object.

Q. But you demanded and took Colonel Washington's silver and watch?

A. Yes; we intended freely to appropriate the property of the slaveholders to carry out our object. It was for that, and only that, and with no design to enrich ourselves with any plunder whatever.

Bystander. Did you know Sherrod in Kansas? I understand you killed him.

Brown. I killed no man except in fair fight. I fought at Black Jack Point and at Osawatomie; and if I killed anybody, it was at one of these places.

[The *New York Herald* reported on November 1 that the following exchange also took place during the interview:]

Governor Wise. Mr. Brown, the silver of your hair is reddened by the blood of crime, and it is meet that you should eschew these hard allusions and think upon eternity.

Brown. Governor, I have, from all appearances, not more than fifteen or twenty years the start of you in the journey to that eternity of which you kindly warn me; and whether my tenure here shall be fifteen months, or fifteen days, or fifteen hours, I am equally prepared to go. There is an eternity behind and an eternity before, and the little speck in the centre, however long, is but comparatively a minute. The difference between your tenure and mine is trifling and I want to therefore tell you to be prepared; I am prepared. You all have a heavy responsibility, and it behoves you to prepare more than it does me.

* * * *

The Trial of John Brown, October 25–November 2, 1859

Brown went on trial before Judge Richard Parker in the courthouse at Charlestown just seven days after his capture. His wounds were not yet healed, and his request for a delay until he had recovered "in some degree" was immediately denied (this request is included in the sources here). His death was, as Douglass said in 1881, "a foregone conclusion," his trial "simply one of form," or else there was, as Wendell Phillips said in a speech recorded here, "no decent form observed, and the essence of a fair trial wholly wanting." Brown's opening remarks on his first day in court express a similar contempt for what he knew would be a mockery of a trial. A contemptuous poem appeared in the New York Tribune, *and is printed among the sources. In Boston,* The Liberator *spat the following verse at the officials running the affair:*

> *So you've convicted old John Brown! brave old*
> *Brown of Osawatomie!*
> *And you gave him a chivalrous trial, lying*
> *groaning on the floor,*
> *With his body ripped with gashes, deaf with*
> *pain from sabre slashes,*
> *Over the head received, when the deadly*
> *fight was o'er;*
> *Round him guns with lighted matches, judge*
> *and lawyers pale as ashes*
> *For he might, perhaps, come to again, and put*
> *you all to flight,*
> *Or surround you, as before!*

The press generally recognized the trial as a mockery. On November 17, the Kansas Republican *wrote: "We defy an instance to be shown in a civilized community where a prisoner has been forced to trial for his life, when so disabled by sickness or ghastly wounds as to be unable even to sit up during the proceedings, and compelled to be carried to the judgment hall upon a litter." The* Boston Transcript *promised that "whatever may be his guilt or folly, a man convicted under such circumstances, and, especially, a man executed after such a trial, will be the most terrible fruit that slavery has ever borne, and will excite the execration of the whole civilized world." Sensing the magnitude of what was unfolding in Virginia, reporters flocked to the courthouse and described the scenes so vividly that, as one member of Brown's distant audience in the North put it, readers "could fairly hear the clanking of his chains, could behold him on his bed of suffering, and later could see him toiling with his pen." Newspaper artists sketched Brown, lying wounded*

J. E. Taylor's 1899 painting of the arraignment of Brown. (*Courtesy, Library of Congress.*)

on his cot in the courtroom, a hand to his ear better to hear the proceedings through his blood-soaked bandages. Without a doubt, the winning of American hearts and the martyrdom of John Brown began in the articles and sketches of the awestruck press.

Brown's lawyer claimed Brown was insane, and Brown's angry rejection of the claim, a "miserable artifice and pretext," is amongst the sources here. Journalists interviewed Mary Brown, and thousands scrutinized her response in the New York Times *on November 18: "I never knew of his insanity until I read it in the newspapers. He is a clear-headed man. He has always been, and now is, entirely in his right mind. He is always cool, deliberate and never over-hasty. . . . His last act was the result, as all others have been, of his truest and strongest conscientious convictions."*

On Wednesday, November 2, 1859, Brown made his final address to the court. The impromptu speech, printed here, is one of the great American speeches of all time, ranked by Emerson alongside Lincoln's "Gettysburg Address." Brown mocks the accusations made against him, and, pronounced in his mild and even tones, they must have sounded absurd indeed. He then strikes a Robin-Hood blow at his accusers and, like Jesus pitying his denier Peter or his betrayer Judas, comments on the frailty of his allies.

Judge Thomas Russell wrote in the Boston Traveller *on November 5 that Brown had "delivered [a] remarkable speech, speaking with perfect calmness of voice and mildness of manner, winning the respect of all for his courage and firmness." He concluded, "His self-possession was wonderful, because his sentence, at this time, was unexpected, and his re-*

marks were entirely unprepared." The New York Tribune *wrote on November 3: "The types can give you no intimation of the soft and gentle tones, yet calm and manly, withal, that filled the court-room, and, I think, touched the hearts of many who had come only to rejoice at the heaviest blow their victim was to suffer." The* New York Times *was not so easily swayed, and its account of this last address is included here.*

After making his final address, Brown stood and calmly heard his sentence read. He would be hanged in public on Friday December 2. "Brown received the sentence with composure," a correspondent for the Washington National Intelligencer *reported, "and the only demonstration made was a clapping of hands by a man in the crowd who is not a resident of Jefferson County." Brown returned to his cell in the Charlestown prison and asked his jailer, "Have you any objections to my writing to my wife and telling her that I am to be hanged on the second of December?" It was one of many letters that would wing their way from his cell onto the pages of national newspapers. He had thirty days before his sands would finally run out. And not a grain would go to waste.*

Opening remarks of John Brown to the Virginia Court, October 27, 1859

Virginians, I did not ask for any quarter at the time I was taken. I did not ask to have my life spared. The Governor of the State of Virginia tendered me his assurance that I should have a fair trial; but, under no circumstances whatever, will I be able to have a fair trial. If you seek my blood, you can have it at any moment, without this mockery of a trial. I have had no counsel. I have not been able to advise with any one. I know nothing about the feelings of my fellow-prisoners, and am utterly unable to attend in any way to my own defense. My memory don't serve me. My health is insufficient, though improving. There are mitigating circumstances that I would urge in our favor, if a fair trial is to be allowed us. But if we are to be forced with a mere form—a trial for execution—you might spare yourselves that trouble. I am ready for my fate. I do not ask for a trial. I beg for no mockery of a trial—no insult—nothing but that which conscience gives, or cowardice would drive to practise. I ask again to be excused from the mockery of a trial. . . . I have now little further to ask, other than that I may not be foolishly insulted, only as cowardly barbarians insult those who fall into their power.

John Brown's request for a delay

I do not intend to detain the court, but barely wish to say, as I have been promised a fair trial, that I am not in circumstances that enable me to attend a trial, owing to the state of my health. I have a severe wound in the back, or rather in one kidney, which enfeebles me very much. But I am doing well, and I only ask for a very short delay in my trial, and I may be able to listen to it; and I merely ask this that, as the saying is "the devil may have his dues," no more. I wish to say further that my hearing is impaired and *rendered indistinct in* consequence of wounds I have about my head. I cannot hear distinctly at all; I could not hear what the Court has said this morning. I would be glad to hear what is said on my trial, and am now doing better than I could expect to be under the circumstances. A very short delay would be all I ask. I do not presume to ask more than a very short delay, so that I may in some degree recover, and be able to [at] least listen to my trial, and hear what questions are asked of the citizens, and what their answers are. If that could be allowed me, I should be very much obliged.

John Brown's response to claims of his insanity

I look upon it as a miserable artifice and pretext of those who ought to take a different course in regard to me. . . . Insane persons, so as my experience goes, have but little ability to judge of their own sanity; and if I am insane, of course I should think I know more than all the rest of the world. But I do not think so. I am perfectly unconscious of insanity, and I reject, so far as I am capable, any attempt to interfere in my behalf on that score.

Last address of John Brown to the Virginia Court, November 2, 1859

I have, may it please the Court, a few words to say.

In the first place, I deny everything but what I have all along admitted, of a design on my part to free the slaves. I intended certainly to have made a clean thing of that matter, as I did last winter, when I went into Missouri and there took slaves without the snapping of a gun on either side, moved them through the country, and finally left them in Canada. I designed to have done the same thing again, on a larger scale. That was all I intended. I never did intend murder, or treason, or the destruction of property, or to excite or incite slaves to rebellion, or to make insurrection.

I have another objection; and that is, it is unjust that I should suffer such a penalty. Had I interfered in the manner which I admit, and which I admit has been fairly proved (for I admire the truthfulness and candor of the greater portion of the witnesses who have testified in this case),—had I so interfered in behalf of the rich, the powerful, the intelligent, the so-called great, or in behalf of any of their friends,—either father, mother, brother, sister, wife, or children, or any of that class,—and suffered and sacrificed what I have in this interference, it would have been all right; and every man in this court would have deemed it an act worthy of reward rather than punishment.

This court acknowledges, as I suppose, the validity of the law of God. I see a book kissed here which I suppose to be the Bible, or at least the New Testament. That teaches me that all things whatsoever I would that men should do to me, I should do even so to them. It teaches me, further to "remember them that are in bonds, as bound with them." I endeavored to act up to that instruction. I say, I am yet too young to understand that God is any respecter of persons. I believe that to have interfered as I have done—in behalf of His despised poor, was not wrong, but right. Now, if it is deemed necessary that I should forfeit my life for the furtherance of the ends of justice, and mingle my blood further with the blood of my children and with the blood of millions in this slave country whose rights are disregarded by wicked, cruel, and unjust enactments,—I submit; so let it be done!

Let me say one word further.

I feel entirely satisfied with the treatment I have received on my trial. Considering all the circumstances, it has been more generous than I expected. But I feel no consciousness of guilt. I have stated from the first what was my intention, and what was not. I never have had any design against the life of any person, nor any disposition to commit treason, or excite slaves to rebel, or make any general insurrection. I never encouraged any man to do so, but always discouraged any idea of that kind.

Let me say, also, a word in regard to the statements made by some of those connected with me. I hear it has been stated by some of them that I have induced them to join me. But the contrary is true. I do not say this to injure them, but as regretting their weakness. There is not one of them but joined me of his own accord, and the greater part of them at their own expense. A number of them I never saw, and never had a word of conversation with, till the day they came to me; and that was for the purpose I have stated.

Now I have done.

Report on John Brown's last address in the New York Times, *November 3, 1859*

If any doubts still linger in the minds of thoughtful men as to the real character and aims of John Brown, or as to the best way of dealing with his crime, they must surely be resolved on the reading of his brief speech, made before sentence was passed upon him by the Court. . . .

Brown's speech classifies him at once, and in a class of one. He is a fanatic; *sui generis*. He shows neither the sophistical grasp of mind nor the malignant unfairness of temper which would be necessary to rank him with agitators of theoretical Abolitionism like Wendell Phillips; nor the astute coquetry with explosive passions which alone could affiliate him with Republican Party leaders. He is simply John Brown, of Kansas; a man logical after the narrow fashion of the Puritan individualism; a law unto himself, and a believer with all his might in theological abstractions as applied to human society and politics. He hates Slavery, and thinks all slaves ought to be free. That anybody should think it wrong for him, so hating Slavery and so thinking, to attempt to set free the greatest possible number of slaves in the shortest possible time; or that any organization which may appear to him necessary for carrying out this object should be regarded as treasonable, John Brown cannot understand now that he is to be hung for it, any more than we believe he understood it when he made up his mind to set about the work, and others flocked after him, who now, less brave than he, endeavor to throw their own more rational guilt upon his shoulders. We own ourselves at a loss to see in what way the execution of such a man can be so brought about that it may not [be] converted to the inflammatory purposes of sectional partisans with whom John Brown has plainly nothing in common; and who will be as eager to make him a profitable martyr when dead, as they are to repudiate him while he still lives.

Wendell Phillips, *"The Lesson of the Hour"* *November 1, 1859*

Trial! . . . I protest against the name. *Trial* for life, in Anglo-Saxon dialect, had a proud, historic meaning. It includes indictment by impartial peers; a copy of such indictment and a list of witnesses furnished the prisoner, with ample time to scrutinize both; liberty to choose, and time to get counsel, a sound body and a sound mind to arrange one's defence; I need not add, a judge and a jury impartial as the lot of humanity will admit; honoured bulwarks and safe-guards, each one the trophy and result of a century's struggle. Wounded, fevered, lying half unconscious on his pallet, unable to stand on his feet, the trial half finished before his first request for aid had reached his friends,—no list of witnesses or knowledge of them till the crier, calling the name of some assassin of his comrades, wakes him to consciousness; the judge a tool, and the prosecutor seeking popularity by pandering to the mob; no decent form observed, and the essence of a fair trial wholly wanting, our History and Law alike protest against degrading the honoured name of *Jury Trial* by leading it to such an outrage as this. The Inquisition used to break every other bone in a man's body, and then lay him on a pallet, giving him neither counsel nor opportunity to consult one, and wring from his tortured mouth something like a confession, and call it a trial, or what the New York press call so, that has been going on in crazed and maddened Charlestown.

Edmund Clarence Stedman,
"How Old Brown Took Harper's Ferry"

How the conquerors wore their laurels; how they hastened on the trial;
How Old Brown was placed, half dying, on the Charlestown court-house
    floor;
How he spoke his grand oration, in the scorn of all denial;
What the brave old madman told them,—these are known the country o'er.
        "Hang Old Brown,
        Osawatomie Brown,"
Said the judge, "and all such rebels!" with his most judicial frown.
But Virginians, don't do it! for I tell you that the flagon,
Filled with blood of Old Brown's offspring, was first poured by Southern
    hands;
And each drop from Old Brown's life veins, like the red gore of the dragon,
May spring up a vengeful Fury, hissing through your slave-worn lands!
        And Old Brown,
        Osawatomie Brown,
May trouble you more than ever, when you've nailed his coffin down!

* * * *

John Brown's Prison Letters,
October 21–December 2, 1859

    Brown understood the value of propaganda and the press. He knew that, as Wendell Phillips averred in his funeral oration on December 8, "Hearts are stronger than swords." Brown could easily have perished alongside his sons at Harpers Ferry, but "God ordered better," Phillips added. In the thirty days before his sentencing and execution, Brown achieved the transformation from murderer to martyr.
    Wielding his pen as weapon, he won the battle for public opinion, converting many with his hundreds of letters to family and friends. His

correspondence was swiftly published in dozens of newspapers across the land, including the New York Tribune, *which had the largest circulation at that time. "Having taken possession of Harper's Ferry," Wendell Phillips quipped in a speech in New York on December 15 that year, "he began to edit the* New York Tribune *and the* New York Herald *for the next three weeks."*

Derision and vilification swiftly became respect and praise. In the South, initially contemptuous dismissals of "a miserably weak and contemptible affair," in the Richmond Dispatch, *on October 20, 1859, gave way to fears that Brown was "a portentous omen of the future," in the* Charleston Mercury, *on October 31, 1859. His raid seemed initially insane even in the North, but sympathy and understanding for his actions quickly grew. Sanborn wrote in his book on Brown of a "defeated, dying old man, who had been praying and fighting and pleading and toiling for years to persuade a great people that their national life was all wrong, suddenly converting millions to his cause by the silent magnanimity or the spoken wisdom of his last days as a fettered prisoner." John A. Andrew was one such convert, and he declared at a Boston gathering to aid Brown's family on November 19: "whether the enterprise of John Brown and his associates in Virginia was wise or foolish, right or wrong, I only know that, whether the enterprise itself was the one or the other, John Brown himself is right." The time Brown had left to live shrank smaller and smaller, but his legend was growing.*

The letters are clearly intended to achieve this result. They are written as a public lesson for a broad audience; his cell had become a pulpit. His words would make of his hanging a martyrdom; posterity would recognize his death as such. Knowing the potential value of his martyrdom to the abolitionist cause even as he sought to effect it, he writes on November 30 of his execution that "in no other possible way could I be used to so much advance the cause of God; & of humanity," that he "now has no doubt but that our seeming disaster; will ultimately result in the most glorious success." He told the Tribune *on November 4, "I do not know that I ought to encourage any attempt to save my life. I am not sure that it would not be better for me to die at this time." The scaffold may be a "manner of dying assigned to" him, as he writes on November 28, but he intended to make that death meaningful. His most beautiful assertion of this intention, and of his sense that everything was unfolding as it should, is on November 15, and in 1928 Stephen Vincent Benét rendered such sentiments into verse, writing in his famous work,* John Brown's Body:

> *Brown told them,*
> *"I am worth now infinitely more to die than to live."*
> *And lives his month so, busily.*
> *A month of trifles building up a legend*
> *And letters in a pinched, firm handwriting*
> *Courageous, scriptural, misspelt and terse,*
> *Sowing a fable everywhere they fell.*

While he wrote and waited, building his legend and sowing his fables, a debate raged as to the correct course of action. Some of Brown's friends planned assorted rescue attempts, while others agreed with Brown that he was "worth inconceivably more to hang than for any other purpose." Henry Ward Beecher, in a sermon at Plymouth Church in Brooklyn just before Brown's sentencing, voiced the feelings of many when he pronounced: "Let Virginia make him a martyr. Now he had only blundered. His soul was noble; his work miserable. But a cord and a gibbet would redeem all that, and round up Brown's failure with a heroic success." Brown, browsing through the sermon in prison, found this passage and wrote in the margin: "good." Theodore Parker, another of his friends and one of the Secret Six, saw Brown's death as inconsequential to universal justice, writing from Rome to Francis Jackson in Boston on November 24: "Let the American State hang his body and the American Church damn his soul. Still, the blessing of such as are ready to perish will fall on him, and the universal justice of the Infinitely Perfect God will make him welcome home. The road to heaven is as short from the gallows as from the throne."

Brown's enemies were also aware of the growing legend and the possibilities for a politically effective martyrdom. The proslavery New York Journal *of Commerce warned: "To hang a fanatic is to make a martyr of him and fledge another brood of the same sort. Better send these creatures to the penitentiary, and so make of them miserable felons." The* Richmond Whig *recognized the hazards of hanging Brown, but thought he should die even so, insisting rather illogically: "Though it convert the whole Northern people, without an exception, into furious, armed abolition invaders, yet old Brown will be hung!. . . The miserable old traitor and murderer belongs to the gallows, and the gallows will have its own." The* Savannah Republic *supported these calls for his execution, urging "a terrible example . . . . that will stand out as a beacon-light in all time to come." That Brown's example would do exactly this, and so light the way to the demolition of slavery, did not occur to this journalist.*

Firing up his beacon-light, Brown began to write letters of gold, masterpieces of their genre, like his final address to the court on November 2. Thoreau thought the letters "deserve[d] to be framed and hung over every mantelpiece in the land," pausing to relish them in his lecture "The Last Days of John Brown." They are poignant, sincere, and Biblical in their eloquence. In many he connects his own labor with that of God's prophets and disciples. On November 8 he instructs his family to remember that "Jesus of Nazareth" also "suffered a most excruciating death on the cross as a felon," that Brown shared the fate of "prophets and apostles and Christians of former days." Seeing in his own strange victory an echo of Samson's, he compares himself to this tragic hero on November 15. He writes on November 23 of feeling "as happy as Paul did when he lay in prison," and in the same letter echoes Jesus in expressing a hope that God will forgive his executioners, for "they know not what they do." On November 25 he finds a Biblical counterpart in Moses, another "poor erring servant" with "powers and faculties" similar to Brown.

Brown compares himself to biblical characters

He handed his last letter, just two sentences, to one of the guards on the morning of his execution. Resoundingly, the prophecy anticipates Lincoln's Second Inaugural speech of 1864, and also unknowingly echoes a letter that he hadn't even read, sent by the dying minister Theodore Parker to Francis Jackson on November 24. Parker writes: "A few years ago it did not seem difficult first to check slavery, and then to end it, without any bloodshed. I think this cannot be done now, nor ever in the future. All the great charters of humanity have been writ in blood. I once hoped that American democracy would be engrossed in less costly ink; but it is plain now that our pilgrimage must lead through a Red sea, wherein many a Pharaoh will go under and perish." Brown was an American Samson but also an American Moses and, as he wrote in a letter of November 25, his death would be "of vastly more value" than his life, just like the Old Testament leader whom God told to "begin to deliver Israel out of the hand of the Philistines." He departed for the gallows and there began a "pilgrimage" of blood, so envisaged by Parker— through a Red Sea that would engulf many who followed, and many who refused. This particular "charter of humanity," the abolition of slavery, though writ in blood, was inscribed in a "less costly ink" too—that of John Brown's prison letters.

Charlestown Jefferson County Va. Oct. 21, 1859

Hon. Thos. Russell
Dear Sir

I am here a prisoner with several sabre cuts in my head, & bayonet stabs in my body. My object in writing to you is to obtain able, & faithful counsel for myself; & fellow prisoners five in all, as we have the faith of Virginia, pledged through her Governor and numerous other prominent citizens, to give us a fair trial. Without we can obtain such counsel from without the slave states: neither the facts in our case can come before the world : nor can *we* have the benefit of such facts (as might be considered mitigating in the views of others) upon our trial. I have money on hand *here* to the amount of $250. and personal property sufficient to pay a most liberal fee to yourself; or to any suitable man who will undertake our defence, if I can be allowed the benefit of said property. Can you or some other good man come in immediately for the sake of the young men prisoners at least? My wounds are doing well. Do not send an ultra Abolitionist.

Very respectfully yours,
John Brown

The trial is set for Wednesday next the 25th inst. J.W. Campbell, Sher Jeff. County

* * * *

Charlestown, Jefferson Co., Va., 31st Oct. 1859

My dear Wife, and Children every one

I suppose you have learned before this by the newspapers that two weeks ago today we were fighting for our lives at Harpers ferry: that during the fight Watson was mortally wounded; Oliver killed, Wm Thompson killed, & Dauphin slightly wounded. That on the following day I was taken prisoner immediately after which I received several Sabre cuts in my head; & Bayonet stabs in my body. As nearly as I can learn Watson died of his wound on Wednesday the 2d or on Thursday the 3d day after I was taken. Dauphin was killed when I was taken; & Anderson I suppose also. I have since been tried, & found guilty of treason, &c; and of murder in the first degree. I have not yet received my sentence. No others of the company with who you were acquainted were so far as *I can learn* either killed or taken. Under all these terrible calamities; I feel quite cheerful in the assurance that God reigns; & will overrule all for his glory; & the best possible good. I feel *no* con[s]ciou[s]ness of *guilt* in the matter: nor even mortifycation on account of my imprisonment; & irons; & I feel perfectly assured that very soon no member of my family will feel any possible disposition to "blush on my account." Already dear friends at a distance with kindest sympathy are cheering me with the assurance that *posterity* at least: will do me justice. I shall commend you all together with my beloved; but bereaved daughters in law to their sympathies which I have no doubt will soon reach you. I also commend you all to him "whose mercy endureth forever": to the God of my *fathers* "whose I am; & whom I serve." "He will never leave you or forsake you" unless you forsake him. Finally my dearly beloved be of good comfort. Be as it has been consistent with the holy religion of Jesus Christ in which I remain a most firm, & humble believer. Never forget the poor nor think any thing you bestow on them to be lost to you even though they may be as *black* as Ebedmelch, the Ethiopian eunuch one to whom Phillip preached Christ. Be sure to entertain strangers . . . "Remember them that are in bonds as bound with them." I am in charge of a jailor *like* the one who took charge of "Paul & Silas;" & you may rest assured that both *kind hearts* and *kind faces* are more or less about me: whilst thousands are thirsting for my blood. "These *light* afflictions which are but *for a moment* shall work out for us a far *more exceeding & eternal* weight of glory." I hope to be able to write you again. My wounds are doing well. Copy this & send it to your sorrow stricken brothers, *Ruth*; to comfort them. Write me a few words in regard to the welfare of all. God Almighty bless you all: & make you "joyful in the midst of all your tribulations." Write to John Brown, Charlestown, Jefferson Co, Va, care of Capt John Avis

Your Affectionate Husband, & Father. John Brown

Nov. 3d 1859

P.S. Yesterday Nov 2d I was sentenced to be hanged on 2 Decem next. Do not grieve on my account. I am still quite cheerful.

Go[d] bless you all Your Ever J Brown

* * * *

Charlestown, Jefferson County, Va., Nov. 1, 1859

My Dear Friend E.B. of R.I.,

Your most cheering letter of the 27th of October is received; and may the Lord reward you a thousandfold for the kind feeling you express toward me; but more especially for your fidelity to the "poor that cry, and those that have no help." For this I am a prisoner in bonds. It is solely my own fault, in a military point of view, that we met with our disaster. I mean that I mingled with our prisoners and so far sympathized with them and their families that I neglected my duty in other respects. But God's will, not mine, be done.

You know that Christ once armed Peter. So also in my case I think he put a sword into my hand, and there continued it so long as he saw best, and then kindly took it from me. I mean when I first went to Kansas. I wish you could know with what cheerfulness I am now wielding the "sword of the Spirit" on the right hand and on the left. I bless God that it proves "mighty to the pulling down of strongholds." I always loved my Quaker friends, and I commend to their kind regard my poor bereaved widowed wife and my daughters and daughters-in-law, whose husbands fell at my side. One is a mother and the other likely to become so soon. They, as well as my own sorrow-stricken daughters, are left very poor, and have much greater need of sympathy than I, who, through Infinite Grace and the kindness of strangers, am "joyful in all my tribulations."

Dear sister, write them at North Elba, Essex County, N.Y., to comfort their sad hearts. Direct to Mary A. Brown, wife of John Brown. There is also another—a widow, wife of Thompson, who fell with my poor boys in the affair at Harper's Ferry—at the same place.

I do not feel conscious of guilt in taking up arms; and had it been in behalf of the rich and powerful, the intelligent, the great (as men count greatness), or those who form enactments to suit themselves and corrupt others, or some of their friends, that I interfered, suffered, sacrificed, and fell, it would have been doing very well. But enough of this. These light afflictions, which endure for a moment, shall but work for me "a far more exceeding and eternal weight of glory." I would be very grateful for another letter from you. My wounds are healing. Farewell. God will surely attend to his own cause in the best possible way and time, and he will not forget the work of his own hands.

Your friend, John Brown.

* * * *

Charlestown, Jefferson Co. Va. 4th Nov. 1859

Rev. T. W. Higginson
Dear Friend

If my Wife were to come here just now it would *only tend* to distract *her mind, ten fold*; & would *only add* to my affliction; & cannot *possibly* do me *any good.* It will also use up the scanty means she has to supply Bread & cheap but comfortable clothing, fuel & C) for herself, and Children *through the Winter.* DO PERSUADE her to remain *at home for a time (at least)* till she can learn further from me. She will secure a Thousand times the consolation AT HOME that she can possibly find elsewhere. I have just *written her there & will* write her CONSTANTLY. Her presence *here* will deepen my affliction a thousand fold. I beg of her to be *calm, & submissive;* & not to go *wild* on my account. I lack *for nothing* & was feeling quite cheerful before I learned she talked of *coming on. I ask her to compose her mind* & to remain *quiet* till the last of this *month;* out of pity to me. I can certainly judge better in this matter than *any one else.* My warmest thanks to yourself; & *all other* kind friends. *God bless you all. Please send this line to my afflicted Wife,* by first possible conveyance.

Your friend in truth, John Brown

* * * *

Charlestown, Jefferson Co. Va. 4th Nov. 1859

Mrs L Maria Child, Wayland, Mass

My Dear friend

(Such you prove to be though an entire stranger) Your most kind letter has reached me; with your kind offer to come here & take care of me. Allow me to express my gratitude for your great sympathy: & at the same time to propose to you a different course; together with my reasons for wishing it. I should certainly be greatly pleased to become personally acquainted with one so gifted; & so kind; but I cannot avoid seeing some objections to it under present circumstances. First I am in charge of a most humane gentleman who with his family have rendered me every possible attention I have desired or that could be of the least advantage: and I am so far recovered from my wounds as no longer to require nursing. Then again it would subject you to great personal inconvenience, & quite a heavy expence; without doing me any good. Now allow me to name to you another channel through which you may reach me with your sympathies much more effectually. I have at home a Wife & three young daughters. The youngest of whom is but a little over Five years old; the oldest is nearly Sixteen. I have also two daughters in law whose Husbands have both fallen near me here. One of these is a Mother & the other like to become so. There is also another Widow a Mrs. Thompson whose Husband also fell here. Whether she is a Mother or not I cannot say. They all (my Wife included) live at North Elba, Essex Co. New York. I have or suppose I have a middle aged Son who has been in some degree a cripple from childhood who would have as much as he could well do to earn a living. He was a most dreadful sufferer in Kansas; & lost all he had laid up: & has not enough to clothe himself for the Winter comfortably. I have *no son or son in law living*; who did not suffer terribly in Kansas. Now dear friend would you not as soon contribute Fifty Cents now: & a like sum *yearly* for the relief of those very poor; & deeply afflicted persons to enable to supply themselves, & Children with Bread: & very plain clothing; & to enable the children to receive a common English education: & also to devote your own energies to induce others to join you in giving a like or other amount to constitute a little fund for the purpose named? I cannot see how your coming here can possibly do me the least good: & I feel quite certain you can do me *immence good* where you are. I am quite cheerful under all my afflicting circumstances; & prospects, having as I humbly trust "the peace of God which passeth all understanding, to rule in my heart." You may make just such use of this as you see fit. Yours *in sincerity; & truth,* (God Allmighty bless; and reward you a thousand time fold.)

John Brown

* * * *

Charlestown, Jefferson County, Va., Nov. 8, 1859

Dear Wife and Children, Every One,

I will begin by saying that I have in some degree recovered from my wounds, but that I am quite weak in my back and sore about my left kidney. My appetite has been quite good for most of the time since I was hurt. I am supplied with almost everything I could desire to make me comfortable, and the little I do lack (some articles of clothing which I lost) I may perhaps soon get again. I am, besides, quite cheerful, having (as I trust) "the peace of God, which passeth all understanding," to "rule in my heart," and the testimony (in some degree) of a good conscience that I have not lived altogether in vain. I can trust God with both the time and the manner of my death, believing, as I now do, that for me at this time to seal my testimony for God and humanity with my blood will do vastly more toward advancing the cause I have earnestly endeavored to promote, than all I have done in my life before. I beg of you all meekly and quietly to submit to this, not feeling yourselves in the least *degraded* on the account. Remember, dear wife and children all, that Jesus of Nazareth suffered a most excruciating death on the cross as a felon, under the most aggravating circumstances. Think also of the prophets and apostles and Christians of former days, who went through greater tribulations than you or I, and try to be reconciled. May God Almighty comfort all your hearts, and soon wipe away all tears from your eyes! To him be endless praise! Think, too, of the crushed millions who "have no comforter." I charge you all never in your trials to forget the griefs "of the poor that cry, and of those that have none to help them." I wrote most earnestly to my dear and afflicted wife not to come on for the present, at any rate. I will now give her reasons for doing so. First, it would use up all the scanty means she has, or is at all likely to have, to make herself and children comfortable hereafter. For let me tell you that the sympathy that is now aroused in your behalf may not always follow you. There is but little more of the romantic about helping poor widows and their children than there is about trying to relieve poor "niggers." Again, the little comfort it might afford us to meet again would be dearly bought by the pains of a final separation. We must part; and I feel assured for us to meet under such dreadful circumstances would only add to our distress. If she comes on here, she must be only a gazing-stock throughout the whole journey, to be remarked upon in every look, word, and action, and by all sorts of creatures, and by all sorts of papers, throughout the whole country. Again, it is my most decided judgment that in quietly and submissively staying at home vastly more of generous sympathy will reach her, without such dreadful sacrifice of feeling as she must put up with if she comes on. The visits of one or two female friends that have come on her have produced great excitement, which is very annoying; and they cannot possibly do me any good. Oh, Mary! do not come, but patiently wait for the meeting of those who love God and their fellow-men, where no separation must follow. "They shall go no more out forever." I greatly long to hear from some one of you, and to learn anything that in any way affects your welfare. I sent you ten dollars the other day; did you get it? I have also endeavored to stir up Christian friends to visit and write to you in your deep affliction. I have no doubt that some of them, at least, will heed the call. Write to me, care of Captain John Avis, Charlestown, Jefferson County, Virginia.

"Finally, my beloved, be of good comfort." May all your names be "written in the Lamb's book of life!"—may you all have the purifying and sustaining influence of the Christian religion!—is the earnest prayer of

Your affectionate husband and father, John Brown

P.S.—I cannot remember a night so dark as to have hindered the coming day, nor a storm so furious and dreadful as to prevent the return of warm sunshine and a cloudless sky. But, beloved ones, do remember that this is not your rest,—that in this world you have no abiding place or continuing city. To God and his infinite mercy I always commend you.

* * * *

Charlestown, Jefferson County, Va., Nov. 12, 1859

Dear Brother Jeremiah,

Your kind letter of the 9th inst. is received, and also one from Mr. Tilden; for both of which I am greatly obliged. You inquire, "Can I do anything for you or your family?" I would answer that my sons, as well as my wife and daughters, are all very poor; and that anything that may hereafter be due me from my father's estate I wish paid to them, as I will endeavor hereafter to describe, without legal formalities to consume it all. One of my boys has been so entirely used up as very likely to be in want of comfortable clothing for winter. I have, through the kindness of friends, fifteen dollars to send him, which I will remit shortly. If you know where to reach him, please send him that amount at once, as I shall remit the same to you by a safe conveyance. If I had a plain statement from Mr. Thompson of the state of my accounts with the estate of my father, I should then better know what to say about that matter. As it is, I have not the least memorandum left me to refer to. If Mr. Thompson will make me a statement, and charge my dividend fully for his trouble, I would be greatly obliged to him. In that case you can send me any remarks of your own. I am gaining in health slowly, and am quite cheerful in view of my approaching end,—being fully persuaded that I am worth inconceivably more to hang than for any other purpose. God Almighty bless and save you all!

Your affectionate brother, John Brown.

November 13.

P.S. Say to my poor boys never to grieve for one moment on my account; and should many of you live to see the time when you will not blush to own your relation to Old John Brown, it will not be more strange than many things that have happened. I feel a thousand times more on account of my sorrowing friends than on my own account. So far as I am concerned, I "count it all joy." "I have fought the good fight," and have, as I trust, "finished my course." Please show this to any of my family that you may see. My love to all; and may God, in his infinite mercy, for Christ's sake, bless and save you all!

Your affectionate brother, J. Brown.

* * * *

Charlestown, Jefferson Co. Va, 15th Nov. 1859

Rev. H L Vaill

My Dear Stedfast Friend

Your most *kind & most welcome* letter of the 8th inst reached me in due time. *I am very grateful* for all the good feeling you express & also for the kind counsels you give together—with your prayers in my behalf. Allow me here to say notwithstanding "my soul is amongst lions," still I believe that "God in very deed is with me." You will not therefore feel surprised when I tell you that I am "joyful in all my tribulations": that I do not feel condemned of Him whose judgment is just; nor of my own conscience. Nor do I feel degraded by my imprisonment, my chains or prospect of the Gallows. I have not only been (*though utterly unworthy*) permitted to suffer affliction with God's people," but have also had *a great many rare* opportunities for "preaching *righteousness* in the great congregation." I trust it will not all be lost. *The jailor* (in whose charge I am) & *his family; & assistants* have all been most kind: & notwithstanding he was one of the bravest of all who *fought me:* he is *now* being abused for humanity. So far as my observation goes; *none but brave* men: are likely to be *humane*; to a fallen foe. "Cowards *prove* their *courage* by their *ferocity.*" It may be done in that way with but little risk. I wish I could write you about a few only of the interesting times, I here experience with different classes of men; *clergymen* among others. Christ the great Captain of *liberty*; as well as of salvation; & who began his mission, as foretold of him; by proclaiming it, *saw fit* to take from me a sword of steel after I had carried it for a time but he has put another in my hand ("The sword of the Spirit;") & I pray God to make me a faithful soldier wherever he may send me, not less on the scaffold, then when surrounded by the warmest sympathizers. My dear old friend I do assure you I have not forgotten our last meeting nor our retrospective look over the route by which God had then led us; & I bless his name that he has again enabled me to hear your words of cheering; & comfort, at a time when I at least am on the "brink of Jordan." See Bunyan's Pilgrim. God in Infinite mercy grant us *soon* another meeting on the opposite shore. I have often passed under the rod of him whom I *call my* Father; & certainly no son ever needed it oftener; & yet I have enjoyed much of life, as I was enabled to discover the secret of this; somewhat early. It has been in making the prosperity, & the happiness of others *my own*: so that really I have had a great deal of prosperity. I am very prosperous still; & looking forward to a time when "peace on Earth & good will to *men* shall every where prevail." I have no murmuring thoughts of *envyous* feelings to fret my mind. "I'll praise my *maker* with my *breath.*" I am *an unworthy* nephew of Deacon John; & I loved him much; & in view of the many choice friends *I have had* here I am led the more earnestly to pray; "gather *not* my soul with the *unrighteous.*" Your assurance of the earnest sympathy of the friends in my native land is very greatful to my feelings; & allow me to say a word of comfort to them. As I believe most firmly that God reigns; I cannot believe that any thing I have *done suffered or may yet suffer will be lost*; to the *cause of God or of humanity*: & before I began my work at Harpers Ferry; I felt assured that in the *worst event;* it would certainly PAY. I often expressed that belief; & I can now see no possible cause to alter my mind. I am not as yet in the *main* at all disappointed. I have been *a good deal* disappointed as it regards *myself* in not keeping up to *my own plans;* but I now feel entirely reconciled to that even: for Gods plan, was Infinitely better; *no doubt*: or I should have kept to my own. Had Samson kept to his *determination* of not telling Delilah wherein his great strength lay; he would probably have never overturned the house. I did not tell Delilah; but I was induced to act very *contrary* to my *better judgment*: & I have lost my two noble boys; & *other friends, if not my two eyes.*

But "Gods will not *mine* be done." I feel a comfortable hope that like the *erring servant* of whom I have just been writing *even I* may (through Infinite mercy in Christ Jesus) yet "die in faith." As to both the time, & manner of my death: I have but very little trouble on that score; & *am able* to be (as you exhort) "of good cheer." I send through you my best wishes to Mrs. Woodruff & her son George; & to all dear friends. May the God of the *poor* and *oppressed*; be the God & Saveior of you all. Farewell till we *"meet again."*

Your friend in truth, John Brown

* * * *

Charlestown, Jefferson Co., Va. 16th Nov., 1859
My Dear Wife:—I write you in answer to a most kind letter, of Nov. 13, from dear Mrs. Spring. I owe her ten thousand thanks; for her kindness to *you particularly and more especially* than for what she has done, and is doing, in a more direct way for me personally. Although I feel grateful for every expression of kindness or sympathy towards me, yet nothing can so effectually minister to my comfort as acts of kindness done to relieve the wants, or mitigate the sufferings of my poor distressed family. May *God Almighty* and *their own consciousness* be their eternal rewarders. I am exceedingly rejoiced to have you make the acquaintance and be surrounded by such choice friends, as I have *long known* some of those to be, with whom you are staying, by reputation. I am most glad to have you meet with one of a *family* (or I would rather say of two families) *most beloved and never to be forgotten by me.* I mean *dear gentle* Sarah Wattles. *Many and many* a time has *she, her father, mother, brothers, sisters, uncle and aunt,* (like angels of mercy) ministered to the wants of myself and of my poor sons, both in sickness and in health. Only last year I lay sick for quite a number of weeks with them, and was cared for *by all,* as though I had been a most affectionate brother or father. *Tell her* that I ask God to bless and reward them *all* forever. "I *was* a stranger, and they took me in." It may possibly be that Sarah would like to copy this letter, and send it to her home. If so, by all means, let her do so. *I would write them* if I had the power.

Now let me say a word about the effort to educate our daughters. I am no longer able to provide means to help towards that object, and it therefore becomes me not to dictate in the matter. I shall gratefully submit the direction of the whole thing to those whose generosity may lead them to undertake in their behalf, while I give *anew* a little expression of my own choice respecting it. You, my wife, *perfectly well* know that I have always expressed a decided preference for a very *plain but perfectly practical* education for both *sons and daughters.* I do not mean an education so very miserable as that *you and I* received in early life; nor as some of our children enjoyed. When I say plain but practical, I mean enough of the learning of the schools to enable them to transact the common business of life, comfortably and respectably, together with that thorough training to good business habits which prepares both men and women to be *useful though poor,* and to meet the *stern* Realities of life with a *good* grace. You well know that I always claimed that the *music* of the broom, washtub, needle, spindle, loom, axe, scythe, hoe, flail, etc., Afterwards. I put them in that order as most conducive to health of body and mind; and for the obvious reason, that after a life of some *experience and of much observation,* I have found *ten women* as well as *ten men* who have made their mark in life *Right,* whose early training was of that *plain, practical* kind, to *one* who had a more popular and fashionable *early* training. But enough of that.

Now, in regard to your coming here; If you feel sure that you can endure the trials and the shock, which will be *unavoidable* (if you come), I should be most glad to see you *once more;* but when I think of your being insulted on the road, and perhaps *while here,* and of only seeing your wretchedness made complete, I *shrink* from it. Your composure and fortitude of mind may be *quite equal to it all;* but I am in *dreadful* doubt of it. *If you do come,* defer your journey till about the 27th or 28th of this month. The scenes which you will have to pass through on coming here will be *anything but those* you now pass, with tender, kind-hearted friends, and kind faces to meet you everywhere. *Do consider the matter well* before you make the *plunge.* I think I had better say *no more on this most painful* subject. My health improves a little; my mind is very tranquil, I may say joyous, and I continue to receive every kind attention that I have any possible need of. I wish you to send copies of all my letters to all our poor children. What I write to one must answer for all, till I have more strength. I get numerous kind letters from friends in almost all directions, to encourage me to "be of good cheer," and I still have, *as I trust,* "the peace of God to rule in my heart." May God, for Christ's sake, ever make his face to shine on you all.

Your affectionate husband, John Brown

* * * *

Charlestown, Jefferson Co. Va. 17th Nov. 1859

J B Musgrave Esqr
My Dear Young Friend

I have just received your most kind; & welcome letter of the 15th inst but did not get any other from you. I am under many obligations *to you & to your Father* for all the kindness you have shown me, especially since my disaster. *May God* & your own consciousness ever be your rewarders. Tell your Father that I am quite cheerful that I do not feel myself in the least degraded by my imprisonment, my chain, or the *near prospect* of the Gallows. *Men* cannot *imprison, or chain; or hang the soul.* I go joyfuly in behalf of Millions that "have no rights" that this "great, & glorious"; "this Christian Republic," "is bound to respect." Strange *change in morals political*; as well as *Christian;* since 1776. I look forward to *other changes* to take place *in "Gods good time;"* fully believing that "the fashion of this world passeth away." (I am unable *now* to tell you where my friend is; that you inquire after. Perhaps my Wife who I suppose is still with Mrs. Spring, may have some information of him. I think it quite uncertain however.) Farewell; may God abundantly bless You all.

Your Friend, John Brown

* * * *

Charlestown, Jefferson Co. Va. 19th Nov. 1859

Rev. Luther Humphrey.
My dear friend,

Your kind letter of 12th inst. is now before me. So far as my knowledge goes as to our mutual kindred, I suppose *I am the first* since the landing of

Peter Brown from the Mayflower that *has either been sentenced to imprisonment; or to the Gallows.* But my dear old friend, let not that fact *alone* grieve you. You cannot have forgotten *how; & where our Grandfather* (Capt. John Brown) fell in 1776; *& that he too* might have perished on the scaffold had circumstances been but *very little* different. *The fact* that a man dies under the hand of an executioner (or other wise) has but little to do with his true character, as I suppose. John Rogers perished at the stake *a great & good* man as I suppose: but *his being* so does *not prove* that any other man who has died in the same way was *good or otherwise.* Whether I have any reason to "be of good cheer" (or not) in view of my end; I can assure you that *I feel so*; & that I am totally *blinded* if I do not really *experience* that *strengthening; & consolation* you so faithfully implore on my behalf. God of *our Fathers*; reward your fidelity. I neither feel *mortified, degraded, nor in the least ashamed* of my imprisonment, my chain, or my prospect of *death by hanging.* I feel assured "that not one hair shall fall from my head without my heavenly Father." I also feel that I have *long been endeavoring* to hold exactly "such a *fast* as God has chosen." See the passage in Isaiah which you have quoted. No part of my life has been more hapily spent; than that I have spent here; & I humbly *trust* that no past has been spent to better purpose. *I would not say boastingly*: but "thanks be unto God who giveth us the victory: *through infinite grace.*" I should be sixty years old were I to live till May 9th 1860. I have enjoyed much of life as it is: & have been remarkably prosperous; having *early learned* to regard the welfare & property of others as *my own.* I have never since I can remember required a great amount of sleep: so that I conclude that I have already enjoyed *full an average* number of waking hours with those who reach their "Three Score years, & ten." I have not as yet been driven to the use of glasses; but can still see to read, & write quite comfortably. But more than that I have *generally* enjoyed remarkably good health. I might go on to recount unnumbered *& unmerited* blessings among which would be some very severe afflictions: & those the most needed blessings of all. And now when I think how easily I might *be left to spoil* all I have done, or suffered in the cause of freedom; I hardly dare risk another voyage; if I even had the opportunity. It is a long time since we met; but we shall now soon come together in our "Father's House," *I trust.* "Let us hold fast that we already have," "remembering that we shall reap in due time if we faint not." Thanks be *ever* unto God; who giveth us the victory through Jesus Christ our Lord." And now my old warmhearted friend, "Good bye." Your Affectionate Cousin, John Brown

* * * *

Charlestown, Jefferson County, Va., Nov. 21, 1859

My Dear Wife,

Your most welcome letter of the 13th instant I got yesterday. I am very glad to learn from yourself that you feel so much resigned to your circumstances, so much confidence in a wise and good Providence, and such composure of mind in the midst of all your deep afflictions. This is just as it should be; and let me still say, "Be of good cheer," for we shall soon "come out of all our great tribulations;" and very soon, if we trust in him, "God shall wipe away all tears from our eyes." Soon "we shall be satisfied when we are awake in His likeness." There is now here a source of disquietude to me,—namely, the fires which are almost of daily and nightly occurrence in this immediate neighborhood. While I well know that no one of them is the work of our friends, I know at the same time that by more or less of the inhabitants we shall be charged with them,—the same as with the ominous and threatening letters to Governor Wise. In the existing state of public feeling I can easily see a further objection to your coming here at present; but I did not intend saying another word to you on that subject.

Why will you not say to me whether you had any crops mature this season? If so, what ones? Although I may nevermore intermeddle with your worldly affairs, I have not yet lost all interest in them. A little history of your failures I should very much prize; and I would gratify you and other friends some way were it in my power. I am still quite cheerful, and by no means cast down. I "remember that the time is short." The little trunk and all its contents, so far as I can judge, reached me safe. May God reward all the contributors! I wrote you under cover to our excellent friend Mrs. Spring on the 16th instant. I presume you have it before now. When you return, it is most likely the lake will not be open; so you must get your ticket at Troy for Moreau Station or Glens Falls (for Glens Falls, if you can get one), or get one for Vergennes in Vermont, and take your chance of crossing over on the ice to Westport. If you go soon, the route by Glens Falls to Elizabethtown will probably be the best.

I have just learned that our poor Watson lingered until Wednesday about noon of the 19th of October. Oliver died near my side in a few moments after he was shot. Dauphin died the next morning after Oliver and William were killed,—namely, Monday. He died almost instantly; was by my side. William was shot by several persons. Anderson was killed with Dauphin. Keep this letter to refer to. God Almighty Bless and keep you all!

Your affectionate husband, John Brown

Dear Mrs. Spring—I send this to your care, because I am at a loss where it will reach my wife. Your friend in truth, John Brown

* * * *

Charlestown, Jefferson County, Va., Nov. 22, 1859

Dear Children, All,

I address this letter to you, supposing that your mother is not yet with you. She has not yet come here, as I have requested her not to do at present, if at all. She may think it best for her not to come at all. She has (or will), I presume, written you before this. Annie's letter to us both, of the 9th, has but just reached me. I am very glad to get it, and to learn that you are in any measure cheerful. This is the greatest comfort I can have, except it would be to know that you are all Christians. God in mercy grant you all may be so! That is what you all will certainly need. When and in what form death may come is but of small moment. I feel just as content to die for God's eternal truth and for suffering humanity on the scaffold as in any other way; and I do not say this from any disposition to "brave it out." No; I would readily own my wrong were I in the least convinced of it. I have now been confined over a month, with a good opportunity to look the whole thing as "fair in the face" as I am capable of doing; and I now feel it most grateful that I am counted in the least possible degree worthy to suffer for the truth. I want you all to "be of good cheer." This life is intended as a season of training, chastisement, temptation, affliction, and trial; and the "righteous shall come out of" it all. Oh, my dear children, let me again entreat you all to "forsake the foolish, and live." What can you possibly lose by such a course? "Godliness with contentment is great gain, having the promise of the life that now is, and of that which is to come." "Trust in the Lord and do good, so shalt thou dwell in the land; and verily thou shalt be fed." I have enjoyed life much; why should I complain on leaving it? I want some of you to write me a little more particularly about all that concerns your welfare. I intend to write you as often as I can. "To God and the word of his grace I commend you all."

Your affectionate father, John Brown

* * * *

Charlestown, Jefferson County, Va., Nov. 22, 1859

Dear Children,

Your most welcome letters of the 16th inst. I have just received, and I bless God that he has enabled you to bear the composure of mind. That is exactly the thing I have wished you all to do for me,—to be cheerful and perfectly resigned to the holy will of a wise and good God. I bless his most holy name that I am, I trust, in some good measure able to do the same. I am even "joyful in all my tribulations" ever since my confinement, and I humbly trust that "I know in whom I have trusted." A calm peace, perhaps like that which your own dear mother felt in view of her last change, seems to fill my mind by day and by night. Of this neither the powers of "earth or hell" can deprive me. Do not, my dear children, any of you grieve for a single moment on my account. As I trust my life has not been thrown away, so I also humbly trust that my death will not be in vain. God can make it to be a thousand times more valuable to his own cause than all the miserable service (at best) that I have rendered it during my life. When I was first taken, I was too feeble to write much; so I wrote what I could to North Elba, requesting Ruth and Anne to send you copies of all my letters to them. I hope they have done so, and that you, Ellen, will do the same with what I may send to you, as it is still quite a labor for me to write all that I need to. I want your brothers to know what I write, if you know where to reach them. I wrote Jeremiah a few days since to supply a trifling assistance, fifteen dollars, to such of you as might be most destitute. I got his letter, but do not know as he got mine. I hope to get another letter from him soon. I also asked him to show you my letter. I know of nothing you can any of you now do for me, unless it is to comfort your own hearts, and cheer and encourage each other to trust in God and Jesus Christ whom he hath sent. If you will keep his sayings, you shall certainly "know of his doctrine, whether it be of God or no." Nothing can be more grateful to me than your earnest sympathy, except it be to know that you are fully persuaded to be Christians. And now, dear children, farewell for this time. I hope to be able to write you again. The God of my fathers take you for his children.

Your affectionate father, John Brown.

* * * *

Charlestown, Jefferson County, Va.,
November 22, 1859
Dear Sir

I have just had my attention called to a seeming confliction between the statement I at first made to Governor Wise and that which I made at the time I received my sentence, regarding my intentions respecting the slaves we took *about the Ferry.* There need be no such confliction, and a few words of explanation will, I think, be quite sufficient. I had given Governor Wise a *full and particular* account of that, and when called in court to say whether I had anything further to urge, I was taken wholly by surprise, as I did not expect my sentence before the others. In the hurry of the moment, I forgot much that I had before *intended to say,* and did *not* consider the full bearing of what *I then said.* I intended to convey this idea, that it was my object to place the slaves in a condition to defend their liberties, if they would, *without any bloodshed, but not* that I intended *to run them out of the slave States.* I was not *aware* of any such apparent confliction until my attention was *called* to it, and I do not suppose that a man in *my then circumstances* should be *superhuman* in respect to the *exact report* of every word he might utter. What I said to Governor Wise was spoken with all the deliberation I was master of, *and was intended for truth;* and what I said in court was *equally intended for truth,* but required a more full explanation *than I then gave.* Please make such use of this as you think calculated to correct any *wrong* impressions I may have given.

Very respectfully yours, JOHN BROWN
ANDREW HUNTER, Esq., *Present.*

* * * *

Charlestown, Jefferson Co. Va. 22d, Nov. 1859
Rev TW Higginson
Dear Sir

I write you a few lines to express to you my deep feeling of gratitude for your journey to visit & comfort my family as well as myself in different ways & at different times; since *my* imprisonment here. Truly you have proved yourself to be "a friend in need;" & *I feel* my many obligations for all your kind *attentions, none the less:* for my wishing my Wife *not* to come on when she first set out. I would it were in my power to make to *all* my kind friends: some *other acknowledgements* than a mere tender of *our & my* thanks. I can assure *all* : Mrs. Stearns, my young friend Hoyt; & many others I have been unable to write as of yet : that I *certainly do not forget;* their love, & kindness. God *Allmighty* bless; & save them *all;* & grant *them to see;* a fulfilment of all their reasonable desires. My daughter writes me that you have sent $25. Twenty Five Dollars in a letter with a bundle of papers. I wish to thank you in particular for sending *them papers,* & hope you will continue this kindness. Friends in the cities who get more papers than they can read; cannot think how much it may add to the comfort of a bereaved family to receive a good paper from time to time from distant friends *even though* those friends may be entire strangers. I am getting much better at my wounds; but am *yet rather lame.*

Am very cheerful & *trust* I may continue so "to the end." My Love to all dear friends. Yours for *God & the right*. John Brown

* * * *

Jail, Charlestown, Wednesday, Nov.23, 1859

Rev. McFarland,
Dear Friend:

Although you write to me as a stranger, the spirit you show towards me and the cause for which I am in bonds, makes me feel towards you as a dear friend. I would be glad to have you, or any of my liberty-loving ministerial friends here, to talk and pray with me. I am not a stranger to the way of salvation by Christ. From my youth I have studied much on that subject, and at one time hoped to be a minister myself; but God had another work for me to do. To me it is given in behalf of Christ, not only to believe in him, but also to *suffer* for his sake. But while I trust that I have some experimental and saving knowledge of religion, it would be a great pleasure to me to have some one better qualified than myself to lead my mind in prayer and meditation, now that my time is so near a close. You may wonder, are there no ministers of the gospel here? I answer, No. There are no ministers of *Christ* here. These ministers who profess to be Christian, and hold slaves or advocate slavery, I cannot abide them. My knees will not bend in prayer with them while their hands are stained with the blood of souls. The subject you mention as having been preaching on, the day before you wrote to me, is one which I have often thought of since my imprisonment. I think I feel as happy as Paul did when he lay in prison. He knew if they killed him it would greatly advance the cause of Christ; that was the reason he rejoiced so. On that same ground "I do rejoice, yea, and will rejoice." Let them hang me; I forgive them, and may God forgive them, for they know not what they do. I have no regret for the transaction for which I am condemned. I went against the laws of men, it is true; but "whether it be right to obey *God* or *men*, judge ye." Christ told me to remember them that are in bonds, as *bound with them,* to do towards them as I would wish them to do towards me in similar circumstances. My conscience bade me do that. I tried to do it, but failed. Therefore I have no regret on that score. I have no sorrow either as to the result, only for my poor wife and children. They have suffered much, and it is hard to leave them uncared for. But God will be a husband to the widow, and a father to the fatherless.

I have frequently been in Wooster; and if any of my old friends from Akron are there, you can show them this letter. I have but a few more days, and I feel anxious to be away, "where the wicked cease from troubling, and the weary are at rest." Farewell.

Your friend, and the friend of all friends of liberty, John Brown.

* * * *

Charlestown, Jefferson County, Va., Nov. 24, 1859

My Dear Mrs. Spring,

Your ever welcome letter of the 19th inst., together with the one now enclosed, were received by me last night too late for any reply. I am always grateful for anything you either do or write. I would most gladly express my gratitude to you and yours by something more than words; but it has come to that, I now have but little else to deal in, and sometimes they are not so kind as they should be. You have laid me and my family under many and great obligations. I hope they may not soon be forgotten. The same is also true of a vast many others, that I shall never be able even to thank. I feel disposed to leave the education of my dear children to their mother, and to those dear friends who bear the burden of it; only expressing my earnest hope that they may all become strong, intelligent, expert, industrious, Christian housekeepers. I would wish that, together with other studies, they may thoroughly study Dr. Franklin's "Poor Richard." I want them to become matter-of-fact women. Perhaps I have said too much about this already; I would not allude to this subject now but for the fact that you had most kindly expressed your generous feelings with regard to it.

I sent the letter to my wife to your care, because the address she sent me from Philadelphia was not sufficiently plain, and left me quite at a loss. I am still in the same predicament, and were I not ashamed to trouble you further, would ask you either to send this to her or a copy of it, in order that she may see something from me often.

I have very many interesting visits from proslavery persons almost daily, and I endeavor to improve them faithfully, plainly, and kindly. I do not think that I ever enjoyed life better than since my confinement here. For this I am indebted to Infinite Grace, and the kind letters of friends from different quarters. I wish I could only know that all my poor family were as much composed and happy as I. I think that nothing but the Christian religion can ever make any one so much composed. "My willing soul would stay / In such a frame as this."

There are objections to my writing many things while here that I might be disposed to write were I under different circumstances. I do not know that my wife yet understands that prison rules require that all I write or receive should first be examined by the sheriff or State's attorney, and that all company I see should be attended by the jailer or some of his assistants. Yet such is the case; and did she know this, it might influence her mind somewhat about the opportunity she would have on coming here. We cannot expect the jailer to devote very much time to us, as he has now a very hard task on his hands. I have just learned how to send letters to my wife near Philadelphia.

I have a son at Akron, Ohio, that I greatly desire to have located in such a neighborhood as yours; and you will pardon me for giving you some account of him, making all needful allowance for the source the account comes from. His name is Jason; he is about thirty-six years old; has a wife and one little boy. He is a very laborious, ingenious, temperate, honest, and truthful man. He is very expert as a gardener, vine-dresser, and manager of fruit-trees, but does not pride himself on account of his skill in anything; always has underrated himself; is bashful and retiring in his habits; is not (like his father) too much inclined to assume and dictate; is too conscientious in his dealings and too tender of people's feelings to get from them his just deserts, and is very poor. He suffered almost everything on the way to and while in Kansas but death, and returned to Ohio not a spoiled but next to a ruined man. He never quarrels, and yet I know that he is both morally and physically brave.

He will not deny his principles to save his life, and he "turned not back in the day of battle." At the battle of Oswatomie he fought by my side. He is a most tender, loving, and steadfast friend, and on the right side of things in general, a practical Samaritan (if not Christian); and could I know that he was located with a population who were disposed to encourage him, without expecting him to pay too dearly in the end for it, I should feel greatly relieved. His wife is a very neat, industrious, prudent woman, who has undergone a severe trial in "the school of affliction."

You make one request of me that I shall not be able to comply with. Am sorry that I cannot at least explain. Your own account of my plans is very well. The son I mentioned has now a small stock of choice vines and fruit-trees, and in them consists his worldly store mostly. I would give you some account of others, but I suppose my wife may have done so.

Your friend, John Brown.

* * * *

Charlestown, Jefferson County, Va., Nov. 25, 1859
Rev. Heman Humphrey, D.D.
My Dear and Honored Kinsman,

Your very sorrowful, kind, and faithful letter of the 20th instant is now before me. I accept it with all kindness. I have honestly endeavored to profit by the faithful advice it contains. Indeed, such advice could never come amiss. You will allow me to say that I deeply sympathize with you and all my sorrowing friends in their grief and terrible mortification. I feel ten times more afflicted on their account than on account of my own circumstances. But I must say that I am neither conscious of being "infatuated" nor "mad." You will doubtless agree with me in this,—that neither imprisonment, irons, not the gallows falling to one's lot are of themselves evidence of either guilt, "infatuation, or madness."

I discover that you labor under a mistaken impression as to some important facts, which my peculiar circumstances will in all probability prevent the possibility of my removing; and I do not propose to take up any argument to prove that any motion or act of my life is right. But I will here state that I know it to be wholly my own fault as a leader that caused our disaster. Of this you have no proper means of judging, not being on the ground, or a practical soldier. I will only add, that it was in yielding to my feelings of humanity (if I exercised such a feeling), in leaving my proper place and mingling with my prisoners to quiet their fears, that occasioned our being caught. I firmly believe that God reigns, and that he overrules all things in the best possible manner; and in that view of the subject I try to be in some degree reconciled to my own weaknesses and follies even.

If you were here on the spot, and could be with me by day and by night, and know the facts and how my time is spent here, I think you would find much to reconcile your own mind to the ignominious death I am about to suffer, and to mitigate your sorrow. I am, to say the least, quite cheerful. "He shall begin to deliver Israel out of the hand of the Philistines." This was said of a poor erring servant many years ago; and for many years I have felt a strong impression that God had given me powers and faculties, unworthy as I was, that he intended to use for a similar purpose. This most unmerited honor

He has seen fit to bestow; and whether, like the same poor frail man to whom I allude, my death may not be of vastly more value than my life is, I think quite beyond all human foresight. I really have strong hopes that notwithstanding all my many sins, I too may yet die "in faith."

If you do not believe I had a murderous intention (while I *know* I had not), why grieve so terribly on my account? The scaffold has but few terrors for me. God has often covered my head in the day of battle, and granted me many times deliverances that were almost so miraculous that I can scarce realize their truth; and now, when it seems quite certain that he intends to use me in a different way, shall I not most cheerfully go? I may be deceived, but I humbly trust that he will not forsake me "till I have showed his favor to this generation and his strength to every one that is to come." Your letter is most faithfully and kindly written, and I mean to profit by it. I am certainly quite grateful for it. I feel that a great responsibility rests upon me as regards the lives of those who have fallen and may yet fall. I must in that view cast myself on the care of Him "whose mercy endureth forever." If the cause in which I engaged in any possible degree approximated to be "infinitely better" than the one which Saul of Tarsus undertook, I have no reason to be ashamed of it; and I cannot now, after more than a month for reflection, find in my heart (before God in whose presence I expect to stand within another week) any cause for shame. [. . .]

I got a long and most kind letter from your pure-hearted brother Luther, to which I replied at some length. The statement that seems to be going around in the newspapers that I told Governor Wise that I came on here to seek revenge for the wrongs of either myself or my family, is utterly false. I never intended to convey such an idea, and I bless God that I am able even now to say that I have never yet harbored such a feeling. See testimony of witnesses who were with me while I had one son lying dead by my side, and another mortally wounded and dying on my other side. I do not believe that Governor Wise so understood, and I think he ought to correct that impression. The impression that we intended a general insurrection is equally untrue.

Now, my much beloved and much respected kinsman, farewell. May the God of our fathers save and abundantly bless you and yours!

John Brown.

* * * *

Charlestown, Jefferson Co. Va. 26th Nov. 1859
(Nov. 27th I mean to write again with some care)

My dear Wife

I wrote our dear friend McKim a few lines yesterday saying I had got his kind letter informing me of where you then were; & how to direct to you while in his neighborhood. I also said to him that I would be glad to have you remain about there; until I was disposed of : *or untill*; I could send you a few little articles by Express : & also write you further; if that (could be) without your becoming burdensome to friends. Our friend McKim wrote me you had gone; *or was going* to stay a while with *Lucretia Mott.* I remember the faithful old Lady well; but presume she has no recollection of me. I once set myself to oppose a *mob* at Boston; where she was. After I interfered the police immediately took up the matter; & soon put a stop to mob proceedings. The meeting was I think in *Marlboro Street* Church, or *Hotel perhaps.* I am glad to have you make the acquaintance of such old "Pioneers" in the cause. I have just received from Mr. John Jay of New York a draft for $50, Fifty Dollars for the benefit of my family; & will enclose *it;* made payable to your order. I have also $15, Fifteen Dollars to send our cripled, & *destitute* unmarried son; when I can I intend to send you by Express Care of Mr. McKim Two or Three little articles to carry home. Should you happen to meet with Mr. Jay say to him that I fully appreciate his great kindness both to *me; & my family.* God bless *all* such friends. It is out of my power to reply to *all* the kind, & encouraging letters *I get; Wish* I could do so. I have been so much relieved from my lameness for the last Three or Four days as to be able to sit up to read; & write pretty much all day : as well as part of the Night; & I do assure you *& all other* friends that I am quite busy; & *none the less happy* on that account. The time passes *quite pleasantly;* & the near aproach of my great change is not the occasion of any particular dread. I trust that *God* who has sustained me *so long;* will not *forsake* me when I most feel my need of *Fatherly aid; & support.* Should he hide his face; my spirit will droop, & die : *but not otherwise : be assured.* My only anxiety is to be properly assured of my *fitness* for the company of those who are "washed from *all filthiness*:" & *for the presence of Him who is Infinitely pure.* I certainly *think* I do have *some* "hunger, & *thirst* after righteousness." If it be only *genuine* I make *no doubt I "shall be filled."* Please let all our friends read my letters when you can; & ask them to accept of it *as in part for them.* I am inclined to think you will not be likely to succeed well about getting away the bodies of your family; but should that *be so: do not let that grieve you.* It can make but little difference *what is done with them.* I would advise that you take any little funds you may have to carry home in Gold (smallish sized) *in good part*; which some kind friend will obtain at a Bank for you. You can continue to carry *(the most of it)* about your person in some *safe way* : & it will not be best for me to advise you about making the little you now get; reach as far as you consistently can. You can well remember the changes you have passed through. Life is made up of a series of changes: & let us try to meet them in the best maner possible. You will not wish to make yourself & children any more burdensome to friends than you are really compelled to do. *I would not.*

I will close this by saying that if you *now feel* that you are *equal* to the undertaking do *exactly as you FEEL disposed to do* about coming to see me before I suffer. *I am entirely willing.*

Your Affectionate Husband, John Brown

* * * *

Charlestown, Jefferson Co. Va. 27th Nov. 1859. Sabbath

My dearly beloved Sisters Mary A, & Martha.

I am obliged to occupy a part of what is probably (my last) Sabbath on Earth in answering the *very kind & very comforting* letters of Sister Hand & Son of the 23d inst or I must fail to do so at all. I do not think it any violation of the day that "God made for man." Nothing could be more grateful to my feelings than to learn that you do *not* feel *dreadfully mortified & even dis-*

graced on account of what I feared would be the *terrible feelings of my kindred* on my account than from *all other* causes. I am most glad to learn *from you* that my fears on *your own* account were ill founded. I was afraid that a little *seeming present* prosperity might have carried you away from realities so that the honor that comes from men might lead you in *some measure* to undervalue that which "cometh from God." I bless God who has *most abundantly supported & comforted me; all along* to find *you* are not ensnared. Dr. Heman Humphrey has just sent me a *most doleful Lamentation* over my *"infatuation" & "madness"* (very kindly expressed :) in which I cannot doubt he has given expression to the *extreme grief* of others of our kindred. I have endeavoured to answer him kindly *also:* & at the same time to deal faithfully with my old friend. I think I will send you his letter; & if you deem it worth the trouble you can probably get my reply or a copy of it. Suffise it for me to say none of these things move me. I here experienced a consolation; & peace which I fear he has not yet known. Luther Humphrey wrote me a very comforting letter There are "things dear Sisters that God hides *even* from the wise & prudent" I feel astonished that one *so exceedingly vile & unworthy as I am* would even be suffered to have a place *anyhow or any where* amongst the *very least of All* who when they came to die (as all must :) *were permitted* to pay the debt of nature in defence of the *right*: & of Gods *eternal & immutable truth.* Oh my dear friends can you believe *it possible* that the Scaffold *has no terrors* for your *own* poor, old, unworthy brother? *I thank God* through Jesus Christ *my Lord : it is even so* I am now sheding tears : but they *are no longer* tears of *grief or sorrow.* I trust I have nearly DONE with those. I am weeping for *joy : & gratitude* that I can *in no other way* express. I get many *very kind & comforting* letters that I cannot possibly reply to. Wish I had time & strength to answer all. I am obliged to ask those whom I do write to let friends read what I send as much as they well can. *Do write* my deeply & oft afflicted Wife: It will greatly comfort her to have you write her freely. She has born up *manfully* under accumulated trials. She will be most glad to know that she has not been entirely forgotten by relatives and say to all my friends that I am "waiting cheerfully" & "patiently the days of my appointed time" : fully believing that for me now "to die will be to me an Infinite gain;" & of *untold* benefit to the cause *we love.* Wherefore "be of good cheer" & "let not your hearts be troubled." "To him that overcometh will I grant to sit with me; in my throne even as I also overcame; & am set down with my Father in his throne." I wish my friends could know but a little of the same opportunities I now get for *Kind & faithful* labour in *Gods cause.* I hope they have not been entirely lost. Now dear friends I have done "May the God of peace bring us all again from the dead."

Your Affectionate Brother, John Brown

* * * *

Charlestown, Jefferson Co., Va., Monday, Nov. 28, 1859

Hon. D. R. Tilden.
My Dear Sir,

    Your *most kind and comforting* letter of the 23d inst. is received.

    I have no language to express the feelings of gratitude and obligation I am under for your kind interest in my behalf ever since my disaster.

The great bulk of mankind estimate each other's actions *and motives* by the measure of success or *otherwise* that attends them through life. By that rule I have been one of the *worst* and one of the *best* of men. I *do* not claim to have been one of the latter; and I leave it to an impartial tribunal to decide whether the world has been the *worse* or the better of my *living* and *dying* in it. My present great anxiety is to get as near in readiness for a different field of action as I well *can* since being in a good measure *relieved from the fear* that my poor, *broken-hearted wife and children* would come to immediate want. May God reward, *a thousand fold,* all the kind efforts made in their behalf. I have enjoyed *remarkable cheerfulness and composure of mind* ever since my confinement; and it is a great comfort to *feel assured* that *I am permitted* to die (for a *cause)* not *merely* to pay the debt of nature, (as all must.) I feel myself to be *most* unworthy of *so great* distinction. The particular manner of dying *assigned* to me, gives me but very little *uneasiness.* I wish I had the time and the ability to give you (my dear friend) some little idea of what is *daily, and, I might also say, hourly,* passing within my *prison walls;* and could my friends but witness only a few of those scenes just as they occur, I think they would feel very reconciled to my being here *just what I am, and just as I am.* My *whole* life *before* had not afforded me one half the opportunity to plead *for the right. In this,* also, *I find* much to reconcile me to both my present condition and my immediate prospect. I may be *very insane,* (and I *am so,* if insane at all.) But if that be so, *insanity* is like a very pleasant dream to me. I am not in the least degree conscious of my *ravings,* of my fears, or of any terrible visions whatever; but *fancy* myself entirely composed, and that my *sleep, in particular,* is as sweet as that of a healthy, joyous little infant. I pray God that he will grant me a continuance of the same calm, but delightful, *dream,* until I come to know of those realities which "eyes have not seen, and which ears have not heard." I have scare realized that I am in prison, or in irons, at all. I certainly think I was never more cheerful in my life. I intend to take the liberty of sending, by express, to your care, some trifling articles for those of my family who may be in Ohio, which you can hand to my brother JERE-MIAH, when you may see him, together with fifteen dollars I have asked him to advance to them. Please excuse me so often troubling you with my letters, or any of my matters. Please also remember me *most* kindly to MR.GRIS-WOLD, and to all others who love their neighbors. I write JEREMIAH to your care.

Your friend, in truth, John Brown.

* * * *

Charlestown, Jefferson Co Va. 29th Nov. 1859

Mrs George L Stearns, Boston Mass
My Dear Friend

No letter I have received since my imprisonment here, has given me more satisfaction, or comfort; then yours on the 8th inst. I am quite cheerful; & was never more happy. Have only time [to] write you a word. May God forever reward you & *all yours. My love to all* who love their neighbors. I have asked to be *spared* from having any *mock; or hypocritical prayers made over me,* when I am publicly *murdered* : & that my only *religious attendants* be poor

little, dirty, ragged, bare headed, & barefooted Slave boys; & Girls; led by some old *grey headed Slave Mother.*
Farewell. Farewell.   Your Friend, John Brown.

* * * *

Charlestown, Jefferson Co., Va., Nov.29, 1859
S. E. Sewall, Esq.
My dear Sir: Your most kind letter of the 24^(th) inst. is received. It does, indeed, give me "pleasure," and the greatest encouragement to know of any efforts that have been made in behalf of my poor and deeply afflicted family. It takes from my mind the greatest cause of sadness I have experienced during my imprisonment here. I feel quite cheerful, and ready to die. I can only say, for want of time, may the *God of the oppressed* and the poor, *in great mercy, remember* all those to whom we are so deeply indebted!
Farewell!
Your friend, John Brown.

* * * *

Charlestown, Prison, Jefferson Co. Va. 30^(th) Nov. 1859
My Dearly beloved Wife, Sons: & Daughters, *every one*
As I now begin what is probably the last letter I shall ever write to any of you; I conclude to write you all at the same time. I will mentions some little matters particularly applicable to little property concerns in another place. I yesterday received a letter from my wife from near Philadelphia: dated Nov 27^(th), by which it would seem that she has about given up the idea of seeing me again. I had written her to come on; if *she* felt equal to the undertaking; but I do not know as she will get my letter in time. It was on her *own account chiefly* that I asked her to stay *back* at first. I had a most strong desire to see her again; but there appeared to be very serious objections; & should we never meet in *this life*; I trust she will in the end be satisfied it was *for the best at least;* if not most for her comfort. I enclosed in my last letter to her a Draft of $50, Fifty Dollars from John Jay made payable to her order. I have now another to send her from my excellent old friend Edward Harris of Woonsocket Rhode Island for $100, One Hundred Dollars; which I shall *also make payable to her* order. I am writing the hour of my public *murder* with great composure of mind, & cheerfulness; feeling the strongest assurance that in no other possible way could I be used to so much advance the cause of God; & of humanity; & that nothing that either I or all my family have sacrifised or suffered: *will be lost.* The reflection that a *wise, & merciful, as well as Just, & holy God:* rules not only the affairs of *this world;* but of all worlds; is a rock to set our feet upon; under all circumstances; *even* those more severely *trying ones:* into which our own follies; & [w]rongs have placed us. I have now no doubt but that our seeming *disaster:* will ultimately result in the most *glorious success.* So my dear *shattered; & broken* family; be of good cheer; & believe & trust in God; "with all your heart; & with all your soul; for *he* doeth *All things well.*" Do not feel ashamed on my account; nor *for one moment* despair of the cause; or grow *weary* of *well doing.* I bless God; I never felt stronger confidence in the certain & near approach of a *bright Morning;*

& *glorious day;* then I have felt; & do now feel; since my confinement here.
I am endeavouring to "return" like a "poor Prodigal" *as I am;* to my Father :
against whom I have *always* sined: *in the hope;* that he may kindly, & for-
givingly "meet me: though; *a verry great way off."* Oh my dear Wife & Children would "to God" you could know how I have been "traveling in birth for
you" all; that no one of you "my fail of the grace of God, through Jesus Christ:"
that no one of you may be blind to the truth: & glorious "light of *his* word;"
in which Life; & Immortality; are brought to light." I beseech you *every one*
to make the bible your *dayly & Nightly study;* with a *childlike honest, candid,
teachable spirit:* out of love and respect for your Husband; & Father: & I beseech *the God* of *my Fathers;* to open all your eyes to a discovery of *the truth.*
You *cannot imagine* how much *you* may *soon need* the consolations of the
Christian religion.

Circumstances like my own; for more than a month past; convince me be-
yound *all doubt* of our great need: of something more to rest our hopes on;
than merely our own vague theories framed up, while our *prejudices* are excited; *or* our *Vanity* worked up to its highest pitch. Oh do not trust your eternal all upon the boisterous Ocean, without *even a Helm;* or *Compass* to *aid*
you in steering. I do *not ask any* of you; to throw *away your reason* : I only
ask you, to make a candid, & sober *use of your reason* : My dear younger
children will you listen to this last poor admonition of one who can *only* love
you? Oh be determined at once to give your whole hearts to God; & let *nothing shake; or alter;* that resolution. You need have no fear *of* REGRETING
it. Do not be in vain; and thoughtless : but *sober minded.* And let me entreat
you all to love *the whole remnant* or our once great family: "with a pure *heart
fervently."* Try to *build again* : your broken walls: & to make *the utmost* of
every *stone* that is left. Nothing can so tend to make life a blessing as the consciousness that you *love: & are beloved* : & "love ye the stranger" *still.* It is
a ground of the utmost comfort to *my mind:* to know that so many of you as
have had *the opportunity;* have given full proof of your fidelity to the great
family of man. *Be faithful* until *death.* From the exercise of habitual love to
man : *it cannot* be very *hard* : to *learn to love* his *maker.* I must *yet* insert a
reason for my firm belief in the Divine inspiration of the Bible : notwithstanding I am (perhaps naturally) skeptical. (certainly not, *credulous.*) I wish
you all to consider *it most thoroughly;* when you read that blessed book; &
see whether you *can not* discover such evidence yourselves. It is the purity of
heart, feeling, or motive : as well as *word, & action* which is every where insisted on; that distinguish it from *all other teachings;* that *commends it* to *my
conscience* : whether *my heart* be "willing, & obedient" *or not.* The induce-
ments that it holds out; are another reason *of my conviction* or its *truth: &
genuineness;* that I cannot here *omit;* in this my *last argument,* for the Bible
Eternal life: is that my soul *is "panting after"* this moment. I mention this; as
reason for endeavouring to leave a valuable copy of the Bible to be carefully
preserved in remembrance of *me* : to so many of my posterity; *instead* of some
other thing : of equal *cost.* I beseech you all to live in habitual contentment
with verry *moderate* circumstances : & gains, of *worldly store* : & most
earnestly to teach this : to your *children; & Childrens, Children;* after you: by
example: as well; as precept. Be determined to know by experience *as soon*

as may be : whether bible instruction is of *Divine origin* or not; *which says;* "*Owe no man anything but* to love one another." John Rogers wrote to his children, "Abhor that arrant whore of Rome." John Brown writes to his children to abhor with *undiing hatred,* also : that "sum of all vilanies;" Slavery. *Remember* that "he that is *slow* to *anger* is *better* than the mighty : and he that ruleth his *spirit;* than he that taketh a city." Remember also : *that* "they that be *wise* shall *shine* : and they that *turn* many to *righteousness:* as the stars forever; & ever." And now dearly beloved *Farewell* To God & the word of his grace I comme[n]d you all.

Your Affectionate Husband & Father, John Brown

* * * *

Charlestown, Jefferson, Co Va, 2d, Dec.1859

Lora Case Esqr
My Dear Sir
Your most kind & cheering letter of the 28[th] Nov is received Such an outburst of warm hearted sympathy not only for myself; but also for those who "have no helper" compels me to steal a moment from those allowe[d] me; in which to prepare for my last great change to send you a few words. Such a feeling as you manifest makes you to "*shine* (in my estimation) in the midst of this wicked; & perverse generation as a light in the world" May you ever prove yourself equal to the high estimate I have placed on you. Pure & undefiled religion befor God & the Father is as I understand it : an *active* (not a dormant) *principle.* I do not undertake to direct any more about my Children. I leave that now entirely to their excellent Mother from whom I have just parted. I send you my "salutation with my own hand." Remember me to all *yours, & my dear friends.* Your Friend John Brown

* * * *

Charlestown, Va, 2d, December, 1859

I John Brown am now quite *certain* that the crimes of this *guilty land: will* never be purged *away;* but with **Blood.** I had as *I now think; vainly* flattered myself that without *verry much* bloodshed; it might be done.

* * * *

The Execution of John Brown, December 2, 1859

Dawn broke on Friday, December 2, 1859. The "clock [was] striking the fatal hour that begins a new era in the conflict with slavery," or so said Lucius Bierce of that morning, in a speech on December 7, printed here. The whole country awaited the moment of Brown's execution. In Europe, where the light of dawn had heralded the day of Brown's death some five hours earlier, Victor Hugo awaited news that, as he put it, "a portion of the light of humanity [had been] eclipsed." In a letter to the London News *that he wrote at some point during the morning (also printed here), he is "inspired with the conscience of humanity" and concerned for "the safety of the universal moral law if the "first fratricide be outdone." There can be, he counselled the murderers of Brown, "something more terrible than Cain slaying Abel—it is Washington slaying Spartacus."*

Figure 20: Victor Hugo, frontispiece from *John Brown par Victor Hugo*, 1861. (*Courtesy Lilly Library.*)

Hugo heard confirmation of Brown's death a few weeks later, while a gray winter storm swept over Guernsey, and Hauteville House. For the rest of the day, as he made a wash drawing of Brown on the scaffold, the storm seemed to echo his mood, and the dark drawing resonates with both mood and storm (fig. 20). In the top left corner dawn breaks or sunlight bursts through the gloom in which Brown hangs, but the darkness is heavy, for "the entire American Democracy" is convulsing, as Hugo wrote in his letter of December 2. The features of the small hanging figure are hidden, the shape more abstract than realistic: the hanging is, his letter explains, "the assassination of the Emancipation of Liberty" by "the whole American Republic," and so the figure hanging is not only Brown but also the "fasces of that splendid Republic . . . bound together with the running noose that hung from the gibbet of Brown." At the bottom of the drawing, Hugo wrote the Latin word "Ecce," so further lifting Brown's execution into the realm of myth and symbol: Pontius Pilate introduced Jesus to the mob calling for His death with the words "Ecce homo—Behold the man." December 2 was, for this European at least, the day when Christ would die a second time. As on that first occasion two thousand years ago, the skies would darken as he died—becoming as dreary as the gray wash drawing.

Very much aware of the potential symbolism of his death, Brown woke on December 2 determined to do the occasion justice; a short time later, his body cut down from where it swayed, none could disagree that he had done just that. While North and South fretted over the ramifications of his execution, he had been peacefully preparing to meet his Maker for weeks. An article in the Boston Daily Advertiser, *printed here, described the intense preparations that took place before Virginia was ready to receive its victim. The article, published just before Brown began his journey to the scaffold on the morning of his death, goes on to ask: "Was the gallows built for such men?" and warns that, though now "inevitable," the execution will add "fuel to the fire of hatred and contempt on the part of the extreme abolitionists at the North." Expressing a widely-held hope, the article concludes by anticipating that the execution "will turn out, in its ultimate consequences, to have done more to hasten the extinction of slavery than any other event of the present century."*

Anticipating these exact consequences, Brown calmly wrote some final letters and awaited the arrival of the execution wagon. Then he gave a book to his guard, and a silver watch to his jailer John Avis, who had grown to like and admire the prisoner. Legend has it that on his way out of the prison to climb onto the coffin and cart, he stopped and bent to kiss a slave child; but this was impossible, for no civilians were allowed near the proceedings. The story, which originated in the New York Tribune *article that is reprinted here, fired the public imagination. James Redpath, who used newspaper articles and other testimonies to put together a chapter on the execution (also included here) in his swiftly published biography of Brown of 1860, borrows heavily from the* Tribune *article and so perpetuated the myth. John Greenleaf Whittier wrote the* poem, "Brown of Ossawatomie," around the incident. The story spawned three important works of art, which are printed and discussed alongside Whittier's poem in Part Four of this anthology. Lydia Maria Child also penned a famous poem about the mythical kiss; the work, printed here, appeared in The Freedmen's Book of 1866.

Arriving at the scaffold, Brown took a last look at the view. A correspondent for the Baltimore Daily Exchange would remember the next few moments: "I see him as he places his foot on the first step. No bravado, but a calm mien and exquisite poise, step after step he takes, as though he were ascending the stairs in a gentleman friend's home to a chamber in which he was to rest." There was no minister present. Brown had written to Mrs. George L. Stearns on November 29: "I have asked to be spared from having any mock; or hypocritical prayers made over me, when I am publicly murdered : & that my only religious attendants be poor little, dirty, ragged, bare headed, & barefooted Slave boys; & Girls; led by some old grey headed Slave Mother." Though denied his request for religious attendants of that kind, Brown was spared from the attentions of slave-owning or proslavery ministers. The attempts of such clergymen to pray on his behalf had agitated him during his weeks in prison. When, towards the end of Brown's incarceration, a Methodist clergyman, Norval Wilson, proposed a prayer for Brown's soul, the condemned man asked "do you believe in slavery?" and heard in reply: "I do, under the present circumstances," to which he responded, "I do not want your prayers. I don't want the prayers of any man that believes in slavery. You can pray to your Father that heareth in secret."

So Brown received the noose and hood unattended by ministers. But his audience was not entirely military. Edmund Ruffin, the secessionist, had borrowed a cadet's uniform so that he could attend. He remarked afterwards: "He is as thorough a fanatic as ever suffered martyrdom and a very brave and able man. . . . It is impossible for me not to respect his thorough devotion to his bad cause." John Wilkes Booth, soon-to-be assassin of Lincoln, also slipped in. By all accounts, there was little for Brown's enemies to despise in these his last minutes. The journalist and newspaper artist David Strother "watched narrowly . . . to see if there was any indication of his giving way" but, as he related in an article for Harpers Weekly printed here, he "detected nothing of the sort." Professor Thomas J. Jackson, later "Stonewall" of the first Battle of Bull Run, watched the scene with the cadets under his command and admired Brown's "unflinching firmness". Another admirer was Francis Lieber, who wrote to Dr. Henry Drisler two days later that Brown "died like a man and Virginia fretted like an old woman." He added, "The deed was irrational, but it will be historical. Virginia has come out of it damaged, I think. She has forced upon mankind the idea that slavery must be, in her own opinion, but a rickety thing." In the act of breaking his body, Brown proved the "rickety" breakability of the slave-system.

There was a painfully long interval between the blindfolding and the swinging out. Brown stood erect and completely still, looking like the monument to liberty that he was to become—perhaps ready, as Bierce *claimed in the speech printed here, to "rise up before the world with his calm, marble features." It was an impressive sight. William A. Phillips, in a lecture extracted here, described the "protracted" moment as deliberate and Brown's calm response as a victory. No one was allowed within hearing distance of the gallows. Any words spoken by Brown would—for once—go unheard. Then he swung out.*

The body hung for thirty-seven minutes. The hangman took a piece of the scaffold and sent it to James Redpath, who labeled it: "A Bit of the True Cross, a Chip from the Scaffold of John Brown," and cherished it for years. Church bells tolled across the Northern states. In Massachusetts, Henry David Thoreau announced, "This morning, Captain Brown was hung. He is not Old Brown any longer; he is an angel of light." Like Moses, Brown never saw the Promised Land. But it was just ahead, and others would march toward it, singing of John Brown's Body as they went.

Article in the Boston Daily Advertiser; Friday Morning, December 2, 1859

. . . [T]his execution of Brown will add fuel to the fire of hatred and contempt on the part of the extreme abolitionists at the North, of which so much complaint has justly been made, and which does so much to exasperate well-disposed persons at the South, and to retard any spontaneous movement in that region for the abolition of slavery. It will tend to reproduce other attempts like that of Brown, equally unjustifiable, but perhaps less rash and more successful. The ultra abolitionists regard Brown as a martyr and a hero; they do so honestly; and it is no wonder. The execution of such a man will add tenfold to the ardor of their ill-judged efforts, and the intemperance of the spirit that animates them. If any one regards that as a small evil, we do not. For although the number of these men is small and their indirect influence in stirring up ill blood and fomenting all those elements of the slave controversy which tend to exasperate and divide, is very great. What is more needed now than anything is a broad, catholic, charitable, and at the same time, a firm discussion and treatment of this question of slavery at the North. But the execution of John Brown does a great deal to check any attempts at such a treatment of it, and goes far to diminish the influence of every one who would undertake it. But this event is inevitable; indeed before these lines are seen by many of our readers, it will have occurred already. It will prove to be no ordinary occurrence. And, after all, much as we may now regret it, perhaps it will turn out, in its ultimate consequences, to have done more to hasten the extinction of slavery than any other event of the present century.

Report in the New York Tribune, December 5, 1859

On leaving the Jail, John Brown had on his face an expression of calmness and serenity characteristic of the patriot who is about to die with a living consciousness that he is laying his life down for the good of his fellow creatures. . . . As he stepped out of door a black woman, with her little child in her arms, stood near his way. The twain were of the despised race for whose

emancipation and elevation to the dignity of children of God he was about to
lay down his life. . . . He stopped for a moment in his course, stooped over,
and with the tenderness of one whose love is as broad as the brotherhood of
man, kissed [the child] affectionately.

David Strother (a.k.a Porte Crayon), account written for Harper's Weekly *[not published until February 1955, in* American Heritage*]*

I stood with a group of half dozen gentlemen near the steps of the scaffold
when the Prisoner was driven up. . . . He stepped from the wagon with sur-
prising agility and walked hastily toward the scaffold, pausing a moment as he
passed our group to wave his pinioned arm and bid us good morning. I thought
I could observe in this a trace of bravado—but perhaps I was mistaken.

The view was of surpassing beauty. Broad and fertile fields dotted with corn
stocks and white farm houses glimmering through the leafless trees—emblems
of prosperity and peace.

I stood within a few paces of him and watched narrowly during these trying moments to see if there was any indication of his giving way. I detected
nothing of the sort. He had stiffened himself for the drop and waited motion-
less 'till it came.

Thomas J. Jackson ("Stonewall"), letter to his wife, December 2, 1859

John Brown was hung today at about 11 1/2 A.M. He behaved with unflinching firmness. The arrangements were well made under the direction of
Col. Smith. Brown's wife visited him last evening. The body is to be deliv-

Figure 21: David Strother (a.k.a Porte Crayon), sketch for *Harper's Weekly*,
December 1859. (*Courtesy, Library of Congress.*)

ered to her. The gibbet was south east of the town in a large field. Brown rode on the head of his coffin, from his prison to the place of execution. The coffin was of black walnut, enclosed in a poplar box of the same shape as the coffin.

He was dressed in carpet slippers of predominating red, white socks, black pants, black frock coat, black vest & black slouch hat. Nothing around his neck beside his shirt collar. The open wagon in which he rode was strongly guarded on all sides. Capt. Williams, formerly one of the assistants of the Institute, marched immediately in front of the wagon. The jailer and high sheriff and several others rode in the wagon with the prisoner.

Brown had his arms tied behind him, & ascended the scaffold with apparent cheerfulness. After reaching the top of the platform, he shook hands with several who were standing around him. The sheriff placed the rope around his neck, then threw a white cap over his head & asked him if he wished a signal when all should be ready—to which he replied that it made no difference, provided he was not kept waiting too long.

In this condition he stood on the trap door, which was supported on one side by hinges, and on the other (south side) by a rope, for about 10 minutes, when Col. S. told the Sheriff "all is ready," which apparently was not comprehended by the Sheriff, and the Col. had to repeat the order, when the rope was cut by a single blow, and Brown fell through about 25 inches, so as to bring his knees on a level with the position occupied by his feet before the rope was cut. With the fall his arms below the elbow flew up, hands clenched, & his arms gradually fell by spasmodic motions—there was very little motion of his person for several minutes, after which the wind blew his lifeless body to & fro.

His face, upon the scaffold, was turned a little east of south, and in front of him were the cadets commanded by Major Gilham. My command was still in front of the cadets, all facing south. One howitzer I assigned to Mr. Truheart on the left of the cadets, and with the other I remained on the right. Other troops occupied different positions around the scaffold, and altogether it was an imposing but very solemn scene.

I was much impressed with the thought that before me stood a man, in the full vigor of health, who must in a few minutes be in eternity. I sent up a petition that he might be saved. Awful was the thought that he might in a few minutes receive the sentence "Depart ye wicked into everlasting fire." I hope that he was prepared to die, but I am very doubtful—he wouldn't have a minister with him.

His body was taken back to the jail, and at 6 p.m. was sent to his wife at Harper's Ferry. When it reached Harper's Ferry the coffin was opened and his wife saw the body—the coffin was again opened at the depot, before leaving for Baltimore, lest there should be an imposition.

James Redpath, **The Public Life of Capt. John Brown,** *1860*

At eleven o'clock, John Brown came out of jail. An eye witness said of his appearance at this solemn moment: "He seemed to walk out of the Gates of Fame; his countenance was radiant; he walked with the step of an conqueror."

Another spectator—everyone, in truth, who saw the old man—corroborated the report: On leaving the jail, he wrote, John Brown had his face an expression of calmness and serenity characteristic of the patriot who is about to die, with a living consciousness that he is lying down his life for the good of his fellow-creatures. His face was even joyous, and a forgiving smile rested upon his lips. His was the lightest heart, among friend or foe, in the whole of Charlestown that day; and not a word was spoken that was not intuitive appreciation of his manly courage. Firmly, with elastic step, he moved forward. No flinching of a coward's heart there. He stood in the midst of that organised mob, from whose despotic hearts petty tyranny seemed for the nonce eliminated by the admiration they had on once beholding A MAN; for John Brown was there every inch a man.

As he stepped out of the door, a black woman, with a little child in her arms, stood near his way. The twain were of the despised race for whose emancipation and elevation to the dignity of children of God he was about to lay down his life. His thoughts at that moment none can know except as his acts interpret them. He stopped for a moment in his course, stooped over, and with the tenderness of one whose love is as broad as the brotherhood of man, kissed it affectionately. That mother will be proud of that mark of distinction for her offspring; and some day, when over the ashes of John Brown the temple of Virginia liberty is reared, she may join in the joyful song of praise which on that soil will do justice to his memory. As he passed along, a black woman with a child in her arms, ejaculated, "God bless you, old man; I wish I could help you, but I cannot." He heard her, and, as he looked at her, a tear stood in his eye.

The vehicle which was to convey John Brown to the scaffold was a furniture wagon. On the front seat was the driver, a man named Hawks, for many years a resident of Virginia, but said to be a native of Massachusetts, and by his side was seated by Mr. Saddler, the undertaker. In the box was placed the coffin, made of black walnut, enclosed in a poplar box with a flat lid, in which coffin and remains were to be transported to the North. John Brown mounted the wagon, and took his place in the seat with Captain Avis, the jailer, whose admiration of his prisoner is of the profoundest nature. Mr. Saddler, too, was one of John Brown's staunchest friends in his confinement, and pays noble tribute to his manly qualities.

He mounted the wagon with perfect calmness. It was immediately surrounded with cavalry. This military escort of the warrior of the Lord to the scene of his last earthly victory, consisted of Captain Scott's company of cavalry, one company of Major Loring's battalion of defensibles, Captain William's Montpelier Guard, Captain Scott's Petersburg Greys, Company D, Captain Miller, of the Virginia Volunteers, and the Young Guard, Captain Rady; the whole under the command of Colonel T.P. August, assisted by Major Loring—the cavalry at the head and rear of the column.

The wagon was drawn by two white horses. From the time of leaving jail [until] he mounted the gallows stairs, he wore a smile upon his countenance, and his keen eye took in every detail of the scene. There was no blenching, nor the remotest approach to cowardice nor nervousness. As he was leaving

myth

the jail, when asked if he thought he could endure his fate, he said "I can endure almost any thing but parting from friends; that is very hard." On the road to the scaffold, he thus replied to an inquiry, "It has been a characteristic of me, from infancy, not to suffer from physical fear. I have suffered a thousand times more from bashfulness than from fear."

"I was very near the old man," writes an eyewitness, "and scrutinized him closely. He seemed to take in the whole scene at a glance; and he straightened himself up proudly, as if to set an example of a soldier's courage. The only motion he made, beyond a swaying to and fro of his body, was that same patting of his knees with his hands that we noticed throughout his trial and while in jail. As he came upon an eminence near the gallows, he cast his eye over the beautiful landscape, and he followed the windings of the Blue Ridge Mountains in the distance. He looked up earnestly at the sun, and sky, and all about, and then remarked, 'This is a beautiful country. I have not cast my eyes over it before—that is, while passing through the field.'"

"Yes," was the sad reply of the brave Captain Avis.

"You are a game man, Captain Brown," said Mr. Saddler.

"Yes," he said, "I was so trained up; it was one of the lessons of my mother; but it is hard to part from friends, though newly made."

"You are more cheerful than I am, Captain Brown," responded Mr. Saddler.

"Yes," said the hero, "*I ought to be.*"

[. . .] As the procession entered the field, the old hero, as if surprised at the absence of the people, remarked:

"I see no citizens here—where are they?"

"The citizens are not allowed to be present—none but the troops," was the reply.

"That ought not to be," said the old man; "citizens should be allowed to be present as well as others."

The wagon halted. The troops composing the escort took up their assigned position; but the Petersburg Greys, as the immediate body guard, remained as before, closely hemming the old hero in—as if still as afraid of his sword of Gideon, as the State had proved itself to be of his sword of the Lord, by preventing the people from listening to his last words. They finally opened ranks to let him pass out; when, with the assistance of two men, he descended from the wagon. Mr. Hunter and Mayor Green were standing near by. "Gentlemen, good bye," the old man said in an unfaltering tone; and then, with firm step and erect form, he calmly walked past jailers, sheriff, and officers, and mounted the steps of the scaffold. He was the first man that stood on it. As he quietly awaited the necessary arrangements, he surveyed the scenery unmoved, looking principally in the direction of the people in the far distance. "There is no faltering in his step," wrote one who saw him, "but firmly and erect he stands amid the almost breathless lines of soldiery that surround him. With a graceful motion of his pinioned right arm he takes the slouched hat from his head and carelessly casts it upon the platform by his side." "I know," said another witness, "that every one within view was greatly impressed with the dignity of his bearing. I have since heard men of the South say that his courageous fortitude and insensibility to fear filled them with amazement."

The hour had now come. The officer approached him. To Captain Avis he said: "I have no words to thank you for kindness to me."

His elbows and ankles are pinioned, the white cap is drawn over his eyes, the hangman's rope is adjusted around his neck. John Brown is ready to be ushered into the land of hereafter.

"Captain Brown," said the Sheriff, "you are not standing on the drop. Will you come forward?"

"I can't see, gentlemen," was the old man's answer unfalteringly spoken, "you must lead me."

The Sheriff led his prisoner forward to the centre of the drop.

"Shall I give you a handkerchief?" asked the Sheriff, "and let you drop it as a signal?"

"No; I am ready at any time; but do not keep me needlessly waiting."

This was the last of John Brown's requests of Virginia; and this, like all others, was refused. When he pleaded for the delay during the progress of his trial, the State refused it, and hurried him to his doom; and now, when he asked, standing on the gallows, blindfolded and with the rope that was to strangle him around his neck, for no unnecessary delay, the demoniacal spirit of slavery again turned a deaf ear to his request. Instead of permitting the execution to be at once consummated, the proceedings were checked by the martial order—"Not ready yet," and the hideous mockery of a vast military display began. For ten minutes at least, under the orders of the commanding officer, the troops trod heavily over the ground, hither and thither, now advancing towards the gallows, now turning about in sham defiance of an imaginary enemy.

Each moment to every humane man seemed an hour, and some of the soldiers, unable to restrain an expression of their sense of the outrage, murmured— *Shame! Shame!*

At last the order was given, and the rope was severed with a hatchet. As the trap fell, its hinges gave a wailing sort of creak, that could be heard at every point in the fields.

John Brown is slowly strangling—for the shortness of the rope prevents a speedy death.

There was but one spasmodic effort of the hands to clutch at the neck, but for nearly five minutes the limbs jerked and quivered. He seemed to retain an extraordinary hold upon life. One who has seen numbers of men hung before, told me he had never seen so hard a struggle. After the body had dangled in mid air for twenty minutes, it was examined by the surgeons for signs of life. First the Charlestown physicians went up and made their examination, and after them the military surgeons; the prisoner being exhausted by civil power, and with military assistance as well. To see them lifting up the arms, now powerless, that once were so strong, and placing their ears to the breast of the corpse, holding it steady by passing an arm around it, was revolting in the extreme. And so the body dangled and swung by its neck, turning to this side or that when moved by surgeons, and swinging pendulum-like, from the force of the south wind that was blowing, until, after thirty-eight minutes from the time of swinging off, it was ordered to be cut down, the authorities being quite satisfied that their dreaded enemy was dead. The body was lifted upon the scaffold, and fell into a heap.

Victor Hugo, letter to the editor of the London News, *December 2, 1859*

Hauteville House, Dec. 2, 1859

Sir:

When one thinks of the United States of America, a majestic figure rises to mind—Washington. Now, in that country of Washington, see what is going on at this hour! . . . At this moment the gaze of Europe is fixed on America. John Brown condemned to die, was to have been hanged on 2nd of December—this very day. . . . The executioner of Brown—let us avow it openly (for the days of kings is past, and the day of the people dawns, and to the people we are bound frankly to speak the truth)—the executioner of Brown would be neither the Attorney Hunter, nor the judge Parker, nor the Governor Wise, nor the State of Virginia; it would be, we say it, and we think it with a shudder, the whole American Republic. . . .

When we reflect on what Brown, the liberator, the champion of Christ, has striven to effect, and when we remember that he is about to die, slaughtered by the American Republic, the crime assumes the proportions of the Nation which commits it; and when we say to ourselves that this Nation is a glory of the human race; that—like France, like England, like Germany—she is one of the organs of civilisation; that she sometimes even out-marches Europe by the sublime audacity of her progress; that she is the queen of an entire world; and that she bears on her brow the immense light of freedom . . . we recoil, horror-struck, from the idea of so great a crime committed by so great a People.

In a political light, the murder of Brown would be an irreparable fault. It would penetrate the Union with a secret fissure, which would in the end tear it asunder. It is possible that the execution of Brown might consolidate Slavery in Virginia, but it is certain that it would convulse the entire American Democracy. You preserve your shame, but you sacrifice your glory.

In a moral light it seems to me, that a portion of the light of humanity would be eclipsed; that even the idea of justice and injustice would be obscured on the day which should witness the assassination of Emancipation of Liberty. . . .

Lydia Maria Child, *"John Brown and the Colored Child,"* **1866.**

A winter sunshine, still and bright,
The Blue Hills bathed with golden light,
And earth was smiling to the sky,
When calmly he went forth to die.

Infernal passions festered there,
Where peaceful Nature looked so fair;
And fiercely, in the morning sun,
Flashed glitt'ring bayonet and gun.

The old man met no friendly eye,
When last he looked on earth and sky;
But one small child, with timid air,
Was gazing on his hoary hair.

As that dark brow to his upturned,
The tender heart within him yearned;
And, fondly stooping o'er her face,
He kissed her for her injured race.

The little one she knew not why
That kind old man went forth to die;
Nor why, 'mid all that pomp and stir,
He stooped to give a kiss to *her*.

But Jesus smiled that sight to see,
And said, "He did it unto *me*."
The golden harps then sweetly rung,
And this the song the angels sung:

"Who loves the poor doth love the Lord;
Earth cannot dim thy bright reward:
We hover o'er yon gallows high,
And wait to bear thee to the sky."

Lucius Bierce, speech reported in Summit Beacon *in Ohio, December 7, 1859*

The tragedy of Brown is freighted with awful lessons and consequences. It is like the clock striking the fatal hour that begins a new era in the conflict with slavery. Men like Brown may die, but their acts and principles will live forever. Call it fanaticism, folly, madness, wickedness, but until virtue becomes fanaticism, divine wisdom folly, obedience to God madness, and piety wickedness, John Brown, inspired with these high and holy teachings, will rise up before the world with his calm, marble features, most terrible in death and defeat, than in life and victory. It is one of those acts of madness which history cherished and poetry loves forever to adorn with her choicest wreaths of laurel.

William A. Phillips, extracts from "The Age and the Man," lecture in Lawrence, Kansas, January 20, 1860

They [men and women of future ages] will see the military power of the Slave State of Virginia ranged around his gallows. They will see how studiously they strove to wring one emotion of fear from that brave old man. The Slave authorities had brow-beaten and intimidated so many Northern men, that they were frantic at the idea that one could die, calmly despising their power. And what a refinement of cruelty and culmination of power. And what a refinement of cruelty and culmination of heroism does that last scene reveal! The martyr to the cause of Liberty stands with his hands bound behind his back,—the death cap over his eyes,—the rope around his neck. It is a solemn moment in which the bravest and best human soul meets death face to face. It was his last moment of life—the nest for eternity. But that moment is protracted,—cunningly, cruelly. The military power of Virginia is wheeling and circling around the base of the scaffold. The artillery rattles—the arms clank.

John Brown does not see it. He can hear, but knows not what it is. It is only the Slave power protracting that solemn moment, in hopes of wringing one quiver of fear from that brave old man. One groan—one spasm, would be worth all the manacles in Virginia. They failed. He died calmly and humbly, without a quiver on his lips. [. . .]

Ah, my friends, we had but little faith in God, or humanity. How unerringly grand the finger that guided all these events! Look to John Brown, surviving that desperate charge, covered with wounds and yet recovering, and escaping the fury of the Virginians after he was disarmed and helpless. Why was it? He was spared to write those grand letters. To utter those simple but solemn Protests against the crime of Slavery. To stand as the representative of the Anti-Slavery sentiment. To Protest against the wrong of his life, and to meet *such* a death undismayed. Two months ago respectable papers were fain to stigmatize him, that they might haply escape the suspicion of sympathizing with him. Now, no respectable paper would like to do such a thing. Then, honourable members of Congress compared him to a highwayman, who now trace the mainsprings of his action to Jefferson, Christianity, and God.

PART FOUR

Immediate responses to John Brown were as polarized as ours in the twenty-first century continue to be: Brown the guardian of American values and the definitive martyr-hero figure is also Brown the unbalanced monomaniac, and even a forerunner to the terrorists of 9/11. Responses to Brown during his lifetime and immediately after his death were divided, unsurprisingly, along the borders of North and South. This final section represents both sides. The Northern sources are writings or speeches by the men who fought beside him, his co-conspirators in the North, and associates and admirers intimate and casual. The Southern sources include, among other selections, responses from politicians and the press. Part Four completes the portrait of a complex man with an even more complex role in American history. The legend of John Brown soon took on different meanings, and these sources reveal where myth and legend intersect with Brown's biography and his own construction of public personae. "The Poet's Song and History's Page," as a poem about Brown's trial in the Boston Liberator *put it, catch John Brown's life and actions as they merge with the coming of the Civil War.*

Figure 22: Jacob Lawrence, *The Life of John Brown*, 1941, No. 1: John Brown, a man who had a fanatical belief that he was chosen by God to overthrow black slavery in America. (*Courtesy, Jacob and Gwendolyn Lawrence Foundation.*)

172

THE MAKING OF A MYTH

Responses to John Brown in the Northern States
* * * *

Osborne Anderson, extract from A Voice From Harper's Ferry, 1861

Just a few days before his death, in a letter from prison on November 28, John Brown declared that he would "leave it to an impartial tribunal to decide whether the world has been the worse or the better of my living and dying in it." The "tribunal" that reflected on John Brown's life in the days, weeks, months, and years that followed his raid and execution, was, however, far from impartial. Passionate and noisy, the company was packed with eminent figures and eloquent voices, nearly all of whom felt strongly either way about the effect on the world of Brown's living and dying in it. Osborne Anderson was no exception.

The only man left alive who was at Harpers Ferry throughout the whole raid, Anderson was an "actor in the scene," as he put it in the preface to A Voice From Harper's Ferry, *as well as one of the "tribunal."* A Voice From Harper's Ferry *is an extended pamphlet of 1861 that recounts the unfolding of the raid in Virginia from Anderson's unique position of participant and observer. He was a freed black who had met Brown while working as a printer in Chatham, Canada. One of five black members of Brown's band, Anderson received the sword of Frederick the Great from Colonel Lewis W. Washington on Brown's behalf, and was the only black raider to escape from the Ferry alive. He returned from Canada to the United States in 1864 and joined the Union Army, then died of consumption in 1872. He writes below as the voice of all African Americans, offering the world "the opinion common among my people of one so eminently worthy of the highest veneration."*

It seems from Anderson's account that it was not only Brown's political philosophy and military strategies that were progressive, but also the attitudes towards race with which he infused his whole Virginia operation: Anderson writes in chapter five of A Voice From Harper's Ferry *of the remarkable interracial dynamic of the band of raiders, calling it an "Anti-slavery family," where "men from widely different parts of the continent met and united into one company, wherein no hateful prejudice*

Figure 23: Osborne Perry Anderson, daguerreotype, 1859. (*Courtesy, Library of Congress.*)

dared intrude its ugly self—no ghost of a distinction found space to enter." While preparations for the raid continued at the Kennedy Farm during the summer of 1859, there was, he continues, "no offensive contempt for the negro, while working in his cause; the pulsations of each and every heart beating in harmony for the suffering and pleading slave."

So Anderson paints a picture of an almost utopian interracial community at the Kennedy Farm, with Brown at its center. He also deepens the impression of Brown's raid as an event of archetypal significance, insisting: "The idea underlying the outbreak at Harper's Ferry is not peculiar to that movement, but dates back to a period very far beyond the memory of the 'oldest inhabitant.'" He lingers on the similarities between Brown and the Old Testament leader Moses. These connections were made by several observers, and by Brown himself (see John Brown's Prison Letters, October 21–December 2, 1859, letter of November 25), and Anderson draws together the threads of symbolism. Taking up another common comparison, Anderson also links Brown and Oliver Cromwell. Brown's ideas were "universal," the language he spoke "understood by the haters of tyranny." Far from a lone fanatic, Brown emerges from Anderson's account as part of a vital and venerable tradition.

Chapters I–II

The idea underlying the outbreak at Harper's Ferry is not peculiar to that movement, but dates back to a period very far beyond the memory of the "oldest inhabitant," and emanated from a source much superior to the Wises and Hunters, the Buchanans and Masons of today. It was the appointed work for life of an ancient patriarch spoken of in Exodus, chap. ii., and who, true to his great commission, failed not to trouble the conscience and to disturb the repose of the Pharaohs of Egypt with that inexorable, "Thus saith the Lord: Let my people go" until even they were urgent upon the people in its behalf. Coming down through the nations, and regardless of national boundaries or peculiarities, it has been proclaimed and enforced by the patriarch and the warrior of the Old World, by the enfranchised freeman and the humble slave of the New. Its nationality is universal; its language every where understood by the haters of tyranny; and those that accept its mission, everywhere understand each other. There is an unbroken chain of sentiment and purpose from Moses of the Jews to John Brown of America; from Kossuth, and the liberators of France and Italy, to the untutored Gabriel, and the Denmark Veseys, Nat Turners and Madison Washingtons of the Southern American States. The shaping and expressing of a thought for freedom takes the same consistence with the colored American—whether he be an independent citizen of the Haytian nation, a proscribed but humble nominally free colored man, a patient, toiling, but hopeful slave—as with the proudest or noblest representative of European or American civilization and Christianity. Lafayette, the exponent of French honor and political integrity, and John Brown, foremost among the men of the New World in high moral and religious principle and magnanimous bravery, embrace as brothers of the same mother, in harmony upon the grand mission of liberty; but, while the Frenchman entered the lists in obedience to a desire to aid, and by invitation from the Adamses and Hamiltons, and thus pushed on the political fortunes of those able to help themselves, John Brown, the liberator of Kansas, the projector and commander of the Harper's Ferry expedition, saw in the most degraded slave a man and a brother, whose appeal for his God-ordained rights no one should disregard; in the toddling slave child, a captive whose release is as imperative, and whose prerogative is as weighty, as the most famous in the land. When the Egyptian pressed hard upon the Hebrew, Moses slew him; and when the spirit of slavery invaded the fair Territory of Kansas, causing the Free-State settlers to cry out because of persecution, old John Brown, famous among the men of God for ever, though then but little known to his fellow-men, called together his sons and went over, as did Abraham, to the unequal contest, but on the side of the oppressed white men of Kansas that were, and the black men that were to be. Today, Kansas is free, and the verdict of impartial men is, that to John Brown, more than any other man, Kansas owes her present position.

I am not the biographer of John Brown, but I can be indulged in giving here the opinion common among my people of one so eminently worthy of the highest veneration. Close observation of him, during many weeks, and under his orders at his Kennedy Farm fireside, also, satisfies me that in comparing the noble old man to Moses, and other men of piety and renown, who were chosen by God to his great work, none have been more faithful, none have given a brighter record.

[. . .] The first visit of John Brown to Chatham was in April, 1858. Wherever he went around, although an entire stranger, he made a profound impression upon those who saw or became acquainted with him. Some supposed him to be a staid but modernized Quaker; others, a solid business man, from "somewhere," and without question a philanthropist. His long white beard, thoughtful and reverent brow and physiognomy, his sturdy, measured tread, as he circulated about with hands, as portrayed in the best lithograph, under the pendant coat-skirt of plain brown Tweed, with other garments to match, revived to those honored with his acquaintance and knowing to his history, the memory of a Puritan of the most exalted type.

After some important business, preparatory to the Convention, was finished, Mr. Brown went West, and returned with his men, who had been spending the winter in Iowa. The party, including the old gentleman, numbered twelve, as brave, intelligent and earnest a company as could have been associated in one party. There were John H. Kagi, Aaron D. Stevens, Owen Brown, Richard Realf, George B. Gill, C. W. Moffitt, Wm. H. Leeman, John E. Cook, Stewart Taylor, Richard Richardson, Charles P. Tidd and J. S. Parsons—all white except Richard Richardson, who was a slave in Missouri until helped to his liberty by Captain Brown. At a meeting held to prepare for the Convention and to examine the Constitution, Dr. M. R. Delany was Chairman, and John H. Kagi and myself were the Secretaries.

When the Convention assembled, the minutes of which were seized by the slaveholding "cravens" at the Farm, and which, as they have been identified, I shall append to this chapter, Mr. Brown unfolded his plans and purpose. He regarded slavery as a state of perpetual war against the slave, and was fully impressed with the idea that himself and his friends had the right to take liberty, and to use arms in defending the same. Being a devout Bible Christian, he sustained his views and shaped his plans in conformity to the Bible; and when setting them forth, he quoted freely from the Scripture to sustain his position. He realized and enforced the doctrine of destroying the tree that bringeth forth corrupt fruit. Slavery was to him the corrupt tree, and the duty of every Christian man was to strike down slavery, and to commit its fragments to the flames. He was listened to with profound attention, his views were adopted, and the men whose names form a part of the minutes of that in many respects extraordinary meeting, aided yet further in completing the work.

* * * *

Richard Realf, comment in James Redpath's Echoes of Harper's Ferry (1860)

On the night that he killed himself in 1878, the poet and abolitionist Richard Realf lashed out in verse at the "little voluble, chattering daws of men" who pecked at him "curiously." This final poem, his beautiful untitled swan song that provides an image of the poet through his own eyes, is also eerily (though probably not intentionally) appropriate as a comment on John Brown's death—and afterlife—in the "chattering daws of men." Also a "great soul killed by cruel wrong," hung after his disastrous raid with the word "Failure written on his brow," neither did John Brown wait "till / Freedom had become / The popular shibboleth of courtier's lips." Here are two verses from the untitled poem:

> De mortuis nil nisi bonum.
> [Say naught but good of the dead]. When
> For me this end has come and I am dead,

And the little voluble, chattering daws of men
  Peck at me curiously, let it then be said
By some one brave enough to speak the truth:
  Here lies a great soul killed by cruel wrong;
Down all the balmy days of his fresh youth
  To his bleak, desolate noon, with sword and song,
And speech that rushed up wildly from his heart,
  He wrought for liberty, till his own wound
(He had been stabbed), concealed with painful art,
  Through wasting years, mastered him and he swooned,
And sank there where you see him lying now,
With the word Failure written on his brow.

      . . .

So he died rich. And if his eyes were blurred
  With big films—silence! He is in his grave:
Greatly he suffered; greatly, too, he erred;
  Yet broke his heart in trying to be brave.
Nor did he wait till Freedom had become
  The popular shibboleth of courtier's lips;
He smote for her when God himself seemed dumb
  And all His arching skies were in eclipse.
He was a-weary, but he fought his fight,
  And stood for simple manhood; and was joyed
To see the august broadening of the light,
  And new Earths heaving heavenward from the void.
He loved his fellows, and their love was sweet;
Plant daisies at his head and at his feet.

Martin Eden, in Jack London's novel, considers this poem, and adds a line that resonates strongly with the writings of numerous men who used the metaphor of a meteor to refer to John Brown and his life (from Whitman and Melville to Thoreau and Reverend J. S. Martin): " ""The little chattering . . . daws of men," Richard Realf called them the night he died.' " 'Pecking at star-dust,'" Martin took up the strain warmly; " 'at the meteoric flight of the master-men."'"[1]

    The most interesting observations of Brown's "star-dust" and his "meteoric flight," didn't peck at his persona but marked out its largest features. They are extracted in this final section of the anthology. Realf himself was one of these. This short note, written for James Redpath's collection, Echoes of Harper's Ferry, *describes the worst of the "chattering daws of men" who pecked at Brown, in an interesting parallel complaint to that of his final poem: "Men have grown hoarse with calumniating his memory, who were never worthy to unloose the latchet of his shoes . . . men who cannot perform an act that is not stained with some deadly sin, have lifted up their hands in holy horror, and yelled out their execrable against his name."*

---

1. Jack London, *Martin Eden*, New York: Penguin, 1993 (first published 1909), p.343.

The note also offers a new perspective on Brown's motivations in fight-
ing for the abolition of slavery. Realf explains: "He believed that unless
the interference of some third party should anticipate and thus prevent
the interference of slaves themselves, these latter would, one day, over-
throw the institution by a bloody war of extermination against their mas-
ters; and it was to prevent havoc and carnage which, as he conceived,
threatened the South, that he entered upon his ill-fated movement."

Though largely forgotten today, in his own time Realf was well-known
in Europe and America, a celebrated poet and sculptor, and a close friend
of Lady Byron. He was born in Sussex, England, in 1834, and emigrated
to America in April 1855 where he worked as a missionary in the slums
of New York and started an abolitionist newspaper. In October 1856, he
moved to Kansas and fought with Brown in the border wars. He was
soon recognized as one of the best men on the free-state side and Brown
made him Secretary of State in his Provisional Government of 1858 (see
John Brown, Provisional Constitution and Ordinances for the People of
the United States, May 8, 1858). Though not at Harpers Ferry, Realf was
charged with treason in connection with the raid, and was released by
the United States Senate investigating committee after giving his testi-
mony. After the outbreak of war he joined the Union Army, and from
1865 worked as a journalist and a Republican speaker, also establish-
ing a school for freed slaves. In 1878 he died by his own hand at his
home in Oakland, California.

1860

They who assert that, in this enterprise, he was moved rather by hatred of
the slaveholder than affection for the slave, do his memory most foul wrong.
The love of his heart comprehended and comprehended both. He believed that
unless the interference of some third party should anticipate and thus prevent
the interference of slaves themselves, these latter would, one day, overthrow
the institution by a bloody war of extermination against their masters; and it
was to prevent havoc and carnage which, as he conceived, threatened the South,
that he entered upon his ill-fated movement. For, he argued, the same elements
of resistance to oppression which would result in all bloody excesses if not
wisely and properly directed, might be made subservient to the accomplishment of high purposes of humanity, if the governing intelligence was at their
side. Wherefore, in order to supply that intellectual sagacity which the slaves
lacked, and thus enable them to achieve their freedom, while restraining them
from the cruelties into which their instincts would hurry them, he gave himself to this enterprise. In regard to his personal character, I must, though I re-
side in the South, where I expect to live and die, be permitted to say that it
has been studiously and elaborately misrepresented. There never lived a man
whose desire to promote human welfare and human happiness was more in-
extinguishable. Men have grown hoarse with calumniating his memory, who
were never worthy to unloose the latchet of his shoes. Venal politicians, grown
sleek upon public plunder, and men who cannot perform an act that is not
stained with some deadly sin, have lifted up their hands in holy horror, and

yelled out their execrable execrations against his name. John Brown was no tongue-hero—no virtue-prattler. He was a reticent man; and when he did speak, the utterance was from his heart, and not his lungs. His faith was very simple. He desired society to be pure, free, unselfish—full of liberty and love. He believed it capable of such realization. The whole history of his life is that of an upward endeavor. "Liberty!" that was the key to his soul; the master-passion that controlled all his other ambitions—personal, social, or political. It swayed him like a frenzy.

* * * *

George B. Gill, letter to Richard Hinton, July 7, 1893

The emotionally complex letter reprinted here is from a onetime associate of Brown who discovered at the critical moment that he could only follow partway on Brown's single-minded quest. George B. Gill was the Secretary of the Treasury for the provisional government formed at John Brown's Constitutional Convention, in Chatham, Canada. He helped Brown liberate eleven Missouri slaves in 1858, then accompanied the group to Canada during the winter of 1858–1859. But, like several whom Brown approached about the Virginia mission, he refused to participate at Harpers Ferry. He wrote the following letter to Brown's biographer thirty-four years later, an "expression of truthfulness," perhaps designed in part as an explanation for his absence from the raid.

By his own sarcastic admission, Gill was "sadly deficient as a god or hero worshiper." His Brown is selfish, intolerant, egotistical, superstitious, and vindictive. Gill even exposes cracks in the Brown family unit, reporting complaints by Owen Brown about his father's "arbitrary" methods within the family. Perhaps hinting at the real source of his resentment, Gill complains: "I cannot now recall an instance in which he gave to another the unstinted and unqualified praise that you and I would give." Brown's "imperial egotism" and exacting standards seem to have rubbed the ambitious Gill the wrong way. The letter is an attempt to telescope Brown to an average size and portray him as neither hero nor villain, but instead, as Gill puts it, "very human."

July 7, 1893

My dear friend;

It seems that all great men have their foibles or what we in our difference from them call their weaknesses. In our intimacy we find the vulnerable points, hence "A man is never a hero to his valet." And I am about to give you an expression of truthfulness which I have never given to anyone yet.

The great father of his country was not personally a loveable man, but an aristocrat in all that the title can claim where it implies selfishness and intolerance. Men to make their marks in the world must have some leading characteristic, prominent either in its great strength or its great weakness. I admit that I am sadly deficient as a god or hero worshiper. I cannot avoid the feeling that men have their merits or demerits without any volition of their own. We may love one for his pretty attractiveness, and abhor another for his repulsiveness, yet neither the one or the other is responsible for these divergent ways. Egotism, love of approbation, love of adventure, love of command and many personal characteristics coupled with firmness, combativeness, destructiveness and sometimes vindictiveness may prompt us to act. These promptings whatever they may be come from a source which we did not originate and are as natural to our being as the flow of blood in our veins, hence we merit neither praise or blame for our acts, and the man who may do his fellows or the world the most good may be far from the goody goody kind but may be personally absolutely offensive.

My intimate acquaintance with Brown demonstrated to me that he was very human. The angel wings were so dim and shadowy as to be almost unseen, very superstitious, very selfish and very intolerant with great self esteem. His immense egotism coupled with love of approbation and his god idea begot in him a feeling that he was the Moses that was to lead the Exodus of the colored people from their southern taskmasters. Brooding on this, in time he believed that he was God's chosen instrument, and the only one, and that whatever methods he used, God would be his guard and shield, rendering the most illogical movements into a grand success. Other ways than his own, other men than himself were not awarded one iota of credit from him. When the colored people would designate him as the second Moses, which they frequently did, it would elate him through and through. He could not brook a rival. At first he was very fond of Montgomery, but when he found that Montgomery had thoughts of his own and could not be dictated to, why he loved him no longer. Montgomery Lane and all other leaders went down before his imperial self. He was intolerant in little things, and in little ways, for instance his drink was tea, others wanted coffee. He would wrangle and compel them to drink tea or nothing as he was cook and would not make coffee for them. I had it from Owen in a quiet way, and from other sources in quite a loud way, that in his family his methods were of the most arbitrary kind. The row that he raised in the Masonic fraternity was most probably a resultant of his imperial egotism. I have known Stevens to sometimes raise merry hell when the old man would get too dictatorial. He was iron and had neither sympathy or feeling for the timid and weak of will. Notwithstanding claims to the contrary, he was essentially vindictive in his nature. Just before we left Kansas during a trip that Brown and myself were some days away from the rest, the boys arrested a man (I think by the name of Jackson). Montgomery gave him a trial and he was released by general consent as not meriting punishment. When we returned Brown was furious because the man had not been shot. His Calvinism and general organism would have treated Servetus as Calvin did. I cannot now recall an instance in which he gave to another the unstinted and unqualified praise that you and I would give.

And yet this very concentration in self commanded the grand advance on American slavery. It bearded the lion in his den, the monster in his home and in the end vindicated an apparent absurd assault by accelerating the forces which in the end gave Success. I still feel that Brown "builded wiser than he knew." The dream which peopled the mountains with dusky freemen and created an army all his own, led as only a Moses could lead, sustained as only a God could sustain, ended only in a dreamless sleep yet the wave moved on upon whose bloody crest the slave rode to freedom.

It seems harsh and cruel in me to tell you of Brown's individuality as I have told you, yet it seemed to me that you, perhaps the last writer on the theme, should know all, whether it be of any use to you or not.

The men in the ranks are too often forgotten in the adulation we give the leaders. Brown's memory will never be as sacred a thing to me as the memory of some who fell with him, for there were some of these whose aspirations were only for others, whose dreams and hopes and loves never centered in self, and whose devotion to friends or cause led them to the deaths that only martyrs and heroes find.

You are the only one that I have ever mentioned these things to, and will be the last. You and I, almost the last links in the chain, and knowing human nature as we do, can never expect to clothe our heroes with the beauty and goodness of mythical angels. Yet henceforth as in the past I'll remember only his or their goodness. Your men will record their virtues. May the lines live when Thermopylaes' myth or Tells' romance will be covered by the dust of centuries, and the fable of the Moses of the Nile will have been forgotten. In all the years to come men will read the story of how these heroes gave their lives for the freedom of a people not their own, when they themselves were free. [. . .]

Yours as ever,
Geo[rge] B. Gill

* * * *

Gerrit Smith, A Ruinous Visit to Monkeyville, November 15, 1851

The philanthropist and abolitionist Gerrit Smith is one of the most compelling and under-researched characters in the John Brown story. Majestic in personal appearance, affable and gracious, Smith was a central figure in reform and a candidate for President in 1848, 1856, and 1860, also serving in Congress. In spite of this he was a private person, much less comfortable than Brown with the spotlight. He barely publicized his philanthropy, but over the course of his reform career spent eight million dollars on various causes, and contributed around a billion in today's currency. Between 1846 and 1850 he gave away two hundred thousand acres of land to poor blacks and whites, one of the largest acts of philanthropy in the world to date. A large portion of this land, 120,000 acres, was in the Adirondacks, and Smith gave it to three thousand New York blacks in 1846. He also sold Brown 244 acres on extended credit in return for the latter's promise to teach the African Americans in the Adirondacks everything he knew about settling and farming land. At the same time Smith built the Liberty Party into a nationally prominent organization, bought the freedom of dozens of slaves, and transformed his home town of Peterboro into one of the most abolitionist and interracial communities in the country.

Smith was a major conspirator in the Harpers Ferry attack, and the only conspirator who thought the raid wrong in retrospect. After Brown's sentencing he suffered an emotional collapse: feeling profound guilt and revulsion at the bloodshed for which he was partly responsible, he was delirious and unable to eat or sleep. On October 18 the New York Herald *provided detailed coverage of the raid, referring to the raiders as "emissaries of the peaceful Gerrit Smith," and to Smith as an "accessory before the fact." In an article of October 20, the paper named Smith as the man who had supplied "the sinews of war."*

On October 30 a reporter interviewed Smith and various Peterboro locals. The report that followed in the New York Herald, *dated October 31, offered this description: "He is a very different man today from what he was twelve months since. His calm, dignified, impressive bearing has given place to a hasty, nervous agitation, as though some great fear was constantly before his imagination. His eye is bloodshot and restless as that of a startled horse. He has lost flesh, and his face looks as red and as rough as though he had just returned from one of old Brown's Kansas's raids." When asked about the raid Smith apparently started "like a frightened deer." A landlord in a Peterboro tavern declared: "He would not be taken away at all, unless those arresting him had more guns than we can muster." The narrating journalist adds: "The men of Peterboro would never consent that Gerrit Smith should be taken to Virginia. They would resist the officers of the law, first, to the extent of their power."*

Though Governor Wise did send federal marshals to seek Smith's arrest, he refrained from indicting the philanthropist, apparently touched by the latter's collapse. Smith's family committed him to the New York State Asylum for the Insane at Utica, a story that was national news in the midst of Brown's trial. He was released in early 1860, and in a crisis of faith and identity pulled away from his friendships with blacks, even embracing a racist belief in innate black inferiority. Something in him had died.

That "something" had perhaps always been under threat from another, murkier part of himself. Probably shocked by the Pottawatomie massacre in 1856, Smith continued to support Brown publicly, but with growing reservations that he expressed privately in his personal writings and letters. As early as 1851 he responded by privately composing the piece that is printed here, transcribed from his notebooks for this anthology. It is Smith's only work of fiction, a short story entitled A Ruinous Visit to Monkeyville. *Written in November 1851 and published for the first time here, it is indicative of Smith's deep uneasiness with the violent antislavery methods increasingly discussed and favored by his friend John Brown. In 1835, Smith had argued against violence as a method, but in 1851 he assisted the violent removal of a fugitive slave from federal custody, and in October of that year, one month before writing the story, he had encouraged all free blacks to fight for their lives, with weapons or otherwise. He may have been troubled by this moral shift in himself, and the story perhaps helped him keep his worries in check, for the walls that hid his private self remained high until they—and he—collapsed in the wake of the Harpers Ferry raid.*

Smith was not a great intellectual, preferring to read newspapers and pamphlets rather than books, and it is clear from this story that he was

*a less talented writer than Brown. But the piece is valuable for its in-
sights into the psychological drama unfolding within Smith even at this
relatively early point. It is a parable of Smith's abolitionism and reveals
his fears about identifying with blacks and John Brown, his horror at the
thought that both might corrupt him, and his massive reservations about
an increasing involvement with violence.*

*The fictive John Brown in the story is a mélange of John Brown him-
self, Gerrit Smith, and Smith's son Greene. The fictional John Brown
meets the "rude, ignorant, low-bred boys" in Monkeyville, and acquires
their "strange and disgusting speech," which leads to bloodshed and
murder, amongst other sins: the real John Brown had settled among
blacks in North Elba and acquired the strange and disturbing speech of
violence. Timbucto, as Smith and Brown called the community at North
Elba, was Monkeyville in the story; the name of the town hints of the
common racist association in antebellum America of blacks with mon-
keys. Smith may, though, be integrating with that racist representation
the black self-identification with the rebellious trickster monkey, or "sig-
nifying monkey," a potent figure in black folklore. The fictive John Brown
learns to lie and steal, and the real John Brown learned rebellious trickster methods with which to defeat slavery. The story is also uncannily
prophetic. The fictional Brown figure goes to Monkeyville, picks up the
speech of the inhabitants, and nine years later commits murder. He then
pleads "not kilty" and accepts his death with alacrity. And the real John
Brown went to North Elba, got closer to black culture and consciousness, began to see the world from a black perspective, increasingly employed the speech of violence and insurrection, and around nine years
later committed murder at Harpers Ferry. He too pleaded "not guilty"
and accepted his death willingly.*

*The invocation at the end of the story is Smith's warning to himself
not to misuse his public voice in the service of John Brown's violent means.
He cautions himself that it would be better not to speak out against
slavery at all than to contaminate with violence his gifted abolitionist
voice: "[E]vil-speaking and evil-doing go together," he commented in his
1864 book,* Religion of Reason; *"profane, polluting, shameless words"
indicated a "bad character."*

*Finally, Smith stirred his son Greene Smith into the mix. Greene was
nine years old in 1851, a problem child at school in New Jersey, and
Smith wrote the story while visiting his son there. According to the headmaster, the boy was prone to telling tall tales—like the fictive nine-year-
old John Brown. He was also something of a clown, engaging in what
the headmaster called "monkeyishness," and "monkey talk," buffoonery
and a version of racist blackface minstrelsy. The Peterboro boys who had
apparently corrupted Smith's son became the Monkeyville boys who "pol-
luted" little John Brown, as Smith phrases it in the story. He was pro-
jecting onto Greene his fears about his own black identification, and onto
the central character in his story his anxieties about his son, combining
all this with a projection onto his real-life friend John Brown of his guilt*

*about using violence. Out of this brew came the nine-year-old figure in
the story.*

A Story. The Ruinous Visit to Monkeyville²
15 November 1851

Once there was a boy of the name of John Brown. He could hear but he
could not speak, although he had got to be nine years old. His family and
brothers and sisters were much [upset] that he could not speak. They all prayed
very earnestly that God would give him the faculty of speech. God heard their
prayers, and on a pleasant May morning, at the breakfast table, John, to the
surprise and joy of all around him, said: "Mother, I love you." The whole family burst into tears, and joined in prayer, and thanked God for having given
power to little John to speak.

John Brown pronounced correctly. His speech was deliberate and beautiful.
Weeks and months rolled on. The people came from all the neighborhood, and
some of them 8 or 10 miles, to witness the wonderful goodness of God to little John. This pleasant boy [gave wisely] in useful knowledge. Some said: "He
will make a great preacher." Others said: "He will make a great statesman."
And they said: "He will make a great lawyer."

Never was there a happier family than that of which John Brown was a
member. All that had been lacking to fill up the measure of their happiness
was that little John should be able to speak what he thought and what he felt;
and now, through the kindness of the Lord, this was no longer lacking.

But alas, much disappointment and especially sorrow visited this happy family. Half a dozen miles from the home of John Brown was the village of Monkeyville. There lived several of John's uncles and aunts; and among them his
aunt Lucy who begged, that John might be permitted to spend a few weeks
among his relatives in Monkeyville. His parents consented; and after many
kisses and tears, little John started for Monkeyville.

In Monkeyville was a set of rude, ignorant, low-bred boys. They had a dialect or language peculiar to themselves. For instance, these foolish, ill-man-
nered boys thought it very smart to say "datch" for "that," "nishe" for "nice";
and "granfader" for grandfather. Little John was suffered to run in the streets,
and to associate with these miserable boys. Such is the speedy and pernicious
effect of evil communications, that, in the course of two or three weeks, John
had caught the strange and disgusting speech of these Monkeyville boys. His
parents heard of it, and hurried with unhappy hearts to Monkeyville. As they
met their son, he said: "How [dutch] you do, Faider and Mudder?" His poor
parents burst into tears: and as they took him home, they wept all the way. On
reaching the house, he called his sisters "shisters," and his brothers, "brud-
ders."

Time passed on. Sometimes, John would try to [speak nice], as his parents
and his God would have him. But the force of his new habit was too strong
for him—and especially so because he had learned from the Monkeyville boys

---

2. Brackets designate illegible words or phrases. Words inside the brackets are best
guesses, based on context and decipherable letters.

to regard it as very smart and very cunning to talk in this disagreeable way. As was to be expected, his head and his heart began to sympathize with his crooked speech. His thoughts and his affections became crooked also. He misstated facts. He told untruths. He told scarcely anything correctly. He learned scarcely anything correctly. Before, his [dispositions] were yearning, loving, beautiful. Now, they were impaired, fearing, hateful. In short, in less than ten years from the time he visited Monkeyville, he was a ruined boy.

At the age of 12, John had become a great liar. At the age of 15 he was a notorious thief. At the age of 18, a man had been murdered for his money, and it was found that John was one of the two murderers. He continued his Monkeyville dialect to the last. In the court where he was tried, he said to the Grand Jury: "I am not kilty": and when, upon the gallows, he was told by the minister, that he had come to a bad end, he replied, "I hash come to the gallows at lasht."

A stone was put upon his grave, on which were inscribed these words:

> "Here lies the wicked boy,
> Whose lying and stealing and murdering,
> All began in his Monkeyville talk.
> May his fate be a warning
> to others —."

John's broken-hearted parents survived him but 6 months. From the time he became a liar until his death they could be heard [yearning] out night and day: "Oh, that our son had never gone to Monkeyville! Oh, that God had never given him a voice!"

John's parents died the same day, and were buried in the same grave. That grave was adjoining wicked John's. The coming of the day which followed the burial of John's parents, was mild and still, and it was bright with the shining of a full and cloudless morn. The eight surviving children went to the cemetery, and joining hands, formed a circle around the three graves. They all fell upon their knees, and lifting up their streaming eyes to Heaven, they all cried, that no Monkeyville talk would ever pollute their lives and send its perverting influence into their minds and hearts; and they all prayed, that if ever they should deliberately and perniciously so sin, God would take away their voices.

Fifty years now have gone by since these graves were wet with the tears of that morning. But in all those fifty years, not a single member, or descendant, of the Brown family, has ever been known to talk the Monkeyville talk.

Remember, Reader, is it not better never to have a voice, than to misuse it, as John Brown did. Remember, Reader, is it not better to have your voice taken away from you, than to have it left to you and so misused by you?

* * * *

Thomas Wentworth Higginson,
"A Visit to John Brown's Household," 1859

The Secret Six, John Brown's most trusted and generous supporters in the North, were scattered by the force of the Harpers Ferry raid. Gerrit Smith suffered a breakdown and spent several months in the New York state asylum at Utica. The Reverend Parker made himself as comfortable as possible in Rome, suffering as he was from terminal tuberculosis, and commented from afar on Brown's death: "The road to heaven is as short from the gallows as from the throne." Howe and Sterns fled to Canada and remained there until after Brown's execution, and Sanborn also headed for Canada, though was present in Concord in April 1860 when local townspeople thwarted an attempt by federal marshals to arrest him, their notorious neighbor. Only Thomas Wentworth Higginson, a member of one of the oldest and most distinguished families in New England and one conspirator who openly supported the raid, did not flee or collapse, instead chewing over a last-minute plan to save Brown by kidnapping Governor Wise. He gave this up, but continued to feel responsible for Brown, regretting that he hadn't "realized the need to protect John Brown from himself."

Though never called to testify before the Senate committee investigating the raid, Higginson, who had been a prominent abolitionist for several years, was quoted as saying that "the worst trait of the American race [is an] infernal colorphobia." He led a raid on the courthouse in Boston to free fugitive slave Anthony Burns in 1854, then aided the Kansas free state movement during 1856, also participating actively in the Underground Railroad. An out-and-out radical, he was committed to religious pluralism and Transcendentalism throughout his time in the Massachusetts Unitarian ministry, having given up his pastorate at Newburyport at the age of twenty-seven because he alienated his congregation with frequent antislavery sermons. He was a fervent campaigner for women's suffrage and the rights of women, calling this "the next great question" for America after the liberation of the slaves. During the Civil War he took on an appointment to command a regiment of freed blacks.

Higginson was a great admirer of Brown, though was perhaps not as thoroughly swept away by him as some others were. He visited Brown's homestead immediately after the Harpers Ferry raid and in December 1859 published this essay describing his visit in the Atlantic Monthly. *He was a prolific scholar and famously altered Emily Dickinson's words when publishing her poems, also causing controversy with his history of Nat Turner. This essay was one of five hundred that he wrote for various publications during his lifetime, and ranks with the best of these and his thirty books.*

Such articles as this helped along the preservation of Brown's farm and burial-site, dedicated in March 1896. The headstone and massive rock that overhangs Brown's grave, the latter with simple but deeply etched letters J. B., carved by Brown on his last visit to North Elba so that his family would know where to lay his body in death, attracted many visitors. But when Higginson visited in late 1859, the house, where Brown's family still lived, was a "home of sacred sorrow," as he puts it.

He unravels the Brown family "genealogy of sorrow." We are right inside the lives of those who received Brown's last letters. The surrounding land is impenetrable, the household's location remote and the buildings bleak. But Mary is stoic and loyal, the children are devoted and calm. Higginson is impressed by the "utter absence of the slightest vindictive spirit, even in words," and also dwells on the family's absolute disinterest in public judgment, present or future. Mary and her children are oblivious of William A. Phillips' "impartial posterity" and "ages yet [to] come," Richard Realf's "chattering daws of men," Frederick Douglass' "impartial justice," the "polishing wheels of after-coming centuries," and Wendell Phillips' "absolute History." Suddenly this seems a glorious oblivion. ³

1859

[. . .] There stands the little house, with no ornament nor relief about it— it needs none with the setting of mountain horizon. Yes, there is one decoration which at once takes the eye, and which, stern and misplaced as it would seem elsewhere, seems appropriate here. It is a strange thing to see any thing so old, where all the works of man are new! but it is an old, mossy, time-worn *tombstone*—not marking any grave, not set in the ground, but resting against the house as if its time were either past or not yet come. Both are true—it has a past duty and a future one. It bears the name of Captain John Brown, who died during the Revolution, eighty-three years ago; it was his tombstone brought hither by his grandson bearing the same name and title; the latter caused to be inscribed upon it, also, the name of his son Frederick, "murdered at Osawatomie for his adherence to the cause of freedom" (so reads the inscription); and he himself has said, for years, that no other tombstone should mark his grave.

. . . Do you ask why they live in such a bleak spot? With John Brown and his family there is a reason for everything, and it is always the same reason. Strike into their lives anywhere, and you find the same firm purpose at bottom, and to the widest questioning the same, prompt answer comes ringing back,—the very motto of the tombstone,—"For adherence to the cause of freedom." The same purpose, nay, the selfsame project that sent John Brown to Harper's Ferry sent him to the Adirondacks.

Twenty years ago John Brown made up his mind that there was an irrepressible ·conflict between freedom and slavery, and that in that conflict he must take his share. He saw at a glance, moreover, what the rest of us are only beginning to see, even now—that slavery must be met, first or last, on its own ground. The time has come to tell the whole truth now—that John Brown's whole Kansas life was the result of this self-imposed mission, not the cause of it. Let us do this man justice; he was not a vindictive guerrilla, nor a maddened Indian; nor was he of so shallow a nature that it took the death of a son to convince him that right was right, and wrong was wrong. He had long before made up his mind to sacrifice every son he ever had, if necessary, in fighting slavery. If it was John Brown against the world, no matter; for, as his friend Frederick Douglass had truly said, "In the right one is a majority." On this conviction, therefore, he deliberately determined, twenty years ago this sum-

---

3. See editors' notes to William A. Phillips, "Three Interviews with Old John Brown," December 1879 and to Richard Realf, comment in James Redpath's *Echoes of Harpers Ferry* (1860).

mer, that at some future period he would organize an armed party, go into a slave State, and liberate a large number of slaves. Soon after, surveying professionally in the mountains of Virginia, he chose the very ground for his purpose. Visiting Europe afterwards, he studied military strategy for this purpose, even making designs (which I have seen) for a new style of forest fortification, simple and ingenious, to be used by parties of fugitive slaves when brought to bay. He knew the ground, he knew his plans, he knew himself; but where should he find his men? He came to the Adirondacks to look for them.

Ten years ago, Gerrit Smith gave to a number of colored men tracts of ground in the Adirondack Mountains. The emigrants were grossly defrauded by a cheating surveyor, who, being in advance of his age, practically anticipated Judge Taney's opinion, that black men have no rights which white men are bound to respect. By his villainy the colony was almost ruined in advance; nor did it ever recover itself; though some of the best farms which I have seen in that region are still in the hands of colored men. John Brown heard of this; he himself was a surveyor, and he would have gone to the Adirondacks, or anywhere else, merely to right this wrong. But he had another object: he thought that among these men he should find coadjutors in his cherished plan. He was not wholly wrong, and he afterwards learned something more. Such men as he needed are not to be *found* ordinarily; they must be *reared*. John Brown did not merely look for men, therefore: he reared them in his sons. During long years of waiting and postponement, he found others; but his sons and their friends (the Thompsons) formed the nucleus of his force in all his enterprises. What services the females of his family may have rendered, it is not yet time to tell; but it is a satisfaction to think that he was repaid for his early friendship of these New York colored men, by some valuable aid from freed slaves and fugitive slaves at Harper's Ferry; especially from Dangerfield Newby, who, poor fellow! had a slave wife and nine slave children to fight for, all within thirty miles of that town.

To appreciate the character of the family, it is necessary to know these things; to understand that they have all been trained from childhood on this one principle, and for this one special project; taught to believe in it as they believed in their God or their father. It has given them a wider perspective than the Adirondacks. Five years before, when they first went to Kansas, the father and sons had a plan of going to Louisiana, trying this same project, and then retreating into Texas with the liberated slaves. Nurtured on it so long, for years of sacrificing to it all the other objects of life, the thought of its failure never crossed their minds; and it is an extraordinary fact that when the disastrous news first came to North Elba, the family utterly refused to believe it, and were saved from suffering by that incredulity till the arrival of the next weekly mail.

[. . .] Let me pause a moment, and enumerate the members of the family. John Brown was born in 1800 and his wife in 1816, though both might have been supposed older than the ages thus indicated. He has had in all twenty children—seven being the offspring of his first wife, thirteen of his second. Four of each race are living—eight in all. The elder division of the surviving family comprises John and Jason, both married, and living in Ohio; Owen, unmarried, who escaped from Harper's Ferry, and Ruth, the wife of Henry

Thompson, who lives on an adjoining farm at North Elba, an intelligent and noble woman. The younger division consists of Salmon, aged twenty-three, who resides with his young wife in his mother's house, and three unmarried daughters, Anne (sixteen), Sarah (thirteen), and Ellen (five). In the same house dwell also the widows of the two slain sons—young girls, aged but sixteen and twenty. The latter is the sister of Henry Thompson and of the two Thompsons who were killed at Harper's Ferry; they also lived in the same vicinity, and one of them also has left a widow. Thus complicated and intertangled is this genealogy of sorrow.

All these young men went deliberately from North Elba for no other purpose than to join in this enterprise. "They could not," they told their mother and their wives, "live for themselves alone;" and so they went. One young wife, less submissive than the others, prevailed on her husband to remain; and this is the only reason why Salmon Brown survives. Oliver Brown, the youngest son, only twenty, wrote back to his wife from Harper's Ferry in a sort of premonition of what was coming, "If I can do a single good action, my life will not have been all a failure."

[. . .] I thought that I had learned the lesson once for all in Kansas, which no one ever learns from books of history alone, of the readiness with which danger and death fit into the ordinary grooves of daily life, so that on a day of a battle, for instance, all may go on as usual; breakfast and dinner are provided, children cared for, and all external existence has the same smoothness that one observes at Niagara, just above the American Fall; but it impressed me anew on visiting this household at this time. Here was a family out of which four noble young men had, within a fortnight, been killed. I say nothing of a father under sentence of death and a brother fleeing for his life, but only speak of those killed. Now that the word *killed* is a word which one hardly cares to mention in a mourning household circle, even under all mitigating circumstances, when sad, unavailing kisses and tender funeral rites have softened the last memories; how much less here, then, where it suggested not merely wounds, and terror, and agony, but also coffinless graves in a hostile land, and the last ignominy of the dissecting-room.

Yet there was not one of that family who could not pronounce that awful word with perfect quietness; never of course, lightly, but always quietly. For instance, as I sat that evening, with the women busily sewing around me, preparing mother for her sudden departure with me on the morrow, some daguerreotypes were brought out to show me, and some one said, "This is Oliver, one of those who were killed at Harper's Ferry," I glanced up sidelong at the young, fair-haired girl who sat near me at the table—a wife of fifteen, a widow at sixteen; and this was her husband, and he was *killed*. As the words were spoken in her hearing not a muscle quivered, and her finger did not tremble as she drew the thread. For her life had become too real to leave room for wincing at mere words. She had lived through, beyond the word, to the sterner fact, and having confronted *that*, language was an empty shell. To the Browns killing means simply dying—nothing more; one gate into heaven, and that one a good deal frequented by their family: that is all.

[. . .] I was the first person who had penetrated their solitude from the outer world since the thunderbolt had fallen. Do not imagine that they asked, What is the world saying of us? Will justice be done to the memory of our martyrs? Will men build the tombs of the prophets? Will the great thinkers of the age affirm that our father "makes the gallows glorious like the cross?" Not at all; they asked but one question after I had told them how little hope there was of acquittal or rescue. "Does it seem as if freedom were to gain or lose by this?" That was all. Their mother spoke the spirit of them all to me, next day, when she said, "I have had thirteen children, and only four are left; but if I am to see the ruin of my house, I cannot but hope that Providence may bring out of it some benefit to the poor slaves."

No; this family work for a higher price than fame. You know it is said that in all Wellington's despatches you never meet with the word GLORY—it is always DUTY. In Napoleon's you never meet with the word DUTY—it is always GLORY. The race of John Brown is of the Wellington type. *Principle* is the word I brought away with me, as most familiar in their vocabulary. That is their standard of classification. A man may be brave, ardent, generous—no matter if he is not all this from principle, it is nothing. The daughters, who knew all the Harper's Ferry men, had no confidence in Cook, because "he was not a man of principle." They would trust Stevens around the world, because "he was a man of principle." "He tries his hardest to be good," said Annie Brown in her simple way, "of any man I ever saw."

[. . .] The children spoke of their father as a person of absolute rectitude, thoughtful kindness, unfailing foresight, and inexhaustible activity. On his flying visits to the farm, every moment was used; he was "up at three A.M., seeing to everything himself," providing for everything, and giving heed to the minutest point. It was evident that some of the older ones had stood a little in awe of him in their childish years. "We felt a little pleased sometimes, after all," said the son, "when father left the farm for a few days." "We girls *never* did," said the married daughter, reproachfully, the tears gushing to her eyes. "Well," said the brother, repenting, "we were always glad to see the old man come back again; for if we *did* get more holidays in his absence, we always missed him."

Those dramatic points of character in him, which will of course make him the favorite hero of all American romance hereafter, are nowhere appreciated more fully than in his own family. In the midst of all their sorrow, their strong and healthy hearts could enjoy the record of his conversations with the Virginians, and applaud the keen, wise, simple answers which I read to them, selecting here and there from the ample file of newspapers I carried with me. When, for instance, I read the inquiry, "Did you go out under the auspices of John Brown," three voices eagerly burst in with "That's true," and "That's so." And when it was related that the young Virginia volunteer taxed him with want of military foresight in bringing so small a party to conquer Virginia, and the veteran imperturbably informed the young man that probably their views on military matters would materially differ, there was a general delighted chorus of "That sounds just like father." And his sublimer expressions of faith and self-devotion produced no excitement or surprise among them, since they knew in advance all which we now know of him, and these things only elicited at times a half stifled sigh as they reflected that they might never hear that beloved voice again.

[. . .] I see, on looking back, how bare and inexpensive this hasty narrative is; but I could not bear to suffer such a privilege as this visit to pass away unrecorded. I spent but one night at the house, and drove away with Mrs. Brown, in the early frosty morning, from the breezy mountain home which her husband loved (as one of them told me) "because he seemed to think there was something romantic in that kind of scenery." There was, indeed, always a sort of thrill in John Brown's voice when he spoke of mountains. I shall never forget the quiet way in which he once told me "that God had established the Alleghany Mountains from the foundation of the world, that they might one day be a refuge for fugitive slaves." I did not then know that his own home was among the Adirondacks.

Just before we went, I remember I said something or other to Salmon Brown about the sacrifices of their family, and he looked up in a quiet, manly way, which I shall never forget, and said briefly, "I sometimes think that is what we came into the world for—to make sacrifices." And I know that the murmuring echo of those words went with me all that day as we came down from the mountains and out through the iron gorge, and it seemed to me that anyone must be very unworthy of the society which I had been permitted to enter who did not come forth from it a wiser and better man.

* * * *

William A. Phillips, "Three Interviews with Old John Brown," December 1879

Just six weeks after John Brown's death, some were already pondering what future ages would make of him. In his lecture in Kansas on January 20, 1860 William A. Phillips looked ahead to a time when "impartial posterity" would scrutinize Brown's words and actions and find them worthy of admiration: "Ages will yet come, not subject to such influence; they will read that a poor old man, with a handful of brave companions, threw themselves away in a protest against Slavery. They will read the old man's letters. They will ponder on his words. . . . The time is coming, when an impartial posterity will calmly review the career of John Brown... and looking from this generation to his sacrifice, will recognize in them the AGE and the MAN."He spoke of Brown's role in history: "the history of the ages was but the history of a few men. Each recorded age has its man. He is the lesson of its history. This age has had its man. . . . An iron man of the old Puritan stock emerges from the struggle between Freedom and Slavery in Kansas. . . . He lives today, my friends—and he will live forever. Like Enoch and Elijah he did not merely have to die. He sublimated, and gave all the life that was left in him to an immortal lesson."

A successful and highly-regarded correspondent for the New York Tribune and a congressman between 1873 and 1877, Phillips had experienced Brown up close and personal, and so his decision to make Brown a symbolic and representative man does not stem from an unfamiliarity with Brown as life-sized and individual. In fact his friendship with Brown had been extremely intimate, with tinges of that between Melville's Ishmael and Queequeg. Phillips's article, here, a collection of reminiscences

*about three occasions across several years on which he met and spoke
with Brown, is one of the best depictions we have of Brown's philosophical and idealistic nature.*

*Phillips was impressed by Brown's tenderness and poetry, and also by
his prophecy, for the "Old Man" warned, with chilling foresight, that
"the war is not over. It is a treacherous lull before the storm. We are on
the eve of one of the greatest wars in history." He saw in Brown "a theorist" and "a visionary," and listened with rapt attention as the man
whose singular and brilliant meteoric flight was to stun the nation told
him: "If one star is more brilliant than others, it is continually shooting
in some erratic way into space." A meteor of the war that he prophesied and worked towards, Brown's "erratic" but "brilliant" light sparkles
from the pages of Phillips's reminiscences.*[4]

Atlantic Monthly, December 1979

Three Interviews with Old John Brown

Upon the 2d of July, 1856, Captain John Brown called on me at the Eastern House, in Lawrence, Kansas. He had left his company, twenty-two men,
camped on the Wakerusa, a few miles from town.... During the day he stayed
with me in Lawrence I had my first good opportunity to judge the old man's
character. I had seen him in his camp, had seen him in the field, and he was
always an enigma, a strange compound of enthusiasm and cold, methodic sto-
lidity,—a volcano beneath a mountain of snow. He told me of his experiences
as a wool merchant and manufacturer in Ohio, and of his travels in Europe. I
soon discovered that his tastes ran in a military rather than a commercial channel. He had visited many of the fortifications in Europe, and criticised them
sharply, holding that the modern system of warfare did away with them, and
that a well armed, brave soldier was the best fortification. He criticised all the
arms then in use, and showed me a fine specimen of repeating-rifle which had
long-range sights, and, he said, would carry eight hundred yards; but, he added,
the way to fight was to press to close quarters. He had a couple of small pamphlets or circulars; one he had had printed on the armies and military systems
of Europe; the other was addressed to the soldiers of the armies of the United
States, and was an odd mixture of advice as to discipline and soldierly habits,
and wound up by advising them to desert whenever there was an attempt made
to use them against a free government and human liberty. He looked upon
passing political movements as mere preliminaries or adjuncts to more important events in the future. With him men were nothing, principles everything.

I had intended to drive from Lawrence to Topeka with a friend that day,
but he urged me to wait until evening and go with him, and I was so interested in him that I did so. We rode down Massachusetts Street, followed by
one of his men, a sort of orderly, if I may so designate him. We ascended
Mount Oread, and proceeded to the point where the state university now stands,
and there reined our horses and looked at the scene, while we waited for the
company, which was now slowly winding towards the base of the hill, where

---

4. "Meteor of the War" is taken from Melville's poem "The Portent"; see in this anthology: Herman Melville, "The Portent (1859)," 1866.

the old California road ascended it. It was a glorious landscape. Lawrence lay to the northeast, at our feet. Kaw River, like a sheet of silver, could be seen here and there through breaks in the forest. Away to our right was the Wakerusa, winding and twisting to meet it. A few miles distant rose the double-peaked Blue Mound. The streams and creeks were marked by feathery lines of trees, and away five or six miles before us, where the Kaw and Wakerusa met, there was an immense mass of timber veiling the meeting of the waters. The sun went down as we looked at it, and as I turned my eyes to his I saw he had drunk in the glorious beauty of the landscape.

"What a magnificent scene, captain!" I exclaimed.

"Yes," he said, in his slow, dry way; "a great country for a free State."

The company had climbed the hill, riding by twos, and we rode towards them. There was no recognition. We silently took our places at the head of the little column; he gave the command to march, and we rode up the California road. Darkness set in long before we reached "Coon Point." While on the march the captain was reticent, and apologized to me for being so on the ground of discipline. The road runs, or ran, some four miles to the south of Lecompton, the pro-slavery capital, and as we neared that region he carefully examined his men, and all appeared to be more vigilant. It was late when we reached Big Springs, and there we left the road, going in a southwesterly direction for a mile, when we halted on a hill, and the horses were stripped of their saddles and other articles, and picketed out to graze. The grass was wet with dew. The men ate of what provision they had with them, and I received a portion from the captain. I was not at all hungry, and if I had been I doubt if I could have eaten it. It was dry beef, which was not so bad; but the bread had been made from corn bruised between stones, and then rolled in balls and cooked in the coal and ashes of the camp fire. These ashes served for saleratus. Captain Brown observed that I nibbled it very gingerly, and said,—

"I am afraid you will be hardly able to eat a soldier's harsh fare."

"I must be frank enough to say that I have doubts on that subject myself," I responded.

We placed our two saddles together so that our heads lay only a few feet apart. He spread his blanket on the wet grass, and, when we lay together upon it, mine was spread over us. Previous to doing this he had stationed a couple of guards. It was past eleven o'clock, and we lay there until two in the morning, scarcely time enough for sleep; indeed, we slept none. He seemed to be as little disposed to sleep as I was, and we talked; or rather he did, for I said little more than enough to keep him going. I soon found that he was a very thorough astronomer and he enlightened me on a good many matters in the starry firmament above us. He pointed out the different constellations and their movements. "Now," he said, "it is midnight," and he pointed to the finger marks of his great clock in the sky.

In his ordinary moods the man seemed so rigid, stern, and unimpressible when I first knew him that I never thought a poetic and impulsive nature lay behind that cold exterior. The whispering of the wind on the prairie was full of voices to him, and the stars as they shone in the firmament of God seemed to inspire him. "How admirable is the symmetry of the heavens; how grand and beautiful. Everything moves in sublime harmony in the government of

God. Not so with us poor creatures. If one star is more brilliant than others, it is continually shooting in some erratic way into space."

He discussed and criticised both parties in Kansas. Of the pro-slavery men he spoke in bitterness. He said that slavery besotted everything, and made men more brutal and coarse. Nor did the free-state men escape his sharp censure. He said that we had many noble and true men, but that we had too many broken-down politicians from the older States. These men, he said, would rather pass resolutions than act, and they criticised all who did real work. A professional politician, he went on, you never could trust; for even if he had convictions, he was always ready to sacrifice his principles for his advantage.

One of the most interesting things in his conversation that night, and one that marked him as a theorist (and perhaps to some extent he might be styled a visionary), was his treatment of our forms of social and political life. He thought society ought to be organized on a less selfish basis; for while material interests gained something by the deification of pure selfishness, men and women lost much by it. He said that all great reforms, like the Christian religion, were based on broad, generous, self-sacrificing principles. He condemned the sale of land as a chattel, and thought that there was an infinite number of wrongs to right before society would be what it should be, but that in our country slavery was the "sum of all villainies," and its abolition the first essential work. If the American people did not take courage and end it speedily, human freedom and republican liberty would soon be empty names in these United States.

He ran on during these midnight hours in a conversation I can never forget. The dew lay cold and heavy on the grass and on the blanket above us. The stars grew sharper and clearer, and seemed to be looking down like watchers on that sleeping camp. My companion paused for a short time, and I thought he was going to sleep, when he said,—

"It is nearly two o'clock, and as it must be nine or ten miles to Topeka it is time we were marching," and he again drew my attention to his index marks in the sky. He rose and called his men. They responded with more alacrity than I expected. In less than ten minutes the company had saddled, packed, and mounted, and was again on the march.

He declined following the road any farther, but insisted on taking a straight course over the country, guided by the stars. It was in vain that I expostulated with him, and told him that three or four creeks were in the way, and that the country was rough and broken, and that it would be difficult to find our way in the dark. He was determined not to go by Tecumseh. We had, it is needless to say, a rough time of it that night, and day broke while we were floundering in the thickets of a creek bottom some miles from Topeka. As soon as daylight came and we could see our way, we rode more rapidly; but the sun had risen above the horizon before we rode down the slopes to Thung-gah-nung. Across the creek and nearly two miles to the right we saw the tents, and in the morning stillness could hear the bugles blow in Colonel Sumner's camp.

John Brown would not go into Topeka, but halted in the timber of the creek, sending one of his men with me, who was to be a messenger to bring him word when his company was needed. He had his horse picketed, and walked down by the side of my horse to the place where I crossed the creek. He sent messages to one or two of the gentlemen in town, and, as he wrung my hand at parting, urged that we should have the legislature meet, and resist all who should interfere with it, and fight, if necessary, even the United States troops.

The second interview occurred, I think, in February, 1857. It was a cold, snowy Sabbath morning, about eight o'clock, when a son of Mr. Whitman rode into Lawrence, and told me the "old man" was at his father's, and wanted to see me. He brought a led horse for me. It was a cold and disagreeable ride that morning, but as I had not heard of the whereabouts of Captain Brown for some time, I concluded to go.

When I reached Mr. Whitman's I found him, and with him Kagi and Whipple, or Stevens, and Cook; in fact, most of the men who were with him at Harper's Ferry. He took me to an apartment where we could be alone, and then he first inquired as to the condition of the free-state cause. He was very apprehensive that many of the free-state leaders would jeopardize the principles of the party in order to get power. He said whenever the free-state party gave itself over to selfish interests, its virtue and usefulness ended, and for good results it was far more desirable that it should be kept on the strain and suffer than make selfish compromises with the enemy. He asked earnestly many questions about the free-state leaders. One very good man he criticised for several things he had done, and in response to my assurances about him he used one of his striking comparisons. He took out a large pocket compass, and unscrewing its brass lid laid it down on the table before me, and pointing at the needle fixed his eyes on me, while he said:—

"You see that needle; it wobbles about and is mighty unsteady, but *it wants to point to the north.* Is he like that needle?"

He told me that some friends in the East had raised for him and placed in his hands a very large sum of money, in all nearly five thousand dollars. He had picked his company, and would like a few more, if he could get the right kind of men. He had spent some time in Iowa and some on the Kansas border. He was drilling and educating his company, and training them to hardship and to be perfectly faithful and reliable. He desired, he said, to get my advice as to the best way of using his force and resources, so as to advance the great interests of freedom and humanity.

Long before that time I had understood John Brown well enough to know that there was little probability about our agreeing on that subject, or of his being governed by the advice of anybody. He urged me so strenuously, however, that for a short time I actually permitted myself to suppose that he might really take advice. I had just previously discovered the site and location for a town, where the city of Salina now stands, and as it was then fifty miles beyond the settlement I told him I would give him any interest I then had in the place, and advised him to go there with his company. Each of them, I said, could take claims on the rich farming lands adjacent; they could be the pioneer builders of the town, could invest their funds in a stock of goods and a mill, and drill, if he thought it best, an hour each morning, and maintain in everything perfect discipline, and be ready for any emergency.

Before I had concluded my rather practical and conservative advice, I could perceive that it did not at all harmonize with the views and purposes of Captain Brown, and I suspected that a location one hundred and eighty miles from the Missouri border was in his opinion rather remote from the scene of operations. He suggested that it was only fair, as Missouri had undertaken to make a slave State of Kansas and failed, that Kansas should make a free State of Missouri, and proceeded at length to show, in the most logical manner, that it was not for the interests of Kansas to have a powerful slave State so close to it, and that the process of putting an end to slavery there was exceedingly simple. He said that he intended to spend some time near Tabor, Iowa where he expected to be joined by others, who would need discipline and organization; and that he expected also to visit Canada, with the view of studying personally its suitability for receiving, and protecting negro emigration. And so we parted on that occasion.

[. . .] The most important interview, the one that has peculiar historical significance was the last I ever had with him. It occurred during the same year of the Harper's Ferry affair, although several months before. He had been absent from Kansas for some time. Now we could hear of him in New England, now in Canada, now in Ohio or Pennsylvania. I had lost track of him, when one day Kagi came to my house in Lawrence, and told me that the old man had arrived and was at the Whitney House, and wished to see me. At first I refused to go, and sent him word by Kagi that as he never took my advice I did not see any use in giving him any. Kagi soon returned, and said that the old man must see me; he was going away, and might never see me again.

I found him in a small room at the Whitney House, then one of the Lawrence hotels, down towards the river. He had changed a little. There was in the expression of his face something, even more dignified than usual; his eye was brighter, and the absorbing and consuming thoughts that were within him seemed to be growing out all over him. He evinced his customary caution by telling Kagi to go out and close the door, and watch on the outside, for fear that some one should come to listen. Then he began.

He sketched the history of American slavery from its beginnings in the colonies, and referred to the States that were able to shake it off. He recalled many circumstances that I had forgotten, or had never heard of. He said the founders of the republic were all opposed to slavery, and that the whole spirit and genius of the American constitution antagonized it, and contemplated its early overthrow. He said this remained the dominant sentiment for the first quarter of a century of the republic. Afterwards slavery became more profitable, and as it did the desire grew to extend and increase it. The condition of the enslaved negroes steadily became worse, and the despotic necessities of a more cruel system constantly pressed on the degraded slaves. Rights they at first possessed were taken from them. The little of domestic happiness and independence that had been left them was taken away. The slave-trade being ended, it was profitable to breed negroes for sale. Gradually the pecuniary interests that rested on slavery seized the power of the government. Public opinion opposed to slavery was placed under ban. The politicians of the South became slavery propagandists, and the politicians of the North trimmers. When the religious and moral sentiment of the country indicated a desire to check this alarming growth, a threat of secession was uttered, and appeals were made not to risk the perpetuation of this glorious republic by fanatical antislavery-ism. Then began an era of political compromises, and men full of professions of love of country were willing, for peace, to sacrifice everything for which the republic was founded.

"And now," he went on, "we have reached a point where nothing but war can settle the question. Had they succeeded in Kansas, they would have gained a power that would have given them permanently the upper hand, and it would have been the death-knell of republicanism in America. They are checked, but not beaten. They never intend to relinquish the machinery of this government into the hands of the opponents of slavery. It has taken them more than half a century to get it, and they know its significance too well to give it up. If the republican party elects its president next year, there will be war. The moment they are unable to control they will go out, and as a rival nation along-side they will get the countenance and aid of the European nations, until American republicanism and freedom are overthrown."

I have endeavored to quote him, but it is quite impossible to quote such a conversation accurately. I well remember all its vital essentials and its outlines. He had been more observant than he had credit for being. The whole powers of his mind (and they were great) had been given to one subject. He told me that a war was at that very moment contemplated in the cabinet of President Buchanan; that for years the army had been carefully arranged, as far as it could be, on a basis of Southern power; that arms and the best of the troops were being concentrated, so as to be under control of its interests if there was danger of having to surrender the government; that the secretary of the navy was then sending our vessels away on long cruises, so that they would not be available, and that the treasury would be beggared before it got into Northern hands.

All this has a strangely prophetic look to me now; then it simply appeared incredible, or the dream and vagary of a man who had allowed one idea to carry him away. I told him he surely was mistaken, and had confounded every-day occurrences with treacherous designs.

"No," he said, and I remember this part distinctly,—"no, the war is not over. It is a treacherous lull before the storm. We are on the eve of one of the greatest wars in history, and I fear slavery will triumph, and there will be an end of all aspirations for human freedom. For my part, I drew my sword in Kansas when they attacked us, and I will never sheathe it until this war is over. Our best people do not understand the danger. They are besotted. They have compromised so long that they think principles of right and wrong have no more any power on this earth."

My impression then was that it was his purpose to carry on incursions on the borders of the free and slave States, and I said to him,—

"Let us suppose that all you say is true. If we keep companies on the one side, they will keep them on the other. Trouble will multiply; there will be collision, which will produce the very state of affairs you deprecate. That would lead to war, and to some extent we should be responsible for it. Better trust events. If there is virtue enough in this people to deserve a free government, they will maintain it."

"You forget the fearful wrongs that are carried on in the name of government and law."

"I do not forget them,—I regret them."

"I regret and will remedy them with all the power that God has given me."

He then went on to tell me of Spartacus and his servile war, and was evidently familiar with every step in the career of the great gladiator. I reminded him that Spartacus and Roman slaves were warlike people in the countries from which they were taken, and were trained to arms in the arena, in which they slew or were slain, and that the movement was crushed when the Roman legions were concentrated against it. The negroes were a peaceful, domestic, inoffensive race. In all their sufferings they seemed to be incapable of resentment or reprisal.

"You have not studied them right," he said, "and you have not studied them long enough. Human nature is the same everywhere." He then went on in a very elaborate way to explain the mistakes of Spartacus, and tried to show me how he could easily have overthrown the Roman empire. The pith of it was that the leader of that servile insurrection, instead of wasting his time in Italy until his enemies could swoop on him, should have struck at Rome; or, if not strong enough for that, he should have escaped to the wild northern provinces, and there have organized an army to overthrow Rome.

I told him that I feared he would lead the young men with him into some desperate enterprise, where they would be imprisoned and disgraced.

He rose. "Well," he said, "I thought I could get you to understand this. I do not wonder at it. The world is very pleasant to you; but when your household gods are broken, as mine have been, you will see all this more clearly."

I rose, somewhat offended, and said, "Captain, if you thought this, why did you send for me?" and walked to the door.

He followed me, and laid his hand on my shoulder, and when I turned to him he took both my hands in his. I could see that tears stood on his hard, bronzed cheeks. "No," he said, "we must not part thus. I wanted to see you and tell you how it appeared to me. With the help of God, I will do what I believe to be best." He held my hands firmly in his stern, hard hands, leaned forward and kissed me on the cheek, and I never saw him again.

* * * *

Frederick Douglass, "Old Brown In Rochester," Frederick Douglass' Paper, April 15, 1859; Letter to the Rochester Democrat, October 31, 1859; "Capt. John Brown Not Insane," Douglass' Monthly, November 1859; "John Brown: An Address at the Fourteenth Anniversary of Storer College," May 30, 1881

From their first meeting in 1847 until his own death in 1885, Frederick Douglass saw John Brown from differing perspectives. Sometimes frustrated by Brown's ideas, and willing to admit that discussions with his friend "began to be something of a bore," at other moments he knew himself to be absolutely in Brown's "stately shadow" and saw that Brown's zeal was greater than his, a "burning sun to my taper light," as he puts it in his 1881 lecture at Storer College, continuing: "mine was bounded by time, his stretched away to the boundless shores of eternity. I could live for the slave, but he could die for him."

Most often Douglass was keen to express admiration for Brown. His first impression of Brown, recalled in The Life and Times of Frederick Douglass, *was of a singularly alive human being, and accordingly he describes Brown as a "mountain pine" and a "race horse," with eyes of "light and fire", "one of the most marked characters, and greatest heroes known to American fame." In the years that followed Douglass remarked that Brown was the only white man he had ever met who was without racism, and in 1855 he called Brown an "active and self-sacrificing abolitionist." In 1858, he invited Brown into his home in Rochester, later telling a crowd in Edinburgh, after the formal segment of his lecture there in January 1860, of his observations during those seven weeks. He had encountered "what indeed he had amply shown at his last moments,—an honest, truthful, earnest, God-fearing man,—a man who felt conscious of having discharged his duty towards his God and his duty towards his fellow-men."*

Brown was just as impressed by Douglass's character and conduct, a keen devourer of anything he said or wrote and an early advocate of his newspaper, the North Star *(titled* Frederick Douglass' Paper *after 1851). Born a slave in 1818, Douglass had made a famous escape in 1838, and became the most famous and respected black leader in the country, heavily involved in the Underground Railroad, and opposed to African colonization schemes. Brown desperately wanted to recruit him. But the pair continued in their own spheres until Brown's death, mutually appreciative but never quite cohorts, mainly because of Douglass's ambivalence about Brown's course. The intricacies of his personality, and his sense of gray areas where Brown seemed to see only black and white, meant Douglass's praise of Brown was occasionally a veiled criticism. His lecture at Harpers Ferry in 1882 suggests some limitation to Brown's vision: "He saw the evil through no mist, haze or cloud, but in a broad light of infinite brightness, which left no line of its ten thousand horrors, out of sight." The first source, here, which pours shame on the townspeople of his hometown that did not turn out to receive and hear John Brown, is also complicated: Douglass's indignation at the Rochester locals' "indifference," and his warning that "this time is coming when we shall be quite ashamed of the reception given to John Brown," are perhaps also directed at his own hesitant heart.*

He gave a far from warm reception to Brown's plea four months later that he join the band of raiders in their expedition to Harpers Ferry, a scheme he could see only as a "trap of steel, and ourselves in the wrong side of it," as he explained in his Storer College address of 1881 (printed here). The plea came during a carefully arranged meeting in August 1859, in an unused quarry pit in Chambersburg, Pennsylvania. Brown outlined his plans and urged Douglass to join the group already installed at the Kennedy Farm. He entreated: "I will defend you with my life. I want you for a special purpose. When I strike, the bees will begin to swarm, and I shall want you to help me hive them." Douglass refused, to the bitter disappointment of Brown, and rose to leave, but his companion, a young black by the name of Shields Green, recently escaped from slavery, hung back. Douglass asked, "Shields, are you coming?" "No," came the reply, "I b'lieve I'll go wid de ole man." Brown left the "council of war," as Douglass called it later, and returned to Virginia with Green but without Douglass, feeling that his friend had faltered at the worst possible moment. Douglass's self-confessed attempt, in his lecture at Storer College, to "pay a just debt long due", was perhaps made with this painful meeting looming large in his memory.

And yet Douglass's attitude towards militant abolitionism had gone through a profound transformation since 1847, in part as a result of his contact with Brown, taking him a lot further along the road to Harpers Ferry than might have been expected. From the man who, as he recounted in The Life and Times of Frederick Douglass, had suggested in 1847 that they might "convert the slaveholders" instead of trying to free the slaves by force (at which Brown "became much excited, and said that could never be, 'he knew their proud hearts and that they would never be induced to give up their slaves, until they felt a big stick about their heads'"), Douglass became an advocate for the merits of violent action, saying in his Storer Address of 1881: "The irrepressible conflict was one of words, votes and compromises. When John Brown stretched forth his arm the sky was cleared." Brown's response was no longer simplistic, but instead refreshingly decisive. The gray areas and alternate routes— "words, votes and compromises"—had eventually revealed themselves as dead ends.

* * * *

"Old Brown In Rochester," Frederick Douglass' Paper, April 15, 1859

We have had a hero among us, and we wish to make a note of the fact for *future* reference. "Old Brown," of Kansas memory, has been here. He was received at the City Hall on Saturday evening by an audience exceedingly and discreditably small, considering the Republican professions of our citizens, and the character and history of the brave old man, to whose courage and skill, more than to those of any other man in Kansas, the freedom of that Territory is now indebted. It is hard to account for the indifference of Republicans to the claims of John Brown, on any grounds which do not imply an impeachment of their sincerity and honesty. Have they been sincere in what they have said of their love of freedom? Have they really desired to head off, hem in, and dam up the desolating tide of slavery? If so, does it not seem that one who has suffered, and periled everything in accomplishing these very ends, has some claims upon their grateful respect and esteem? Where were they on Saturday night? Why were they not present to grasp the hand that disarmed the Border Ruffian, Henry Clay Pate, and captured his company of Missouri invaders? The hand that cut up General Read's army of four hundred ruffians, who were running roughshod over the trembling Free State settlements in Kansas in 1856? The hand that made it possible for Free State men to remain in that Territory at all; we say, why were they not in favour of freedom in Kansas?

Had John Brown been a man of words, rather than deeds, had he been noted for opposing slavery with his breath, rather than with blows, some apology might be made for the indifference with which he has been received in this city. It might be said that we have enough of that sort of courage among us for all the homage and admiration we have to lavish upon courage of that quality. Had he come to us from Washington, where he has spoken eloquently for free Kansas, instead of from the dangers and hardships of border life, where he had acted his part bravely, his reception here would have been cordial, and perhaps enthusiastic. Only give us a sham instead of a real man and Rochester is not behind the chief cities of the Republic. Even our newly appointed Republic Janitor of the City Hall ran off with the key of the bell of the City Hall, and refused to ring it on the occasion! Shame upon his little soul, and upon all the little souls who sustained him in his conduct!

John Brown does not only need the sympathy such souls can give. Though he comes here from a three years' campaign in the cause of justice and liberty, and stripped of all earthly possessions, he has with him that which is more precious than silver or gold, or the hollow hearted approbation of the crowd. The consciousness of having honestly and fearsomely performed his duty, in a crisis which demanded the courage and skill of a hero, is his. A man who will forsake home, family, ease, and security, and in the cause of liberty go forth to spill his blood, if need be, is a man who can look down upon a large part of this world as ours. This time is coming when we shall be quite ashamed of the reception given to John Brown, for the country has not reached such an absolute security from the aggressions of slavery as to make it safe and wise to discharge a man so noble, and a soldier so brave . . .

* * * *

Letter to the Rochester Democrat, *October 31, 1859*

Canada West, Monday, Oct. 31, 1859

I notice that the telegram makes Mr. Cook (one of the unfortunate insurgents at Harpers Ferry, and now a prisoner in the hands of the thing calling itself the Government of Virginia, but which is but an organized conspiracy by one party of the people against the other and weaker) denounce me as a coward—and so assert that I promised to be present in person at the Harper Ferry insurrection. This is certainly a very grave impeachment, whether viewed in its bearings upon friends or upon foes, and you will not think it strange that I should take a somewhat serious notice of it. Having no acquaintance whatever with Mr. Cook, and never having exchanged a word with him about the Harpers Ferry insurrection, I am disposed to doubt that he could have used the language concerning me which the wires attributed to him. The lightning, when speaking for itself, is among the most direct, reliable and truthful of things; but when speaking for the terror-stricken slave-holders at Harpers Ferry it has been made the swiftest of liars. Under their nimble and trembling fingers it magnified seventeen men into seven hundred—and has since filled the columns of New York Herald for days with interminable contradictions. But assuming that it has told the truth as to the sayings of Mr. Cook in this instance, I have this answer to make to my accuser: Mr. Cook may be perfectly right in denouncing me as a coward. I have not one word to say in defense or vindication of my character for courage. I have always been more distinguished for running than fighting—and tried by the Harpers Ferry insurrection test, I am most miserably deficient in courage—even more so than Cook, when he deserted his brave old Captain and fled to the mountains. To this extent Mr. Cook is entirely right, and will meet no contradiction from me or from anybody else. But wholly, grievously and most unaccountably wrong is Mr. Cook, when he asserts that I promised to be present in person at the Harpers Ferry insurrection. Of whatever other imprudence and indiscretion I may have been guilty, I have never made a promise so rash and wild as this. The taking of Harpers Ferry was a measure never encouraged by my word or by my vote, at any time or place. My wisdom, or my cowardice, has not only kept me from Harpers Ferry, but has equally kept me from making any promise to go there. I desire to be quite emphatic here—for of all guilty men he is the guiltiest who lures his fellow men to an undertaking of this sort, under promise of assistance, which he afterwards fails to render, I therefore declare that there is no man living, and no man dead, who, if living, could truthfully say that I ever promised him or anybody else, either conditionally or otherwise, that I would be present in person at the Harpers Ferry insurrection. My field of labor for the abolition of Slavery has not extended to an attack upon the United States Arsenal. In the teeth of the documents already published, and of those which may hereafter be published, I affirm that no man connected with that insurrection, from its noble and heroic leader down, can connect my name with a single broken promise of any sort whatever. So much I may deem it proper to say negatively.

The time for a full statement of what I know, and of all I know, of this desperate but sublimely disinterested effort to emancipate the slaves of Maryland and Virginia from their cruel task-masters has not yet come, and may never come. In the denial which I have now made my motive is more a respectful consideration for the opinions of the slave's friends than from my fear of being made an accomplice in the general *conspiracy* against Slavery. I am ever ready to write, speak, publish, organize, combine, and even to conspire against Slavery, when there is a reasonable hope of success. Men who live by robbing their fellow-men of their labor and liberty, have forfeited their right to know anything of the thoughts, feelings, or purposes of those whom they rob and plunder. They have, by the single act of slave-holding, voluntarily placed themselves beyond the laws of justice and honor, and have become only fitted for companionship with thieves and pirates—the common enemies of God and of all mankind. While it should be considered right to protect one's self against thieves, burglars, robbers, and assassins, and to slay a wild beast in the act of devouring his human prey, it can never be wrong for the imbruted and whip-scarred slaves, or their friends, to hunt, harass, and even strike down the traffickers in human flesh. If anybody is disposed to think less of me on account of this sentiment, or because I may have had a knowledge of what was about to occur, and did not assume the base and detestable character of an informer, he is a man whose good or bad opinion of me may be equally repugnant and despicable. Entertaining this sentiment, I may be asked why I did not join John Brown—the noble old hero whose one right hand has shaken the foundation of the American Union, and whose ghost will haunt the bed-chambers of all the born and unborn slaveholders of Virginia through all their generations, filling them with alarm and consternation! My answer to this has already been given, at least impliedly given. "The tools to those who can use them." Let every man work for the abolition of Slavery in his own way. I would help all and hinder none. My position in regard to the Harpers Ferry insurrection may be easily inferred from these remarks, and I shall be glad if those papers which have spoken of me in connection with it, would find room for this statement . . .

* * * *

"Capt. John Brown Not Insane," Douglass' Monthly, November 1859

One of the most painful incidents connected with the name of this old hero, is the attempt to prove him insane. Many journals have contributed to this effort from a friendly desire to shield the prisoner from Virginia's cowardly vengeance. This is a mistaken friendship, which seeks to rob him of his true character and dim the glory of his deeds, in order to save his life. Was there the faintest hope of securing his release by this means, we would choke down our indignation and be silent. But a Virginia court would hang a crazy man without a moment's hesitation, if his insanity took the form of hatred of oppression; and this plea only blasts the reputation of this glorious martyr of liberty, without the faintest hope of improving his chance of escape.

It is an appalling fact in the history of the American people, that they have so far forgotten their own heroic age, as readily to accept the charge of insanity against a man who has imitated the heroes of Lexington, Concord, and Bunker Hill.

It is an effeminate and cowardly age, which calls a man a lunatic because he rises to such self-forgetful heroism, as to count his own life as worth nothing in comparison with the freedom of millions of his fellows. Such an age would have sent Gideon to a mad-house, and put Leonidas in a straight-jacket. Such a people would have treated the defenders of Thermopylae as demented, and shut up Caius Marcus in bedlam. Such a marrowless population as ours has become under the debaucheries of Slavery, would have struck the patriot's crown from the brow of Wallace, and recommended blisters and bleeding to the heroic Tell. Wallace was often and again desperately forgetful of his own life in defense of Scotland's freedom, as was Brown in striking for the American slave; and Tell's defiance of the Austrian tyrant, was as far above the appreciation of cowardly selfishness as was Brown's defiance of the Virginia pirates. Was Arnold Winkelried insane when he rushed to his death upon an army of spears, crying "make way for Liberty!" Are heroism and insanity synonyms in our American dictionary? Heaven help us! When our loftiest types of patriotism, our sublimest historical ideals of philanthropy, come to be treated as evidence of moonstruck madness. Posterity will owe everlasting thanks to John Brown for lifting up once more to the gaze of nation grown fat and flabby on the garbage of lust and oppression, a true standard of heroic philanthropy, and each coming generation will pay its installment of the debt. No wonder that the aiders and abettors of the huge, overshadowing and many-armed tyranny, which he grappled with in its own infernal den, should call him a mad man; but for those who profess a regard for him, and for human freedom, to join in the cruel slander, "is the unkindest cut of all."

Nor is it necessary to attribute Brown's deeds to the spirit of vengeance, invoked by the murder of his brave boys. That the barbarous cruelty from which he has suffered had its effect on intensifying his hatred of slavery, is doubtless true. But his own statement, that he had been contemplating a bold strike for the freedom of the slaves for ten years, proves that he had resolved upon his present course long before he, or his sons, ever set foot in Kansas. His entire procedure in this matter disproves the charge that he was prompted by an impulse of mad revenge, and shows that he was moved by the highest principles of philanthropy. His carefulness of the lives of unarmed persons—his humane and courteous treatment of his prisoners—his cool self-possession all through his trial—and especially his calm, dignified speech on receiving his sentence, all conspire to show that he was neither insane or actuated by vengeful passion; and we hope that the country has heard the last of John Brown's madness. The explanation of his conduct is perfectly natural and simple on its face. He believes the Declaration of Independence to be true, and the Bible to be a guide to human conduct, and acting upon the doctrines of both, he threw himself against the serried ranks of American oppression, and translated into heroic deeds the love of liberty and hatred of tyrants, with which he was inspired by both these forces acting upon his philanthropic and heroic soul. This age is too gross and sensual to appreciate his deeds, and so calls him mad; but the future will write his epitaph upon the hearts of a people freed from slavery, because he struck the first effectual blow.

Not only is it true that Brown's whole movement proves him perfectly sane and free from merely revengeful passion, but he has struck the bottom line of the philosophy which underlies the abolition movement. He has attacked slavery with the weapons precisely adapted to bring it to the death. Moral considerations have long since been exhausted upon slaveholders. It is in vain to reason with them. One may as well hunt bears with ethics and political economy for weapons, as to seek to "pluck the spoiled out of the hand of the oppressor" by the mere force of moral law. Slavery is a system of brute force. It shields itself behind *might,* rather than right. It must be met with its own weapons. Capt. Brown has initiated a new mode of carrying out the crusade of freedom, and his blow has sent dread and terror throughout the entire ranks of the piratical army of slavery. His daring deeds may cost him his life, but priceless as is the value of that life, the blow he has struck, will, in the end, prove to be worth its mighty cost. Like Samson, he has laid his hands upon the pillars of this great national temple of cruelty and blood, and when he falls, that temple will speedily crumble to its final doom, burying its denizens in its ruins.

* * * *

"John Brown: An Address at the Fourteenth Anniversary of Storer College," May 30, 1881

Not to fan the flame of sectional animosity now happily in the process of rapid and I hope permanent extinction; not to revive and keep alive a sense of shame and remorse for a great national crime, which has brought its own punishment, in loss of treasure, tears and blood; not to recount the long list of wrongs, inflicted on my race during more than two hundred years of merciless bondage; nor yet to draw, from the labyrinths of far-off centuries, incidents and achievements wherewith to rouse your passions, and enkindle your enthusiasm, but to pay a just debt long due, to vindicate in some degree a great historical character, of our own time and country, one with whom I was myself well acquainted, and whose friendship and confidence it was my good fortune to share, and to give you such recollections, impressions and facts, as I can, of a grand, brave and good old man, and especially to promote a better understanding of the raid upon Harper's Ferry of which he was the chief, is the object of this address. [. . .]

What ground there was for *this* distinguished consideration shall duly appear in the natural course of this lecture. I wish however to say just here that there was no foundation whatever for the charge that I in any wise urged or instigated John Brown to his dangerous work. I rejoice that *it* is my good fortune to have seen, not only the end of slavery, but to see the day when the whole truth can be told about this matter without prejudice to either the living or the dead. I shall however allow myself little prominence in these disclosures. Your interests, like mine, are in the all-commanding figure of the story, and to him I consecrate the hour. His zeal in the cause of my race was far greater than mine—it was as the burning sun to my taper light—mine was bounded by time, his stretched away to the boundless shores of eternity. I could live for the slave, but he could die for him. The crown of martyrdom is high, far beyond the reach of ordinary mortals, and yet happily no special greatness or superior moral excellence *is* necessary to discern and in some measure appreciate a truly great soul. Cold, calculating and unspiritual as most of us are, we are not wholly insensible to real greatness; and when we are brought in contact with a man of commanding mold, towering high and alone above the millions, free from all conventional fetters, true to *his* own moral convictions, a "law unto himself," ready to suffer misconstruction, ignoring torture and death for what he believes to be right, we are compelled to do him homage.

In the stately shadow, in the sublime presence of such a soul I find myself standing to-night; and how to do it reverence, how to do it justice, how to honor the dead with due regard to the living, has been a matter of most anxious solicitude. Much has been said of John Brown, much that is wise and beautiful, but in looking over what may be called the John Brown literature, I have been little assisted with material, and even less encouraged with any hope of success in treating the subject. Scholarship, genius and devotion have hastened with poetry and eloquence, story and song to this simple altar of human virtue, and have retired dissatisfied and distressed with the thinness and poverty of their offerings, as I shall with mine.

The difficulty in doing justice to the life and character of such a man is not altogether due to the quality of the zeal, or of the ability brought to the work, nor yet to any imperfections in the qualities of the man himself; the state of the moral atmosphere about us has much to do with it. The fault is not in our eyes, nor yet in the object, if under a murky sky we fail to discover the object. Wonderfully tenacious is the taint of a great wrong. The evil, as well as "the good that men do, lives after them." Slavery is indeed gone; but its long, black shadow yet falls broad and large over the face of the whole country. It is the old truth oft repeated, and never more fitly than now, "a prophet is without honor in his own country and among his own people." Though more than twenty years have rolled between us and the Harper's Ferry raid, though since then the armies of the nation have found it necessary to do on a large scale what John Brown attempted to do on a small one, and the great captain who fought his way through slavery has filled with honor the Presidential chair, we yet stand too near the days of slavery, and the life and times of John Brown, to see clearly the true martyr and hero that he was and rightly to estimate the value of the man and his works. Like the great and good of all ages, the men born in advance of their times, the men whose bleeding footprints attest the immense cost of reform, and show us the long and dreary spaces, between the luminous points in the progress of mankind, this our noblest American hero must wait the polishing wheels of after-coming centuries to make his glory more manifest, and his worth more generally acknowledged. Such instances are abundant and familiar. If we go back four and twenty centuries, to the stately city of Athens, and search among her architectural splendor and her miracles of art for the Socrates of today, and as he stands in history, we shall find ourselves perplexed and disappointed. In Jerusalem Jesus himself was only the "carpenter's son," a young man wonderfully destitute of worldly prudence, a pestilent fellow, "inexcusably and perpetually interfering in the world's business," "upsetting the tables of the money-changers," preaching sedition, opposing the good old religion, "making himself greater than Abraham," and at the same time "keeping company" with very low people; but behold the change! He was a great miracle-worker, in his day, but time has worked for him a greater miracle than all his miracles, for now his name stands for all that is desirable in government, noble in life, orderly and beautiful in society. That which time has done for other great men of his class, that will time certainly do for John Brown. The brightest gems shine at first with subdued light, and the strongest characters are subject to the same limitations. Under the influence of adverse education and hereditary bias, few things are more difficult than to render impartial justice. Men hold up their hands to Heaven, and swear they will do justice, but what are oaths against prejudice and against inclination! In the face of high-sounding professions and affirmations we know well how hard it is for a Turk to do justice to a Christian, or for a Christian to do justice to a Jew. How hard for an Englishman to do justice to an Irishman, for an Irishman to do justice to an Englishman, harder still for an American tainted by slavery to do justice to the Negro or the Negro's friends. "John Brown," said the late Wm. H. Seward, "was justly hanged." "John Brown," said the late John A. Andrew, "was right." It is easy to perceive the sources of these two opposite judgments: the one was the verdict of slaveholding and panic-stricken Virginia, the other was the verdict of the best heart and brain of free old Massachusetts. One was the heated judgment of the passing and passionate hour, and the other was the calm, clear, unimpeachable judgment of the broad, illimitable future.

[. . .]Another feature of the times, worthy of notice, was the effect of this blow upon the country at large. At the first moment we were stunned and bewildered. Slavery had so benumbed the moral sense of the nation, that it never suspected the possibility of an explosion like this, and it was difficult for Captain Brown to get himself taken for what he really was. Few could seem to comprehend that freedom to the slaves was his only object. If you will go back with me to that time you will find that the most curious and contradictory versions of the affair were industriously circulated, and those which were the least rational and true seemed to command the readiest belief. In the view of some, it assumed tremendous proportions. To such it was nothing less than a wide-sweeping rebellion to overthrow the existing government, and construct another upon its ruins, with Brown for its President and Commander-in-Chief; the proof of this was found in the old man's carpet-bag in the shape of a constitution for a new Republic, an instrument which in reality had been executed to govern the conduct of his men in the mountains. Smaller and meaner natures saw in it nothing higher than a purpose to plunder. To them John Brown and his men were a gang of desperate robbers, who had learned by some means that government had sent a large sum of money to Harper's Ferry to payoff the workmen in its employ there, and they had gone thence to fill their pockets from this money. The fact is, that outside of a few friends, scattered in different parts of the country, and the slave-holders of Virginia, few persons understood the significance of the hour. That a man might do something very audacious and desperate for money, power or fame, was to the general apprehension quite possible; but, in face of plainly written law, in face of constitutional guarantees protecting each State against domestic violence, in face of a nation of forty million of people, that nineteen men could invade a great State to liberate a despised and hated race, was to the average intellect and conscience, too monstrous for belief. In this respect the vision of Virginia was clearer than that of the nation. Conscious of her guilt and therefore full of suspicion, sleeping on pistols for pillows, startled at every unusual sound, constantly fearing and expecting a repetition of the Nat Turner insurrection, she at once understood the meaning, if not the magnitude of the affair. It was this understanding which caused her to raise the lusty and imploring cry to the Federal government for help, and it was not till he who struck the blow had fully explained his motives and object, that the incredulous nation in any wise comprehended the true spirit of the raid, or of its commander. Fortunate for his memory, fortunate for the brave men associated with him, fortunate for the truth of history, John Brown survived the saber gashes, bayonet wounds and bullet holes, and was able, though covered with blood, to tell his own story and make his own defense. Had he with all his men, as might have been the case, gone down in the shock of battle, the world would have had no true basis for its judgment, and one of the most heroic efforts ever witnessed in behalf of liberty would have been confounded with base and selfish purposes. [. . .]

To the outward eye of men, John Brown was a criminal, but to their inward eye he was a just man and true. His deeds might be disowned, but the spirit which made those deeds possible was worthy [of] highest honor. It has been often asked, why did not Virginia spare the life of this man? why did she not avail herself of this grand opportunity to add to her other glory that of a lofty magnanimity? Had they spared the good old man's life, had they said to him, "You see we have you in our power, and could easily take your life, but we have no desire to hurt you in any way; you have committed a terrible crime against society; you have invaded us at midnight and attacked a sleeping community, but we recognize you as a fanatic, and in some sense instigated by others; and on this ground and others, We release you. Go about your business, and tell those who sent you that we can afford to be magnanimous to our enemies." I say, had Virginia held some such language as this to John Brown, she would have inflicted a heavy blow on the whole Northern abolition movement, one which only the omnipotence of truth and the force of truth could have overcome. I have no doubt Gov. Wise would have done so gladly, but, alas, he was the executive of a State which thought she could not afford such magnanimity. She had that within her bosom which could more safely tolerate the presence of a criminal than a saint, a highway robber than a moral hero. All her hills and valleys were studded with material for a disastrous Conflagration, and one spark of the dauntless spirit of Brown might set the whole State in flames. A sense of this appalling liability put an end to every noble consideration. His death was a foregone conclusion, and his trial was simply one of form. [. . .]

Slavery was the idol of Virginia, and pardon and life to Brown meant condemnation and death to slavery. He had practically illustrated a truth stranger than fiction, a truth higher than Virginia had ever known, a truth more noble and beautiful than Jefferson ever wrote. He had evinced a conception of the sacredness and value of liberty which transcended in sublimity that of her own Patrick Henry and made even his fire-flashing sentiment of "Liberty or Death" seem dark and tame and selfish. Henry loved liberty for himself, but this man loved liberty for all men, and for those most despised and scorned, as well as for those most esteemed and honored. Just here was the true glory of John Brown's mission. It was not for his own freedom that he was thus ready to lay down his life, for with Paul he could say, "I was born free." No chain had bound his ankle, no yoke had galled his neck. History has no better illustration of pure, disinterested benevolence. It was not Caucasian for Caucasian— white man for white man; not rich man for rich man, but Caucasian for Ethiopian, white man for black man, rich man for poor man, the man admitted and respected, for the man despised and rejected. "I want you to understand, gentlemen," he said to his persecutors, "that I respect the rights of the poorest and weakest of the colored people, oppressed by the slave system, as I do those of the most wealthy and powerful." In this we have the key to the whole life and career of the man. Than in this sentiment humanity has nothing more touching, reason nothing more noble, imagination nothing more sublime; and if we could reduce all the religions of the world to one essence we could find in it nothing more divine. It is much to be regretted that some great artist, in sympathy with the spirit of the occasion, had not been present when these and similar words were spoken. The situation was thrilling. An old man in the center of an excited and angry crowd, far away from home, in an enemy's country, with no friend near, overpowered, defeated, wounded, bleeding, covered with reproaches, his brave companions nearly all dead, his two faithful sons stark and cold by his side—reading his death-warrant in his fast, oozing blood and increasing weakness as in the faces of all around him, yet calm, collected, brave, with a heart for any fate, using his supposed dying moments to explain his course and vindicate his cause: such a subject would have been at once an inspiration and a power for one of the grandest historical pictures ever painted.

With John Brown, as with every other man fit to die for a cause, the hour of his physical weakness was the hour of his moral strength, the hour of his defeat was the hour of his triumph, the moment of his capture was the crowning victory of his life. With the Alleghany mountains for his pulpit, the country for his church and the whole civilized world for his audience, he was a thousand times more effective as a preacher than as a warrior, and the consciousness of this fact was the secret of his amazing complacency. Mighty with the sword of steel, he was mightier with the sword of the truth, and with this sword he literally swept the horizon. [. . .]

Nothing should postpone further what was to him a divine command, the performance of which seemed to him his only apology for existence. He often said to me, though life was sweet to him, he would willingly lay it down for the freedom of my people; and on one occasion he added, that he had already lived about as long as most men, since he had slept less, and if he should now lay down his life the loss would not be great, for in fact he knew no better use for it. During his last visit to us in Rochester there appeared in the newspapers a touching story connected with the horrors of the Sepoy War in British India. A Scotch missionary and his family were in the hands of the enemy, and were to be massacred the next morning. During the night, when they had given up every hope of rescue, suddenly the wife insisted that relief would come. Placing her ear close to the ground she declared she heard the Slogan, the Scotch war song. For long hours in the night no member of the family could hear the advancing music but herself. "Dinna ye hear it? Dinna ye hear it?" she would say, but they could not hear it. As the morning slowly dawned a Scotch regiment was found encamped indeed about them, and they were saved from the threatened slaughter. This circumstance, coming at such a time, gave Capt Brown a new word of cheer. He would come to the table in the morning his countenance fairly illuminated, saying that he had heard the Slogan, and he would add, "Dinna ye hear it? *Dinna* ye hear it?" Alas! like the Scotch missionary I was obliged to say "No." Two weeks prior to the meditated attack, Capt Brown summoned me to meet him in an old stone quarry on the Conecochequi river, near the town of Chambersburgh, Penn. His arms and ammunition were stored in that town and were to be moved on to Harper's Ferry. In company with Shields Green I obeyed the summons, and prompt to the hour we met the dear old man, with Kagi, his secretary, at the appointed place. Our meeting was in some sense a council of war. We spent the Saturday and succeeding Sunday in conference on the question, whether the desperate step should then be taken, or the old plan as already described should be carried out. He was for boldly striking Harper's Ferry at once and running the risk of getting into the mountains afterwards. I was for avoiding Harper's Ferry altogether. Shields Green and Mr. Kagi remained silent listeners throughout. It is needless to repeat here what was said, after what has happened. Suffice it, that after all I could say, I saw that my old friend had resolved on his course and that it was idle to parley. I told him finally that it was impossible for me to join him. I could see Harper's Ferry only as a trap of steel, and ourselves in the wrong side of it. He regretted my decision and we parted.

[. . .] But the question is, Did John Brown fail? He certainly did fail to get out of Harper's Ferry before being beaten down by United States soldiers; he did fail to save his own life, and to lead a liberating army into the mountains of Virginia. But he did not go to Harper's Ferry to save his life. The true question is, Did John Brown draw his sword against slavery and thereby lose his life in vain? and to this I answer ten thousand times, No! No man fails, or can fail who so grandly gives himself and all he has to a righteous cause. No man, who in his hour of extremest need, when on his way to meet an ignominious death, could so forget himself as to stop and kiss a little child, one of the hated race for whom he was about to die, could by any possibility fail. Did John Brown fail? Ask Henry A. Wise in whose house less than two years after, a school for the emancipated slaves was taught. Did John Brown fail? Ask James M. Mason, the author of the inhuman fugitive slave bill, who was cooped up in Fort Warren, as a traitor less than two years from the time that he stood over the prostrate body of John Brown. Did John Brown fail? Ask Clement L. Vallandigham, one other of the inquisitorial party; for he too went down in the tremendous whirlpool created by the powerful hand of this bold invader. If John Brown did not end the war that ended slavery, he did at least begin the war that ended slavery. If we look over the dates, places and men, for which this honor is claimed, we shall find that not Carolina, but Virginia—not Fort Sumter, but Harper's Ferry and the arsenal—not Col. Anderson, but John Brown, began the war that ended American slavery and made this a free Republic. Until this blow was struck, the prospect for freedom was dim, shadowy and uncertain. The irrepressible conflict was one of words, votes and compromises. When John Brown stretched forth his arm the sky was cleared. The time for compromises was gone, the armed hosts of freedom stood face to face over the chasm of a broken Union, and the clash of arms was at hand. The South staked all upon getting possession of the Federal Government, and failing to do that, drew the sword of rebellion and thus made her own, and not Brown's, the lost cause of the century.

* * * *

Wendell Phillips, eulogy for John Brown, December 8, 1859

Governor Wise had originally planned to hand Brown's body over to surgeons for use in dissection, so that Brown would be without a grave on the day of resurrection. But he changed his mind. John Brown's funeral began at one o'clock on December 8, 1859, at his home in North Elba. Present were family friends and neighbors, Salmon Brown, Henry Thompson, and the Brown women, numbering several widows. The service opened with one of Brown's favorite hymns, "Blow Ye the Trumpet, Blow." Then the minister prayed that God would "cause the oppressed to go free" and "hasten on the day when no more wrong or injustice shall be done in the earth," and several family friends spoke words of comfort to Mary Brown and her children.

Wendell Phillips's eulogy, the centerpiece of the service, came next. Phillips was one of the foremost anti-slavery leaders of his day, and a masterful orator; his eulogy is triumphal yet unassuming. Another hymn followed, during which the casket was brought outside and opened so that all present could say their goodbyes. Brown apparently had a healthy flush and a lifelike complexion, to the perplexity of whoever expected a pallid death mask. As the casket was lowered into the grave by the huge stone near the house, the minister read from 2 Timothy 4:7–8. "I have fought a good fight. I have finished my course. I have kept the faith..." This minister, a Reverend Young, would be hauled over the coals for his part in Brown's funeral. Though the abolition community in Burlington supported his involvement, many in his congregation snubbed him and sought other places to worship. Eventually Young could stand the enmity no longer, and in 1863 left his Burlington ministry for one in Massachusetts.

By contrast Wendell Phillips continued to employ his silver tongue unimpaired and with enthusiasm after the funeral, on behalf of his "hero-saint," as he put it on December 8. A week later he gave a virtuoso speech in New York City. This speech, during which he called himself the "mouthpiece of John Brown," concluded: "when he ascended to Heaven, in the eye of God that sees the oak in the acorn, in the eye of history that is looking back at that moment, he ascended with three hundred thousand fetters of Virginia's slaves in his right hand." Brown's lean and work-worn body was finally at rest, beneath the aged headstone that he had lain himself a few years previous. But "in the eye of history" he was on the ascendant, and, as soldiers sang repeatedly during the years of war that followed, his soul was marching on. Brown was "not buried but planted" on December 8, 1859, as George William Curtis commented, continuing, in this lecture in Worcester four days after Brown's funeral: "He will spring up a hundred-fold." As Theodore Parker observed in a letter of November 1858, in a phrase analogous to both Curtis's planting metaphor and Phillips's image of "the oak in the acorn," Brown was "an oak at last."

December 8, 1859

How feeble words seem here! How can I hope to utter what your hearts are full of? I fear to disturb the harmony which his life breathes round this home. One and another of you, his neighbors, say, "I have known him five years," "I have known him ten years." It seems to me as if we had none of us known him. How our admiring, loving wonder has grown, day by day, as he has unfolded trait after trait of earnest, brave, tender, Christian life! We see him walking with radiant, serene face to the scaffold, and think what an iron heart, what devoted faith! We take up his letters, beginning "My dear wife and children, everyone,"—see him stoop on his way to the scaffold and kiss that negro child,—and this iron heart seems all tenderness. Marvellous old man! We have hardly said it when the loved forms of his sons, in the bloom of young devotion, encircle him, and we remember he is not alone, only the majestic center of a group. Your neighbor farmer went, surrounded by his household, to tell the slaves there were still hearts and right arms ready and nerved for their service. From this roof four, from a neighboring roof two, to make up that score of heroes. How resolute each looked into the face of Virginia, how loyally each stood at his forlorn post, meeting death cheerfully, till that master-voice said, "It is enough." And these weeping children and widow seem so lifted up and consecrated by long, single-hearted devotion to his great purpose, that we dare, even at this moment, to remind them how blessed they are in the privilege of thinking that in the last throbs of those brave young hearts, which lie buried on the banks of the Shenandoah, thoughts of them mingled with love to God and hope for the slave.

He has abolished slavery in Virginia. You may say this is too much. Our neighbors are the last men we know. The hours that pass us are the ones we appreciate the least. Men walked Boston streets, when night fell on Bunker's Hill, and pitied Warren, saying, "Foolish man! Thrown away his life! Why didn't he measure his means better?" Now we see him standing colossal on that blood-stained sod, and severing that day the tie which bound Boston to Great Britain. That night George III ceased to rule in New England. History will date Virginia Emancipation from Harper's Ferry. True, the slave is still there. So, when the tempest uproots a pine on your hills, it looks green for months, a year or two. Still, it is timber, not a tree. John Brown has loosened the roots of the slave system; it only breathes,—it does not live,—hereafter.

Men say, "How coolly brave!" But matchless courage seems the least of his merits. How gentleness graced it! When the frightened town wished to bear off the body of the Mayor, a man said, "I will go, Miss Fowke, under their rifles, if you will stand between them and me." He knew he could trust their gentle respect for woman. He was right. He went in the thick of the fight and bore off the body in safety. That same girl flung herself between Virginia rifles and your brave young Thompson. They had no pity. The pitiless bullet reached him, spite of woman's prayers, though the fight had long been over. How God has blessed him! How truly he may say, "I have fought a good fight, I have finished my course." Truly he has finished, done his work. God granted him the privilege to look on his work accomplished. He said, "I will show the South that twenty men can take possession of a town, hold it twenty-four hours, and carry away all the slaves who wish to escape." Did he not do it? On Monday night he stood master of Harper's Ferry,—could have left unchecked with a score or a hundred slaves. The wide sympathy and secret approval are shown by the eager, quivering lips of lovers of slavery, asking, "O why did he not take his victory and go away?" Who checked him at last? Not startled Virginia. Her he had conquered. The Union crushed, seemed to crush him. In reality God said, "That work is done; you have proved that a Slave State is only fear in the mask of despotism; come up higher, and baptize by your martyrdom a million hearts into holier life." Surely such a life is no failure. How vast the change in men's hearts! Insurrection was a harsh, horrid word to millions a month ago. John Brown went a whole generation beyond it, claiming the right for white men to help the slave to freedom by arms. And now men run up and down, not disputing his principle, but trying to frame excuses for Virginia's hanging of so pure, honest, high-hearted, and heroic a man. Virginia stands at the bar of the civilized world on trial. Round her victim crowd the apostles and martyrs, all the brave, high souls who have said, "God is God," and trodden wicked laws under their feet. As I stood looking at his grandfather's gravestone, brought here from Connecticut, telling, as it does, of his death in the Revolution, I thought I could hear our hero-saint saying, "My fathers gave their swords to the oppressor,—the slave still sinks before the pledged force of this nation. I give my sword to the slave my fathers forgot."

If any swords ever reflected the smile of Heaven, surely it was those drawn at Harper's Ferry. If our God is ever the Lord of Hosts, making one man chase a thousand, surely that little band might claim him for their captain. Harper's Ferry was no single hour, standing alone, taken out from a common life, it was the flowering out of fifty years of single-hearted devotion. He must have lived wholly for one great idea, when these who owe their being to him, and these whom love has joined to the circle, group so harmoniously around him, each accepting serenely his and her part.

I feel honored to stand under such a roof. Hereafter you will tell children standing at your knees, "I saw John Brown buried, I sat under his roof." Thank God for such a master. Could we have asked a nobler representative of the Christian North putting her foot on the accursed system of slavery? As time passes, and these hours float back into history, men will see against the clear December sky that gallows, and round it thousands of armed men guarding Virginia from her slaves. On the other side, the serene brow of that calm old man, as he stoops to kiss the child of a forlorn race. Thank God for our emblem. May he soon bring Virginia to blot out hers in repentant shame, and cover that hateful gallows and soldiery with thousands of broken fetters.

What lesson shall those lips teach us? Before that still, calm brow let us take a new baptism. How can we stand here without a fresh and utter consecration? These tears! how shall we dare even to offer consolation? Only lips fresh from such a vow have the right to mingle their words with your tears. We envy you your nearer place to these martyred children of God. I do not believe slavery will go down in blood. Ours is the age of thought. Hearts are stronger than swords. That last fortnight! How sublime its lesson! the Christian one of conscience,—of truth. Virginia is weak, because each man's heart said amen to John Brown. His words, they are stronger even than his rifles. These crushed a State. Those have changed the thoughts of millions, and will yet crush slavery. Men said, "Would he had died in arms!" God ordered better, and granted to him and the slave those noble prison hours, that single hour of death; granted him a higher than the soldier's place, that of teacher; the echoes of his rifles have died away in the hills, a million hearts guard his words. God bless this root, make it bless us. We dare not say bless you, children of this home! you stand nearer to one whose lips God touched, and we rather bend for your blessing. God make us all worthier of him whose dust we lay among these hills he loved. Here he girded himself and went forth to battle. Fuller success than his heart ever dreamed God granted him. He sleeps in the blessings of the crushed and the poor, and men believe more firmly in virtue, now that such a man has lived. Standing here, let us thank God for a firmer faith and fuller hope.

* * * *

Reverend J. S. Martin, speech on December 2, 1859
African American communities across the United States prepared carefully for Brown's execution on December 2, and the date swiftly became known as "Martyr's Day." On November 29 the black congregation at the Wylie Street A.M.E. Church, in Pittsburgh, met and resolved: "We, the colored people of Pittsburgh . . . acknowledge in the person of John

Brown a hero, patriot, and Christian—a hero because he was fearless to defend the poor; a patriot because he loves his countrymen; and a Christian because he loves his neighbor as himself, and remembered those in bonds as bound with them." They declared that "in the event of the execution of John Brown upon the 2d of December, the anniversary of that day be hereafter perpetually observed among us as a day of humiliation and prayer." African Americans held similar meetings elsewhere, and the gathering in Detroit resolved: "That we hold the name of Old Capt. John Brown in the most sacred remembrance, now the first disinterested martyr for our liberty . . . Therefore will we ever vindicate his character through all coming time, as our temporal redeemer whose name shall never die . . . therefore are we now loudly called upon to arouse to our own interest, and to concentrate our efforts in keeping the Old Brown liberty-ball in motion."

And so, on the eve that followed John Brown's execution, African Americans contemplated the meaning of the day that was drawing to a close. Businesses closed early, men and women wore black armbands and collected money for Brown's widow. The Pittsburgh congregation came together to begin a time "of humiliation and prayer," as their document called for, and their leader, the Reverend J. S. Martin, gave a thrilling sermon, printed here. It is bursting with spectacular conceits. Martin uses an extended metaphor of disease and surgery and returns repeatedly to farming and planting imagery. Also highly dramatic is his comparison of Brown to John the Baptist. But perhaps the best part of Martin's speech is when he turns to the metaphor that is used most often to describe Brown—that of a meteor. Like Whitman, Melville, Thoreau, and others, Martin sees star-dust in Brown's flight across the national sky.

Martin and his Pittsburgh congregation, and the eloquent community of Detroit, intended that blacks "ever vindicate [Brown's] character through all coming time, as our temporal redeemer whose name shall never die," so the Detroit resolutions declared. African Americans have been the only group in America consistently to esteem Brown. The years have since seen W. E. B. Du Bois's famous biography of Brown, which finds the martyr's message ever relevant to the situation of black Americans. Countee Cullen's famous poem of 1942, "A Negro Mother's Lullaby," published in Opportunity, declares: "Though some may be bonded, you shall be free, / Thanks to a man, Osawatamie Brown." In an article for the Chicago Defender in 1959 Langston Hughes reconfirmed: "John Brown's name is one of the great martyr names of all history and the men who fought with him rank high on the scrolls of freedom. . . . This month marks one hundred years since John Brown struck his blow for freedom. . . . I hope that a great many Afro-Americans will attend this commemoration [at Harpers Ferry]. Those of us who cannot attend will remember with reverence this white man, John Brown, who laid down his life that his brothers might be free."[5] Though the tides of historical

---

5. Langston Hughes, *Chicago Defender*, October 17, 1959.

judgment continually shifted, African Americans claimed Brown as a martyr, a hero and a brother in 1859 and 1959—and declare him so today.

Friday evening, December 2, 1859, Pittsburgh

Mr. President, Ladies and Gentlemen, Today, a solemn question has been asked this nation. The Pilate of Providence has asked America—"Whom will you that I deliver unto you—the Barabbas of Slavery, or the John Brown of Freedom?" And, intimidated by the false majesty of despotic enactments, which have usurped the place of Christianity, corrupted a false policy, and stung to frenzy by the insinuations of our political high priests, we have cried out, as a nation, "Release unto us the Barabbas of slavery, and destroy John Brown." And, true to this horrible, this atrocious request, John Brown has been offered up. Thank God, he said, "I am ready to be offered up."

Men say that his life was "a failure." I remember the story of one of the world's moral heroes, whose life was just such a "failure." I remember one who, having retired to the deserts of Judea, to wring from the hard, stony life of those deserts the qualifications, and with all this purity, was brought into a corrupt and voluptuous court. I remember, too, that in that court, notwithstanding he was its favorite, notwithstanding the corruption and luxury of the times, he preserved himself the same stern man, and said to the King, "It is not lawful for you to live with your brother Phillip's wife." These were the stern words of John the Baptist and John Brown, for John Brown, like John the Baptist, retired into the hard and stony desert of Kansas, and there, by the weapons of heroism, by the principles of freedom, and the undaunted courage of a man, wrung from the bloody soil the highest encomiums of Freedom and the most base acknowledgements of slavery, that the one was right and the other wrong. (Applause.) I know that John Brown, in thus rebuking our public, in thus facing the monarch, has had to bear just what John the Baptist bore. His head today, by Virginia, that guilty maid of a more guilty mother, the American Government, (cheers, mingled with a few hisses, which were at once drowned in an outburst of vehement applause)—has been cut off, and it has been presented to the ferocious and insatiable hunger, the terrible and inhuman appetite, of this corrupt government. Today, by the telegraph, we have received the intelligence that John Brown has forfeited his life—all this honesty, all this straight-forwardness, all this self-sacrifice, which has been manifested in Harper's Ferry.

My friends, his life was just such a "failure" as all great movements have been. The physical failure has been the death of the seed, externally, which has given life to the germ, which has sprung forth to spread its moral boughs all over this corrupt nation. (Applause.) I have not the slightest doubt that this will be the result . . . John Brown has died, but the life of Freedom, from his death, shall flow forth to this nation.

[. . .] I do not believe the dagger should be drawn, until there is in the system to be assailed such terrible evidences of its corruption, that it becomes the *dernier resort*. And my friends, we are not to blame the application of the instrument, we are to blame the disease itself. We blame a physician for the use of the knife; but the impure blood, the obstructed veins, the disordered system, have caused the cancer, and rendered the use of the instrument necessary. The physician has but chosen the least of two evils. So John Brown chose the least of two evils. To save the country, he went down to cut off the Virginia cancer. (Applause.)

I say, that I am prepared to endorse John Brown's course fully. He has said that he did not intend to shed blood. In my opinion, speaking as a military critic, this was one of the faults of his plan. In not shedding blood, he left the slaves uncertain how to act; so that the North has said that the Negroes there are cowards. They are not cowards, but great diplomats. When they saw their masters in possession of John Brown, in bonds like themselves, they would have been perfect fools had they demonstrated any willingness to join him. They have got sense enough to know, that until there is a perfect demonstration that the white man is their friend—a demonstration bathed in blood—it were foolishness to cooperate with them. They have learned this much from the treachery of white men at the North, and the cruelty of the white men at the South, that they cannot trust the white man, even when he comes to deliver them. So it was not their cowardice, not their craven selfishness, but it was their caution, that prevented them from joining Brown. I say this because I think it is necessary to vindicate the character of the Negro for courage. I know very well that in this country, the white people have said that the Negroes will not fight; but I know also, that when the country's honor has been at stake, and the dire prejudice that excludes the colored man from all positions of honor, and all opportunities for the advancement, has not interfered to exclude him from the military, he was gone with the army, and there displayed as much courage as his white brother.

[. . .] The people of the North have said John Brown was a madman—I suppose mostly because it is on the eve of an election: but if he was mad, his madness not only had a great deal of "method" in it, but a great deal of philosophy and religion. I say, my friends, that no man ever died in this country as John Brown has died today. I say it because John Brown was a praying man. I remember hearing an incident in reference to his praying, from the lips of a man in whose presence and in whose house it occurred, and I loved him the more when I heard it. Coming to Henry Highland Garnet, of New York, some two years ago, he said to him, after unfolding all his plans, "Mr. Garnet, what do you think?" Said Mr. Garnet, who is at once a Christian, a gentleman, and a scholar, "Sir, the time has not come yet for the success of such a movement. Our people in the South are not sufficiently appraised of their rights, and of the sympathy that exists on the part of the North for them; our people in the North are not prepared to assist in such a movement, in consequence of the prejudice that shuts them out from both the means and the intelligence necessary. The breach between the North and the South has not yet become wide enough." Mr. Brown, looking him in the face as his keen eye was lit up with its peculiar fire, and his soul seemed to come forth with all its intellectual energy to look out and scan, if possible, the whole horizon of Providence, said, "Mr. Garnet, I will ask God about it"; and he got down upon his knees, and there poured out his heart to that God who is peculiarly the God of the bondman. He then showed the depth of his religious feeling, the intense interest that he had in the emancipation of mankind, and the heroism of his soul. Mr. Garnet says that never in his life has he been so moved by a prayer as he was by that prayer of John Brown's.

When such a man as this dies as he has died to-day, with the prayers of five millions of people going up to Heaven in his behalf—for I know that at least that number of Christians here have prayed for him—when such a man dies, I am sure that his death under such circumstances affords us a great, an almost demonstrable evidence of the success of the movement that he has inaugurated and of the final accomplishment of the great object of his soul. (Applause.) I say that no man has ever died in this country as John Brown has died. While his soul has gone up to God, and his body has been taken down a lifeless corpse, thank God all over the country meetings are being held to-night to give expression to that great feeling of sympathy which is to swell the great tornado. Let Virginia thank herself for it! In her guilty planting she has sown the wind; let her thank herself if in her terrible harvest she reaps the whirlwind of destruction.

Go down to Virginia, and see that firm old man as he comes out from his prison, leaning upon the arm of the sheriff and with his head erect, ascends the dreadful steps of the gibbet. We see as he goes his way to the top, and every step he takes seems to be inspired with that feeling which the poet Longfellow describes as animating the heart of the young man climbing to the top of the mountain, "Excelsior," until planting himself on the top, he is ready for his martyrdom. Though his body falls, the spirit of slavery and despotism falls with it, while John Brown goes up to heaven. Thank God! thank God! (Applause.)

I have detained you long enough. This is not the time to vindicate his cause. I have made these remarks only because they seem to be suggested here. I close by saying, my friends, that John Brown . . . shall slay more in his death than he ever slew in all his life. It is thought by the slaves—and it is a beautiful conceit, though coming from slaves—that the meteors from the heavens are sparks that . . . strike upon the craters of volcanoes, and that is the cause of their eruption. From the firmament of Providence today, a meteor has fallen. It has fallen upon the volcano of American sympathies, and though, for awhile, it may seem to sleep, yet its igneous power shall communicate . . . to the slumbering might of the volcano, and it shall burst forth in one general conflagration of revolution that shall bring about universal freedom. (Applause.)

* * * *

Anglo-African Magazine, *"Brown & Nat Turner,"* *December 31, 1859*

The year 2000 marked the bicentennial of the births of two important radicals in American history, and speakers at various commemoration services across the United States drew numerous parallels between the pair. This was not the first time that Nat Turner and John Brown were discussed in the same breath. Their legacies have grown up together side by side, quickly coming to symbolize the abolitionist cause of the nineteenth century. The first significant comparison was made in December 1859 by the Anglo-African Magazine, *in an anonymous article possibly written by James McCune Smith, an editor of the publication (which ran from 1859 to 1865 in New York City), and the most educated black American before W. E. B. Du Bois. The article, entitled "Brown & Nat*

Turner: An Editor's Comparison," is included in full here. In the same issue the magazine printed Turner's public confession so that readers could compare the method of Nat Turner with that of John Brown, for the two stories were interrelated and mutually dependent events in American history.

If the country didn't respond to Brown's methods, Turner's would take over, the article declares. And Turner's methods were terrifying indeed: in 1831 he led seventy slaves in a rebellion in Southampton Country, Virginia. The rampage left sixty whites and a hundred blacks dead, and is still the most famous slave revolt in American history. It made the South hysterical and clumsily shrill, and the threat of more of the same presumably made Brown's attack feel more dangerously convincing as a serious rallying call to the slaves. Wendell Phillips, in a lecture entitled "The Lesson of the Hour," from November 1, 1859, was able to refer back to Turner and so raise the stakes on Brown: "Nat Turner's success, in 1831, shows [slave insurrection] would have been possible," he reminds his audience, "Virginia had not slept sound since Nat Turner led an insurrection in 1831, and she bids fair never to have a nap now." In 1881 Frederick Douglass remembered that in October 1859, "expecting a repetition of the Nat Turner insurrection, [the South] at once understood the meaning, if not the magnitude of the affair."

So Turner made Brown's insurrection more horrifying. He may also have enabled Brown's actions in the first place. The epitome of the rebellious slave, Turner proved to Brown that slaves would fight. Brown admired Turner as much as he admired George Washington, and both were at the forefront of his mind as he planned his own violent insurrection of twenty-eight years later. Brown's self-consciously Christ-like manner during his imprisonment and execution may have been an imitation of Turner, who, when in 1831 was asked what he thought of his fast-approaching execution, answered: "Was not Christ crucified?"

December 31, 1859

There are two reasons why we present our readers with the "Confessions of Nat Turner." First, to place upon record this most remarkable episode in the history of human slavery, which proves to the philosophic observer that in the midst of this most perfectly contrived and apparently secure system of slavery, humanity will out, and engender from its bosom forces that will contend against oppression, however unsuccessfully; and secondly, that the two methods of Nat Turner and of John Brown may be compared. The one is the mode in which the slave seeks freedom for his fellows, and the other mode in which the white man seeks to set the slave free. There are many points of similarity between these two men; they were both idealists; both governed by their views of the teachings of the Bible; both had harbored for years the purpose to which they gave up their lives; both felt themselves swayed as by some divine, or at least, spiritual impulse; the one seeking in the air, the earth, and the heavens for signs which came at last; and the other, obeying impulses which he believes to have been foreordained from the eternal past; both cool, calm, and heroic in prison and in the prospect of inevitable death; both confess with child-like frankness and simplicity the object they had in view, the pure and simple emancipation of their fellow men; both win from the judges who sentenced them expressions of deep sympathy—and here the parallel ceases. Nat Turner's terrible logic could only see the enfranchisement of one race compassed by the extirpation of the other; and he followed his gory syllogism with rude ex-actitude. John Brown, believing that the freedom of the enthralled could only be effected by placing them on an equality with the enslavers, and unable in the very effort at emancipation to tyrannize himself, is moved with compassion for tyrants, as well as slaves, and seeks to extirpate this formidable cancer, without spilling one drop of Christian blood.

These two narratives present a fearful choice to the slaveholders, nay, to this great nation—which of the two modes of emancipation shall take place? The method of Nat Turner, or the method of John Brown?

Emancipation must take place, and soon. There can be no long delay in the choice of methods. If John Brown's be not soon adopted by the free North, then Nat Turner's will be by the enslaved South.

Had the order of events been reversed—had Nat Turner been in John Brown's place at the head of these twenty-one men, governed by his inexorable logic and cool daring, the soil of Virginia and Maryland and the far South would by this time be drenched in the blood and the wild and sanguinary course of these men, no earthly power could stay.

The course which the South is now frantically pursuing will engender in its bosom and nurse into maturity a hundred Nat Turners, whom Virginia is infinitely less able to resist in 1860, than she was in 1831.

So, people of the South, people of the North! Men and brethren, choose ye which method of emancipation you prefer—Nat Turner's or John Brown's?

* * * *

Ralph Waldo Emerson, address at Salem, January 6, 1860

Ralph Waldo Emerson's literary and poetic vision resembled the political and social vision of John Brown. Emerson crossed the boundary between aesthetics and politics: better known as a Transcendentalist than an abolitionist, during the 1850s he was a fervent opponent of slavery. He came to abolitionism late in life; in 1840 he did not approve of the abolitionist methods of Garrison and others but, over the years that followed, abolitionists—including his close friend Theodore Parker—consistently pursued him as a potential supporter. The radical new individualism of the Transcendentalists, which exalted private conscience and experience as intuiting universal truths, made it logical that Emerson enlist in the abolitionist cause, which could free slave-owners as well as slaves to cultivate their moral and spiritual selves. He wrote: "I think we must get rid of slavery or we must get rid of freedom. . . . If you put a chain around the neck of a slave, the other end fastens itself around your own." He admired Gerrit Smith, Brown's close friend and supporter, because he recognized Smith's vision of a world that sought "something not selfish, not geographical, but human and divine," as he wrote in a journal entry of 1854.

Once converted, Emerson spoke out against the Fugitive Slave Law, that "filthy enactment," as he called it, adding: "I will not obey it, by God." As he made the transition from revolutionary aesthetics to revolutionary politics, he did vacillate somewhat, writing in a journal entry of 1852: "I waked at night and bemoaned myself that I had not thrown myself into this deplorable question of slavery. . . . But then in hours of sanity I recover myself . . . I have quite other slaves to free than those negroes, to wit, imprisoned spirits, imprisoned thoughts far back in the Brain of man . . ." He was shocked anew by the Kansas-Nebraska Act and predicted a second American Revolution, this time against slavery.

He first met Brown in March 1857 at Thoreau's home, after the drama in Kansas, and then heard him speak at the town hall in Concord. Brown seemed that day to breathe the air of liberty, and Emerson thought the Kansas war hero "the rarest of heroes, a pure idealist." Emerson was less enthusiastic about Brown's actions at Harpers Ferry, and wrote to his son on October 23, 1859: "We are all very well, in spite of the sad Harper's Ferry business, which interests us all who had Brown for our guest twice. . . . He is a true hero, but lost his head there." He nevertheless collected money for Brown's trial and admired Brown's calm eloquence after his imprisonment. He made several speeches in Brown's defense, the most famous on November 8 when he described the condemned man as "The Saint whose fate yet hangs in suspense, but whose martyrdom, if it shall be perfected, will make the gallows as glorious as the Cross." He respected Brown's private laws and divine principles, and perhaps saw in him the hero he had envisaged as early as 1841, in the essay "Heroism": "Heroism feels and never reasons, and therefore is always right; and although a different breeding, different religion and greater intellectual activity would have modified or even reversed the particular action, yet, for the hero, that thing he does is the highest deed, and is not open to the censure of philosophers or divines." Perhaps Emerson recognized in Brown a transcendental symbol; something of the "divine life" that Thoreau discusses in his journal entry on Emerson. "Emerson . . . [l]ives a far more intense life; seeks to realize a divine life . . . Love and friendship, Religion, Poetry, the Holy are familiar to him," Thoreau writes. Looking for "Love and Friendship" in the world, Emerson saw them personified in Brown.

Clearly the speech here was written with close reference to Brown's autobiographical essay, which Emerson kept in his possession for several years (see Autobiographical Letter of John Brown). To focus on the biographical details of a man's life, and then expand out to discuss that man's role as a representation of universal forces, as Emerson does in this Salem address, is not as incongruous as it might seem. For Emerson, individualism was not the opposite of communalism, but rather the means to the achievement of true community. A greater knowledge of self would lead to a deeper understanding of the Over-Soul, of which all selves partake. Nature generally affirms a belief in the necessary and beautiful relationship of the part to the whole, and "The American Scholar," for example, returns repeatedly to the idea that "you must take the whole society to find the whole man," that there is a "oneness or . . . identity of the mind through all individuals." An individual can survive only when he is made of the same material as the universal mind, which in his essay, "Fate," Emerson likens to the ocean: "A tube made of a film of glass can resist the shock of the ocean, if filled with the same water." A richly developed individual mind can through speech and action awaken in other minds an experiencing of the transcendent. The progress of a nation or generation is to be achieved through the effort and pain of an individual, and Brown, in whom transcendental truth was powerfully present, as Emerson declares in his Salem address, was that individual for antebellum America. Brown was, Emerson wrote to Lydia Maria Child just before the execution, "one of those on whom miracles wait."

The radical abolitionists were as admiring of Emerson as he was— eventually—of them. Brown considered Emerson among his best New England friends, and Smith and his comrades often quoted or para- phrased Emerson's writings during the 1850s, as, for example, in 1859 when Smith in a sermon summarized the Transcendentalist view of na- ture: "Every man is, in an important sense, bound to make up a Bible for himself." Central to both Emerson's aesthetic revolution and the rad- ical abolitionist political revolution was a subjective notion of the self in a state of continuous flux. A conception of the self as fluid allowed Brown, in particular, to break down racial hierarchies and envision a pluralist society.

But Emerson couldn't go as far as Brown and his supporters: the rad- ical abolitionists surpassed his rhetoric and broke down not only the di- chotomies separating the ideal and the real, body and soul, but also the separations of black from white, civilization from savagery. Emerson's revolution remained largely aesthetic. He could not make the passage Brown achieved from white conventions to a fully transracial activism. Brown lived up to Emerson's doctrine of self-reliance and sacred self- sovereignty more fully than Emerson did himself.

January 6, 1860

Mr. Chairman:

I have been struck with one fact, that the best orators who have added their praise to his fame,—and I need not go out of this house to find the purest elo- quence in the country—have one rival who comes off a little better, and that is JOHN BROWN. Every thing that is said of him leaves people a little dis- satisfied; but as soon as they read his own speeches and letters they are heartily contented,—such is the singleness of purpose which justifies him to the head and the heart of it all. Taught by this experience, I mean, in the few remarks I have to make, to cling to his history, or let him speak for himself.

John Brown, the founder of liberty in Kansas, was born in Torrington, Litch- field County, Conn., in 1800. When he was five years old his father emigrated to Ohio, and the boy was there set to keep sheep and to look after cattle and dress skins; he went bareheaded and barefooted, and clothed in buckskin. He said that he loved rough play, could never have rough play enough; could not see a seedy hat without wishing to pull it off. But for this it needed that the playmates should be equal: not one in fine clothes and the other in buckskin; not one his own master, hale and hearty, and the other watched and whipped. But it chanced that in Pennsylvania, where he was sent by his father to collect cattle, he fell in with a boy whom he heartily liked and whom he looked upon as his superior. This boy was a slave; he saw him beaten with an iron shovel, and otherwise maltreated; he saw that this boy had nothing better to look forward to in life, whilst he himself was petted and made much of; for he was much considered in the family where he then stayed, from the circumstance that this boy of twelve years had conducted alone a drove of cattle a hundred miles. But the colored boy had no friend, and no future. This worked such indignation in him that he swore an oath of resistance to Slavery as long as he lived. And thus his enterprise to go into Virginia and run off five hundred or a thousand slaves was not a piece of spite or revenge, a plot of two years or of twenty years, but the keeping of an oath made to Heaven and earth forty-seven years before. Forty-seven years at least, though I incline to accept his own account of the matter at Charlestown, which makes the date a little older, when he said, "This was all settled millions of years before the world was made."

He grew up a religious and manly person, in severe poverty; a fair specimen of the best stock of New England; having that force of thought and that sense of right which are the warp and woof of greatness. Our farmers were Orthodox Calvinists, mighty in the Scriptures; had learned that life was a preparation, a "probation," to use their word, for a higher world, and was to be spent in loving and serving mankind.

Thus was formed a romantic character absolutely without any vulgar traits; living to ideal ends, without any mixture of self-indulgence or compromise, such as lowers the value of benevolent and thoughtful men we know; abstemious, refusing luxuries, not sourly and reproachfully but simply as unfit for his habit; quiet and gentle as a child in the house. And, as happens usually to men of romantic character, his fortunes were romantic. Walter Scott would have delighted to draw his picture and trace his adventurous career. A shepherd and herdsman, he learned the manners of animals and knew the secret signals by which animals communicate. He made his hard bed on the mountains with them; he learned to drive his flock through thickets all but impassable; he had all the skill of a shepherd by choice of breed and by wise husbandry to obtain the best wool, and that for a course of years. And the anecdotes preserved show a far-seeing skill and conduct which, in spite of adverse accidents, should secure, one year with another, an honest reward, first to the farmer, and afterwards to the dealer. If he kept sheep, it was with a royal mind; and if he traded in wool, he was a merchant prince, not in the amount of wealth, but in the protection of the interests confided to him.

I am not a little surprised at the easy effrontery with which political gentlemen, in and out of Congress, take it upon them to say that there are not a thousand men in the North who sympathize with John Brown. It would be far safer and nearer the truth to say that all people, in proportion to their sensibility and self-respect, sympathize with him. For it is impossible to see courage, and disinterestedness, and the love that casts out fear, without sympathy. All women are drawn to him by their predominance of sentiment. All gentlemen, of course, are on his side. I do not mean by "gentlemen," people of scented hair and perfumed handkerchiefs, but men of gentle blood and generosity, "fulfilled with all nobleness," who, like the Cid, give the outcast leper a share of their bed; like the dying Sidney, pass the cup of cold water to the wounded soldier who needs it more. For what is the oath of gentle blood and knighthood? What but to protect the weak and lowly against the strong oppressor?

Nothing is more absurd than to complain of this sympathy, or to complain of a party of men united in opposition to Slavery. As well complain of gravity, or the ebb of the tide. Who makes the Abolitionist? The Slaveholder. The sentiment of mercy is the natural recoil which the laws of the universe provide to protect mankind from destruction by savage passions. And our blind statesmen go up and down, with committees of vigilance and safety, hunting for the origin of this new heresy. They will need a very vigilant committee indeed to find its birthplace, and a very strong force to root it out. For the arch-Abolitionist, older than Brown, and older than the Shenandoah Mountains, is Love, whose other name is Justice, which was before Alfred, before Lycurgus, before Slavery, and will be after it.

* * * *

Henry David Thoreau, "A Plea for Captain John Brown," October 30, 1859, and "The Last Days of John Brown," July 4, 1860

Henry David Thoreau struggled for some time to keep clear of the whirlpool of activism threatening to pull him from the calm waters of Walden Pond. He wrote in his journal on June 16, 1854, while in Concord: "There is a fine ripple and sparkle on the pond, seen through the mist. But what signifies the beauty of nature when men are base? We walk to lakes to see our serenity reflected in them. When we are not serene, we go not to them . . . The remembrance of politicians spoils my walks. My thoughts are murder to the State; I endeavor in vain to observe nature; my thoughts involuntarily go plotting against the State." Though isolated, Thoreau could not retreat entirely. Inside him the active was at constant war with the contemplative. It was impossible to remain impassive to the daily political dances and games, though the game be a "game of straws," as he put it in his "Plea for Captain John Brown."

During the 1850s the Massachusetts writer, naturalist, and philosopher effected a shift, from his passive resistance to governmental intrusion upon individual rights of 1849, to a radical militancy where slavery was concerned by 1859. Shocked by the Fugitive Slave Law of 1850, he wrote in his journal: "I hear a good deal said about trampling this law under foot. Why, one need not go out of his way to do that. This law lies not at the level of the head or the reason. Its natural habitat is the dirt." His lecture entitled "Slavery in Massachusetts," delivered in

1854, further excoriated the law. Slavery was too deeply rooted an evil to be pulled up by passive resistance, and he welcomed the armed assault on Harpers Ferry. It was not, as he recognized in his journal entry of June 16, 1854, "an era of repose." He thus celebrates Brown in his "Plea" as a soldier of morals, a "Captain," with the "Spartan habits" of "a soldier," "armored" with his cause, fitted with "rifles of principle." His work of 1849, A Week on the Concord and Merrimack Rivers, *speaks of Christ and Brahma as Western and Eastern counterparts, Christ a man of action, a practical rebel, and Brahma a man of contemplation, seeking not to "assault evil, but to patiently starve it out." Brown is perhaps Christ, the fighter, in this equation, and Thoreau himself the Brahma.*

Thoreau may also have found his own doctrine of civil disobedience personified in the same man who personified Transcendentalism for Emerson. In July of 1846, Thoreau had spent a night in the Concord jail for nonpayment of his poll tax, and out of that experience came the famous essay "Civil Disobedience." If a law "is of such a nature that it requires you to be the agent of injustice to another," he wrote, "then, I say, break the law." John Brown embodied and extended this idea, and in justification of Brown's actions at Harpers Ferry, Thoreau asked, in an echo of his "Civil Disobedience" essay: "Is it not possible that an individual may be right and a government wrong? Are laws to be enforced simply because they were made?"

The speech in which he asked this question is one of his most polemical and celebrated. On October 19, 1859, he heard the news of John Brown's raid and leapt to Brown's defense, though most were abandoning ship rapidly—as he describes with anger in his "Plea for Captain John Brown." During this speech, Thoreau's Brown emerges like a silver and gold butterfly from a chrysalis, moral and humane, anti-war and decidedly not insane; Thoreau refutes all claims to that effect, adding with acidity: "when were the good and the brave ever in a majority?"

The piece is in an informal, personal style, full of personal pronouns, particularly in the opening, so that Thoreau can suggest a familiarity with Brown. The speech caused considerable controversy and was instrumental in shaping public perceptions of Brown. Thoreau's self-proclaimed intention was "to plead [Brown's] cause . . . not for his life, but for his character—his immortal life." And he went a long way toward achieving this. He redeemed Brown's character for whoever had remained unimpressed by Brown during his trial and imprisonment.

Thoreau continued this work on behalf of Brown's "character," and gave another luminous speech the following year (also printed here). Entitled "The Last Days of John Brown," it concludes with a statement of faith in Brown's "immortality"—the "immortal life" that he aimed at in "A Plea for Captain John Brown": "I meet him at every turn. He is more alive than ever he was. He has earned immortality." Between the raid on October 16 and the execution on December 2, the Northeast had witnessed a meteor shower on an unprecedented scale, and all the news-

papers that Thoreau read during that time covered the story: in this speech Thoreau connects natural and political phenomena, making of Brown a "meteor" and thus likening him to a bright but transitory flash, the debris of a comet or planet rather than the more immortal comet itself: "John Brown's career for the last six weeks of his life was meteor-like, flashing through the darkness in which we live." Brown's career flashed through the dark skies, with the same rapidity that his body sped from Charleston to North Elba: "like a meteor it shot through the Union from the Southern regions toward the North!"

One newspaper even referred to the bright meteor lights as those of "an avenging angel," a phrase sometimes used with reference to Brown. Some lights seemed to hover and then not fall to earth, instead vanishing or returning to space—perhaps hinting at an immortal existence beyond the skies. Thoreau weaves the themes of light and fire throughout his speech to suggest the possibility of immortality: the meteor burns as a clear "light, shining sun-like, forever, on the land, and also splight." Here is the metaphysical significance of the meteor storm of 1859, and here is the eternal.

A Plea for Captain John Brown

Concord, October 30, 1859

. . .Little as I know of Captain Brown, I would fain do my part to correct the tone and the statements of the newspapers, and of my countrymen generally, respecting his character and actions. It costs us nothing to be just. We can at least express our sympathy with, and admiration of, him and his companions, and that is what I now propose to do.

First, as to his history. I will endeavor to omit, as much as possible, what you have already read. I need not describe his person to you, for probably most of you have seen and will not soon forget him. I am told that his grandfather, John Brown, was an officer in the Revolution; that he himself was born in Connecticut about the beginning of this century, but early went with his father to Ohio. I heard him say that his father was a contractor who furnished beef to the army there, in the War of 1812; that he accompanied him to the camp, and assisted him in that employment, seeing a good deal of military life—more, perhaps, than if he had been a soldier; for he was often present at the councils of the officers. Especially, he learned by experience how armies are supplied and maintained in the field, a work which, he observed, requires at least as much experience and skill as to lead them in battle. He said that few persons had any conception of the cost, even the pecuniary cost, of firing a single bullet in war. He saw enough, at any rate, to disgust him with a military life; indeed, to excite in him a great abhorrence of it; so much so, that though he was tempted by the offer of some petty office in the army, when he was about eighteen, he not only declined that, but he also refused to train when warned, and was fined for it. He then resolved that he would never have anything to do with any war, unless it were a war for liberty.

When the troubles in Kansas began, he sent several of his sons thither to strengthen the party of the Free State men, fitting them out with such weapons as he had; telling them that if the troubles should increase, and there should be need of him, he would follow, to assist them with his hand and counsel. This, as you all know, he soon after did; and it was through his agency, far more than any other's, that Kansas was made free.

For a part of his life he was a surveyor, and at one time he was engaged in wool-growing, and he went to Europe as an agent about that business. There, as everywhere, he had his eyes about him, and made many original observations. He said, for instance, that he saw why the soil of England was so rich, and that of Germany (I think it was) so poor, and he thought of writing to some of the crowned heads about it. It was because in England the peasantry live on the soil which they cultivate, but in Germany they are gathered into villages at night. It is a pity that he did not make a book of his observations.

I should say that he was an old-fashioned man in his respect for the Constitution, and his faith in the permanence of this Union. Slavery he deemed to be wholly opposed to these, and he was its determined foe. He was by descent and birth a New England farmer, a man of great common sense, deliberate and practical as that class is, and tenfold more so. He was like the best of those who stood at Concord Bridge once, on Lexington Common, and on Bunker Hill, only he was firmer and higher-principled than any that I have chanced to hear of as there. It was no abolition lecturer that converted him. Ethan Allen and Stark, with whom he may in some respects be compared, were rangers in a lower and less important field. They could bravely face their country's foes, but he had the courage to face his country herself when she was in the wrong. A Western writer says, to account for his escape from so many perils, that he was concealed under a "rural exterior"; as if, in that prairie land, a hero should, by good rights, wear a citizen's dress only.

He did not go to the college called Harvard, good old Alma Mater as she is. He was not fed on the pap that is there furnished. As he phrased it, "I know no more of grammar than one of your calves." But he went to the great university of the West, where he sedulously pursued the study of Liberty, for which he had early betrayed a fondness, and having taken many degrees, he finally commenced the public practice of Humanity in Kansas, as you all know. Such were his humanities, and not any study of grammar. He would have left a Greek accent slanting the wrong way, and righted up a falling man.

He was one of that class of whom we hear a great deal, but, for the most part, see nothing at all—the Puritans. It would be in vain to kill him. He died lately in the time of Cromwell, but he reappeared here. Why should he not? Some of the Puritan stock are said to have come over and settled in New England. They were a class that did something else than celebrate their forefathers' day, and eat parched corn in remembrance of that time. They were neither Democrats nor Republicans, but men of simple habits, straightforward, prayerful; not thinking much of rulers who did not fear God, not making many compromises, nor seeking after available candidates.

[. . .] He was a man of Spartan habits, and at sixty was scrupulous about his diet at your table, excusing himself by saying that he must eat sparingly and fare hard, as became a soldier, or one who was fitting himself for difficult enterprises, a life of exposure. A man of rare common sense and directness of speech, as of action; a transcendentalist above all, a man of ideas and

principles—that was what distinguished him. Not yielding to a whim or transient impulse, but carrying out the purpose of a life. I noticed that he did not
overstate anything, but spoke within bounds. I remember, particularly, how, in
his speech here, he referred to what his family had suffered in Kansas, without ever giving the least vent to his pent-up fire. It was a volcano with an ordinary chimney-flue. Also referring to the deeds of certain Border Ruffians, he
said, rapidly paring away his speech, like an experienced soldier, keeping a reserve of force and meaning, "They had a perfect right to be hung." He was
not in the least a rhetorician, was not talking to Buncombe or his constituents
anywhere, had no need to invent anything but to tell the simple truth, and communicate his own resolution; therefore he appeared incomparably strong, and
eloquence in Congress and elsewhere seemed to me at a discount. It was like
the speeches of Cromwell compared with those of an ordinary king.

[. . .] On the whole, my respect for my fellow-men, except as one may out-
weigh a million, is not being increased these days. I have noticed the cold-
blooded way in which newspaper writers and men generally speak of this event,
as if an ordinary malefactor, though one of unusual "pluck"—as the Governor
of Virginia is reported to have said, using the language of the cockpit, "the
gamest man be ever saw"—had been caught, and were about to be hung. He
was not dreaming of his foes when the governor thought he looked so brave.
It turns what sweetness I have to gall, to hear, or hear of, the remarks of some
of my neighbors. When we heard at first that he was dead, one of my towns-
men observed that "he died as the fool dieth"; which, pardon me, for an instant suggested a likeness in him dying to my neighbor living. Others, craven-
hearted, said disparagingly, that "he threw his life away," because he resisted
the government. Which way have they thrown their lives, pray?—such as would
praise a man for attacking singly an ordinary band of thieves or murderers. I
hear another ask, Yankee-like, "What will he gain by it?" as if he expected to
fill his pockets by this enterprise. Such a one has no idea of gain but in this
worldly sense. If it does not lead to a "surprise" party, if he does not get a
new pair of boots, or a vote of thanks, it must be a failure. "But he won't gain
anything by it." Well, no, I don't suppose he could get four-and-sixpence a
day for being hung, take the year round; but then he stands a chance to save
a considerable part of his soul—and such a soul!—when you do not. No doubt
you can get more in your market for a quart of milk than for a quart of blood,
but that is not the market that heroes carry their blood to.

Such do not know that like the seed is the fruit, and that, in the moral world,
when good seed is planted, good fruit is inevitable, and does not depend on
our watering and cultivating; that when you plant, or bury, a hero in his field,
a crop of heroes is sure to spring up. This is a seed of such force and vitality, that it does not ask our leave to germinate.

[. . .] A man does a brave and humane deed, and at once, on all sides, we
hear people and parties declaring, "I didn't do it, nor countenance him to do
it, in any conceivable way. It can't be fairly inferred from my past career." I,
for one, am not interested to hear you define your position. I don't know that
I ever was or ever shall be. I think it is mere egotism, or impertinent at this
time. Ye needn't take so much pains to wash your skirts of him. No intelligent man will ever be convinced that he was any creature of yours. He went

and came, as he himself informs us, "under the auspices of John Brown and nobody else." The Republican Party does not perceive how many his failure will make to vote more correctly than they would have them. They have counted the votes of Pennsylvania & Co., but they have not correctly counted Captain Brown's vote. He has taken the wind out of their sails—the little wind they had—and they may as well lie to and repair.

What though he did not belong to your clique! Though you may not approve of his method or his principles, recognize his magnanimity. Would you not like to claim kindredship with him in that, though in no other thing he is like, or likely, to you? Do you think that you would lose your reputation so? What you lost at the spile, you would gain at the bung. If they do not mean all this, then they do not speak the truth, and say what they mean. They are simply at their old tricks still. "It was always conceded to him," says one who calls him crazy, "that he was a conscientious man, very modest in his demeanor, apparently inoffensive, until the subject of Slavery was introduced, when he would exhibit a feeling of indignation unparalleled."

The slave-ship is on her way, crowded with its dying victims; new cargoes are being added in mid-ocean; a small crew of slaveholders, countenanced by a large body of passengers, is smothering four millions under the hatches, and yet the politician asserts that the only proper way by which deliverance is to be obtained is by "the quiet diffusion of the sentiments of humanity," without any "outbreak." As if the sentiments of humanity were ever found unaccompanied by its deeds, and you could disperse them, all finished to order, the pure article, as easily as water with a watering-pot, and so lay the dust. What is that that I hear cast overboard? The bodies of the dead that have found deliverance. That is the way we are "diffusing" humanity, and its sentiments with it.

[. . .] If Walker may be considered the representative of the South, I wish I could say that Brown was the representative of the North. He was a superior man. He did not value his bodily life in comparison with ideal things. He did not recognize unjust human laws, but resisted them as he was bid. For once we are lifted out of the trivialness and dust of politics into the region of truth and manhood. No man in America has ever stood up so persistently and effectively for the dignity of human nature, knowing himself for a man, and the equal of any and all governments. In that sense he was the most American of us all. He needed no babbling lawyer, making false issues, to defend him. He was more than a match for all the judges that American voters, or office-holders of whatever grade, can create. He could not have been tried by a jury of his peers, because his peers did not exist. When a man stands up serenely against the condemnation and vengeance of mankind, rising above them literally by a whole body—even though he were of late the vilest murderer, who has settled that matter with himself—the spectacle is a sublime one—didn't ye know it, ye Liberators, ye Tribunes, ye Republicans?—and we become criminal in comparison. Do yourselves the honor to recognize him. He needs none of your respect.

As for the Democratic journals, they are not human enough to affect me at all. I do not feel indignation at anything they may say. I am aware that I anticipate a little—that he was still, at the last accounts, alive in the hands of his foes; but that being the case, I have all along found myself thinking and speaking of him as physically dead. I do not believe in erecting statues to those who still live in our hearts, whose bones have not yet crumbled in the earth around us, but I would rather see the statue of Captain Brown in the Massachusetts State-House yard than that of any other man whom I know. I rejoice that I live in this age, that I am his contemporary.

[. . .] Insane! A father and six sons, and one son-in-law, and several more men besides—as many at least as twelve disciples—all struck with insanity at once; while the same tyrant holds with a firmer grip than ever his four millions of slaves, and a thousand sane editors, his abettors, are saving their country and their bacon! just as insane were his efforts in Kansas. Ask the tyrant who is his most dangerous foe, the sane man or the insane? Do the thousands who know him best, who have rejoiced at his deeds in Kansas, and have afforded him material aid there, think him insane? Such a use of this word is a mere trope with most who persist in using it, and I have no doubt that many of the rest have already in silence retracted their words.

Read his admirable answers to Mason and others. How they are dwarfed and defeated by the contrast! On the one side, half-brutish, half-timid questioning; on the other, truth, clear as lightning, crashing into their obscene temples. They are made to stand with Pilate, and Gessler, and the Inquisition. How ineffectual their speech and action! and what a void their silence! They are but helpless tools in this great work. It was no human power that gathered them about this preacher.

What have Massachusetts and the North sent a few sane representatives to Congress for, of late years?—to declare with effect what kind of sentiments? All their speeches put together and boiled down—and probably they themselves will confess it—do not match for manly directness and force, and for simple truth, the few casual remarks of crazy John Brown on the floor of the Harper's Ferry engine-house—that man whom you are about to hang, to send to the other world, though not to represent you there. No, he was not our representative in any sense. He was too fair a specimen of a man to represent the like of us. Who, then, were his constituents? If you read his words understandingly you will find out. In his case there is no idle eloquence, no made, nor maiden speech, no compliments to the oppressor. Truth is his inspirer, and earnestness the polisher of his sentences. He could afford to lose his Sharp's rifles, while he retained his faculty of speech—a Sharp's rifle of infinitely surer and longer range.

[. . .] It is a relief to turn from these slanders to the testimony of his more truthful, but frightened jailers and hangmen. Governor Wise speaks far more justly and appreciatingly of him than any Northern editor, or politician, or public personage, that I chance to have heard from. I know that you can afford to hear him again on this subject. He says: "They are themselves mistaken who take him to be a madman. . . . He is cool, collected, and indomitable, and it is but just to him to say that he was humane to his prisoners. . . . And he inspired me with great trust in his integrity as a man of truth. He is a fanatic, vain and garrulous" (I leave that part to Mr. Wise), "but firm, truthful, and intelligent. His men, too, who survive, are like him. . . . Colonel Washington says that he was the coolest and firmest man he ever saw in defying danger and death. With one son dead by his side, and another shot through, he felt the pulse of his dying son with one hand, and held his rifle with the other, and commanded his men with the utmost composure, encouraging them to be firm, and to sell their lives as dear as they could. Of the three white prisoners, Brown, Stevens, and Coppoc, it was hard to say which was most firm."

Almost the first Northern men whom the slaveholder has learned to respect! The testimony of Mr. Vallandigham, though less valuable, is of the same purport, that "it is vain to underrate either the man or his conspiracy. . . . He is the farthest possible removed from the ordinary ruffian, fanatic, or madman."

[. . .] I hear many condemn these men because they were so few. When were the good and the brave ever in a majority? Would you have had him wait till that time came?—till you and I came over to him? The very fact that he had no rabble or troop of hirelings about him would alone distinguish him from ordinary heroes. His company was small indeed, because few could be found worthy to pass muster. Each one who there laid down his life for the poor and oppressed was a picked man, culled out of many thousands, if not millions; apparently a man of principle, of rare courage, and devoted humanity; ready to sacrifice his life at any moment for the benefit of his fellow-man. It may be doubted if there were as many more their equals in these respects in all the country—I speak of his followers only—for their leader, no doubt, scoured the land far and wide, seeking to swell his troop. These alone were ready to step between the oppressor and the oppressed. Surely they were the very best men you could select to be hung. That was the greatest compliment which this country could pay them. They were ripe for her gallows. She has tried a long time, she has hung a good many, but never found the right one before.

When I think of him, and his six sons, and his son-in-law, not to enumerate the others, enlisted for this fight, proceeding coolly, reverently, humanely to work, for months if not years, sleeping and waking upon it, summering and wintering the thought, without expecting any reward but a good conscience, while almost all America stood ranked on the other side—I say again that it affects me as a sublime spectacle. If he had had any journal advocating "his cause," any organ, as the phrase is, monotonously and wearisomely playing the same old tune, and then passing round the hat, it would have been fatal to his efficiency. If he had acted in any way so as to be let alone by the government, he might have been suspected. It was the fact that the tyrant must give place to him, or he to the tyrant, that distinguished him from all the reformers of the day that I know.

[. . .] The same indignation that is said to have cleared the temple once will clear it again. The question is not about the weapon, but the spirit in which you use it. No man has appeared in America, as yet, who loved his fellow-man so well, and treated him so tenderly. He lived for him. He took up his life and he laid it down for him. What sort of violence is that which is encouraged, not by soldiers, but by peaceable citizens, not so much by laymen as by ministers of the Gospel, not so much by the fighting sects as by the Quakers, and not so much by Quaker men as by Quaker women?

This event advertises me that there is such a fact as death—the possibility of a man's dying. It seems as if no man had ever died in America before; for in order to die you must first have lived. I don't believe in the hearses, and palls, and funerals that they have had. There was no death in the case, because there had been no life; they merely rotted or sloughed off, pretty much as they had rotted or sloughed along. No temple's veil was rent, only a hole dug somewhere. Let the dead bury their dead. The best of them fairly ran down like a clock. Franklin—Washington—they were let off without dying; they were merely missing one day. I hear a good many pretend that they are going to die; or that they have died, for aught that I know. Nonsense! I'll defy them to do it. They haven't got life enough in them. They'll deliquesce like fungi, and keep a hundred eulogists mopping the spot where they left off. Only half a dozen or so have died since the world began. Do you think that you are going to die, sir? No! there's no hope of you. You haven't got your lesson yet. You've got to stay after school. We make a needless ado about capital punishment— taking lives, when there is no life to take. Memento mori! We don't understand that sublime sentence which some worthy got sculptured on his gravestone once. We've interpreted it in a grovelling and snivelling sense; we've wholly forgotten how to die.

But be sure you do die nevertheless. Do your work, and finish it. If you know how to begin, you will know when to end. These men, in teaching us how to die, have at the same time taught us how to live. If this man's acts and words do not create a revival, it will be the severest possible satire on the acts and words that do. It is the best news that America has ever heard. It has already quickened the feeble pulse of the North, and infused more and more generous blood into her veins and heart than any number of years of what is called commercial and political prosperity could. How many a man who was lately contemplating suicide has now something to live for!

One writer says that Brown's peculiar monomania made him to be "dreaded by the Missourians as a supernatural being." Sure enough, a hero in the midst of us cowards is always so dreaded. He is just that thing. He shows himself superior to nature. He has a spark of divinity in him. *"Unless above himself he can / Erect himself, how poor a thing is man!"* Newspaper editors argue also that it is a proof of his insanity that he thought he was appointed to do this work which he did—that he did not suspect himself for a moment! They talk as if it were impossible that a man could be "divinely appointed" in these days to do any work whatever; as if vows and religion were out of date as connected with any man's daily work; as if the agent to abolish slavery could only be somebody appointed by the President, or by some political party. They talk as if a man's death were a failure, and his continued life, be it of whatever character, were a success.

[. . .] Who is it whose safety requires that Captain Brown be hung? Is it indispensable to any Northern man? Is there no resource but to cast this man also to the Minotaur? If you do not wish it, say so distinctly. While these things are being done, beauty stands veiled and music is a screeching lie. Think of him—of his rare qualities!—such a man as it takes ages to make, and ages to understand; no mock hero, nor the representative of any party. A man such as the sun may not rise upon again in this benighted land. To whose making went the costliest material, the finest adamant; sent to be the redeemer of those in captivity; and the only use to which you can put him is to hang him at the end of a rope! You who pretend to care for Christ crucified, consider what you are about to do to him who offered himself to be the savior of four millions of men.

[. . .] I am here to plead his cause with you. I plead not for his life, but for his character—his immortal life; and so it becomes your cause wholly, and is not his in the least. Some eighteen hundred years ago Christ was crucified; this morning, perchance, Captain Brown was hung. These are the two ends of a chain which is not without its links. He is not Old Brown any longer; he is an angel of light. I see now that it was necessary that the bravest and humanest man in all the country should be hung. Perhaps he saw it himself. I almost fear that I may yet hear of his deliverance, doubting if a prolonged life, if any life, can do as much good as his death.

"Misguided!" "Garrulous!" "Insane!" "Vindictive!" So ye write in your easy-chairs, and thus he wounded responds from the floor of the armory, clear as a cloudless sky, true as the voice of nature is: "No man sent me here; it was my own prompting and that of my Maker. I acknowledge no master in human form." And in what a sweet and noble strain he proceeds, addressing his captors, who stand over him . . . You don't know your testament when you see it . . . "You may dispose of me very easily. I am nearly disposed of now; but this question is still to be settled—this negro question, I mean; the end of that is not yet." I foresee the time when the painter will paint that scene, no longer going to Rome for a subject; the poet will sing it; the historian record it; and, with the Landing of the Pilgrims and the Declaration of Independence, it will be the ornament of some future national gallery, when at least the present form of slavery shall be no more here. We shall then be at liberty to weep for Captain Brown. Then, and not till then, we will take our revenge.

* * * *

The Last Days of John Brown

John Brown's career for the last six weeks of his life was meteor-like, flashing through the darkness in which we live. I know of nothing so miraculous in our history.

If any person, in a lecture or conversation at that time, cited any ancient example of heroism, such as Cato or Tell or Winkelried, passing over the recent deeds and words of Brown, it was felt by any intelligent audience of Northern men to be tame and inexcusably far-fetched.

For my own part, I commonly attend more to nature than to man, but any affecting human event may blind our eyes to natural objects. I was so absorbed in him as to be surprised whenever I detected the routine of the natural world surviving still, or met persons going about their affairs indifferent. It appeared strange to me that the "little dipper" should be still diving quietly in the river, as of yore; and it suggested that this bird might continue to dive here when Concord should be no more.

I felt that he, a prisoner in the midst of his enemies and under sentence of death, if consulted as to his next step or resource, could answer more wisely than all his countrymen beside. He best understood his position; he contemplated it most calmly. Comparatively, all other men, North and South, were beside themselves. Our thoughts could not revert to any greater or wiser or better man with whom to contrast him, for he, then and there, was above them all. The man this country was about to hang appeared the greatest and best in it.

[. . .] Most Northern men, and a few Southern ones, were wonderfully stirred by Brown's behavior and words. They saw and felt that they were heroic and noble, and that there had been nothing quite equal to them in their kind in this country, or in the recent history of the world. But the minority were unmoved by them. They were only surprised and provoked by the attitude of their neighbors. They saw that Brown was brave, and that he believed that he had done right, but they did not detect any further peculiarity in him. Not being accustomed to make fine distinctions, or to appreciate magnanimity, they read his letters and speeches as if they read them not. They were not aware when they approached a heroic statement,—they did not know when they *burned*. They did not feel that he spoke with authority, and hence they only remembered that the *law* must be executed. They remembered the old formula, but did not hear the new revelation. The man who does not recognize in Brown's words a wisdom and nobleness, and therefore an authority, superior to our laws, is a modern Democrat. This is the test by which to discover him. He is not willfully but constitutionally blind on this side, and he is consistent with himself. Such has been his past life; no doubt of it. In like manner he has read history and his Bible, and he accepts, or seems to accept, the last only as an established formula, and not because he has been convicted by it. You will not find kindred sentiments in his common-place book, if he has one.

When a noble deed is done, who is likely to appreciate it? They who are noble themselves. I was not surprised that certain of my neighbors spoke of John Brown as an ordinary felon, for who are they? They have either much flesh, or much office, or much coarseness of some kind. They are not ethereal natures in any sense. The dark qualities predominate in them. Several of them are decidedly pachydermatous. I say it in sorrow, not in anger. How can a man behold the light who has no answering inward light? They are true to their *sight*, but when they look this way they *see* nothing, they are blind. For the children of the light to contend with them is as if there should be a contest between eagles and owls. Show me a man who feels bitterly toward John Brown, and let me hear what noble verse he can repeat. He'll be as dumb as if his lips were stone.

[. . .] When I looked into a liturgy of the Church of England, printed near the end of the last century, in order to find a service applicable to the case of Brown, I found that the only martyr recognized and provided for by it was King Charles the First, an eminent scamp. Of all the inhabitants of England and of the world, he was the only one according to this authority, whom that church had made a martyr and saint of; and for more than a century it had celebrated his martyrdom, so called, by an annual service. What a satire on the Church is that!

Look not to legislatures and churches for your guidance, nor to any soulless *incorporated* bodies, but to *inspirited* or inspired ones. What avail all your scholarly accomplishments and learning, compared with wisdom and manhood? To omit his other behavior, see what a work this comparatively unread and unlettered man wrote within six weeks. Where is our professor of *belles-lettres,* or of logic and rhetoric, who can write so well? He wrote in prison, not a History of the World, like Raleigh, but an American book which I think will live longer than that. I do not know of such words, uttered under such circumstances, and so copiously withal, in Roman or English or any history. What a variety of themes he touched on in that short space! There are words in that letter to his wife, respecting the education of his daughters, which deserve to be framed and hung over every mantelpiece in the land. Compare this earnest wisdom with that of Poor Richard.

The death of Irving, which at any other time would have attracted universal attention, having occurred while these things were transpiring, went almost unobserved. I shall have to read of it in the biography of authors.

Literary gentlemen, editors and critics, think that they know how to write, because they have studied grammar and rhetoric; but they are egregiously mistaken. The art of composition is as simple as the discharge of a bullet from a rifle, and its masterpieces imply an infinitely greater force behind them. This unlettered man's speaking and writing are standard English. Some words and phrases deemed vulgarisms and Americanisms before, he has made standard American; such as "*It will pay.*" It suggests that the one great rule of composition—and if I were a professor of rhetoric, I should insist on this—is, to *speak the truth.* This first, this second, this third pebbles in your mouth or not. This demands earnestness and manhood chiefly.

We seem to have forgotten that the expression "a *liberal* education" originally meant among the Romans one worthy of *free* men; while the learning of trades and professions by which to get your livelihood merely, was considered worthy of *slaves* only. But taking a hint from the word, I would go a step further and say, that it is not the man of wealth and leisure simply, though devoted to art, or science, or literature, who, in a true sense, is *liberally* educated, but only the earnest and *free* man. In a slaveholding country like this, there can be no such thing as a *liberal* education tolerated by the State; and those scholars of Austria and France who, however learned they may be, are contented under their tyrannies, have received only a *servile* education.

Nothing could his enemies do but it redounded to his infinite advantage,—that is, to the advantage of his cause. They did not hang him at once, but reserved him to preach to them. And then there was another great blunder. They did not hang his four followers with him; that scene was still postponed; and so his victory was prolonged and completed. No theatrical manager could have arranged things so wisely to give effect to his behavior and words. And who, think you, *was* the manager? *Who* placed the slave woman and her child, whom he stooped to kiss for a symbol, between his prison and the gallows?

We soon saw, as he saw, that he was not to be pardoned or rescued by men. That would have been to disarm him, to restore to him a material weapon, a Sharp's rifle, when he had taken up the sword of the spirit,—the sword with which he has really won his greatest and most memorable victories. Now he has not laid aside the sword of the spirit, for he is pure spirit himself, and his sword is pure spirit also.

[. . .] What a transit was that of his horizontal body alone, but just cut down from the gallows-tree! We read that at such a time it passed through Philadelphia, and by Saturday night had reached New York. Thus like a meteor it shot through the Union from the Southern regions toward the North! No such freight had the cars borne since they carried him southward alive.

On the day of his translation, I heard, to be sure, that he was *hung*, but I did not know what that meant; I felt no sorrow on that account; but not for a day or two did I even *hear* that he was *dead*, and not after any number of days shall I believe it. Of all the men who were said to be my contemporaries, it seemed to me that John Brown was the only one who *had not died*. I never hear of a man named Brown now,—and I hear of them pretty often,—I never hear of any particularly brave and earnest man, but my first thought is of John Brown, and what relation he may be to him. I meet him at every turn. He is more alive than ever he was. He has earned immortality. He is not confined to North Elba nor to Kansas. He is no longer working in secret. He works in public, and in the clearest light that shines on this land.

* * * *

Stephen Douglas, remarks to the U.S. Senate, January 23, 1860

Abraham Lincoln's longtime personal and political rival was a rabidly racist five-foot tall Democrat from Illinois. Stephen Douglas drafted the 1854 Kansas-Nebraska Bill that caused the civil war in Kansas in which John Brown and his sons first made their names as freedom fighters, and also tussled with Lincoln over the role of the Republican Party in John Brown's raid. In the short speech printed here, made to the Senate almost two months after John Brown's execution, he makes Brown a Republican, and the Republican Party a breeding ground for radicals. "Harpers Ferry crime was the natural, logical, inevitable result of the doctrines and teachings of the Republican party," he states. "The causes that produced the Harpers Ferry invasion are now in active operation." This was an opinion shared by the Joint Committee of the General Assembly of Virginia, which commented on January 26, 1860: "The crimes of John Brown were neither more nor less than practical illustrations of the Republican Party."

The exchange between Douglas and Lincoln over the Harpers Ferry raid has its roots further back. In 1858 Lincoln had challenged Douglas for his Senate seat, and both candidates earned much notoriety and popularity through their debates of that year, an exchange that has been called "the most famous war of words in history." One local resident said of Illinois during that period: "the prairies are on fire." The series of seven public debates on the issue of slavery, each session lasting three hours long, began on August 21 and ended on October 15, 1858. Lincoln was opposed to popular sovereignty, a policy that allowed new states to choose for themselves on the issue of slavery, and in particular Douglas's proposal that the people living in the Louisiana Purchase should be allowed to own slaves. The seasoned Democrat had an advantage over his relatively unknown opponent. The debates were held outside so that anyone could attend, then transcribed in national newspapers, and Douglas's familiarity with the Illinois people in the audience allowed him successfully to judge their responses. The better-known candidate, he had more opening and closing speeches, more speaking time, and the choice of venues.

He won the Senate election, as a result forcing the divisions within the Democratic Party even wider. But Lincoln, who gained widespread recognition, and began on the path to Presidency, shrugged. "I am killing larger game," he said. "The great battle of 1860 is worth a thousand of this senatorial race."

January 23, 1860

It cannot be said with truth that the Harper's Ferry case will not be repeated, or is not in danger of repetition. It is only necessary to inquire into the causes which produced the Harper's Ferry outrage, and ascertain whether those causes are yet in active operation, and then you can determine whether there is any ground for apprehension that that invasion will be repeated. Sir, what were the causes which produced the Harper's Ferry outrage? Without stopping to adduce evidence in detail, I have no hesitation in expressing my firm and deliberate conviction that the Harper's Ferry crime was the natural, logical, inevitable result of the doctrines and teachings of the Republican party, as explained and enforced in their platform, their partisan presses, their pamphlets and books, and especially in the speeches of their leaders in and out of Congress. (Applause in the galleries) . . .

I am not making this statement for the purpose of crimination or partisan effect. I desire to call the attention of the members of that party to a reconsideration of the doctrines that they are in the habit of enforcing, with a view to a fair judgment whether they do not lead directly to those consequences on the part of those deluded persons who think that all they say is meant in real earnest and ought to be carried out. The great principle that underlies the organization of the Republican party is violent, irreconcilable, eternal warfare upon the institution of American slavery, with the view of its ultimate extinction throughout the land; sectional war is to be waged until the cotton fields of the South shall be cultivated by free labor, or the rye fields of New York and Massachusetts shall be cultivated by slave labor. In furtherance of this article of their creed, you find their political organization not only sectional in its location, but one whose vitality consists in appeals to northern passion, northern prejudice, northern ambition against southern States, southern institutions, and southern people. . . .

Can any man say to us that although this outrage has been perpetrated at Harper's Ferry, there is no danger of its recurrence? Sir, is not the Republican party still embodied, organized, confident of success and defiant in its pretensions? Does it not now hold and proclaim the same creed that it did before this invasion? It is true that most of its representatives here disavow the acts of John Brown at Harper's Ferry. I am glad that they do so; I am rejoiced that they have gone thus far; but I must be permitted to say to them that it is not sufficient that they disavow the act, unless they also repudiate and denounce the doctrines and teachings which produced the act. Those doctrines remain the same; those teachings are being poured into the minds of men throughout the country by means of speeches and pamphlets and books and through partisan presses. The causes that produced the Harper's Ferry invasion are now in active operation.

* * * *

Abraham Lincoln, address at the Cooper Institute, February 27, 1860

As the leading Republican in Illinois in 1859 and a possible nominee for high office, Lincoln responded swiftly to the Democratic effort to identify Brown with the Republicans. Although Brown had shown "great courage" and "rare unselfishness," Lincoln observed, he committed high crimes and received just punishment. The day after Brown was executed, Lincoln warned Southerners that they would be dealt with in much the same way if they tried to break up the Union: "Old John Brown has just been executed for treason against a state. We cannot object, even though he agreed with us in thinking slavery wrong. That cannot excuse violence, bloodshed, and treason."

Three months later, in his famous speech at the Cooper Union that contributed to his nomination for President, he answered accusers such as Stephen Douglas who would lay the blame for the raid at the feet of the Republican Party. He compares Brown to a fanatic who attempted to assassinate the nation's leader, and thus anticipates John Wilkes Booth's actions. Just days after the end of the Civil War, Booth gunned down the sixteenth president of the United States.

Brown, the victim of "slavery in its supremacy," and Lincoln, the victim of "slavery in its extremity," as William Dean Howells put it in the North American Review *in 1911, have been a strange partnership of proximal and co-dependent icons, each functioning alternately as the good cop and the bad cop of American abolitionism, and moving in and out of shadow and spotlight as their myths marched on. John Brown's final address to the court ranked, for Emerson, Higginson, and others, alongside Lincoln's "Gettysburg Address" as one of the best speeches of the nineteenth century.*

In 1863, Edna Dean Proctor wrote a poem entitled "The President's Proclamation" to commemorate Lincoln's Emancipation Proclamation, but put Brown very much at the poem's center. While the martyr of 1859 is mentioned by name nine times, the soon-to-be martyr of 1865 appears only twice, as "The President" and "our noble Ruler." "John Brown sowed," the poet declares, and it was all Lincoln could do to reap the harvest. In a similar resizing of the two men, Eitaro Ishigaki's mural of 1937 for the Harlem Courthouse, sponsored by the Works Project Administration, physically joins Nat Turner, Frederick Douglass, and Lincoln by way of John Brown and, though Lincoln stands taller, indicating his higher footing and more prominent place in American history, Brown stands forward, defining his more progressive and radical politics.

Diego Rivera's mural for the Rockefeller Center, "Portrait of America," completed four years before Ishigaki's mural, has two John Browns in panel VI, "The Civil War" (fig. 24). Brown is in both upper and lower foreground on the left, so emphasizing his importance to the beginnings of the narrative of war and emancipation told across the canvas from left to right. The Brown in the upper foreground is higher than any other figure, apparently with no eyes; his vision entirely eradicated, perhaps by Lincoln, whose eyes are remarkable for their dullness and lack of comprehension and here addresses a dead man, frozen in legend. The scaffold frames the second figure of Brown in the lower section, so forming a picture within a picture that is captioned by a quote from Marx, who was highly critical of Lincoln: "a white skin cannot emancipate itself where labor with a black skin is branded."

This second Brown is the most compelling in the whole panel: calm and intensely knowing, seemingly aware of the coming removal of his eyes on the scaffold. The many other pairs of eyes in the mural focused on Brown all contain some degree more of engagement than Lincoln, who stands with Generals William Sherman and Ulysses Grant, and holds before the hanging figure of Brown two columns of words. These twin tablets indicate that Lincoln is trying to be Moses now that John Brown,

Figure 24: Diego Rivera, *Potrait of America: Civil War*, 1933. (International Ladies Garment Workers Union, Rivera Murals, 1942).

a Moses figure, is crucified; and yet the juxtaposition of the columns ironically indicates how far from either Brown or Moses Lincoln is in consistency or sincerity: "I have no purpose to introduce political and social equality between the white and black race . . . If I could save the Union without freeing any slaves I would do it . . . If I could save it by freeing all I would do it . . . If I could do it by freeing some and leaving others alone, I would also do that," reads the first, and the other side is the Emancipation Proclamation. In his panel "The Tree of Liberty," part of his 1,650 square foot mural "Pan American Unity" of 1948, Rivera returned to the theme of the relative relationships of Brown and Lincoln to American history. In the bottom section are such liberators as Simón Bolívar, Miguel Hidalgo, José María Morelos, George Washington, Thomas Jefferson, and Abraham Lincoln, but the way to liberty is pointed by John Brown, at the center.

[. . .] You charge that we stir up insurrections among your slaves. We deny it; and what is your proof? Harper's Ferry! John Brown!! John Brown was no Republican; and you have failed to implicate a single Republican in his Harper's Ferry enterprise. If any member of our party is guilty in that matter, you know it or you do not know it. If you do know it, you are inexcusable for not designating the man and proving the fact. If you do not know it, you are inexcusable for asserting it, and especially for persisting in the assertion after you have tried and failed to make the proof. You need not be told that persisting in a charge which one does not know to be true, is simply malicious slander.

Some of you admit that no Republican designedly aided or encouraged the Harper's Ferry affair; but still insist that our doctrines and declarations necessarily lead to such results. We do not believe it. We know we hold to no doctrine, and make no declaration, which were not held to and made by "our fathers who framed the Government under which we live." You never dealt fairly by us in relation to this affair. When it occurred, some important State elections were near at hand, and you were in evident glee with the belief that, by charging the blame upon us, you could get an advantage of us in those elections. The elections came, and your expectations were not quite fulfilled. Every Republican man knew that, as to himself at least, your charge was a slander, and he was not much inclined by it to cast his vote in your favor. Republican doctrines and declarations are accompanied with a continual protest against any interference whatever with your slaves, or with you about your slaves. Surely, this does not encourage them to revolt. True, we do, in common with "our fathers, who framed the Government under which we live," declare our belief that slavery is wrong; but the slaves do not hear us declare even this. For anything we say or do, the slaves would scarcely know there is a Republican party. I believe they would not, in fact, generally know it but for your misrepresentations of us, in their hearing. In your political contests among yourselves, each faction charges the other with sympathy with Black Republicanism; and then, to give point to the charge, defines Black Republicanism to simply be insurrection, blood and thunder among the slaves.

Slave insurrections are no more common now than they were before the

Republican party was organized. What induced the Southampton insurrection, twenty-eight years ago, in which, at least, three times as many lives were lost as at Harper's Ferry? You can scarcely stretch your very elastic fancy to the conclusion that Southampton was "got up by Black Republicanism." In the present state of things in the United States, I do not think a general, or even a very extensive slave insurrection, is possible. The indispensable concert of action cannot be attained. The slaves have no means of rapid communication; nor can incendiary freemen, black or white, supply it. The explosive materials are everywhere in parcels; but there neither are, nor can be supplied, the indispensable connecting trains.

Much is said by Southern people about the affection of slaves for their masters and mistresses; and a part of it, at least, is true. A plot for an uprising could scarcely be devised and communicated to twenty individuals before some one of them, to save the life of a favorite master or mistress, would divulge it. This is the rule; and the slave revolution in Hayti was not an exception to it, but a case occurring under peculiar circumstances. The gunpowder plot of British history, though not connected with slaves, was more in point. In that case, only about twenty were admitted to the secret; and yet one of them, in his anxiety to save a friend, betrayed the plot to that friend, and, by consequence, averted the calamity. Occasional poisonings from the kitchen, and open or stealthy assassinations in the field, and local revolts extending to a score or so, will continue to occur as the natural results of slavery; but no general insurrection of slaves, as I think, can happen in this country for a long time. Whoever much fears, or much hopes for such an event, will be alike disappointed.

In the language of Mr. Jefferson, uttered many years ago, "It is still in our power to direct the process of emancipation, and deportation, peaceably, and in such slow degrees, as that the evil will wear off insensibly; and their places be, pari passu, filled up by free white laborers. If, on the contrary, it is left to force itself on, human nature must shudder at the prospect held up."

Mr. Jefferson did not mean to say, nor do I, that the power of emancipation is in the Federal Government. He spoke of Virginia; and, as to the power of emancipation, I speak of the slaveholding States only. The Federal Government, however, as we insist, has the power of restraining the extension of the institution—the power to insure that a slave insurrection shall never occur on any American soil which is now free from slavery.

John Brown's effort was peculiar. It was not a slave insurrection. It was an attempt by white men to get up a revolt among slaves, in which the slaves refused to participate. In fact, it was so absurd that the slaves, with all their ignorance, saw plainly enough it could not succeed. That affair, in its philosophy, corresponds with the many attempts, related in history, at the assassination of kings and emperors. An enthusiast broods over the oppression of a people till he fancies himself commissioned by Heaven to liberate them. He ventures the attempt, which ends in little else than his own execution. Orsini's attempt on Louis Napoleon, and John Brown's attempt at Harper's Ferry were, in their philosophy, precisely the same. The eagerness to cast blame on old England in the one case, and on New England in the other, does not disprove the sameness of the two things.

And how much would it avail you, if you could, by the use of John Brown,

Helper's Book, and the like, break up the Republican organization? Human action can be modified to some extent, but human nature cannot be changed. There is a judgment and a feeling against slavery in this nation, which cast at least a million and a half of votes. You cannot destroy that judgment and feeling—that sentiment—by breaking up the political organization which rallies around it. You can scarcely scatter and disperse an army which has been formed into order in the face of your heaviest fire; but if you could, how much would you gain by forcing the sentiment which created it out of the peaceful channel of the ballot-box, into some other channel? What would that other channel probably be? Would the number of John Browns be lessened or enlarged by the operation?

* * * *

John Greenleaf Whittier, "Brown of Ossawatomie," December 22, 1859

With reference to a particularly impressive moment in John Brown's life, Henry David Thoreau spoke of "the time when the painter will paint that scene," when "the poet will sing it; the historian record it; and, with the Landing of the Pilgrims and the Declaration of Independence, it will be the ornament of some future national gallery." He was referring to the scene of Brown's interview at Harpers Ferry, but the same sentiment also applies to the famous scene on the morning of Brown's execution, when Brown allegedly stopped on the way to the gallows to kiss the child of a slave woman. Though initially reported by the New York Tribune, *on December 5, 1859, and then reprinted in other newspapers and early Brown biographies, the event most likely didn't take place. Nevertheless, the painter and the poet have returned again and again to the image. Lydia Maria Child composed the poem "John Brown and the Colored Child," and Thoreau, in "The Last Days of John Brown," wondered "Who placed the slave woman and her child, whom he stooped to kiss for a symbol, between his prison and the gallows?" In his eulogy at Brown's funeral, Wendell Phillips exclaimed: "We . . . see him stoop on his way to the scaffold and kiss that negro child,—and this iron heart seems all tenderness. Marvellous old man! . . . the serene brow of that calm old man, as he stoops to kiss the child of a forlorn race. Thank God for our emblem." Frederick Douglass, in an address years later, concluded that "No man, who in his hour of extremest need, when on his way to meet an ignominious death, could so forget himself as to stop and kiss a little child, one of the hated race for whom he was about to die, could by any possibility fail".*

The poet John Greenleaf Whittier, a pacifist Quaker and gradualist abolitionist, though horrified by Brown's "rash and insane attempt . . . dangerous and unjustifiable act" at Harpers Ferry, was impressed by his character as expressed by the apocryphal kiss. At the center of his poem, "Brown of Ossawatomie," printed here, is "that kiss, from all its guilty means / Redeemed the good intent." The most widely read comment on Brown in the nineteenth century, Whittier's poem was first published in the New York Independent *three weeks after Brown's execution, and cemented the story that was fast becoming a national myth. But some be-*

lieved that Whittier had, in his ambivalence, failed to express the requisite level of unequivocal support for Brown, and William Lloyd Garrison launched a particularly thorough attack on the poem. "There is an apparent invidious or severity of imputation in these epithets, which does not seem to be called for," Garrison complained in his article for the Liberator, *with reference to lines like "the folly that seeks through evil good," and "the raid of midnight terror."*

*Artists in the years that followed used Whittier's "Brown of Ossawatomie" to form their own complex interpretations of Brown's life and death. Whittier himself in his collection "National Lyrics" of 1865, included an unsigned woodcut of the scene (fig. 29), a work in which, unusually, the viewer is positioned above rather than below Brown. As late as the 1930s and 40s artists continued to reinterpret the meaning of the kiss: Eitaro Ishigaki included the mother and child pair in his 1937 mural for the Harlem Courthouse, and William H. Johnson's 1945 paint-*ing John Brown's Legend *(fig. 35, see p. 268) puts it at the very center of Brown's life: his family and friends, his life at North Elba, the raid at Harpers Ferry, his trial and execution, are all peripheral to the kiss. Three John Browns coexist within the one frame, reminding the public of Brown's multiple roles and personae during his lifetime, but Brown kissing the slave child is foregrounded and centered. The viewer follows the diagonal line through John Brown's sons, the rifle held by the disembodied hand, the slave mother, the slave child, to find Brown's face as a visual climax; his shoulders and bent head mirrored and so reframed in importance by the angle of the sun to Harpers Ferry in the top right.*

The most well-known artistic interpretations of the kissing scene are by Louis Ransom in 1860, Thomas S. Noble in 1867, and Thomas Hovenden in 1884. Ransom's painting, John Brown Meeting the Slave Mother and Her Child on the Steps of Charleston Jail on His Way to Execution, *translated into a widely-distributed lithograph by Currier and Ives in 1863 (fig. 25), was the first visual rendering of the scene, and met with huge controversy. Issued in the North during the Civil War, with heavy propagandistic overtones, it drew a favorable review from* Harper's Weekly, *which commented at the end of its appraisal on June 13, 1863, "It is one of the incidents that history will always fondly record and art delineate. The fierce and bitter judgment of the moment upon the old man is already tempered. Despised and forsaken in his own day, the heart of another generation may treat him as he treated the little outcast child." Nevertheless authorities removed the painting itself from the American Museum, fearing during the July 1863 New York City draft riots that it would draw angry crowds. In 1870 Currier and Ives issued a version of the print without the sectionalist references (fig. 26).*

The image features a majestic Brown, six inches taller than he had been in life, with head framed by the yellow flag of Virginia, so seeming to form a halo above him. A Madonna-like slave woman holds up a child in the likeness of Christ, and the only man looking at Brown bears a striking expression, enhanced by the glow around his eyes as though

Figure 25: *John Brown Meeting the Slave Mother and Her Child on the Steps of Charleston Jail on His Way to Execution*, Currier and Ives lithograph, 1863, from Louis Ransom painting, 1860. (*Courtesy, Library of Congress.*)

Figure 26: *John Brown—the Martyr*, Currier and Ives lithograph, 1870, from Louis Ransom painting, 1860. (*Courtesy, Library of Congress.*)

he has looked upon something holy. This watching figure is in fact a character from the American Revolution, with a tricornered hat emblazoned with "76." A statue of Justice in the corner has the same pose as Brown, arms cut off, right leg forward and eyes hidden, so reminding the viewer of Brown's statuesque bearing on the scaffold. The band around the eyes of the statue evokes Brown's gallows hood, and also charges America with being blind to the truth with regard to Brown's sacrifice.

Religious tones pervade Thomas Satterwhite Noble's painting of 1867, John Brown's Blessing *(fig. 27), in which Brown looks like an honorable old patriarch of the church and, rather than kiss the child, simply places a priestly hand on its head. Thomas Hovenden's* Last Moments of John Brown *of 1884 (fig. 28) refocuses attention on the racial dynamics of the scene—unsurprisingly, for the family of Hovenden's wife had been involved with the abolitionist cause and his studio was once used as a stop along the Underground Railroad. The rifle and bayonet on the left are at same angle as Brown's leaning torso and form an X with Brown's right arm and the sheriff's head and left arm. The natural center of the painting is thus the bright white death warrant in the middle of this X, but the action of Brown kissing the black child, at which all the watching faces stare, shift attention from the document. The slave mother holds her elbow at the same angle as the sheriff holds his, and the child in her hands counterbalances the death warrant in the sheriff's. De-centered, the painting enacts a struggle between life and death, black and white, freedom and the slavery of Southern law.[6] The rebalancing of the scene between white death warrant and black slave child hints at the fusion of races in Brown's life. Though probably aware that the scene was fictional, Hovenden embraces its rich symbolism and makes of his gentle, beslippered old Brown a weapon more commanding than the bayonet that parallels Brown's torso, more powerful than the death warrant that Brown simply supplants as the scene's centerpiece with a black child.*

New York Independent, December 22, 1859

Brown of Ossawatomie

John Brown of Ossawatomie spake on his dying day:
"I will not have to shrive my soul a priest in Slavery's pay;
But let some poor slave-mother whom I have striven to free,
With her children, from the gallows-stair put up a prayer for me!"
John Brown of Ossawatomie, they led him out to die;
And lo! a poor slave-mother with her little child pressed nigh:
Then the bold, blue eye grew tender, and the old harsh face grew mild,
As he stooped between the jeering ranks and kissed the negro's child!
The shadows of his stormy life that moment fell apart,
And they who blamed the bloody hand forgave the loving heart;

---

6. In one recently unearthed reproduction of the painting a remarque head of Lincoln hovers in the bottom left corner, confirming the painting's proximity to the *Realpolitik* of the nation's political and racial struggle rather than any religious, mythical, or classical themes.

Figure 27: Thomas S. Noble,
John Brown's Blessing, 1867.
(*Courtesy, Library of Congress.*)

"BROWN OF OSSAWATOMIE"

Figure 28: Thomas Hovenden, *The
Last Moments of John Brown*, 1884.
(*Courtesy, Library of Congress.*)

Figure 29: "Brown of Ossawatomie,"
unsigned woodcut in John Greenleaf
Whittier's *National Lyrics*, 1865.
(*Courtesy, Library of Congress.*)

That kiss from all its guilty means redeemed the good intent,
And round the grisly fighter's hair the martyr's aureole bent!
Perish with him the folly that seeks through evil good!
Long live the generous purpose unstained with human blood!
Not the raid of midnight terror, but the thought which underlies;
Not the borderer's pride of daring, but the Christian's sacrifice.
Nevermore may yon Blue Ridges the Northern rifle hear,
Nor see the light of blazing homes flash on the negro's spear;
But let the free-winged angel Truth their guarded passes scale,
To teach that right is more than might, and justice more than mail!
So vainly shall Virginia set her battle in array;
In vain her trampling squadrons knead the winter snow with clay!
She may strike the pouncing eagle, but she dares not harm the dove;
And every gate she bars to Hate shall open wide to Love!

* * * *

Herman Melville, "The Portent (1859)," 1866

As Frederick Douglass noted in 1881, John Brown was quickly popular as a subject for "the poet, scholar, philosopher and statesman." A
man whom "poetry loves forever to adorn with her choicest wreaths of
laurel," or so Lucius Bierce predicted in 1859, Brown was featured in
numerous poems and paintings. After the scene with the slave child on
the way to gallows, the most artistically appealing moment of his execution was simply that of the corpse hanging, often depicted as a Christ
figure on the cross. Jacob Lawrence's interpretation of this moment, the
cover illustration to this anthology, is discussed in the book's introduction, as is the association of Brown with the sky, by Frederick Douglass
and Wendell Phillips in particular. Phillips was drawn to the image of
the gallows against the sky, seeing in that death a sign and a symbol:
"As time passes, and these hours float back into history, men will see
against the clear December sky that gallows. . . . Thank God for our
emblem," said Phillips in his eulogy at Brown's funeral, echoing his own
use of a similar image in a lecture on November 1: "It is the only universal history," he had said of Brown's life. In their attempts to rescue
Brown from the "dim unknown," the messy impenetrable past and the
graveyard of obscurity, poets, scholars, and speech-makers extended the
image of the sky to encompass one of the firmament's brightest lights,
the meteor. James Schouler, the Reverend J. S. Martin, Henry David
Thoreau, Walt Whitman, and Herman Melville all saw in Brown's life
and death a meteoric flight. Melville's interpretation of Brown as meteor
comes in his famous poem, "The Portent," originally published in 1866
in Battle-Pieces and Aspects of the War.
    His "Weird John Brown" is an instrument of Fate, like Shakespeare's
three "Weird Sisters" in Macbeth. As such, he is more important as symbol and portent than man: his weirdness sets him out of the ordinary
course of earthly activity, makes of him a meteor. Unlike Whitman's
Brown, in his poem of 1881, "Year of Meteors [1859–60]," who is en-

tirely human, vulnerable and "trembling with age" and wounds as he ascends the scaffold, the face of Melville's Brown is hidden in the execution hood, thus emphasizing his role as abstraction. Melville picks up on Phillips' swaying scaffold and the "dim unknown" of the "future", veiled as it is in "The Portent" too, as well as the "shadow" cast by Brown on the gallows.

As "shadow," Melville's "Weird John Brown" falls across "your green", forcing an end to what Melville calls in his poem "Misgivings" the "optimist-cheer" of America. The unearthly dark shadow reveals Nature's "dark-side," and brings a fall from innocence, a disruption of the "pastoral green" of his poem "An Apparition." Brown is perhaps the "ocean-clouds" that "sweep storming in late autumn brown" in "Misgivings", for this poem uses his name and the time of year he raided Harpers Ferry, "autumn brown", and the "moody brow" in this poem might again refer back to his name and to his "crown" and face, veiled now with storm clouds rather than a "cap." "Weird John Brown" is a new prophecy for America, a shadow on its previous understanding of its fate, its belief in Manifest Destiny. "Shenandoah" marks the location of Harpers Ferry and Charlestown court-house, for both were along the Shenandoah River, and also function as the death-cry of the South and of the old ways of American exceptionalism.

Melville had prophesied the dissolution of the utopic Union in works like Benito Cereno, Moby Dick, Pierre, Israel Potter and The Confidence Man, and in John Brown's raid and execution he recognized the beginning of this end. Later Henry James would write of the Civil War that it "introduced into the national consciousness a certain sense of proportion and relation, of the world being a more complicated place than it had hitherto seemed, the future more treacherous, success more difficult . . . The good American, in days to come, will be a more critical person than his complacent and confident grandfather. He has eaten of the tree of knowledge." Following all the details of Brown's last weeks and hours, Melville would have read of the condemned man's comment as he traveled to the gallows: seeing the countryside with new eyes, as though he had eaten of James' "tree of knowledge", Brown commented to the undertaker, "This is a beautiful country. I never had the pleasure of seeing it before." Melville's "green", referring to America's fallen Eden but more literally to this "beautiful country", is suddenly more poignant.

Brown's beard becomes a meteor, white and streaming, and his hooded face, "Hidden in the cap," recalls the blind prophets in Greek tragedy, most famously Tiresias of Sophocles's Oedipus Rex. Firmly located in myth and literature, the poem references the portentous meteor that appeared above Rome just before the assassination of Julius Cæsar, Melville's Brown was perhaps the source for John Steuart Curry's twentieth century painting, John Brown of Osawatomie (fig. 6, see p. 8), where a mythical and "weird" John Brown gazes wildly about, beard streaming, a natural sign symbolizing the coming of the war, this time a tornado rather than a meteor. The movement of Melville's Brown, "slowly *swaying," also evokes Jacob Lawrence's painting, for the coattails in this more abstract work suggest motion, extended as they are on the right. Both Lawrence's painting and Melville's poem use the swinging motion of the symbolic figure to suggest that the country too is in flux.*

Newspaper articles described the meteor-shower that took place during October, November, and December 1859, as white and luminous, often of an immense size, perhaps recalling for Melville that other great, white, luminous portent, the whale Moby Dick, of his novel of 1851. Melville may have recognized aspects of Brown's character in his character Ahab: both have been called monomaniacs, and Melville's narrator could almost be referring to Brown when he says of Ahab: "there was an infinity of firmest fortitude, a determinate, unsurrenderable willfulness, in the fixed and fearless, forward dedication of that glance." The bewitched crew of the Pequod *was Brown's band of men, to whom he cried "God hunt us all, if we do not hunt Moby Dick to his death!" His wrecked ship was the Harpers Ferry project, the whole slave-holding South his immense white whale. Like Ahab, Brown began the destruction of his enemy with his final blow, though it took him down too.*

The Portent (1859)

Hanging from the beam,
Slowly swaying (such the law),
Gaunt the shadow on the green,
Shenandoah!
The cut is on the crown
(Lo, John Brown),
And the stabs shall heal no more.
Hidden in the cap
Is the anguish none can draw;
So your future veils its face,
Shenandoah!
But the streaming beard is shown
(Weird John Brown),
The meteor of the war.

* * * *

Walt Whitman, "Year of Meteors (1859–60)," 1881

Walt Whitman often seems like John Brown's poetic alter ego. Whitman's Leaves of Grass, *published on July 4, 1855, just a few days after the inaugural convention of the Radical Abolitionists, which dissolved the boundaries between black and white just as Brown did with his life and actions. Like Brown, Whitman looked to an age of individual and national liberation. Brown's politics and Whitman's poetry sought to abolish sin through individual and collective regeneration, to establish a democracy of inclusion embracing women and blacks, and to proclaim the divinity in all people. Set against the backdrop of the broader culture of dissent in America, Whitman and Brown share a similar vision of America. Reuben Ludwig, a Yiddish poet of New York, created in his*

1923 poem, "Symposium," a harmony of three voices,—Whitman, Brown, and Lincoln—all mourning the destruction of their America by capitalism. Whitman's "tremendous dream," the Harpers Ferry raid, and the Emancipation Proclamation, are, in Ludwig's poem, three elements in the same vision and symposium.

Yet, while Brown and the Radical Abolitionists worked to bring about the new age, Whitman believed it had already arrived; poetry had created a pluralist society. In the introduction to Leaves of Grass *he writes in the present tense of a nation reborn: "Here at last is something in the doings of man that corresponds with the broadcast doings of the day and night. . . . Here is [a] nation of nations. . . . Here is action untied from strings." Whitman's is not a vision of the future but a celebration of the present moment. For Brown, the break with the past was still to come. The political process had failed both men, but while one turned to violence for resolution, the other had already found it in poetry.*

Though Whitman told a friend that he distanced himself from the abolitionists not "because they were too radical [but] because they were not radical enough," he also warned the same friend: "Be radical—be radical—be not too damned radical." He once declared, "I am somehow afraid of agitators, though I believe in agitation," and he adopted no programs for social change. He refused to join the abolitionist movement, the women's rights movement and the labor movement, finding his utopia, and his heaven on Earth, through poetic form instead. In an 1857 Daily Times *article he calculated that slavery would probably disappear in a hundred years. The spirit of* Leaves of Grass *is in the announcement: "Evil propels me, and reform of evil propels me. . . . I stand indifferent." It was the life and mystery in all things, all contradictory things, that moved him. Though he knew Franklin Sanborn, Richard Hinton, and James Redpath, Brown's friends and co-conspirators, Whitman rejected Brown's militancy and commented that Brown lacked "evidence of great human quality." "I am never convinced by the formal martyrdoms alone," he added. "I see martyrdoms wherever I go: it is an average factor in life: why should I go off emotionally half-cocked only about the ostentatious cases?"*

Far from the translation of Brown into the form of a poet, Whitman was in certain ways, then, Brown's opposite. Wishing to identify with all so that division might thus be imaginatively resolved, Whitman denounced the extremes of both proslavery Southerners and Northern abolitionists that threatened the rich and various democracy of the Union. The poet "is the arbiter of the diverse and he is the key," he emphasized in the 1855 preface to Leaves of Grass. *"He is the equalizer of his age and land . . . he supplies what wants supplying and checks what wants checking"; he should "not be for the eastern states more than the western or the northern states more than the southern."*

Unable to celebrate Brown's political martyrdom, Whitman in his poem "Year of Meteors [1859–60]," dated 1881, therefore fixes on Brown's humanity and vulnerability. The speaker is set somewhat in opposition to Brown, for his teeth are "shut close" as he watches Brown hang, while Brown's would presumably be forced open by his tongue as he strangled and died. This detail reminds the reader that in reality Brown is silenced while the poet speaks on. A similar ambivalence toward the status and significance of Brown is again apparent when, in a poem about arrivals—ships, cargoes, the English prince, the "Great Eastern" and "myriads of small craft," the comet—Brown is the only figure departing. Equally, the poem's pattern, of accompaniments or components, breaks down in the section on Brown. The Nineteenth Presidentiad has Lincoln and Douglas; the ship has cargo; the Prince of Wales, who visited New York on October 11, 1860, has nobles; the tables have data; the "Great Eastern" has small crafts; the comet has meteors; and the year itself has fragments adding up to this poem—characters and incidents patched and "mottled." Brown seems to have no such components, or perhaps only the "trembling," as accompaniment to his indifferent death.

So the poem is not a celebration of Brown, or of the year "1859–1860." It was a "brooding year," a year to brood upon, a full or pregnant year (a broody year, a year with a brood), a year that passed stormily, menacingly, brooding like a stormy sky. And it was a year full of reversals: the speaker says of the Prince of Wales, "There in the crowds stood I, and singled you out with attachment," thereby reversing the usual order of things, in which one in the crowd is singled out by the public figure. Disrupting the chronology of the year, so that historical events that actually came later in the year here feature earlier, Whitman denies linear progress. In the year of Brown's raid and execution, humanity did not sail forward so smoothly as the "proud black ships of Manhattan," the prince "surging Manhattan's crowds," "the ship as she swam up my bay / Well-shaped and stately," the comet that "sail'd its balls of unearthly light over / our heads." The year was of "fitful" movement, and Brown, who mounts the scaffold twice in the poem and so is its most "fitful" feature, a poetic spasm, was perhaps the source of the year's seizure.

Year of Meteors [1859–60]

Year of meteors! brooding year!
I would bind in words retrospective some of your deeds and signs,
I would sing your contest for the 19th Presidentiad,
I would sing how an old man, tall, with white hair, mounted the
  scaffold in Virginia,
(I was at hand, silent I stood with teeth shut close, I watch'd,
I stood very near you old man when cool and indifferent, but trembling
  with age and your unheal'd wounds you mounted the scaffold;)
I would sing in my copious song your census returns of the States,
The tables of population and products, I would sing of your ships
  and their cargoes,
The proud black ships of Manhattan arriving, some fill'd with
  immigrants, some from the isthmus with cargoes of gold,
Songs thereof would I sing, to all that hitherward comes would welcome
  give,

And you would I sing, fair stripling! welcome to you from me, young
    prince of England!
(Remember you surging Manhattan's crowds as you pass'd with your
    cortege of nobles?
There in the crowds stood I, and singled you out with attachment;)
Nor forget I to sing of the wonder, the ship as she swam up my bay,
Well-shaped and stately the Great Eastern swam up my bay, she was
    600 feet long,
Her moving swiftly surrounded by myriads of small craft I forget not
    to sing;
Nor the comet that came unannounced out of the north flaring in heaven,
Nor the strange huge meteor-procession dazzling and clear shooting
    over our heads,
(A moment, a moment long it sail'd its balls of unearthly light over
    our heads,
Then departed, dropt in the night, and was gone;)
Of such, and fitful as they, I sing—with gleams from them would
    gleam and patch these chants,
Your chants, O year all mottled with evil and good—year of forebodings!
Year of comets and meteors transient and strange—lo! even here one
    equally transient and strange!
As I flit through you hastily, soon to fall and be gone, what is this chant,
What am I myself but one of your meteors?

Responses to John Brown in the Southern States

* * * *

John Wilkes Booth, letter to the National Intelligencer, *April 14, 1865*

*At least one man in the Virginia militia was profoundly moved as he
watched John Brown swing from the gallows. He was close enough to
see the slight grasping of Brown's hands and the twitching of his limbs
as the rope jerked taut and the boards of the gallows creaked from the
force of the hundred-and-fifty-pound body coming to a sudden stop. John
Wilkes Booth would later say that he had helped capture Brown, but he
was playing a stock character at the Marshall Theatre in Richmond when
Brown was captured. Booth was fascinated by Brown, however, and was
anxious to attend his hanging. On November 24, as a train of uniformed
militia prepared to leave for Harpers Ferry, Booth asked whether he
could join them. After learning that only men in uniform were allowed
on the train, he expressed his desire to buy a uniform, and acquired the
necessary items from a number of different men.*

*Booth saw much of himself in Brown, even though they differed com-
pletely in social conviction. Although he had recently moved to the North
and was rich and relatively famous as an actor there, Booth identified
himself as a Southerner. He considered slavery a positive good, believed*

that a rigid social hierarchy was essential to civilization, and assumed that the United States was for white men only. But he lauded Brown's pluck, his willingness to act on his beliefs in a daring way, and his performance at Harpers Ferry, and he seemed almost envious of Brown's martyrdom, despite opposing what it stood for. In a draft of a December 1860 speech Booth said Brown was justly executed for attempting "in another way" what Lincoln and the Republican Party were now doing. Brown's method of "open force" was "holier than" the "hidden craft" of the Republicans. Four years later, in 1864, Booth told his sister that Lincoln was "walking in the footprints of old John Brown, but no more fit to stand with that rugged old hero—Great God! no. John Brown was a man inspired, the grandest character of the century!" Brown served as an important source of inspiration for Booth's own efforts to redeem his country and become a martyr to his cause.

The letter here that Booth submitted to the National Intelligencer *on April 14, 1865, the day he murdered Lincoln, resembles Gerrit Smith's public letter foretelling an insurrection, as well as Brown's numerous prison letters. The society it favors is exactly opposite to that for which Brown struggled, but like the warrior of Harpers Ferry, he considers himself a champion of liberty. The reference to Brown suggests that the heroism of that increasingly mythic figure has continued to haunt him.*

Booth and Brown were enormously successful at re-creating themselves and assuming authentic personae. Booth knew Shakespeare the way Brown knew the Bible: Brown associated himself with Biblical heroes, Booth with the characters in Julius Caesar. In November 1864, five months before he assassinated Lincoln, Booth and his brothers starred in Julius Caesar *before an audience of two thousand at the Winter Garden in New York to raise money for a statue of Shakespeare in Central Park. Although Booth played Mark Anthony that night, he preferred the role of Brutus, for he ended his letter to the* National Intelligencer *by saying: "When Caesar had conquered the enemies of Rome and the power that was his menaced the liberties of the people, Brutus arose and slew him. The stroke of his dagger was guided by his love of Rome. It was the spirit and ambition of Caesar that Brutus struck at." Later that night, at Ford's Theatre, Booth played an all-too-authentic Brutus, with Lincoln as his Caesar.*

Booth also identified himself as God's messenger, but in this role he was disingenuous and unconvincing. Unlike Brown and his comrades, Booth could neither assume an authentic spiritual self nor imagine a sacred reality. John Brown never wavered in his belief that he was an instrument in God's hand, and he therefore felt sure that he was doing the right thing by invading Harpers Ferry. Booth, however, states in the source that follows: "Right or wrong, God judge me, not man." He was unsure of God's judgment and of the purity of his intentions. Three days after he murdered Lincoln he wrote in his diary: "Our country [the South] owed all her troubles to him [Lincoln], and God simply made me the instrument of [H]is punishment." He sounds similar to Brown, until his next diary entry: "I do not repent the blow I struck. I may before God but not to man." He wanted to wear his mask of Brutus before men but knew that God could see through it, for in the very next line of his diary he acknowledges his sin by likening himself to Cain: "I think I have done well, though I am abandoned, with the curse of Cain upon me." God, not man, cursed Cain, made him a fugitive and an outcast, and marked him. Booth understood that he had sinned against God but was horrified at the thought of being an outcast and fugitive. Brown embraced his outsider status, for he felt sure that he was following God's will and not the rules and conventions of his world.

The most important difference between the two men was in the source, or location, of their values. What was important to Booth is how his fellow men viewed him. He sought to redeem the South in the eyes of his countrymen rather than in the eyes of God, and consequently he appears particularly concerned about his own status and fame. He lamented in his diary that people would consider him "a common cutthroat." Brutus was honored for striking down a tyrant; why should not he achieve similar honor and glory for killing "a greater tyrant"? By contrast, Brown and his comrades relied—in theory—on their sacred self-sovereignty rather than on social status and worldly fame as the locus of value. They sought to realize a heaven on earth where peace and good-will prevailed, and they cared little for how society viewed them. But like Booth, they used violence to achieve their ends, thereby compromising their belief in the fundamental sacredness of all human beings. In practice, then, Brown was not entirely unconcerned with status; but his quest for fame at Harpers Ferry was a byproduct rather than a central feature of his fundamental beliefs and values.

Washington, D.C., April 14, 1865

To the Editors of the *National Intelligencer*

To My Countrymen: [. . .] When I aided in the capture and execution of John Brown (who was a murderer on our western border, and who was fairly tried and convicted before an impartial judge and jury of treason, and who, by the way, has since been made a God.) I was proud of my little share in the transaction, for I deemed it my duty. and that I was helping our common country to perform an act of justice, but what was a crime in poor John Brown is now considered (by themselves) as the greatest and only virtue of the whole Republican party.

Strange transmigration! Vice to become a virtue, simply because more indulge in it. I thought then, as now, that the Abolitionists were the only traitors in the land, and that the entire party deserved the same fate as poor old Brown. Not because they wished to abolish slavery. but on account of the means they have ever endeavored to use to effect that abolition. If Brown were living I doubt whether he himself would set slavery against the Union. Most, or nearly all the North, do openly curse the Union if the South are to return and retain a single right guaranteed to them by every tie which we once revered as sacred. The South can make no choice. It is either extermination or slavery for themselves (worse than death) to draw from. I know my choice, and hasten to accept it. I have studied hard to discover upon what grounds the right of a State to secede has been denied, whether our very name, United State, and the Declaration of Independence both provide for secession. but there is now no time for words. I know how foolish I shall be deemed for undertaking such a step as this, where on the one side I have many friends and every thing to make me happy, where my profession alone has gained me an income of more than twenty thousand dollars a year, and where my great personal ambition in my profession has been a great field for labor. On the other hand, the South have never bestowed upon me one kind word; a place now where I have no friends, except beneath the sod; a place where I must either become a private soldier or a beggar. To give up all of the former for the latter, (besides my mother and sisters whom I love so dearly although they so widely differ with me in opinion), seems insane; but God is my judge. I love justice more than I do a country that disowns it; more than fame and wealth; more (heaven pardon me if wrong) more than a happy home. I have never been upon a battlefield, but oh! my countrymen, could you all but see the reality or effects of this horrid war. As I have seen them in every state save Virginia, I know you would think like me, and would pray the Almighty to create in the Northern mind a sense of right and justice (even should it possess no seasoning of mercy) and that he would dry up the sea of blood between us which is daily growing wider. Alas, I have no longer a country. She is fast approaching her threatened doom. Four years ago, I would have given a thousand lives to see her remain (as I had always known her) powerful and unbroken. And even now I would hold my life as naught, to see her what she was. Oh! my friends, if the fearful scenes of the past four years had never been enacted, or if what has been had been but a frightful dream, from which we could now awake, with what overflowing hearts could we bless our God and pray for his continued favor.

How I have loved the old flag can never now be known. A few years since and the entire world could boast of [none] so pure and spotless. But I have of late been seeing and hearing of the bloody deeds of which she has been made the emblem. And would shudder to think how changed she had grown. Oh! how I have longed to see her break from the mist of blood and death so circled around her folds, spoiling her beauty and tarnishing her honor. But no; day by day has she been dragged deeper and deeper into cruelty and oppression, till now (in my eyes) her once bright red stripes look like bloody gashes on the face of heaven. I look now upon my early admiration of her glories as a dream. My love (as things stand today) is for the South alone, and to her side I go penniless.

Her success has been near my heart, and I have labored faithfully to further an object which would more than have proved my unselfish devotion. Heartsick and disappointed I turn from the path which I have been following into a bolder and more perilous one. Without malice I make the change. I have nothing in my heart except a sense of duty to my choice. If the South is to be aided it must be done quickly. It may already be too late. When Caesar had conquered the enemies of Rome and the power that was his menaced the liberties of the people, Brutus arose and slew him. The stroke of his dagger was guided by his love of Rome. It was the spirit and ambition of Caesar that Brutus struck at. "Oh that we could come by Caesar's spirit, / And not dismember Caesar! / But, Alas! / Caesar must bleed for it." I answer with Brutus, He who loves his country better than gold or life.

John W. Booth

* * * *

Edmund Ruffin, "Resolution of the Central Southern Rights Association," March 1860

Edmund Ruffin was much excited by Brown's raid. Though sixty-five years old, he enlisted in the Corps of Cadets of the Virginia Military Institute for one day so as to attend Brown's execution, and afterwards arranged to have sent to each governor of a slaveholding state one of Brown's pikes, bought for use by slaves who rebelled in the wake of the raid. Ruffin labeled them: "Sample of the favors designed for us by our Northern Brethren." But unlike John Wilkes Booth, Ruffin did not admire the figure ascending the scaffold. The Harpers Ferry raid had been, as far as Ruffin was concerned, "malignant, atrocious, and devilish," so expressed in the "Resolution of the Central Southern Rights Association," printed here.

Ruffin was, in fact, something of a John Brown for Southern nationalism. The life-trajectory of this eccentric, wild-haired, strongly opinionated old man paralleled Brown's: while the latter farmed sheep, Ruffin developed fertilizer, and then both reinvented themselves as active political radicals in the 1850s. Ruffin, a Virginian slaveholder and wealthy plantation owner, was a respected agriculturalist until the 1850s, and at one point the president of the Virginia State Agricultural Society. But secession became for Ruffin a reform cause as central to the survival and development of the South as agricultural improvement, and by 1855 he believed that slavery, the cornerstone of Southern society, was unsustainable within the existing Union. He gave up agriculture to agitate for secession.

In 1831 he interceded on behalf of a black wrongly accused of involvement in the Nat Turner revolt. But he was a highly vocal advocate of the racial inferiority of blacks, and an outspoken secessionist. A better writer than he was speaker, he produced numerous editorials, three lengthy pamphlets, two major articles, and a long political epistolary novel, Anticipations of the Future. *He organized the Central Southern Rights Association, in Virginia in 1851, then reorganized it in December, 1859, publishing the "Resolution" of the Association in* DeBow's Review *in March 1860, reprinted here. He was the hero of fire-eating southern radicals, invited to attend three secession conventions, and eventually given the honor of firing one of the first batteries against Fort Sumter.*

When it was clear that the South was about to lose the war, Ruffin began to plan his suicide. He thought about it for two months, and on June 17, 1865, after Lee surrendered to Grant, he wrapped himself in the Confederate flag and put a bullet through his brain. The shot is sometimes considered the last of the Civil War. Just as Brown had made his body on the gallows a symbol of the Northern blood that must be shed to free the slaves, and a Christ-like symbol of sacrifice and regeneration, Ruffin made his scattered brains a symbol of the lost cause, an expression of the Southern code of honor. The last words in his diary, penned minutes before killing himself, are: " . . .what will be near my latest breath, I here repeat and would willingly proclaim my unmitigated hatred to Yankee rule—to all political, social and business connections with Yankees, and the perfidious, malignant and vile Yankee race."

DeBow's Review, March 28, 1860.
"Resolution of the Central Southern Rights Association,"

Resolved, That the late outbreak at Harper's Ferry, of a long-concocted and wide-spread Northern conspiracy, for the destruction by armed violence and bloodshed of all that is valuable for the welfare, safety, and even existence of Virginia and the other Southern States, was, in the prompt and complete suppression of the attempt, and in all its direct results, a failure no less abortive and contemptible than the design and means employed, and objects aimed at, were malignant, atrocious, and devilish.

Resolved, That, nevertheless, the indirect results of this Northern conspiracy, and attempted deadly assault and warfare on Virginia, are all-important for the consideration and instruction of the Southern people, and especially in these respects, to wit: 1st, As proving to the world the actual condition of entire submission, obedience, and general loyalty of our negro slaves, in the fact that all the previous and scarcely impeded efforts of Northern abolitionists and their emissaries, aided by all that falsehood and deception could effect, did not operate to seduce a single negro in Virginia to rebel, or even to evince the least spirit of insubordination. 2d, As showing, in the general expression of opinion in the Northern States, through the press and from the pulpit, from prominent or leading public men, and also in the only public meetings yet held, and generally by the great popular voice of the North, that the majority, or at least the far greater number of all whose opinions have yet been expressed, either excuse, or desire to have pardoned, or sympathise with, or openly and heartily applaud the actors in this conspiracy and attack, which could have been made successful only by the means of laying waste the South and extinguishing its institutions and their defenders by fire and sword, and with outrages more horrible than merely general massacre—while the Northern friends of the South, and of the cause of right and law are too few, or too timid to speak openly in our support, or even to make their dissent heard, and too weak to contend with the more numerous and violent assaults of the South.

Resolved, That the time has come when every State and every man of the South should determine to act promptly and effectively for the defense of our institutions and dearest rights, as well as for other important, though less vital interests; and we earnestly appeal, especially to the legislature of Virginia, and also to the legislatures of all others of the slaveholding States, that they will hasten to consult and to deliberate, and will maturely consider and discuss the condition of the Southern States, under all past aggressions and wrongs, especially this last and crowning aggression of Northern usurpation and hatred, and devise suitable and efficient measures for the defense of the Southern people and their institutions, from the unceasing hostility and unscrupulous assaults of Northern enemies, fanatics and conspirators.

* * * *

Governor Henry Wise, speech in Virginia, October 21, 1859

Governor Henry Wise was the Pontius Pilate of Brown's passion play. Elected governor of Virginia in 1856, he had to meet Brown's raid, trial, and execution head-on, in his own territory, and take up a large measure of responsibility for deciding Brown's fate. He rose to the challenge and insisted on prosecuting Brown in a Virginia court, instead of turning him over to federal authorities. Thus he enhanced the prestige of Virginia, furthered his own career, and ensured a speedy trial, so preventing a lynching. He thought carefully about the decision to execute Brown. He saw, as he put it in his "Message to the Virginia Legislature" on December 5, 1859, that "causes and influences lie behind [the raid] more potent far than the little band of desperadoes who were sent ahead to kindle the sparks of a general conflagration." He acknowledged the risk of martyrdom, asking in the same "Message": "will execution of the legal sentence of a humane law make martyrs of such criminals? . . . Shall John Brown be pardoned, lest he might be canonized by execution of felony for confessed murder, robbery treason in inciting servile insurrection in Virginia?" He decided to let Brown hang. But his considered conduct, and his nuanced response to Brown, expressed in the speech given in Richmond on October 21 and published in the Richmond Enquirer, *printed here, won him both Northern and Southern admirers. He was mentioned as a Democratic presidential candidate in 1860.*

Wise's response is particularly interesting because of its clear-sighted even-handedness. A great individualist, Wise had enormous respect for Brown, though he considered him a fanatic. In Brown he encountered "a man of clear head, of courage, fortitude, and simple ingenuousness . . . cool, collected and indomitable . . . vain and garrulous, but firm, and truthful, and intelligent," as he explained in the speech of October 21. He added in his "Message to the Virginia Legislature" of December 5: "it is mockery to call [the raiders] monomaniacs . . . monomaniacs they were, only as the subject of slavery makes men more insensate than any other one subject can. If these men were monomaniacs, then are a large portion of the people of many of the states monomaniacs." He respected Gerrit Smith for the same reasons that he respected Brown: because he appeared honest, intelligent, and courageous. But Wise's admirable perspective failed when he considered Brown's black comrades and supporters, for apparently he could not conceive of a black man as being respectable and honorable. He refused to indict Gerrit Smith, and contemplated having Brown declared insane, thereby sparing his life, but did all he could to capture and execute Frederick Douglass.

Wise's fate remained intertwined with Brown's for some years after Harpers Ferry. In 1861 he conspired with members of the Virginia militia to seize the government armory and arsenal at Harpers Ferry, for

*the defense of Virginia in the American Civil War. When Wise attempted
to return after the war to his plantation in Princess Anne County, which
had been occupied by Union troops since 1862, he found members of the
American Missionary Association, among them one of John Brown's
daughters, running a school for emancipated slaves there. Wise did not
regain possession of the property until 1868. Each morning, the black
students began their school day with several rounds of "John Brown's
Body."*

October 21, 1859

"Old Brown," the fanatic of Osawatomie and Lawrence and Fort Scott memory who denounced the Missourians as "Border Ruffians," became himself the Border Ruffian of Virginia, and is now a prisoner of Treason to her authority. The slaves he would incite to insurrection and massacre would not take up arms against their masters. His spears were untouched by them. And they are themselves mistaken who take him to be a madman. He is a bundle of the best nerves I ever saw, cut and thrust, and bleeding and in bonds. He is a man of clear head, of courage, fortitude, and simple ingenuousness. He is cool, collected and indomitable, and it is but just to him to say, that he was humane to his prisoners, as attested to me by Col. Washington and Mr. Mills; and he inspired me with great trust in his integrity as a man of truth. He is a fanatic, vain and garrulous, but firm, and truthful, and intelligent. His men too, who survive, except the free negroes with him, are like him. He professes to be a Christian, in communion with the Congregationalist Church of the North, and openly preaches his purpose of universal emancipation: and the negroes themselves were to be the agents by means of arms, led on by white commanders. . . . And Col. Washington says that he, Brown, was the coolest and firmest man he ever saw in defying danger and death. With one son dead by his side and another shot through, he felt the pulse of his dying son with one hand and held his rifle with the other and commanded his men with the utmost composure, encouraging them to be firm, and to sell their lives as dearly as they could. Of the three white prisoners, Brown, Stevens and Coppoc, it was hard to say which was most firm; and of the two negroes it was hard to say which seemed the most cowardly and false. The North Carolina negro offered to betray all persons involved in the affair if spared and the Canada negro, who was, I believe, one of the members of their provisional Congress, was a crouching craven, who lied, as Brown said, for his life.

* * * *

Jefferson Davis, remarks to the U.S. Senate, December 8, 1859

Like Edmund Ruffin, Jefferson Davis was a potent symbol of the Lost Cause. Originally a Democrat from Mississippi, also a Mexican War hero, a member of the House of Representatives, a senator, and the secretary of war under Franklin Pierce, Davis is most famous for having served as president of the Confederacy during the Civil War. In his speech here, he responds to Brown's raid and execution and rails against William H. Seward, Lincoln's rival for the Republican nomination in 1860.

Brown returned to haunt Jefferson Davis some years later. Union forces captured the fallen leader on May 10, 1865, and as they drove him to prison sang "John Brown's Body," placing particular emphasis on the verse that went: "We'll hang Jeff Davis from a sour apple tree." Shortly after his capture a sheet music publisher issued "The Sour Apple Tree; Jeff Davis' Last Ditch." Union soldiers had sung of hanging Davis since the beginning of the war, but Davis's fate was to be Fortress Monroe rather than an apple tree. Legend has it that, in an effort to evade arrest, Davis had donned his wife's dress just before the federal cavalry overtook him that day. The Northern press made much of the image. P. T. Barnum even offered five hundred dollars for the petticoats in which Davis was caught, intending to exhibit them in the American Museum. Minus the elusive petticoats, a wax figure of Davis, christened "The Belle of Richmond," soon appeared there.

G. Querner's lithograph of 1865, John Brown Exhibiting His Hangman *(fig. 30), connects Brown to Davis, though the latter had played no part in Brown's trial or execution and was no "hangman" of Brown. Wearing the requisite dress and bonnet, Davis sits in a birdcage that dangles from a hangman's scaffold, holding a sour apple. Free birds wheel in the sky. Tiny figures of comic blacks, dressed in minstrel stage costumes, dance mockingly beneath. As an exhibit, strung up for viewing rather than torture or death, this caged Jefferson Davis is reminiscent of the historical figure captured on May 10, 1865, vulnerable and exposed to the mockery of the John Brown song as he was transported to*

Figure 30: G. Quener, *John Brown Exhibiting His Hangman*, lithograph, 1865. (*Courtesy, Library of Congress.*)

*prison. In the lithograph, Brown, bearded and in a white robe, rises out
of the ground beside the cage, himself doing the taunting this time. The
figure is an embodiment of the haunting John Brown song.*

U.S. Senate, December 8, 1859

I will show before I am done that Seward, by his own declaration, knew
of the Harper's Ferry affair. If I succeed in showing that, then he, like John
Brown, deserves, I think, the gallows, for his participation in it. (Applause.)

Says Mr. Seward: "There is a meaning in all these facts, which it becomes
us to study well. The nation has advanced another stage; it has reached the
point where intervention by the Government, for slavery and slave States, will
no longer be tolerated."

What is that stage to which the Union has advanced? The slave States had
a majority in both branches of Congress once, whereas now the free States are
seventeen, and the slave States only fifteen in this Union. There has been a
transfer of the majorities in Congress from the slave to the free States. The
Government, Senator Seward tells us, has advanced another stage. The Government is no longer to intervene in favor of protection for our slaves. We may
be robbed of our property, and the General Government will not intervene for
our protection. When the Government gets into the hands of the Republican
party, the arm of the General Government, we are told, will not be raised for
the protection of our slave property. Then intervention in favor of slavery and
slave States will no longer be tolerated. We may be invaded, and the Black
Republican Government will stand and permit our soil to be violated and our
people assailed and raise no arm in our defense. The sovereignty of the State
is no longer to be a bar to encroachments upon our rights when the Government gets into Black Republican hands. Then John Brown, and a thousand
John Browns, can invade us, and the Government will not protect us. There
will be no army, no navy, sent out to resist such an invasion; but we will be
left to the tender mercies of our enemies. Has the South then no right to complain? Has the South then no right to entertain apprehensions when we are told
that we are not to be protected in our property when the Republican party shall
get possession of the Government? You even declare you will not defend the
sovereignty of the States. Have we then no right to announce upon this floor
that if we are not to be protected in our property and sovereignty, we are therefore released from our allegiance, and will protect ourselves out of the Union,
if we cannot protect them in the Union? Have we no right to allege that to secure our rights and protect our honor we will dissever the ties that bind us together, even if it rushes us into a sea of blood. . . .

Again, that Senator said: "Free labor has at last apprehended its rights, its
interests, its powers, and its destiny and is organizing itself to assume the Government of the Republic. It will henceforth meet you boldly and resolutely
here, that is on the floor of the Senate, in the Territories or out of them, wherever you may go to extend slavery. It has driven you back in California and
Kansas; it will invade you soon in Delaware, Maryland, Virginia, Missouri,
and Texas."

Ah! "it will invade you soon in Delaware and Virginia." Has it not already
been done? Has it not invaded us with pike, with spear, with rifles—yes, with

Sharpe's rifles? Have not your murderers already come within the limits of our borders, as announced by the traitor, Seward, that it would be done in a short time. At the time of the speech Forbes was in Washington, and he says he communicated to Seward the fact that an invasion would be made. We have been invaded; and that invasion, and the facts connected with it, show Mr. Seward to be a traitor, and deserving of the gallows. (Applause in the galleries.) Brown had organized his constitution when that speech was made . . . and had a conversation with Seward in reference to the invasion. Seward denies that Forbes told him anything about it; but he admits that he had a conversation with Forbes, and that Forbes wanted money. Well, what was that money wanted for? The Senator confesses he had a conversation with Brown about that time. Forbes says it was about the Virginia invasion, and Seward announces in the Senate that Maryland and Virginia would be invaded.

Are these facts not startling? And ought they not to awaken an apprehension in the minds of southern men? Is it not time that we were armed? But, more than that, gentlemen, he goes on to say: "That invasion will be not merely harmless, but beneficent, if you yield seasonably to its just and moderated demands."

That is exactly what John Brown said. He said if we would allow him to take our niggers off without making any fuss about it, he would not kill anybody. (Laughter.) Brown said he did not mean to kill anybody; Seward says it is harmless and beneficent to us if we yield to their just demands. But if we do not yield, what then? Why, Brown said he would kill our people, butcher our women and children. What does Seward say? "Whether that consummation shall be allowed to take effect and with needful and wise precautions against sudden change and disaster, or be hurried on by violence, is all that remains for you (the people of the South) to decide."

That is the very language of John Brown. Whether we will allow them to do it quietly or not, is the only question for the South to decide. Virginia has decided it, and has hung the traitor Brown; and may, if she can get a chance, hang the traitor Seward. (Laughter.) We have repeatedly refused to yield, and you have sought to force us to yield by violence, and Virginia has met it with violence, and has hung the man; and Virginia has had twenty-five hundred men under arms, and has defied all your efforts to rescue him.

* * * *

David Strother (Porte Crayon), articles in Harper's Weekly, *November 5, 12, 1859, and sketches*

David Strother, better known as Porte Crayon (and not to be confused with David A. Strother, the first black in the United States to vote as a result of the Fifteenth Amendment!) was one of John Brown's keenest observers. This writer and artist sketched Brown from the Harpers Ferry raid to the gallows, using his uncle's personal relationship with Governor Wise to gain rare civilian access to the execution. According to some witnesses, he even approached the hanging body soon after Brown was pronounced dead, lifted the execution cap and quickly sketched Brown's still-warm face, intending to send the drawing to the abolitionist Lydia Maria Child as punishment for her admiration of Brown and her recently expressed desire to possess as many images of him as possible.

His articles and sketches were the most popular items in Harper's
Weekly, *though the magazine eventually came under fire for his articles
on Brown, which seemed to the antislavery forces too harsh and to slavery's defenders too mild. He was a Virginian slave-owner but also a
Unionist, eventually a Union officer in the war and Virginia's first post-
war Adjutant General. Initially caught on the fence as the country polarized around the issues of slavery and secession, he was to recall from
the vantage point of 1866 in a* Harper's *article: "I sympathized with neither of extreme factions which, from opposite quarters, seemed to be mutually intent on breaking down the Government and destroying the peace
and prosperity of the country. Preferring to preserve a reputation for
frankness to the doubtful honor of being enrolled among the ex post facto
prophets, I am fain to acknowledge (in the phraseology of tobacco
planters) that I had very few opinions "ready cut and dry" for the occasion. I heard nothing but a confusion of tongues such as followed the
destruction of Babel".*

*Strother remained one of America's most financially successful writers
throughout the 1850s and early 1860s and had an immense influence on
the national literary culture of the 1850s. He was one of the first writers*
Harper's *commissioned to produce "American" content for the magazine. Under the pen name Porte Crayon, adopted after meeting Washington Irving, who published his own* Sketch Book *as the fictional author
"Geoffrey Crayon," he produced stories of the Shenandoah Valley after
the fashion of Irving's Hudson River Valley stories. The* Harper's *readership loved his series of humorous, thinly-fictionalized, anti-modern,
genteel travel narratives, illustrated by his own sketches and generally
set in the western Virginia mountains, which he then published in book
form.*

*Working in the genteel tradition of so-called "genre paintings," which
were popular in the 1840s and 50s, Strother infused his sketches, like his
writing, with middle-class condescension, hostility towards moderniza-
tion, stereotypes of gender and race, and a celebration of class distinction. Brown cuts a rather pathetic figure. Two sketches in particular work
as a pair, representing as they do the same moment from two different
viewpoints: "Interior of the Engine-House" and "The US Marines Storming the Engine-House (figs. 33 and 34)."[7] The artist makes his attitudes
towards the two groups apparent through the contrast between the
marines who work neatly and efficiently as a team and Brown's group
inside that stands around in disarray. The marine dying on the left outside does so in a classic, heroic posture, nobly and stoically drooping
on the arms of his comrades, while the parallel figure on the inside lifts
an anguished face and dies alone, unsupported. The figure lying on his
back outside on the right contrasts to one of Brown's men who lies on*

---

7. These two images were published anonymously in *Frank Leslie's Illustrated Newspaper* and so there is some possibility that they are by the artist William Waud, who
sketched for *Leslie's*.

Figure 31: David Strother (a.k.a. Porte Crayon), "Osawatomie Brown on his way from the Court to his Prison, after hearing Sentence of Death pronounced upon him," *Harper's Weekly*, November 1859. (*Courtesy, Library of Congress.*)

Figure 32: David Strother (a.k.a. Porte Crayon), Osawatamie Brown, wounded and prisoner," *Harper's Weekly*, November 1859. (*Courtesy, Library of Congress.*)

Figure 33: David Strother (a.k.a. Porte Crayon), "Interior of the Engine-House, just before the gate is broken down by the Storming Party—Col. Washington and his Associates as Captives," *Leslie's Illustrated*, October 1859. (*Courtesy, Library of Congress.*)

Figure 34: David Strother (a.k.a. Porte Crayon), "The U.S. Marines Storming the Engine-House. Insurgents Firing through Holes in the Doors," *Leslie's Illustrated*, October 1859. (*Courtesy, Library of Congress.*)

*his front, his slumped face down on the floor. The posture of the com-
mander outside matches that of Brown inside but also that of the African
American on the right, indicating that authority within the Engine-Room
is hopelessly divided, shared as it is with blacks. The useless and static
line of hostages inside reflects the line of men ramming the ladder outside, except that the latter are an active and useful line. The cart inside
has as its double the ladder, which is similarly angled but from the opposite direction, its rungs a more efficient version of the cart's wheel-
spokes in this case, for it is used against the door while the cart, like
the hostages, just takes up space.*

*Other sketches are similarly unflattering. Lying alone on the floor of
the paymaster's office in one sketch (fig. 32), a vacant-looking Brown
stares in an almost demonic fashion, like the character described in the
article here as "the demon which those border forays had awakened."
His seemingly decapitated head pokes out from sheets that coil around
his whole body, giving him a snake-like appearance. This reptilian creature leans against an overturned chair that symbolizes the small scale of
things that he has managed to turn upside down. Brown is also pathetic
on his way to prison (fig. 31); hunched and small, he is clearly emaci-
ated and possibly still wounded. A white child watches from a distance
(on the right) as Brown is lead away by guards, in a strange anticipated
reversal of the baby-kissing paintings, that also feature watching children, guards, and a procession from one of the locations of Brown's last
days to another (prison to gallows rather than courthouse to prison);
though always with a strong, tall, majestic, hero and a physical connection between Brown and the child. Here space and his bed—carried before him as was his coffin on the morning of the baby-kissing paintings—
divide him from the child.*

Harper's Weekly,
Saturday November 5, 1859

And all about this good-humored, good-for-nothing, half-monkey race—the
negroes. Let us walk through the streets of Harpers Ferry and see what part
they have played in the drama . . . There is not the remotest suspicion that a
single individual among them had any foreknowledge of Brown's movement . . . that neither threats, promises, nor persuasion could induce one of
them to join the movement when it was proposed . . . Hayward was shot dead
while heroically expressing his horror of their nefarious designs. Brown discovered early that he could make no use of such as he had captured, and on
Monday morning sent Cook and two other white men with eleven negro prisoners over to the Maryland side, where they were employed in removing the
arms and munitions of war from the Kennedy farm to the log school-house in
the mountain opposite the town. This was done that they might be more con-
venient for those imaginary recruits which the insane brigands still seemed
confidently to expect. As Cook and his companions went at times to the river
to fire across at the Virginians, these negroes escaped, dodging through the
woods, swimming the river and, running every hazard, returned to their re-
spective homes. I conversed with several of them . . . One fellow said that,
when he was taken, a pike was put into his hands by Brown, who told him to

take it and strike for Liberty. "Good lord, Massa," cried Cuffee, in a tremor, "I don't know nuffin 'bout handlin' dem tings." "Take it instantly," cried the philanthropist, "and strike home. This is a day that will long be remembered in the history of your race—a glorious anniversary." "Please God, Massa, I'se got a sore finger," and Cuffee exhibited a stump, the first joint of which he had lost in a wheat-machine some years before.

Finding that he had no mind to be a hero, Brown took him to the Armory, and during the siege sent him out for water. As soon as he got out of range of their guns he broke the pitcher and fled for his life. I narrate the story faithfully as it was told to me. Many similar anecdotes I gleaned from the darkeys themselves, but have not space to relate them. In the town they were passing to and fro with entire freedom, jubilating over their own escapes and jeering at the dead carcasses of the Liberators. Several told me that Brown, in urging them to arm, said, repeatedly, "Don't you know me? Did you never hear of John Brown of Kansas—old Osawatomie Brown?" This only frightened the negroes more. They dropped the pikes, like the devil's gifts, and took to their heels, hiding every where under straw ricks, barns, and stables. On the other hand, there is sufficient and full evidence to show that, had their masters been present in any instance, the slaves would, in their defense, have very cheerfully thrust the pikes into the bodies of the pseudo-philanthropists, proving that they were not so ignorant of the pitch-fork exercise as they pretended.

As for the non-slaveholding inhabitants, on whom Brown calculated so confidently for assistance, it is estimated that at least four out of five of those who volunteered so promptly were non-slaveholders and of non-slaveholding families. They were the fighting men of the occasion, the stormers, who went to work with a remorseless ferocity equaling that of the outlaws themselves . . .

Harper's Weekly,
Saturday November 12, 1859

The more I see of Brown, the more I am convinced that, in addition to his abolition monomania, he is under the influence of a ferocious vanity. Influenced by the infuriate babblings of persons better educated but no wiser than himself, he goes to Kansas, where he earns a reputation as a partisan leader, and at the same time gets a taste of human blood. "Ira brevis furor est."[8] That miserable contest, fomented by unprincipled politicians for party and personal purposes, at length ceased. The belligerent parties shook hands, took a drink, and peacefully turned their energies to cheating one another and the rest of the world. Not so John Brown. The demon which those border forays had awakened is destined never again to sleep. Old Brown, Osawatomie Brown, Brown of Kansas, the Topeka Governor, the dread of Border Ruffians, the Moses of the higher law—can not descend into the vulgar stagnation of common life.

Aesop tells us of a certain harper who, having pleased the sots in an alehouse with his music, was so conceited as to go upon the stage and play for the great public. Here he failed ignominiously, and was hissed. In his grand scheme to overthrow the Government of the United States and the Anglo-Saxon men in the South, with twenty-two men, Brown has failed as signally as the poor musicians . . . Yet . . . to give the devil his dues, he bears himself stiffly

---

8. Latin: "Anger is a brief madness."

under his misfortunes. Fierce as a gun-lock, cool as a sword, he makes no apologies, and yields no triumph to his enemies. In his bearing there is neither weakness nor bravado. Defiant only when stirred; otherwise civil and straightforward; communicative when questioned; and thankful for small favors. In person, Brown is gaunt and tall—over six feet, I should think. He walks like a man accustomed to the woods. His face indicates unflinching resolution, evil passions, and narrow mind.

* * * *

Richmond Daily Enquirer *and* Southern Watchman, *November 2–3, 1859*

On November 6, 2001, the Kansas City Star *commented of Timothy McVeigh that the Oklahoma City bomber had not "entertained journalists around the clock the way the abolitionist John Brown—another famous federal inmate—did 140 years ago." Certainly the 1850s press had a field day with the raid at Harpers Ferry, and the trial and execution at Charleston. They were the first national media events in American history, and Brown himself recognized the potential value of the press to his self-made martyrdom. He published his prison letters in the abolitionist newspapers of the North and performed his best at trial and execution for the editors of the papers.*

But the Southern press was far beyond his reach. Representative articles from two of the most important newspapers in the South are reprinted here. The Richmond Daily Enquirer *was the major Virginia organ, a Democratic newspaper edited by O. Jennings Wise, the son of Governor Wise. This article of November 2 opposes recent requests to keep Brown alive and must be read in light of this connection to Governor Wise, for he was personally responsible for the decision to hang Brown rather than imprison him for life. The paper was wildly hostile towards Republican newspapers and Northern interests in the press, and forced Southerners to engage with the abolitionist threat.*

Panic pervades the majority of Southern newspaper articles written on Brown in late 1859. The press in the South debated ad nauseam *the issues of whether or not it was advisable to kill Brown, who else might be guilty, and how likely it was that slaves would ever join agitators in rebellion. The* Charleston Mercury *called the raid "a portentous omen of the future," and an article of November 3 in the* Southern Watchman, *published here, also acknowledged the potential danger of the raid to the Union. Far from downplaying Brown's importance, as some Southern newspapers persisted in doing, the article concludes: "Let the people but will it, and agitation must cease. Let it go on, and the sun of liberty will set in blood!"*

Richmond Daily Enquirer,
November 2, 1859

A Suggestion for Governor Wise

Under this head, the "New York commercial Advertiser," a Black Republican Free-soil sheet, puts forth an argument to show that Brown is an "ultrafanatic," "little better than insane," "with mind and heart alike too warped for him to discern evil from good." Under these circumstances, the "Advertiser," argues that it would not be good policy for Virginia to hang Brown and his fellow-murderers. . . .

A cunning policy does the "Advertiser" suggest. Pardon the principal and permit the accessories to escape! Extend clemency to Brown and forgiveness to Seward, Hale, Giddings, Smith and Greeley!—The "Advertiser" begs the Executive of Virginia not to make a martyr of Brown; that being a fanatic he is insane certainly to some degree, and our New York contemporary fears direful consequences will spring from his execution. That as the blood of the martyrs was the seed of the Church, so from the grave of john Brown the "Advertiser" fears a crop of armed fanatics may spring up destructive to Virginia and the South. It would perhaps have been more to the point to have shown that the pardon of Brown would have lessened the number of existing fanatics rather than by suggesting their increase from a due course of justice. But we apprehend the Executive of Virginia will not turn an attentive ear to suggestions coming from such a source as the New York Commercial "Advertiser." The Republican party, of which the "Advertiser" is an organ, is too deeply implicated in the actions of their chief leaders to offer suggestions with regard to the just punishment of one of their numbers. . . .

Violated laws and murdered citizens demand a victim at the hand of justice, if Brown is a crazed fanatic, irresponsible either in morals or law, there are yet guilty parties. He is then the agent of wicked principals. If the Northern people believe Brown insane, what punishment is due to those who have poisoned his mind with the "irrepressible conflict" and spurred his fanaticism to deeds of blood and carnage? He may be insane, but there are other criminals, guilty wretches, who instigated the crimes perpetrated at Harper's Ferry. Bring these men, bring Seward, Greeley, Giddings, Hale and Smith to the jurisdiction of Virginia, and Brown and his deluded victims in the Charlestown jail may hope for pardon. In the opinion of Virginia the five Republican leaders, above mentioned, are more guilty than even John Brown and his associates. An ignorant fanaticism may be pleaded in paliation of the crime of Brown, but the five Republican leaders would spurn such a stultifying plea! They would not compromise their intelligence even at the cost of their morality. Let the friends of Brown, let all who believe him to be insane, and all who intend to represent him as a crazy fanatic, for whose folly no party is responsible, deliver up Seward, Greeley, Giddings, Smith and Hale. A fair trial, at their own time, with their own counsel, will be freely given them, and if Virginia does not prove them guilty, they too shall go unhurt.

The Southern Watchman,
November 3, 1859
The Harper's Ferry Insurrection

This subject still engrosses much of the public attention. It has been condemned, so far as we have observed, by the Black Republican newspapers. They ought, however, to possess sufficient penetration to perceive that however far they might themselves be from engaging directly in the treasonable plots of Ossawatomie Brown, the general tone of their papers, like the sentiments of Seward's speech, has a tendency to incite other fanatics, less prudent, to the commission of acts of treason and bloodshed.

Figure 35: William
H. Johnson, *John
Brown's Legend,*
ca. 1945. **First two
rows, left to right:**
Gerrit Smith,
Theodore Parker,
Samuel Gridley
Howe; Thomas Went-
worth Higginson,
Franklin B. Sanborn,
George L. Stearns.
Third Row, left:
prison, guardhouse,
and courthouse,
Charles Town; Owen
Brown, John Brown's
father. **Next two
rows:** John Brown's
sons Salmon, John
Jr., Jason, and Owen.
Top right: Harpers
Ferry with Shenandoah and Potomac Rivers. **Center, right:** John Brown
about 1857, with sketches of the Kennedy Farm, a nearby cabin, and the
schoolhouse where arms were stored. **Top to bottom, right:** John H Kagi,
A. D. Stevens, Oliver Brown, and Watson Brown. **Lower right:** North Elba
farmhouse and grave. (Adapted from Adelyn D. Breeskin, William H. Johnson, 1901–1970 [Washington, D.C., 1971].) (*Courtesy, Smithsonian American
Art Museum, Gift of the Harmon Foundation.*)

Some of the Northern papers are reading to the South lectures on the subject of the outbreak, and remind our people that they are quietly reposing on
the crust of a volcano, ready at any moment to burst forth and destroy them.
This, they say, is the lesson the late outbreak teaches. No foolhardy enthusi-
asts ever missed the mark further. It teaches a lesson to the fanatics of the
North. It shows them that the slaves their misdirected philanthropy would relieve are so well satisfied with their condition that they will not join them in
their rebellion. And by the time the outraged sovereignty of Virginia has been
satisfied, they will learn one other great lesson, viz: that the South can produce hemp enough to hang all the traitors the great "Northern hive" can send
among her people to stir up sedition and insurrection!

It teaches the whole country—all sections of it—a great lesson, which we
hope all will profit by—that is, that the everlasting agitation of the slavery
question will inevitably lead to civil war and bloodshed! Let the people, then,
of all parties—all those who would preserve the Union as our fathers made
it—indignantly rebuke the agitators and drive them back to their kennels. The
present is a propitious time to begin such a work. Let the people but will it,
and agitation must cease. Let it go on, and the sun of liberty will set in blood!

CODA

"Does anyone even study history anymore?" So inquired Timothy McVeigh, who was soon to become the Oklahoma City bomber, in a 1994 letter to the American Legion.[1] He apparently *did* study history, for after his attack on the federal buildings he wrote to reporters that he hoped America would remember him as a freedom fighter akin to that historical American terrorist, John Brown. "If I am going to hell," he added, "I'm gonna have a lot of company."[2] According to one newspaper he even "cited slavery abolitionist John Brown as an inspiration . . . [though] conveniently forgot or downplayed the fact that his militia philosophy has its repressive roots in a reactionary, rightwing agenda of racism, sexism and cultish religious fundamentalism."[3]

Gore Vidal, who attended McVeigh's execution by invitation of the condemned man, was another who still studied history. Vidal told the American press that "McVeigh saw himself as John Brown of Kansas," and was "reacting to something that is going on in the country, as John Brown reacted against slavery." He added ominously, "one year after [Brown] was executed, we had a Civil War. I trust we don't have one; but we might have one." In an article for *Vanity Fair* in November 1998, Vidal compared the Oklahoma City bombing to "Pearl Harbor, a great shock to an entire nation and, one hopes, a sort of wake-up call to the American people that all is not well with us." He might as well have added John Brown's raid on Harpers Ferry as another precedent, for descriptions of the former as a "shock" and a warning abound in historical writing and cultural criticism.

Journalists writing in the wake of McVeigh's bomb could also have answered in the affirmative his question about the study of history. *The Gully* online magazine noted on June 17, 2001: "The shadow of violent abolitionist John Brown hangs over Timothy McVeigh and the Oklahoma City bombing. . . One of McVeigh's heroes was America's own John Brown." The article went on to describe McVeigh in terms that the introduction to this anthology applies similarly to Brown: "He saw himself as catalyst and teacher, a patriot holding the U.S. government accountable. . . He was a living mirror held in front of our faces, but we pretended it wasn't there. . . Our opinion shapers' refusal to consider that America runs on the same moral and cultural batteries that propelled McVeigh, means they had to turn him into a self-made monster." The magazine *The Reporter* saw McVeigh through a similarly historical

---

1. *New York Times*, June 11, 2001, "History and Timothy McVeigh."
2. According to the *Courier-Journal,* Louisville, Kentucky, Sunday, June 10, 2001.
3. See the *Athens Banner-Herald*, June 16, 2001.

lens: "McVeigh's many contemporary missives take great pains to say that Oklahoma City was a planned, measured act of war against a totalitarian government whose own violence had grown intolerable. Does this sound familiar? In the late 18th century, terrorist acts were committed routinely against the British army, leading to an escalation of hostilities and a full-blown revolutionary war in colonial America. In like manner . . . [John Brown] sought to free slaves and arm them for violent revolution against white oppressors. . . . Oklahoma City was the final desperate chapter . . . of the so-called modern 'patriot' movement in America."[4]

Numerous other journalists emphasized and explored the connections between Brown and McVeigh. The magazine *Race Traitor* said of McVeigh in its Fall 2001 issue: "He might even have become the John Brown of our day. It's a shame he didn't." On December 3, 1998, the online magazine *Salon* noted: "Brown's vision is reminiscent of the logic behind Timothy McVeigh's bombing of the Murrah building in Oklahoma City—the sight of a federal building in rubble was supposed to rally the militia around the country to rise and overthrow Washington." The article goes on to differentiate the pair: "This might have actually happened had McVeigh let God do the planning. The Lord was ostensibly the one responsible for John Brown's acts of righteous terrorism, including his murderous rampage against proslavery settlers in Kansas in 1856. Brown possessed that primal nineteenth century American trait that Joseph Smith and Brigham Young shared: personal communication with God."

To study history, as McVeigh apparently believed we should, is to contextualize its characters; to see the night sky behind the meteors. Through sources and contextualization Brown's apparent explosion onto the night-sky of 1859 becomes a logical and gradual emergence. But his meteor traces a new and complex pattern across the sky in the first decade of the twenty-first century. As we have seen, to read his writings and unravel the details of his life is to come face-to-face with a man who wrote himself into myth and lived with an eye on the movement of history. He was as conscious and manipulative of historical and mythic precedent as McVeigh. Any biographer of Brown inevitably acknowledges that Brown was his own biographer, and any artist interpreting Brown knows that Brown interpreted himself first. The sources that make up this anthology reveal Brown's attitude toward identity and role-playing. They sketch the symbiotic relationship between Brown's sense of self and his actions; his self-presentation to America and America's response; Brown's view of the world and, during his lifetime and after his death, the world's view of him. But the world after McVeigh and 9/11 sees an entirely new John Brown.

As American notions about terrorism, idealistic politics, and individual protest shift and change, and the debate about America's role of a terrorist state or adversary of terrorism continues, David W. Blight asks, "How indeed weigh John Brown's body at the turn of the twenty-first century, a time when our notions of violence in a righteous cause are troubled by a litany of terrorism committed by individuals, religious groups, and governments?"[5] Blight poses

---

4. *TheReporter.com*, May 6, 2001.
5. David W. Blight, article in *The American Prospect*, March 13, 2000. See also reference in this anthology's introduction to Benét's poem ("how weigh John Brown's body?")

a pivotal question: "Can John Brown remain an authentic American hero in an age of Timothy McVeigh, Osama Bin Laden, and the bombers of abortion clinics?" After Oklahoma City, 9/11, and the wars on "terror" in Afghanistan and Iraq, John Brown looks different. Equally, twenty-first century suicide bombers, freedom fighters, and wagers of holy war all change shape when held up to the historic light of that first American terrorist, John Brown. More than ever Brown's words merit a close reading, his role in American myth and history a fresh attention. Confronting Brown afresh brings the whole weight of nineteenth-century history to bear on our contemporary global politics of the early twenty-first century. As Blight explains, "Brown provokes us to think about the meaning and uses of martyrdom. His story is a template for our understanding of revolutionary violence in any age; . . . he represents some of our deepest political ambivalences, standing as he does for high ideals and ruthless deeds." We should use Brown's "template" to remind ourselves that American culture sanctions violence in the name of a cause, and to deepen the ongoing debate about "principled violence"—that emblematic and troubling concept in American history and culture.

It is far more likely, however, that Brown's story will again become that of a madman and villain, taking on the same aspect as that of the Jim Crow and McCarthy years. A horror for the violence at Pottawatomie and Harpers Ferry may supersede any admiration for Brown's humanity toward blacks. We may regret that Brown shifted the antislavery movement from an era of New Testament love and peace to a time of Old Testament vengeance and apocalypse, and that America abolished slavery the John Brown way. Silhouetted against the sky, Brown will continue to shift and sway through history, now and again burning brighter and with the clarity of a meteor; his memory possessing the perpetual motion of a body swinging at the end of a rope from a scaffold, on a crisp December morning in 1859. Though in a later time he may be again a patriot and hero, in the first years of this new century he will likely come to seem anti-democratic and un-American, perhaps even responsible for all the terrorists that came after him. The claim of the *Christian Mirror,* made on December 6, 1859, may come to look believable: that Brown wanted "to put a premium on such measures [like the Harpers Ferry raid] in the future, and to move a host of reckless aspirants to power and fame to attempt the same thing." If, as the *Boston Daily Advertiser* predicted on December 2, 1859, Brown's execution has tended "to reproduce other attempts like that of Brown," then McVeigh is part of Brown's legacy. Certainly, John Brown was "not buried but planted," as George William Curtis commented in 1859, and so may have sprung "up a hundred-fold."[6] Thoreau warned America: "when you plant, or bury, a hero in his field, a crop of heroes is sure to spring up."[7] Brown planted no church with his martyr's seeds of blood, tears, and ink, but rather a crop of division, provocation, and change. It was a riotous harvest.

6. George William Curtis, lecture in Worcester, Massachusetts, December 12, reported in the *Ohio Sentinel*, December 15, 1859.
7. See in this anthology: Henry David Thoreau, "A Plea for Captain John Brown," October 30, 1859.

CHRONOLOGY

	John Brown's life	Major events
1793	*February 13:* Owen Brown marries Ruth Mills in Torrington, Litchfield County, Connecticut.	Fugitive Slave Act makes it a crime to help an escaped slave or prevent his arrest.
1800	*May 9:* John Brown born in Torrington, the son of Owen and Ruth Mills Brown. His father, a strict Calvinist, believed slavery to be a sin against God. Nat Turner is born the same year.	In Philadelphia, free blacks petition Congress to repeal the 1793 Fugitive Slave Act. *August 30*: Gabriel Prosser's plan to lead Virginia slaves in rebellion revealed.
1805	*June:* Brown family moves to Hudson, Ohio, a town eventually known for its abolitionism.	*May:* Lewis and Clark expedition reach the Rocky Mountains and later that year the Pacific Ocean.
1807	John begins to ramble around the countryside alone. He describes his sixth year as his entrance to the "School of adversity."	British Parliament and U.S. Congress vote to end the African slave trade.
1808	*December:* John's mother dies in Hudson, and his father marries again the following year.	Methodist Episcopal Church removes the rules prohibiting slavery from the Disciplines it sends to the South.
1812	Twelve-year-old John travels a hundred miles, from Ohio to Detroit, with a herd of cattle, and sees a child slave beaten with an iron shovel. This event made him, as he explained in his autobiography, "a determined Abolitionist," for it made him "reflect on the wretched, hopeless condition of Fatherless and Motherless slave children," asking, "is God their Father?"	State of Louisiana enters the union. *June 1*: President Madison asks for a declaration of war against Great Britain because of the blockade of American ports. *June 19*: War declared against England.
1816	John becomes a member of his father's Congregational church in Hudson after making a formal profession of faith. *April 15:* Mary Day, John Brown's second wife, was born in Granville, Washington County, New York. *Summer:* John goes to study at Moses Hallock's school in Plainfield,	Seminole Wars begin in Florida, as a result of slaves taking refuge with Seminole Indians. The American Colonization Society is founded to resettle free blacks in Africa. Paul Cuffe, a shipowner and son of a former African American slave,

	Massachusetts, a preparatory school for ministers, artists and writers.	brings thirty-eight free African Americans to settle in the British colony of Freetown, Sierra Leone.
1817	John transfers to the Morris Academy in Litchfield, Connecticut, but inflammation of the eyes forces him to return to Hudson.	James Forten leads blacks in a Philadelphia protest meeting against colonization.
1819	John goes into business with Levi Blakeslee: they build a cabin and tannery, and John cooks for the "Bachelors Hall." He also begins to teach Sunday school in Hudson.	Congress authorizes armed vessels to be sent to Africa to suppress the slave trade, but defeats an amendment that would have prohibited slavery in Arkansas Territory.
1820	John decides to become a surveyor, and teaches himself geometry and trigonometry. *June 21*: John marries Dianthe Lusk, the daughter of the Bachelors Hall housekeeper and cook, in the new Congregational Meeting House at Hudson, Portage County (now Summit), Ohio.	Missouri Compromise admits Missouri and Maine as slave and free states, respectively. The measure establishes the 36 degree, 30 parallel of latitude as a dividing line between free and slave areas of the territories. U.S. Congress defines the slave trade as piracy.
1821	John becomes a freeholder and voter, and is active in the Hudson community, especially in law enforcement. *July 25*: John's first child and namesake, John Brown, Jr., is born in Hudson, Ohio.	Kentucky representatives present resolution to Congress protesting Canada's reception of fugitive slaves. Republic of Liberia in West Africa is established as a refuge for freed American slaves.
1823	*January 19*: Jason Brown born in Hudson.	Monroe Doctrine proclaims that the Americas will no longer be the object of European colonization.
1824	*November 4*: Owen Brown born in Hudson.	Bureau of Indian Affairs organized.
1825	A fugitive slave and his wife, escaped from Kentucky, appear at John's house. John and Dianthe feed and hide the pair.	Fanny Wright, a Scottish reformer, publishes a *Plan for the Gradual Abolition of Slavery* and establishes a cooperative in which slaves could earn their freedom in Tennessee.
1826	Brown and family move to Randolph, now New Richmond, Pennsylvania, where Brown establishes a tannery.	Secretary of State Henry Clay asks Canada to help return escaped slaves and the Canadian government refuses.
1827	*January 9*: Frederick Brown born in New Richmond.	First black newspaper, *Freedom's Journal*, published in New York.
1829	*February 18:* Ruth Brown born in New Richmond.	*August 10:* Race riot in Cincinnati, Ohio. White mobs attack black freedmen, 1000 of whom then left for Canada.

1830	*December 21:* Frederick Brown (second son named Frederick) born in New Richmond.	First National Negro Convention.
1831	John punishes his eldest, John Brown, Jr., for transgressions, and receives, Christ-like, two-thirds of the lashes due to his son on his own back, thus demonstrating the Doctrine of Atonement. *March 31:* Frederick Brown (elder son) dies at New Richmond.	*January 1:* William Lloyd Garrison begins publishing *The Liberator*, the country's first publication to demand an immediate end to slavery. Georgia offers $5000 to anyone bringing him to trial. *August 22:* Nat Turner leads slave uprising in Southampton, Va. 70 whites are killed, & 100 blacks in the search for Turner.
1832	*August 7:* Unnamed son dies at birth in New Richmond. *August 10:* Dianthe Brown, John's wife, dies of heart failure in New Richmond.	New England Anti-Slavery Society founded Louisiana requests Federal Government to arrange with Mexico to allow slaves escaped from Louisiana to be claimed.
1833	John working as the postmaster in New Richmond, as well as running his tannery business. *July 11:* John Brown marries seventeen-year-old Mary Day, sister of his new housekeeper. She bears him thirteen children and takes care of the five children born to Dianthe.	Britain adopts an emancipation and apprenticeship plan that prepares 800,000 slaves for freedom. Oberlin, the first college to admit blacks, opens. *December:* Garrison and 60 delegates found the American Anti-Slavery Society.
1834	*May 11:* Sarah Brown born in New Richmond.	*October:* White anti-abolitionist rioters destroy 45 homes in Philadelphia's black community.
1835	John and family move to Franklin Mills (now Kent), Portage County, Ohio where John enters into a partnership with Zenas B. Kent to build a tannery. They remain here, with John residing off and on, until 1839. *October 7:* Watson Brown born at Franklin Mills.	A mob drags Garrison through Boston and nearly lynches him before authorities remove him. Mob in Charleston, S.C. burns abolitionist literature. Abolitionist writers are ejected from Southern states. Harriet Jacobs goes into hiding until 1842.
1836	*January:* During a period of extreme land speculation, Brown moves his family to Franklin Mills, Ohio, and borrows money to buy land.	The number of antislavery societies reaches 527. By 1838 there will be 1,300 with 109,000 members.

	October 2: Salmon Brown, born at Hudson, Ohio.	Massachusetts Supreme Court rules that a slave brought within its borders by a master is free.
1837	Brown is almost ruined financially by the Panic of 1837. *November 3*: Charles Brown born at Hudson. *November 7:* Upon hearing that abolitionist newspaperman Elijah Lovejoy has been shot and killed in Illinois by a proslavery mob, Brown commits to working for the destruction of slavery.	*May 10:* Beginning of the Panic of 1837, bank failures and unemployment. Andrew Jackson recognizes the Republic of Texas; the U.S. now consists of 13 slave and 13 free states. Presbyterians divide over slavery.
1838	*December:* John goes to Boston and New York to respond in court to several suits against him, and to meet creditors. He also buys and sells sheep.	Underground Railroad is formally organized. *Sept:* Frederick Douglass escapes from slavery in Baltimore.
1839	*March 9:* Oliver Brown born at Franklin Mills. *June:* John makes another trip east, to New York and Boston, on business, seeking money to keep his estate from liquidation.	Spanish slave ship *Amistad*, carrying 53 slaves, is taken over in a mutiny by their leader, Cinqué, who orders the two surviving whites to sail the ship to Africa. The ship is seized off the coast of Long Island and the Africans are jailed.
1840	John and his family move back to Hudson and he is forced into bankruptcy. The family's home is sold and Brown is jailed for resisting. *December 7:* Peter Brown born at Hudson, Summit County, Ohio.	Garrison and others walk out when women abolitionists are not seated as delegates at the World Anti-Slavery Convention in London. Further schisms between Garrison and gradualists develop.
1841	John is legally bankrupt, and cleared of any obligation to repay his debts. He and the family move to Richfield, Summit County, Ohio, where he finally begins to raise sheep, in partnership with Captain Heman Oviatt, to whom he owed several thousand dollars.	Supreme Court frees the *Amistad* prisoners on grounds that the international slave trade is illegal. *7 November:* Slaves aboard the *Creole* en route from Hampton, Va., to New Orleans, mutiny and sail to a British port in the Bahamas, where they are freed.
1842	*September 14*: Austin Brown born at Richfield. *September 28:* A federal court finalizes John's bankruptcy case and he is stripped by creditors of all but bare essentials.	Supreme Court rules in *Prigg* v. *Pennsylvania* that state officials are not required to assist in the return of fugitive slaves. Webster-Ashburton Treaty reinforced Atlantic slave trade ban.

1843	Four of John's children die in an epidemic in Richfield: *September 11:* Charles Brown *September 21:* Austin Brown *September 22:* Peter Brown *September 23*: Sarah Brown *December 23:* Anne Brown born at Richfield.	New England railroads integrate after "ride-ins." Henry Highland Garnet delivers "Address to the Slaves" at the National Negro Convention, advocating a general strike and physical resistance.
1844	The Brown family moved to Akron, Summit County, Ohio. Brown begins work as a partner in the wool business Perkins & Brown.	Methodists divide over slavery. Expansionist Democrat James K. Polk defeats Whig Henry Clay in the presidential elections.
1845	*June 22*: Amelia Brown born at Akron.	Frederick Douglass publishes *Narrative of the Life of Frederick Douglass.*
1846	Perkins sends John to run the business in Massachusetts, and Brown moves to Springfield to be near the Perkins and Brown warehouse. Gerrit Smith gives land to New York blacks in Essex and Franklin Counties, New York, where John Brown settles at North Elba. *September 11*: Sarah Brown born at Akron. *October 30:* Amelia Brown dies in Akron, scalded to death by her older sister Ruth.	*May 11:* United States declares war on Mexico. *June 14:* Settlers proclaim the independent Republic of California, which is annexed by the U.S. in August. *July:* Thoreau is jailed for refusal to pay poll tax, giving rise to his essay of 1849, known as *Civil Disobedience.* *August*: House of Representatives adopts the Wilmot Proviso, which would bar slavery from any territory acquired from Mexico. The Senate rejects the proviso.
1847	In Springfield, John befriends blacks and sometimes preaches at a Methodist church with a black congregation. Frederick Douglass visits John. They begin a friendship and discuss plans to free slaves.	Douglass publishes his abolitionist newspaper, the *North Star.* Senator Lewis Cass proposes "popular sovereignty," which meant residents of territories would decide whether the state should be slave or free.
1848	John composes "Sambo's Mistakes," an essay in which he adopts the persona of an African American. The *Ram's Horn* publishes it anonymously.	The Free Soil Party nominates Martin Van Buren on an antislavery platform. He receives 10 percent of votes cast.

	May 20: Ellen Brown born in Springfield, Massachusetts.	*March*: Treaty ends the Mexican War. U.S. takes a third of Mexico's territory.
1849	*April 30:* Ellen Brown dies in Springfield. *Summer*: John travels to Europe to sell wool. His trips to England, France, Belgium, Germany, and Russia are unsuccessful and he returns in the fall.	Harriet Tubman escapes from slavery in Maryland. She goes on to help at least 300 slaves to freedom before the Civil War. *November:* California applies for admission to Union as a free state.
1850	John starts to close down the Perkins and Brown business during 1850 and 1851. He moves between North Elba and Springfield, also traveling west on business. Early in 1850 Brown hears from his family that the experimental North Elba settlements were faced with ruin. Some of the black settlers were leaving. At Thanksgiving Brown speaks on the Fugitive Slave bill to the congregation at his church.	*January*: Henry Clay introduces the "Compromise of 1850," which admits California as a free state, among other provisions. The new Fugitive Slave Act is passed, allowing slaveholders to retrieve slaves in Northern states and free territories without due process of law, prohibiting anyone from helping fugitives, and requiring citizens to assist in the retrieval of escaped slaves. Captured blacks are denied any legal power to prove their freedom.
1851	John establishes the United States League of Gileadites with the blacks of Springfield, a self-defense organization. He writes the document, "Words of Advice," with an "Agreement" and "Resolutions." The senator Charles Sumner meets with Brown and the Gileadites in Springfield.	A leading antislavery weekly begins to publish Harriet Beecher Stowe's *Uncle Tom's Cabin.* *February 15:* Frederick Jenkins is seized by slave-catchers. Richard Henry Dana, Jr., tries to free him by legal means, but he is rescued by a group of African Americans.
1852	*April 26:* John's unnamed son born at Akron. *May 17:* Unnamed son dies at Akron.	Josiah Priest publishes *The Bible defense of slavery.* *Uncle Tom's Cabin* sells one million copies within the year.
1853	Religious tensions between John and his sons develop. John, now living with his family in Akron, Ohio, becomes involved with the Underground Railroad. He also manages the Perkins flock of sheep.	*August:* John A. Quitman begins his "Filibustering Activities" within the liberation movement in Cuba, to try to eventually bring the area under United States control as a slave state. This continues through April 1855.
1854	Henry Thompson, John's son-in-law, begins to build John a house in North Elba. Frederick Douglass visits John at	*May 25:* Kansas-Nebraska Bill passed, sweeping aside The Missouri Compromise, which restricted the expansion of slavery. Those settling the new territories will decide, by

Akron, and on another occasion so does the abolitionist Henry Highland Garnet.

September 25: Ellen Brown, John's last child, is born in Akron.

The partners dissolve their business, Perkins & Brown. The partnership ends on a positive note, Perkins keen that John remain in Ohio. But John breaks all ties with Akron and finally becomes a permanent resident of North Elba.

October: The unmarried sons, Owen, Frederick, and Salmon leave for Kansas territory in the wake of the Kansas-Nebraska Bill, but are unable to persuade their father to join them, though he is tempted.

popular vote, whether to be "free" or "slave." The violence of "Bleeding Kansas" begins, as hundreds of proslavery and antislavery advocates move into the area.

June 2: 50,000 in Boston watch Anthony Burns, a fugitive slave, taken in shackles to a ship.

July 6: The Republican Party founded in the wake of the Kansas-Nebraska Act convention at Jackson, Michigan.

October 16: Lincoln's "Peoria Speech" makes the moral and political case against slavery and its extension.

Garrison publicly burns a copy of the U.S. Constitution, calling it "a covenant with death and an agreement with Hell."

1855	*Spring 1855:* Two more of John's sons, John Jr. and Jason, come to Kansas and settle with their brothers ten miles west of Osawatomie. *June:* John decides to follow his sons, but leave Mary and the children behind at North Elba. *October 6:* John arrives in Osawatomie. *December 7:* John and four of his sons help defend Lawrence during the Wakarusa War.	Herman Melville publishes *Benito Cereno.* Walt Whitman publishes *Leaves of Grass.* Frederick Douglass publishes *My Bondage and My Freedom.* Radical Abolitionists' Convention. Senator Charles Sumner and black lawyer Robert Morris desegregate Boston schools.
1856	*May:* John and his men defend Lawrence, Kansas, which was threatened by proslavery forces. On May 24 John directs his men in the murder of five proslavery settlers at Pottawatomie Creek. *June 2:* At the Battle of Black Jack in southeastern Douglas County, Brown defeats Henry Clay Pate. *August 30:* John fights at the Battle of	*April 5:* Booker T. Washington born, in Franklin County, Virginia. *May 22:* Charles Sumner, of Massachusetts, is caned almost to death in his office in Washington, D.C., by Congressman Preston Brooks, of South Carolina, after delivering an antislavery speech, "The Crime Against Kansas." *Summer:* Free-state travel blocked on

	Osawatomie, and his second son, Frederick, is killed. ***October:*** Brown leaves Kansas.	the Missouri River by proslavery forces.
1857	***January***: Franklin Sanborn, secretary for the Massachusetts State Kansas Committee, introduces Brown to influential abolitionists in Boston, some of whom will become the "Secret Six." Brown begins to travel through New England, raising money for the Kansas campaign. ***March 12:*** John Brown tells a Concord audience, including Thoreau and Emerson, that he hates violence but accepts it as God's will. ***April 6:*** John hides in the house of Judge Thomas Russell to avoid arrest by a federal marshal.	Economic recession hits. ***March:*** The *Dred Scott Decision* by the Supreme Court rules that Scott, a Missouri slave who sued for freedom on grounds that when his master took him into free territory he had become a free man, was not a citizen, and so not eligible to sue. With a Southern majority, it also ruled that no black, free or slave, was a U.S. citizen, that slaveholders had the right to take slaves into free territory, and that Congress had no power to prevent slavery in the territories. It thereby declared the Missouri Compromise unconstitutional.
1858	***February 22***: Brown meets with Gerrit Smith and Franklin Sanborn in Peterboro, New York, and outlines a plan to raid Harpers Ferry. Sanborn calls a meeting of the "Secret Six." ***May 8:*** Brown's "Constitutional Convention of the Oppressed People of the United States" is held in Chatham, Ontario, Canada. African American leaders attend. Brown produces and presents his Provisional Constitution for a government in a free nation, and plans his Harpers Ferry raid. ***Summer***: Brown seeks support for his raid in New York, Connecticut, Kansas, Ohio. ***December 20–21***: Brown leads a raid on two proslavery homesteads in Missouri, confiscates property, and liberates 11 slaves. He then travels for eighty-two days to escort the slaves along the Underground Railroad to Canada.	President Buchanan's request that Kansas be admitted as a slave state is rejected. Financial panic of 1858. ***May 18***: Five free-state men are killed at the Massacre of Marais des Cygnes, Kansas. ***June 16***: At Springfield, Illinois, senatorial candidate Abraham Lincoln gives the "House Divided" speech at the close of the Republican state convention, thus opening the senatorial campaign: "A house divided against itself cannot stand. I believe this government cannot endure, permanently half slave and half free." ***August to October***: The Lincoln-Douglas Debates, an exchange between Republican Abraham Lincoln and Democrat Stephen Douglas, bring Lincoln into the national spotlight, enabling his nomination for President in 1860, though he loses the election for the

1859

Mid-March: Brown reaches Detroit and moves the slaves into Canada.

July 3: Brown arrives in Harpers Ferry and rents a farm five miles away. His men slowly arrive.

October 16: In the evening the Harpers Ferry Raid begins. Brown's men capture the watchmen and the armory. They take the arsenal and Rifle Works, and capture local militia leaders, including Colonel Lewis W. Washington, a grand nephew of George Washington.

October 17: At 1:30 a.m. a train arrives at the Ferry and in an exchange the raiders kill the black baggage master. At 7 a.m. the conductor alerts railroad officials to the situation, who telegraph President Buchanan. Local militia move to the Ferry. During the day several of Brown's men are killed. At nightfall Brown ignores demands that he surrender. Lieutenant Colonel Robert E. Lee and Lieutenant J. E. B. Stuart arrive at the Ferry.

October 18: At dawn Lee's Marines break into the Engine- House. Lieutenant Israel Green attacks Brown with the dress sword he brought by mistake. It bends on Brown's belt so he hits Brown over the head with the sword's handle, ending the raid.

October 25–November 2: Trial and sentencing of Brown at Charleston.

December 2: Brown is hanged for "murder, treason and slave insurrection," and buried at North Elba.

Senate seat in Illinois to Douglas.

January: In response to Brown's Missouri raid, President Buchanan offers a $250 reward for his capture.

May 9–19: At a meeting of the Southern Commercial Convention in Vicksburg, Mississippi, Southern slaveowners call for the reopening of the African slave trade, banned by Congress in 1808 and made an act of piracy punishable by death in 1820.

October 30: Thoreau delivers his widely-read speech, *A Plea for Captain John Brown* in Concord.

Charles Darwin publishes *Origin of Species.*

Harriet E. Wilson publishes *Our Nig,* the first novel by an African American woman.

The slave ship *Clothilde* lands in Mobile, Alabama, with the last illegal cargo of slaves.

Georgia passes a law forbidding owners from manumitting slaves in their wills.

Convention at Wyandotte, Kansas, brings together free-soil and proslavery forces. They draft a constitution that will make the territory a free state. Voters approve the new constitution, but Southerners in Congress delay its acceptance.

Juan Cortina, of Brownsville on the Rio Grande border, leads an uprising protesting the mistreatment of Mexicans by Texans. Unlike Brown, he retreats, and continues his guerrilla war from Mexico for ten years.

BIBLIOGRAPHY

Creative

Abe Lincoln in Illinois. Dir. John Cromwell. Perf. Raymond Massey, Gene Lockhart, and John Cromwell/John Chenoweth. RKO, 1940. (film)

Banks, Russel. *Cloudsplitter.* New York: Harper Flamingo, 1998. (novel)

Benet, Stephen Vincent. *John Brown's Body.* (poem/play)

Dir. Charles Laughton. Perf. Tyrone Power, Judith Anderson, and Raymond Massey. Prod. Paul Gregory. 1953.

Dir. Curtis Canfield. Music Fenno Heath. Staged at the Yale Drama School and Off-Broadway. New York: Dramatists Play Service, 1961.

Bevier, Robert S. *Briefleigh: A Tale of the Days of Old John Brown.* New York: Minerva, 1889. (novel)

Blankfort, Michael and Michael Gold. *Battle Hymn.* Experimental Theater, (part of the WPA's Federal Theater Project) (play)

The Blue and the Grey. Dir. Andrew V. Mclaglen. Perf. Bruce Abbott, Royce D. Applegates, Diane Baker, and Sterling Hayden. Prod. Columbia Pictures Television, 1982. (television miniseries)

Boggs, O. A. *John Brown.* (song)

Bowles, John. *The Stormy Petrel: An Historical Romance.* New York: Lovell, 1892. (novel)

Boyd, James. *Marching On.* New York: Scribner's, 1927. (novel)

Burns, Ken, "The Meteor", in *The Civil War*, 1990. (documentary)

Channing, William Ellery. John *Brown and the Heroes of Harper's Ferry.* Boston: Cupples, Upham, 1886. (poem) (Lamont: Michofiche W 2652 Reproduction (microfiche): New Canaan, Ct.: Readex, 1996.)

Cliff, Michelle. *Free Enterprise.* New York: Dutton, 1993. (novel)

Cooke, John Esten. *Surry of Eagle's Nest.* New York: G.W. Dillingham, 1866. (novel)

Currier & Ives. *John Brown–The Martyr.* 1870 (lithograph)

— *John Brown Meeting the Slave-mother and her Child on the steps of Charlestown jail on his way to execution.* 1863 (coloured lthograph)

Curry, John Steuart. *Freeing of the Slaves. Law School Library, University of Wisconsin in Madison.* 1942. (oil/tempera on canvas)

— *The Tragic Prelude.* Kansas Statehouse, Topeka. 1937. (mural)

Davis, Julia. *The Anvil.* 1962. (play)

Dixon, Thomas, *The Man in Gray: A Romance of North and South.* New York: D. Appleton, 1921. (novel)

— *The Torch: A Story of the Paranoic Who Caused a Great War.* New York: The Author, 1927. (screenplay)

Dos Passos, John. *Three Soldiers.* New York: George H. Doran, 1921. (novel)

Ehrlich, Leonard. *God's Angry Man.* New York: Simon & Schuster, 1932. (novel)

Fraser, George MacDonald. *Flashman and the Angel of the Lord.* Lord: HarperCollins, 1999. (novel)

Gow, Ronald. *Gallows Glorius: A Play in Three Acts.* London, 1933. (play)

Perf. Howard Bosworth at Pasadena Community Playhouse in 1935.
(Widener: 23625.92.4100)
Hovenden, Thomas. *The Last Movement of John Brown*. Metropolitan Museum of Art,
New York. (painting–oil on canvas)
Hubbard, Elbert. *Time and Chance*. East Aurora, N. Y., Roycrafters, 1899. (novel)
Ishigaki, Eitaro. Unnamed mural, Harlem Magistrate Court in New York City, 1935.
(mural)
Jackson, Phyllis Wynn. *John Brown*. 1938. (play)
Libby, Jean *Black Voices from Harper's Ferry; Osborne Anderson and John Brown
Raid,* (1979)
— editor and compiler, *John Brown Mysteries by Allies for Freedom*. Missoula, Mt:
Pictorial Histories Publishing Co., (1999).
— *"The John Brown Daguerreotypes; a leader uses his likeness for remembrance and
promotion."* The Daguerrian Annual 2002. Pittsburgh, 2004.
John Brown and the Valley of the Shadow. Website:
Links to master list of John Brown Newspaper articles from The Valley Spirit (Cham-
bersburg, Pa), The Staunton Spectator (Staunton, Va), The Republican Vindicator
(Staunton, Va), and the other newspapers from around the nation.
"John Brown's Holy War." *The American Experience*. Narr. Joe Morton. Writ. Ken
Chowder. Dir. Robert Kenner. PBS 2000. (television special)
Website:
John Brown's Raid. Perf. Robert Duvall, James Mason. NBC, 1960. (television miniseries)
Karsner, David. *John Brown: Terrible Saint*. 1934. (novel)
Kellogg, E.C. and E.B. Kellogg. Untitled Lithograph of John Brown. Hartford, Con-
necticut, 1860. (lithograph)
Lawrence, Jacob. *The John Brown Series*. Gouche on paper, 1941, serigraph, 1977.
Memorial Art Gallery, Rochester. (painting)
— With Robert Hayden. *The Legend of John Brown*. Detroit: Detroit Institute of Art
Wayne State UP, 1978.
Lewis, Sinclair. *It Can't Happen Here*. Garden City, N.Y., 1935. (novel)
Lindsay, Vachel. "John Brown." *The Chinese Nightingale and Other Poems*. New York:
Macmillan, 1922. (poem)
McManus, Thomas J.L. *The Boy and the Outlaw: A Tale of John Brown's Raid on
Harpers Ferry*. New York: Grafton Press, 1904. (novel)
Mechem, Kirke. *John Brown: A Play in Three Acts*. In *Kansas Magazine,* Kansas State
College, 1939. (play)
Meriwether, Elizabeth Avery. *The Master of Red Leaf: A Tale*. 1872, rpt. New York:
E.J. Hale, 1880. (novel)
Mott, Frederick B. *Before the Crisis*. New York: The Bodley Head, 1904. (novel)
Nelson, Truman John. *The Surveyor*. Garden City: Doubleday, 1960. (novel)
Noble, Tomas. *John Brown's Blessing*. 1867. (lithograph/painting)
North and South. Dir. Richard T. Heffron. Perf. Patrick Swayze, Kirstie Alley, and
Johnny Cash. Warner Bros. Television, 1985. (television miniseries)
Olds, Bruce. *Raising Holy Hell*. New York: Holt, 1995. (novel)
Realf, Richard. *Free State Poems with Personal Lyrics Written in Kansas*. Ed. Richard
J. Hinton. Topeka: Crane, 1900.
Rivera, Diego. *Portrait of America*. New York: Covici-Fried, 1934.
Rukeyser, Muriel. *Soul and Body of John Brown*. 1940. (poem)
Saddler, Harry Dean. *John Brown, The Magnificent Failure*. Philadelphia: Dorrance,
1951. (novel)
Santa Fe Trail. Dir. Michael Curtiz. Perf. Errol Flynn, Olivia De Havilland, and Ray-
mond Massey. Warner Brothers. 1940. (film)
Schochen, Ceyril. *The Moon Beseiged*. 1950. (play)

Shields Green and the Gospel of John Brown. Dir. Chris Columbus. Perf. Denzel Washington. 20ᵗʰ Century Fox (film)

Seven Angry Men. Dir. Charles Marquis Warren. Pcrf. Raymond Massey, Debra Paget, and Jeffrey Hunter. Allied Artists, 1955. (film)

Strachey, Rachel Costelloe. *Marching On.* New York: Harcourt Brace, 1923. (novel)

Stavis, Barrie, *Harpers Ferry: A Play About John Brown.* New York: A. S. Barnes, 1967. (play)

Strother, David Hunter. In *Harpers Weekly* and *Frank Leslie's Illustrated Newspaper,* 1859. (sketches and articles)

Swayze, J. C. *Mrs Ossawatomie Brown, or, The Insurrection at Harper's Ferry: A Drama in Three Acts.* New York: S. French, 1859. (play)

U.S. Parks Service, *To Do Battle in the Land* (film)

Watkins, Louise Ward. "Old John Brown." *Heroes and Heroines of Yesterday.* Los Angeles: Cannell and Chafin, 1926. (play)

Waud, Alfred Rudolph. *John Brown's Cave Near Harper's Ferry.* C1960-65. (1 drawing on green paper: pencil and Chinese white)

Whittier, John Greenleaf. "Brown of Osawatomie." Pub. In *New York Tribune* 5 Dec. 1859. (poem)

Williams, Ben Ames. *House Divided.* Boston: Houghton Mifflin, 1947. (novel)

Woodman, Selden J. Untitled Painting of John Brown. West Virginia State Museum, Charleston, 1882. (painting)

Primary documents and secondary criticism

Abels, Jules. *Man on fire; John Brown and the cause of liberty.* New York, Macmillan, 1971.

Abbot, Lyman. "John Brown: A Review and an Impression." *The Outlook,* 97 (Jan-Apr 1911), 273–278.

Albrecht, Robert C. "Thoreau and His Audience: 'A Plea for Captain John Brown.'" *American Literature,* 32 (Mar 1960-Jan 1961), 393–402.

Ames, Charles Gordon. *The Death of John Brown; A discourse preached on the occasion of his public execution, delivered at the Free Congregational Church in Bloomington, Ill. Dec. 4. 1859.* Bloomington: Free Congregational Church, 1909.

Anderson, Osbourne P. *A voice from Harper's Ferry.* Boston: Printed for the author, 1861.

Anti-Slavery History of the John Brown Year. New York: Arno Press, 1969.

Aptheker, Herbert. "The Drama of Frederick Douglass and John Brown." *Toward Negro Freedom.* New York: New Century, 1956. Pp. 68–72.

— *John Brown, American Martyr.* New York: New Century, 1960.

Atkinson, Eleanor. "The Soul of John Brown." *American Magazine,* 68 (May-Oct, 1909), 633–643.

Avey, Elijah. *The Capture and Execution of John Brown, A Tale of Martyrdom.* Chicago: The Hyde Park Bindery, 1906.

Balkam, Uriah. The *Harper's Ferry Outbreak and Its Lesson: A sermon preached in the Pine Street chapel, Sabbath afternoon, Dec. 11ᵗʰ 1859.* Lewiston: Journal Office, 1859.

Barry, Joseph. *The Strange Story of Harpers Ferry, With Legends of the Surrounding Country.* Martinsburg, W. Va.: Thompson Brothers, 1903.

Bennett, Lerone, Jr. "God's Angry Man." *Pioneers in Protest.* Chicago: Johnson, 1968. Pp. 161–182.

— "Tea and Sympathy: Liberals and Other White Hopes." *The Negro Mood and Other Essays.* Chicago: Johnson, 1965. Pp. 75–104.

Bercovitch, Sacvan. *The American Jeremiad.* Madison: U of Wisconsin P, 1978.

Blight, David W. Article in *The American Prospect,* March 13, 2000

Bloom, Harold. *The American Religion: The Emergence of the Post-Christian Nation.* New York: Simon, 1992.

Booth, John Wilkes, to John C. Clark, 1864. Rpt. *New York Tribune,* 20 April, 1865.

Boyer, Richard Owen. *The legend of John Brown.* New York, Knopf, 1973.

Bradford, Gamaliel. "John Brown." *Damaged Souls.* Boston: Houghton Mifflin, 1923. Pp. 157–188.

Brewster, W.H., and Beatrice B. Brewster. *John Brown: A Brief Biography, with Letters by the Liberator.* N.p., n.d. [c. 1925]

Bridgeman, Edward Payson. *With John Brown in Kansas; the battle of Osawatomie.* Madison, Wis., J.N. Davidson, 1915.

Brown, George W. *False Claims of Kansas Historians Truthfully Corrected.* Rockford, Ill: The author, 1902.

Brown, H. Rap. *Die Nigger Die!* New York: Dial, 1969.

Cady, Edwin Harrison. *Young Howells & John Brown.* Columbus: Ohio State University Press, 1985.

Chamberlin, Joseph Edgar. *John Brown.* Boston: Small, Maynard, 1899.

Chapin, Lou V. "The Last Days of Old John Brown." *Overland Monthly,* 33, 2nd series (1899), 322–332.

Child, Lydia Maria. *The Letters of Lydia Maria Child.* Intro. By John Greenleaf Whitter. Boston: Houghton Mifflin, 1883.

— *Lydia Maria Child, Selected Letters, 1817–1888,* ed. Milton Meltzer and Patricia Holland (Amherst, 1982)

Clifford, James. "'Hanging up Looking Glasses at Odd Corners': Ethnobiographical Prospects", in *Studies in Biography,* ed. Daniel Aaron. Cambridge: Harvard University Press, 1978.

Congressional Globe: Containing the Debates and Proceedings of the First Session of the Thirty-Sixth Congress, Also of the Special Session of the Senate. Vol 1. Washington D.C.: John C. Rives, 1860

Connelley, William Elsey. *John Brown.* Topeka, Kansas: Crane & Company, 1900.

Cournos, John. "John Brown – Traitor and Patriot." "The Comparison of Brown with Garibaldi". *A Modern Plutarch.* Indianapolis: Bobbs Merrill, 1928.

Daingerfield, John E. P. "John Brown at Harpers Ferry." *The Century,* 30, (May-Oct. 1885), 265–267.

Dana, Richard H., Jr. "How We Met John Brown." *Atlantic Monthly,* 28 (July-Dec. 1871), 1–9.

Davis, David Brion. *Homicide in American Fiction, 1798–1860: A Study in Social Values.* Ithaca: Cornell, 1957.

Debs, Eugene Victor. *The Writings and Speeches of Eugene V. Debs.* New York: Hermitage, 1948.

Douglass, Frederick. John Brown. *An address by Frederick Douglass, at the fourteenth anniversary of Storer College, Harper's Ferry, West Virginia,* May 30, 1881.

Dover, NH: Morning Star Job Printing House, 1881.

— *The Life and Times of Frederick Douglass.* Hartford, Conn.: Park, 1882.

Drescher, Seymour. "Servile Insurrection and John Brown's Body in Europe", in the *Journal of American History,* 80 (1993), 499–534.

Drew, Thomas. *The John Brown Invasion: An Authentic History of the Harpers Ferry Tragedy.* Boston: J. Campbell, 1860.

Du Bois, W. E. B. *John Brown.* Philadelphia: G. W. Jacobs & Company, 1909.

Eby, Cecil D. "John Brown's Kiss." *Virginia Cavalcade* 11 (1961), 42–47.

Emerson, Ralph Waldo. *The Letters of Ralph Waldo Emerson,* ed. Ralph L. Rusk. 6 vols. New York: Columbia Univ. Press, 1939.

— *Works: Journals and Miscellaneous Notebooks,* ed. Ronald A. Bosco and Glen Jackson. Cambridge, Harvard University Press, 1982.

Featherstonhaugh, Thomas. *A bibliography of John Brown*. Baltimore, Md: Friedenwald Co., 1897.

Ferguson, Robert A. "Story and Transcription in the Trial of John Brown." *Yale Journal of Law and the Humanities* 6 (1994), 37–73.

Finkleman, Paul (ed.), His *Soul Goes Marching On: Responses to John Brown and the Harper's Ferry Raid*. Charlottesville: University Press of Virginia, 1995.

Fletcher, Robert S. "Ransom's John Brown Painting." *Kansas Historical Quarterly* 9 (1940), 343–46.

Fogelson, Robert M. and Richard E. Rubenstein, eds, *Invasion at Harpers Ferry. Mass Violence in America*. New York: Arno-NY Times, 1969.

Fouquier, Amand. *Causes Celebres*. Paris: Ad, Laine, c1860s.

Fried, Albert. *John Brown's journey; notes and reflections on his America and mine*. Garden City, N.Y.: Anchor Press/Doubleday, 1978.

Furnas, J.C. *The Road to Harper's Ferry*. New York: W. Sloane Associates, 1959.

Glasgow, J. Ewing. *The Harper's Ferry insurrection: being an account of the late outbreak in Virginia, and the trial and execution of Captain John Brown, its hero*. Glasgow, Edinburgh: M. McPhail, 1860.

Gold, Michael, *The Life of John Brown: Centennial of His Execution*. 1924, rept. New York: Roving Eye Press, 1960.

Graham, Stephen. *The Soul of John Brown*. New York: Macmillan, 1920.

Green, Laurence. *The Raid: A Biography of Harpers Ferry*. New York: Henry Holt, n.d. [1953]

Hall, Nathaniel. *Two sermons on slavery and its hero-victim*. Boston: John Wilson, 1859.

Harris, Thomas Legrand, *John Brown*. Bloomington: Indiana Univ. Press, 1926

Hawthorne, Nathaniel. *The Scarlet Letter* New York: Norton Critical Edition, 1961, first published 1850.

—"Chiefly About War Matters." *Atlantic Monthly*, 10 (July-Dec., 1862), 43–61.

Higginson, Thomas Wentworth. *Cheerful Yesterdays*. Boston: Houghton Mifflin, 1899.

Hinton, Richard J. *John Brown and His Men*. New York: Arno Press, 1968.

Holst, Hermann Von. *John Brown*. Boston: Cupples, 1888.

Howe, Samuel Gridley. *The Letters and Journals of Samuel Gridley Howe*. Ed. Laura E. Richards. 2 vols. Boston: Dana Estes, 1908–1909.

Howells, William Dean. "John Brown After Fifty Years." *North American Review*, 193 (Jan-June 1911), 26–34.

Hugo, Victor. *John Brown*. Ridgewood, NJ: Alwil Shop, 1902.

Huhner, Leon. *Some Jewish associates of John Brown*. New York, 1908.

Iger, Eve M. *John Brown: His Soul Goes Marching On*. New York: Young Scott Books, 1969.

Ingalls, John. "John Brown's Place in History." *North American Review*, 138 (Jan-June 1884), 139–150.

Invasion at Harper's Ferry. New York, Arno Press, 1969.

James, William. *Pragmatism*. Cambridge, Mass: Harvard University Press, 1975, first published 1907.

Jellison, Charles Albert, Jr. "The Martyrdom of John Brown." *West Virginian History*, 18 (Oct 1956 – July 1957), 243–255.

Jenks, Leland H. "The John Brown Myth". *American Mercury*, 1 (1924), 267–273.

"John Brown – Fanatic or Precursor of Freedom?" *Negro History Bulletin*, 30, No. 5 (1967), 4–5.

Jung, Carl Gustav. *C.J. Jung: Psychological Reflections, a New Anthology of His Writings, 1905–1961*. Ed. Jolande Jacobi with R.F.C. Hull. Bollingen Series, XXXI. Princeton: PUP, 1970

— *Modern Man in Search of a Soul*. New York: Harcourt, 1933.

— *Psychology of the Unconscious*. New York: Moffat, 1916.

— *The Spirit in Man, Art and Literature.* New York: Pantheon, 1966.

Keller, Allan. *Thunder at Harper's Ferry.* Englewood Cliffs, N.J., Prentice-Hall, 1958.

Kendell, M. Sue. *Rethinking Regionalism: John Steuart Curry and the Kansas Mural Controversy.* Smithsonian Institute Press, Washington D. C. , 1986.

Kliger, George and Robert C. Albrecht. "A Polish Poet on John Brown." *The Polish Review* 8 (1963), 1–6.

Lee, Cap. Robert E. *Recollections and Letters of General Robert E. Lee.* New York: Doubleday, Page, 1904.

Libby, Jean. *Black Voices From Harper's Ferry: Osbourne Anderson and the John Brown Raid.* Palo Alto: Libby, 1979.

The Life, trial, and execution of Captain John Brown, known as "Old Brown of Ossawatomie." Compiled from official and authentic sources. New York, Da Capo Press, 1969.

Lincoln, Abraham, *The Complete Works of Abraham Lincoln.* Ed John G. Nicolay and John Hay. 12 vols. New York: Century Company, 1905.

Little, Malcolm. *Malcolm X Speaks: Selected Speeches and Statements.* Ed. George Breitman. New York: Grove, 1965

Litvin, Martin. *The Journey: the first full-length documented biography of the American-Jewish freedom fighter who rode with John Brown in Kansas.* Galesburg, Ill: Galesburg Historical Society, 1981.

Ljungquist, Kent. "'Meteor of the War': Melville, Thoreau and Whitman respond to John Brown." *American Literature* 61 (1989), 674–680.

MacDonald, William. "John Brown." *Nation,* 91 (July-Dec 1910), 357–359.

MacDonald, William Naylor. *The Two Rebellions; or Treason Unmasked.* By a Virginian. Richmond, Va.: Smith, Bailey, 1865.

Madison, Charles A. "John Brown: A Fanatic in Action." *Critics and Crusaders.* New York: Holt, 1947.

Malin, James Claude. *John Brown and the legend of fifty-six.* Philadelphia: The American Philosophical Society, 1942.

— "The John Brown Legend in Pictures: Kissing the Negro Baby." *Kansas Historical Quarterly,* 8 (1939), 339–341; 9 (1940), 339–342.

McClellen, Katherine Elizabeth. *A hero's Grave.* Saranac Lake, NY: Pub. By the author, 1896.

McDonald, John J. "Emerson and John Brown." *New England Quarterly,* 44 (1971), 377–396.

McGlone, Robert E. "Rescripting a Troubled Past: John Brown's Family and the Harpers Ferry Conspiracy." *Journal of American History* 75 (March 1989): 1179–1200.

Melville, Hermann, *Moby Dick,* New York: Norton Critical Edition, 2002, first published 1851.

Miller, Ernest C. *John Brown, Pennsylvania citizen; the story of John Brown's ten years in northwestern Pennsylvania.* Warren, Pa: The Penn State Press, 1952.

Moore, Cleon. *John Brown's Attack on Harpers Ferry.* Point Pleasant, W. Va.: Mrs. Livia Simpson Poffenbarger, 1904.

Morrison, Toni. "Living Memory," *City Limits* (31 Mar.-7 Apr. 1988): 10–11.

Nelson, Truman John. "John Brown Revisited." *The Nation* 31, August 1957, 86–8.

—*The Right of Revolution,* Boston: Beacon Press, 1968.

—*The old man; John Brown at Harper's Ferry.* New York: Holt, Rinehart and Winston, 1973.

Newhall, Fales Henry. *The conflict in America; a funeral discourse occasioned by the death of John Brown of Ossawattomie, who entered into rest, from the gallows, at Charlestown, Virginia, Dec. 2, 1859, preached at the Warren St. M.E. Church, Roxbury, Dec. 4 / Rev. Fales Henry Newhall.* Boston: J.M. Hewes, 1859.

Newton, John. *Captain John Brown of Harper's Ferry; a preliminary incident to the great civil war of America.* New York: A Wessels Company, 1902.

New York Times, June 11, 2001, "History and Timothy McVeigh"

Noble, Glenn. *John Brown and Jim Lane trail.* Broken Bow, Neb: Purcells, 1977.

Nolan, Jeanette Covert, *John Brown,* New York: J. Messner, 1950.

Norton, Charles Eliot. "John Brown." *Atlantic Monthly,* 5, (Jan-June 1860), 378–381.

Oates, Stephen B. *Our fiery trial: Abraham Lincoln, John Brown, and the Civil War era.* Amhest: University of Massachusetts Press, 1979.

— *The purge this land with blood: a biography of John Brown.* New York: Harper & Row, 1970.

Ostrander, Gilman M. "Emerson, Thoreau and John Brown." *Mississippi Valley Historical Review,* 39, (June 1952-March 1953), 713–726.

Parker, Theodore. *John Brown's expedition.* Boston: The Fraternity, 1860.

Patton, William W. *The execution of John Brown: a discourse, delivered at Chicago, December 4th, 1859, in the First Congregational Church.* By Rev. W. W. Patton. Chicago: Church, Goodman & Cushing, 1859.

Peterson, Merrill D. *Lincoln in American Memory.* New York: OUP, 1994.

Phillips, Col. William A. "Three Interviews with Old John Brown." *Atlantic Monthly,* 44 (July-Dec, 1879), 738–744.

— Lecture to the Kansas Historical Society, "Lights and Shadows of Kansas History," in *Magazine of Western History* 12 (1890), 6–12.

Quarles, Benjamin. *Allies for Freedom; Blacks and John Brown.* New York: Oxford University Press, 1974.

— *Blacks on John Brown.* Urbana: University of Illinois Press, 1972.

Ransom, Rev. Reverdy C., "The Spirit of John Brown." Delivered at the Niagara Conference, Harpers Ferry, West Virginia, August 17, 1906. *Voice of the Negro,* 3 (1906), 412–417.

Redpath, James. *Echoes of Harper's Ferry.* Boston: Thayer and Eldridge, 1860.

— *The Public life of Capt. John Brown.* Boston: Thayer and Eldridge, 1860

Roe, Alfred S. *John Brown: A Retrospect.* Worcester, MA: Private Press of F.P. Rice, 1885.

Roosevelt, Theodore. "Progressives, Past and Present." *The Outlook,* 96 (Sept–Dec 1910), 19–30.

Rosenburg, Daniel. *Mary Brown: from Harper's Ferry to California.* New York: American Institute for Marxist Studies.

Ross, Alexander Milton. *Memoirs of a reformer.* Toronto, Hunter, Rose, 1893.

— *Recollections and experiences of an abolishionist, from 1855 to 1865.* Toronto: Rowswell & Hutchinson

Rossbach, Jeffrey S. *Ambivalent Conspirators: John Brown, The Secret Six, and A Theory of Slave Violence.* Philadelphia: University of Pennsylvannia Press, 1982.

Ruchames, Louis, ed. *A John Brown Reader.* New York: Abelard-Schuman, 1959.

— ed., *John Brown: the making of a revolutionary; the story of John Brown in his own words and in the words of those who knew him.* New York: Grosset & Dunlap, 1969.

Sanborn, F.B. "John Brown and His Friends." *Atlantic Monthly,* 30 (July-Dec. 1872), 50–61.

— "John Brown in Massachusetts." *Atlantic Monthly,* 29 (Jan-June 1872), 420–433.

— The *life and letters of John Brown, liberator of Kansas, and martyr of Virginia.* Boston: Roberts Brothers, 1885.

— *Memoirs of John Brown.* Albany: J Munsell, 1878.

— *Recollections of seventy years.* Boston, R.G. Badger, 1909.

Scheidenhelm, Richard Joy. *The response to John Brown.* Belmont, Calif., Wadsworth Pub. Co., 1972.

Schnittkind, Henry Thomas. "John Brown, Madman or Saint?" *The Story of the United*

States: A Biographical History of America. New York: Doubleday, Doran, 1938. Pp. 194–201.

Schouler, James. *History of the United States of America Under the Constitution.* New York, 1891

Scott, Otto J. *The secret six: John Brown and the abolitionist movement.* New York: NYT Times Books, 1979.

Shapiro, Samuel. "Fidel Castro and John Brown." *Columbia University Forum,* 6, No. 1 (1963), 22–28.

Sharp, Ellen. "The Legend of John Brown and the Series by Jacob Lawrence." *Bulletin of the Detroit Institute of Arts* 67 (1993), 15–35.

Sheeler, J. Reuben. "John Brown: A Century Later." *Negro History Bulletin,* 24 (Oct 1960-Sept 1961), 7–10.

Six trials. New York: Thomas Y. Cromwell Company, 1969.

Stauffer, John, *The Black Hearts of Men,* Cambridge: Harvard University Press, 2002.

— "Daguerreotyping the National Soul". *Prospects,* 22.

Stavis, Barrie. *John Brown; the sword and the word.* South Brunswick, A.S. Barnes, 1970.

Stone, Edward, ed. *Incident at Harpers Ferry.* Englewood Cliffs, N.J.: Prentice-Hall, 1956.

Stutler, Boyd B. *Captain John Brown and Harpers Ferry: The Story of the Raid and the Old Fire Engine House Known as John Brown's Fort.* Harpers Ferry, W. Va.: Storer College, 1930.

— "Abraham Lincoln and John Brown: A Parallel." *Civil War History* 8, 1962, 290–299.

Styron, William. *The Confessions of Nat Turner.* New York: Random, 1967.

Swennes, Robert H. "Lydia Maria Child: Holographs of 'The Hero's Heart' and 'Brackett's Bust of John Brown.'" *American Literature,* 40 (Mar 1968-Jan 1969), 539–542.

Tafts, S.H. *A discourse on the character and death of John Brown;* delivered in Martinsburgh, N.Y., Dec. 12, 1859. Des Moines: Steam Printing House of Carter, Hussey and Curl, 1872.

Talbert, Joy K. "John Brown in American Literature." 2 vols. Diss. Univ. of Kansas, Lawrence, 1942.

Thoreau, Henry David. *The Writings of Henry David Thoreau.* 20 vols. Boston: Houghton, Mifflin, 1906.

Tufts, Samuel N. *Slavery, and the death of John Brown.* Lewiston, Me: Journal Office, 1859.

Utter, David N. "John Brown of Osawatomie." *North American Review,* 137 (July-Dec 1883), 435–446.

Verney, Victor Vincent, Jr. "John Brown: Cultural Icon in American Mythos." Diss. Buffalo, 1996.

Villard, Oswald Garrison. *John Brown, 1800 – 1859; a biography fifty years after.* Boston: Houghton Mifflin Company, 1910.

Warch, Richard and Fanton, Jonathan F., eds. *John Brown.* Englewood Cliffs, NJ, Prentice-Hall, 1973.

Wardenaar, Leslie Albert, "John Brown: The Literary Image." Diss. UCLA, 1974.

Warren, Robert Penn. *John Brown; the making of a martyr.* New York: Payson & Clarke Ltd., 1929.

Watterson, Henry. "An Abortive Hero." *North American Review,* 193 (Jan-June 1911), 35–46.

Webb, Richard Davis. *The life and letters of Captain John Brown: who was executed at Charlestown, Virginia, Dec. 2, 1859, for an armed attack upon American slavery; with notices of some of his confederates.* London: Smith, Elder & Co., 1861.

Webb, Robert N. *The Raid on Harpers Ferry, October 1859.* New York: Watts, 1971.

Weiss, John. *The Life and Correspondence of Theodore Parker.* 2 vols. New York: D. Appleton, 1864.

Whitridge, Arnold. "The John Brown Legend." *History Today,* 7 (1957), 211–220.

Whitter, John Greenleaf. "The Lesson of the Day." In John A Pollard, *John Greenleaf Whitter: Friend of Man.* Boston: Houghton Mifflin, 1949. Pp. 600–604.

Whitman, Karen. "Re-evaluating John Brown's Raid at Harpers Ferry." *West Virginia History,* 34 (Oct. 1972-July 1973), 46–84.

Williams, George Washington, *History of the Negro Race in America.* New York, Arno Press, 1968, first published 1882.

Wilson, Edmund, *Patriotic Gore: Studies in the Literature of the Civil War.* London: Deutsch, 1962.

Wilson, Hill Peebles. *John Brown, soldier of fortune; a critique.* Boston: The Cornhill Company, 1918.

Winkley, Jonathon Wingate. *John Brown, the hero; personal reminiscences.* Boston: James H. West Company, 1905.

Wise, Henry A. "Message to the Senate and House of Delegates of the General Assembly of the Commonwealth of Virginia." *Journal of the Senate of House of Delegates of the Commonwealth of Virginia: Begun and Held at the Capitol Session, 1859.* Richmond, Va.: James E. Goode, 1859.

Woodward. C. Vann. "John Brown's Private War." *America in Crisis.* Ed. Daniel Aaron. New York: Knopf, 1952. Pp. 109–130.

Wright, Marcus Joseph. *Trial of John Brown.* Richmond, Va., W. E. Jones, printer, 1889.

Wyatt-Brown, Bertram. "John Brown, Weathermen, and the Psychology of Antinomian Violence." *Soundings,* 58 (1975), 426–440.

Zabriskie, George A. "John Brown: Saint or Sinner?" *New York Historical Society Quarterly,* 33 (1949), 31–38.

Zittle, Captain John H. *A Correct History of the John Brown Invasion.* Hagerstown. Md.: Published by his Widow, 1905.